THE STAFFORD & UTTOXETER RAILWAY

Stafford Common Station in August 1952 looking east towards Uttoxeter from under Marston Road overbridge (No. 41); the houses on the right are in Aston Terrace. The covered stairways to each platform from the booking office, which was located on the bridge, can be seen to the left and right. Stafford Common signal box is in the centre of the photograph near to which are rakes of hip-roofed salt vans. All three salt works are featured. Manger's Crown Works (formerly Stubbs & Co.) is on the left behind the station name board; the Tillington Works of ICI (formerly Chance & Hunt) is also on the left beyond the signal box and the Stafford Salt and Alkali Works with its two tall chimneys is on the right opposite the signal box. By this time the latter works together with Manger's had become part of Amasal Ltd. The overbridge in the far distance is No. 38; it carries the Stafford to Sandon Road and is featured at the top of page 52. JOHN ALSOP

© Lightmoor Press, Allan C. Baker and Mike G. Fell, 2014.
Designed by Stephen Phillips.

British Library Cataloguing-in-Publication Data. A catalogue record for this book is available from the British Library.
ISBN 9781 899889 90 7

LIGHTMOOR PRESS
Unit 144B, Lydney Trading Estate, Harbour Road, Lydney, Gloucestershire GL15 5EJ www.lightmoor.co.uk
Lightmoor Press is an imprint of Black Dwarf Lightmoor Publications Ltd.

Printed and bound by
Berforts Information Press Ltd,
Eynsham, Oxford.

THE
STAFFORD & UTTOXETER
RAILWAY

ALLAN C. BAKER & MIKE G. FELL

Contents

Abbreviations, measurements and notes

BCR	Belfast Central Railway
BoT	Board of Trade
BR	British Railways
BRB	British Railways Board
B&SCER	Birmingham & Sutton Coldfield Extension Railway
BTC	British Transport Commission
CMR	Cannock Mineral Railway
CRO	County Record Office, Stafford – now known as Staffordshire & Stoke-on-Trent Archive Service, Staffordhire Record Office, Stafford
DS&WJR	Derbyshire, Staffordshire & Worcestershire Junction Railway
E&WJR	East & West Junction Railway
FD&RC	Felixstowe Dock & Railway Company
GCR	Great Central Railway
GJR	Grand Junction Railway
GNR	Great Northern Railway
GWR	Great Western Railway
HLRO	House of Lords Record Office
ICI	Imperial Chemical Industries
L&RRO	The Record Office for Leicestershire, Leicester and Rutland
LBR	London & Birmingham Railway
LCCA	The Land Clauses Consolidation Act 1845
LM&SR	London Midland & Scottish Railway
LMR	London Midland Region
L&NER	London & North Eastern Railway
L&NWR	London & North Western Railway
LT&SR	London, Tilbury & Southend Railway
MS&LR	Manchester Sheffield & Lincolnshire Railway
NA	National Archives
NLR	North London Railway
NRM	National Railway Museum
NSR	North Staffordshire Railway
OW&WR	Oxford, Worcester & Wolverhampton Railway
RAF	Royal Air Force
RCH	Railway Clearing House
RE	Railway Executive
RPS	Railway Preservation Society
SLS	Stephenson Locomotive Society
SSR	South Staffordshire Railway
S&UR	Stafford and Uttoxeter Railway
TVR	Trent Valley Railway
UKNIWN	United Kingdom National Inventory of War memorials
WTT	Working Time Table

The following Imperial measures of area, length and weight are used in the text.

One acre = 4 roods or 4,840 square yards; one rood = 40 square poles or 1,210 square yards.

One mile = 8 furlongs; one furlong = 220 yards; one chain = 22 yards or 4 poles; one link = 7.92 inches. There are 100 links in a chain.

One ton = 20 cwt; one cwt = 4 quarters; one quarter = 28 lbs.

Notes

Notes are located at the end of each chapter.

THE road from Stafford crosses the River Trent at Weston and does something rather odd. Sixty yards north of the graceful stone bridge which takes it in a single span over the river, now 50 feet wide and visibly polluted, the road clambers laboriously over the arch of another bridge, this time of brick–and set in the middle of an empty field. It seems a good deal of effort to very little purpose, until one realizes that this bridge is one of the strangly evocative remains of a long lost railway; a single track doomed, one would have thought, to unprofitability from the start, which ran from Stafford to Uttoxeter along a sylvan route carved round the foot of Hopton Heath and still clearly definable in abandoned causeway, grass covered ballast and useless bridges for most of its 15 miles. The line of this forgotten relic of an age when railways grew like mushrooms in a horse paddock, crosses the River Trent a few yards upstream of the stone road bridge before passing under the road itself and on the northern bank the stone pier of its bridge remains, more like a medieval ruin than the unwanted debris of the nineteenth century. There is something infinitely sad about a railway abandoned so long ago that is no longer just a derelict remnant of an overtaken age but as much a venerable relic of the past as the Bronze Age barrows and the paving of Roman villas.

Portrait of The River Trent, Peter Lord. Robert Hale, 1968.

Preface

BOTH AUTHORS have an inexhaustible appetite for the history of the former North Staffordshire Railway (NSR) and have written extensively on that subject. The NSR did not own the Stafford and Uttoxeter Railway (S&UR) but the S&UR had running powers from Bromshall Junction into the NSR's station at Uttoxeter, which greatly stimulated our interest. At the other end of the line the S&UR, with the agreement of the London & North Western Railway (L&NWR) accessed Stafford Station which was also used by NSR trains. Our curiosity was aroused and evolved into the detailed primary research necessary to write this book. Earlier histories of the line have appeared in the form of articles, a private publication and a small booklet but we felt that the enterprise was worthy of this more substantial history.

We have enjoyed researching the origins of a small and impecunious railway company that battled its birthright through Parliament in 1862 against strong opposition from its powerful neighbours and then took over five years to build its line of just over 12½ miles. We have made a special point of identifying its directors and management and some key members of its staff. Those are the people that made it work, or nearly so, as unfortunately it spent almost the whole of its independent life in receivership. We have closely unravelled the intrigue that resulted in the S&UR being acquired by the enterprising and highly competitive Great Northern Railway (GNR) in 1881 and how that railway developed its relationship with the NSR over whose line it had to pass in order to reach its own metals

at Egginton Junction. At the grouping of the railways in 1923, the GNR became part of the London & North Eastern Railway (L&NER) whereas the NSR and L&NWR became part of the London Midland & Scottish Railway (LM&SR) and so it was that Stafford and Uttoxeter continued to be locations where the trains and liveries of different railway companies rubbed shoulders. The varnished teak coaching stock of an L&NER train contrasted markedly with LM&SR maroon so sparking an interest in the mind of an inquisitive passenger or enthusiast as to why the two co-existed in North Staffordshire. The former S&UR lost its passenger service in 1939 but the line survived to become nationalised. What would the original subscribers have thought of that?

We obviously hope that this book will appeal to railway enthusiasts but hope that it will also be purchased by those who want to learn more about past commercial and industrial enterprise in the area in which they reside. We do hope that all readers will like what they see and enjoy the fruits of our research. Little did we realise when we commenced our research that our efforts would result in a book of nearly 100,000 words which is equivalent to nearly 8,000 words per mile of railway! We believe that for a standard gauge line with such a short independent existence the result might just be a record.

ALLAN C. BAKER, *High Halden, Kent*
MIKE G. FELL, *Elloughton, East Riding of Yorkshire*

Seal of the Stafford & Uttoxeter Railway Company.

THE G.N. NO. 23. STAFFORD, LEAVES UTTOXETER.

So far as we know, this is the only photograph of a GNR train at Uttoxeter station, a down train departing for Stafford circa 1900. The engine is number 23, one of the Stirling mixed-traffic 0-4-2 tender engines built at Doncaster in 1868 and only the second member of the class. Not one of those rebuilt by Ivatt, it was withdrawn in December 1907. A November 1905 list shows this locomotive as allocated to Colwick shed. McKenzie & Holland lower quadrant signalling practice is very much in evidence. Uttoxeter West Junction signal box can be seen in the left foreground; it had a frame with 41 levers. The left hand arms on the prominent junction signal were for the Churnet Valley line, the right hand arms controlled the main line to Derby and Burton-on-Trent. In the left distance the down starter for the Churnet line can be seen and to the extreme right the up starter for the Derby line is just discernible with the home signal in the off position. Milk traffic was very important at this time as evidenced by the conical churns in Station Road and those lining the milk dock behind the junction signal. The tall warehouse to the right was associated with a dairy and cheese factory.

Introduction

STAFFORD AND UTTOXETER are both located within the County of Stafford, Uttoxeter being 14 miles due east of the county town. For a period of almost 90 years a railway connected the two towns: it was the last main line railway to arrive at each location and the first to go. The first train in public service departed from Stafford on 23 December 1867 while the last train, a Stephenson Locomotive Society 'Special', ran on 23 March 1957 several years after the majority of the line had been closed to traffic. During its period of operation the line had four owners: the independent Stafford & Uttoxeter Railway Company, the Great Northern Railway (GNR), the London & North Eastern Railway (L&NER) and the nationalised British Railways (BR). This book explains why the line was built, who promoted it, what brought about its demise and what happened during its lifetime. It is a fascinating tale.

In 1801 the population of Stafford was just under 4,000 inhabitants. By the time the Grand Junction Railway arrived in the town in 1837 the population had doubled. At that time Stafford was a market town renowned for its shoe making, the tanning of leather and the brewing of ale. The shoe making industry was mechanised in 1855 when sewing machines were introduced much to the dismay of the workers and their trade union representatives. As a result factories were established in the Foregate area of the town which soon became the shoe making suburb. Increased employment stemmed from support businesses including Dorman which made knives and machinery, Evode which made glue, Venables the timber merchants, which produced wooden heels and crates used to export the shoes all over the world and Stafford Box which made the cardboard shoe boxes. The Lotus Shoe business was the last to survive, its red-brick factory on Sandon Road being demolished in 1998.

Stafford also earned a reputation for salt production following the accidental finding of a substantial deposit at Stafford Common during attempts to secure a new source of fresh water for the town in 1893. This discovery led to the decline of the salt workings at Shirleywich and Weston. The workings at Shirleywich on the estate of Earl Ferrers had been in operation since before 1686. The transportation of the salt from Shirleywich benefited from the opening of the nearby Trent and Mersey Canal which in 1771 was opened from the River Trent at Wilden Ferry to Stone. In 1810 the facilities were further improved by the construction of a short branch canal to serve the workings directly. The salt workings at Weston on the estate of Earl Shrewsbury and Talbot were opened in 1821 and by 1851 were producing about 250 tons weekly. In 1874 the Weston Salt Works which, since 1872, had been operated by the Shrewsbury Estates & Manure Company, was connected to the S&UR by a siding which was also used to load gypsum traffic.

There were three separately owned sites for salt production at Stafford Common: two on the north side of the S&UR and one on the south. The latter was the first to be developed by the Stafford Salt & Alkali Company Ltd which opened its factory in 1893 and eventually established eight pans on the site. This company constructed a second salt processing works at Baswich in 1894 and supplied this with brine by means of a two mile long pipeline to its Stafford Common works. The pipeline passed through the centre of Stafford in order to feed the Brine Baths in Greengate Street and then continued to Baswich underneath the towpath of the River Sow Navigation.

The second operation to be developed at Stafford Common was undertaken by Stubbs & Co. in 1895 and the firm operated four pans at its Crown Salt Works on the north side of the S&UR. The third site to be developed at Stafford Common was also located on the north side of the S&UR just to the east of the Crown Salt Works. This third site, known as the Tillington Works, was established in 1907 and was operated by Chance & Hunt Ltd, a chemical company with works at Oldbury and Wednesbury. The subsequent history of these three salt works and their rail connections is dealt with later in the book. Problems with subsidence eventually brought an end to all salt mining in Stafford. In years gone by, traffic awaiting attention in the goods yard at Stafford Common was characterised by the very distinctive hip-roofed salt vans which wore the salt companies' distinctive liveries, some of which feature in the photographs used to illustrate this book.

Stafford also acquired a reputation for engineering. William Henry Dorman (1834-1926) established his business to support the shoe industry in 1870. It soon grew into a large engineering manufacturing business, later specialising in internal combustion engines. By 1875 the Castle Engine Works had been established by William Gordon Bagnall (1852-1907) and was producing portable steam engines and agricultural equipment. W.G. Bagnall Ltd subsequently achieved a world-wide reputation for the design and manufacture of locomotives and railway equipment and at its peak employed about 500 people. A total of 1,855 locomotives were built at Stafford during the firm's lifespan which ended in 1962. The Universal Grinding Wheel Company Ltd was founded in 1914 following the merger of several firms with kindred interests. The products of this company were originally designed for the shoe trade but the abrasives produced at the Doxey Road factory, which by the late 1950s occupied a 44 acre site, were also used in the engineering industry. The firm still survives and since 1997 has been a wholly-owned subsidiary of the French company, Saint-Gobain.

Since the early 1900s a major activity in the town has been heavy electrical engineering. In 1900 Siemens Brothers Ltd purchased 500 acres of land to develop a factory which has subsequently undergone a series of changes in ownership, including English Electric, GEC Alstom, Areva T&D and Alstom Grid & Schneider Electric. In 1925 the British Reinforced Concrete Company established a works at Queensville, an operation which continued into recent times. All of this business activity, past and present, has had a significant influence on the railway industry in Stafford and some of the products generated, for example salt and timber, were an important source of traffic for the S&UR and its successors.

When the NSR opened its main line through Uttoxeter in 1848 the market town had a population of about 5,000 souls. Prior to the arrival of the railway, Uttoxeter was well served by horse-drawn coach services to London, Birmingham, Derby, Newcastle-under-Lyme, Liverpool, Manchester and Sheffield. The town was located in the heart of a rich grazing district and at one time was noted for clock making, tanning, nail making and brewing. The Cattle Market survived until 2005. The main employer in the area today is the well known excavator manufacturer J.C. Bamford Excavators Ltd whose founder, Joseph Cyril Bamford (1916-2001), started this huge international business in a small garage in the town in 1945 and made his JCB initials famous throughout the world. The Bamford family had previously established a farm machinery business in the town at the Leighton Ironworks and became a significant employer from the end of the 19th century. The earlier enterprise was well known for its balers, hay turners, rakes, mangold cutters and stationary steam engines, examples of which were transported by train and exported all over the world. The area traversed by the S&UR was rich in dairy farming and milk became a very important traffic for the railway. Horse traffic was also prominent and was given additional encouragement by the Meynell Hunt which was established in 1872 when new kennels were built at Sudbury. When Uttoxeter Racecourse

opened in 1907 this resulted in further equestrian traffic and excursion trains to transport the racegoers. The Second World War gave another fillip to traffic routed over the S&UR following the establishment of a Royal Ordnance Factory at Bramshall (spelt differently from the NSR's Bromshall Junction) and the creation of 16 Maintenance Unit (16MU) by the Air Ministry at Stafford.

What then is the situation at each end of the S&UR today? The population of both towns has witnessed considerable growth. Uttoxeter now has over 12,000 inhabitants and Stafford supports over 63,000 people. Happily both towns still have railway stations but that at Uttoxeter is but a shadow of its former self and nowadays is unstaffed and only handles passenger traffic. Train operating company, East Midlands Trains, operates a service between Crewe, Stoke-on-Trent and Derby and about 120,000 passengers a year use Uttoxeter station. It is no longer an important junction, the Churnet Valley line connection having closed in 1965. The railway scene at Stafford is very different with the present station, which dates from 1962, handling over 1.2 million passengers a year! Although the S&UR and Shrewsbury line connections have been lost, Stafford is still a major junction for the Birmingham and Trent Valley Lines and supports services throughout the electrified west coast main line with traditional links to London, Birmingham, Stoke-on-Trent, Liverpool and Manchester but also more recent cross country services to Bristol and the south west of England.

Having set the scene we will begin by stepping back in time and describing what was there before the S&UR arrived.

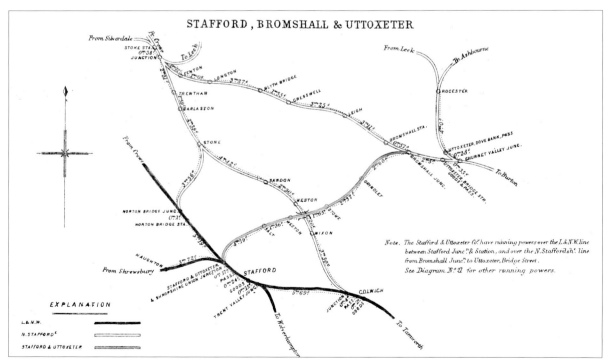

The Railway Clearing House (RCH) Junction Diagrams, under the name of John Airey, first appeared in 1867. Although we don't have a date for the one reproduced here, it is an early edition as it shows the S&UR when still an independent company. Most surviving copies of the diagrams the authors have seen, in fact all except this one, are dated after the line was acquired by the GNR. The diagram also shows the original NSR layout at Uttoxeter. These diagrams which show the mileages between stations and junctions, were used by the RCH and the various railways party to the RCH agreements, to apportion receipts for traffic that passed over two or more different railway companies' lines.

CHAPTER ONE

Canals and Railways at Stafford and Uttoxeter

Staffordshire and Worcestershire Canal

James Brindley (1716-1772) was the Engineer for the Grand Trunk Canal (later known as the Trent and Mersey) which was authorised by an Act of Parliament which received the Royal Assent on 14 May 1766.[1] It was entitled:

An Act for making a navigable Cut or Canal from the River Trent, at or near Wildon Ferry, in the County of Derby, to the River Mersey, at or near Runcorn Gap.

The enterprise took 11 years to complete but by 12 November 1771 was open from the River Trent to Stone, just to the north of Stafford traversing the Ingestre and Sandon estates en route. There is evidence suggesting that the owners of both estates, the Earl of Shrewsbury and Talbot and the Earl of Harrowby, used the canal for the transport of their goods both before and after

the coming of the railways. It took another six years to excavate the Harecastle canal tunnel and so provide a through navigation from Liverpool to Hull via the Rivers Mersey, Trent and Humber. Concurrently with authorisation of the inaugural Act for the Grand Trunk Canal another Act[2] received the Royal Assent on the very same day entitled:

An Act for making and maintaining a navigable Cut, or Canal, from the River Severn, between Bewdley and Titton Brook, in the county of Worcester, to cross the River Trent, near Haywood Mill, in the county of Stafford, and communicate with a Canal intended to be made between the said River Trent and the River Mersey.

This was a further part of Brindley's master plan to link the ports of Liverpool, Bristol and Hull. The Staffordshire and Worcestershire Canal was opened throughout from the River

As related in the text, the Trent & Mersey Canal, formerly the Grand Trunk, passed through Sandon on its way south from the Potteries to where it joined the River Trent at Derwent Mouth, near Shardlow. Parts of it actually ran through Earl Harrowby's estate. At Sandon, forty four miles and 4 chains from Derwent Mouth, this lock, number 25, is situated and at one time there was a coal wharf here too, known as Sproston's. From the Summit lock at Etruria, Stoke-on-Trent, the canal is on a continuous downward course to the River Trent, a total drop of 316 feet. This 1950s view looks north towards Stoke-on-Trent.

Severn to Haywood Junction by May 1772. Unfortunately for the inhabitants of Stafford, the new canal bypassed the town some 1½ miles to the east at Radford Bank.

The principal traffics carried included iron, ironstone, coal, stone, timber, lime and limestone. Interestingly, paving-stones, gravel, sand and other materials for repairing roads (except limestone) and manure for the grounds of persons whose land was taken for the canal, were exempted from tolls, provided there was a surplus of water when such commodities passed through a lock, i.e. when water was flowing over the lock weir.

Stafford's First Railway

Stafford's first railway, which is little known, was opened on 1 November 1805 less than two weeks after Vice Admiral Viscount Lord Nelson's victory at the Battle of Trafalgar. It was rather primitive and took the form of a flanged plateway which connected Stafford with the canal at Radford Bank. It was built by the Stafford Railway Coal & Lime Company and was opened on 1 November 1805 following an abortive proposal to construct a branch canal. The plateway, which was worked by horses, started from a basin behind Radford Wharf, crossed over the River Penk and then ran along Lichfield Road before continuing over that road into the town centre. The terminus was at Railway Wharf (or Stafford Wharf) by Green Bridge.

The owners of the Stafford Railway Coal & Lime Company were John Brown, John Hall, Omar Hall and Edward Harding. The venture was clearly not a success as by July 1811 John Hall had cut his losses and sold his £810 share in the company to James Cramer for £254. In September 1810 the idea of a branch canal was resurrected and Omar Hall approached the proprietors of the Staffordshire and Worcestershire Canal with a proposal to make the Rivers Penk and Sow navigable into Stafford via a lock at Radford but the negotiations were unsuccessful. In August 1812 there was even talk of an inclined plane linking the canal to the two rivers.

By 1813 the owners of the plateway were bankrupt and it closed the following year. The assets were sold at auction by Henshaw & Smith at the Star Inn in Stafford on 15 July 1814. The following items were included in the sale:

The Railway and Sills [sleepers] between Radford and Stafford, laid with flanch [flanged] rails, a Weighing Machine capable of weighing 5 tons, with a Machine House and Blacksmith's Shop at the Green in Stafford; two Canal Boats and two short River Boats; a quantity of Railway Carriages capable of carrying from 20cwt to 30cwt each; a Crane with wheels &c. and other sundry articles.

The plateway was replaced by a waterway linking with the canal at Baswich just to the north of Radford. There was a lock which took boats down to the River Sow which was then 'canalised' (i.e. straightened and deepened) for one mile into the centre of Stafford. This navigation was opened on 19 February 1816 and survived for over 130 years. *Bradshaw's Canals and Navigable Rivers of England and Wales* compiled by Henry Rodolph De Salis and published in 1904 describes the branch as leaving the main line near Baswich, passing through Baswich Lock and

descending to the River Sow, the course of which was followed to Stafford. The book goes on to record that the portion of the River Sow forming the Stafford Branch was leased from Lord Stafford (1833-1913) by the Staffordshire and Worcestershire Canal Company. The following maximum dimensions were given for narrow boats using the navigation: length 72ft 0in; width 6ft 9in; headroom 8ft 8in; draught from 3ft 10in in to 5ft 0in according to the amount of water in the River Sow. In 1948 a survey by Stafford Borough Council noted that the waterway was narrow, weed-grown and neglected and very seldom used for traffic. Dereliction followed but happily there is now a serious project for its revival for pleasure boating to be known as the Stafford Riverway Link.

Grand Junction Railway

On Tuesday, 4 July 1837 Stafford witnessed the opening of the Grand Junction Railway (GJR), authorised by an Act of Parliament which received the Royal Assent on 6 May 1833.[3] This trunk railway initiative had many parallels with the grand schemes of the canal era in that it was intended to connect places of commercial and industrial importance, namely, Liverpool and Manchester (already rail served since 1830) with Birmingham and London, the latter via the London and Birmingham Railway (L&BR) which was opened throughout on 17 September 1838. However, on this occasion, Stafford, instead of being bypassed, as was the case with the canals, found itself located on a major transport artery, a position it retains to this day on the West Coast Main Line. From the outset Stafford was regarded as a *First-class* station, the next such station to the south with similar importance being Wolverhampton and that to the north, Whitmore, which became an interchange point for horse drawn traffic to Newcastle-under-Lyme and the Potteries.[4] Indeed, it was just to the north of Whitmore that the inaugural north and southbound trains passed each other on the opening day.

The first northbound train from Birmingham departed from a temporary station at Vauxhall as the planned station at Curzon Street was still under construction. This is how a contemporary newspaper reported the first departure from Birmingham:

At seven o'clock precisely the bell rang, and the opening train, drawn by the WILDFIRE engine commenced moving. The train consisted of eight carriages, all of the first class, and bearing the following names: the GREYHOUND, the SWALLOW, the LIVERPOOL AND BIRMINGHAM MAIL, the CELERITY, the UMPIRE, the STATESMAN and the BIRMINGHAM AND MANCHESTER MAILS.

The sight of this train entering Stafford station where many local people must have witnessed a steam hauled public service passenger train for the very first time must have been quite something. The *Wildfire* was a 2-2-2 tender engine built by Robert Stephenson and Company in 1837; it weighed less than 10 tons and had driving wheels of five foot diameter. It is interesting to note that the four-wheeled coaches were individually named in the manner of their horse-drawn coach antecedents. The first class coaches accommodated six persons under cover whereas the mail coaches carried only four passengers. Interestingly, the compartment of the mail coaches was convertible into a bed-carriage, accomplished by lifting up one of the false backs of the carriages which formed a sort of couch. On the first day of operations a problem was encountered through the weakness of the coach springs causing them to thump against the axle-trees[5] such that the bottoms of some of the carriages were completely worn away by the friction. This was remedied by transferring the passengers' luggage from the roofs of certain vehicles to others that were less full in order to redistribute the weight. This was truly railway pioneering and Stafford was in the forefront of both accommodating and benefiting from this new mode of transport.

The GJR went from strength to strength. At Stafford a new engine shed was built in 1838 and during 1843-1844 it became necessary to build a new station in order to accommodate the increase in traffic. The new station was designed in the Elizabethan style by architect John Cunningham (1799-1873) of Liverpool.

Trent Valley Railway

In the meantime it had become clear that a more direct link between London and the north was needed and an obvious way to achieve this was to shorten the route to Rugby and London via the Trent Valley. This led to the promotion in 1838 of a scheme which had the support of the main towns which lay on the proposed route, Nuneaton, Tamworth, Lichfield and Rugeley. This early scheme met with opposition from the GJR and the L&BR whose directors were cautious about the new line being in competition with their undertakings but, after several counter proposals, including a project which gained the support of the GJR but not the L&BR, the scheme eventually re-emerged under the title of the Trent Valley Railway (TVR) and succeeded in being authorised by an Act of Parliament which received the Royal Assent on 21 July 1845.[6] Just prior to this the L&BR had altered its position from one of opposition to taking control of the situation. The L&BR Chairman, George Carr Glyn (1797-1873), at the 23rd meeting of the L&BR shareholders held on 12 February 1845 explained:

We had proposals made to us by the Manchester and Birmingham Company, and after a little consideration, we have connected these proposals with those made to us by the Trent Valley and Churnet Valley Companies; and before we conclude our business to-day it will be my duty to propose to you resolutions by which the eventual amalgamation of two of these lines with our own, and the perpetual leasing of the other, shall be carried into effect.

This statement was followed by applause and the Chairman went on to say:

After taking the best advice we have been able to obtain from those most experienced in such matters, we think that, as regards the Trent Valley line, we have made a very safe bargain for you.

The resolution insofar as the Trent Valley Company was concerned was then adopted. However, before the construction of the new line was completed it became part of the newly established L&NWR which was formed on 16 July 1846 by the merger of three major companies: the GJR, which had absorbed the Liverpool & Manchester Railway in 1845; the LBR which had already absorbed the TVR and the Manchester & Birmingham Railway (M&BR) which had opened its line from Manchester to Crewe on 10 August 1842. George Carr Glyn became the first L&NWR Chairman.

The Trent Valley line from Stafford to Rugby was opened on 26 July 1847 and shortened the original GJR/L&BR route to London by eight miles. However, through trains to London did not commence until 1 December 1847 as additional work was required on some of the bridges which had been constructed using cast iron. They were similar to the one built for the Chester & Holyhead Railway to span the River Dee. The Dee Bridge had collapsed in spectacular fashion while a train was crossing on 24 May 1847 resulting in the deaths of six passengers and so it is not surprising that caution was exercised on the newly completed TVR, especially as Robert Stephenson (1803-1859) was the Engineer for both railways.

North Staffordshire Railway

The North Staffordshire Railway (Potteries Line) Act 1846 which received the Royal Assent on 26 June 1846[7] granted powers for the construction of a main line from Macclesfield in Cheshire through Stoke-upon-Trent and Stone to Colwich where it was to join the Trent Valley line of the newly formed L&NWR. There were three branches, one of which was to run from Stone to Norton Bridge where it would also link with the L&NWR, 5¼ miles to the north of Stafford. The very first section of the NSR to be opened was from Stoke to Norton Bridge. The official openings took place on 17 April 1848 when the NSR 2-2-2 locomotive No. 1 *Dragon* (Sharp Bros. 484/1848) hauled a passenger train from a temporary station at Whieldon Grove in Stoke to the NSR's station at Norton Bridge. This station closed in 1850 following which all trains used or passed through the L&NWR station. There is some evidence that through running of NSR trains between Stoke and Stafford had taken place before this date. Thereafter, NSR engines and trains could be seen at Stafford on a daily basis, some running through to Wolverhampton and Birmingham. A new station with four platforms was opened at Norton Bridge on 14 October 1876 following the quadrupling of the line between Stafford and Crewe.

Shropshire Union Railway

An Act of Parliament for the making of a railway from Shrewsbury to Stafford (with a branch to Stone that was never completed) received the Royal Assent on 3 August 1846.[8] The same Act established the Shropshire Union Railways & Canal Company as a legal entity and so brought together a common ownership between the proposed new railway and the Shropshire Union Canal and its branches. Before the new railway was completed another Act which received the Royal Assent on 2 July 1847[9] provided for the L&NWR to lease the newly formed railway and canal company in perpetuity. The formal opening of the line from Stafford to Shrewsbury took place on 1 June 1849. There was great junketing at Wellington and Shrewsbury where the coming of the railway was a new phenomenon, the line from

Shrewsbury to Birmingham having opened simultaneously as far as Oakengates to compliment the line from Chester which had reached Shrewsbury the previous year. However, there was no ceremony at Stafford which is, perhaps, not surprising as the county town had already been on the main line railway map for some twelve years and trains had become commonplace. Indeed by 1861 yet another station on the same site was being built at Stafford to cope with the increasing demand for travel. This time it was built by contractor John Parnell (1817-1885) of Rugby in Italianate style to the designs of the L&NWR Chief Engineer, William Baker (1817-1878).

It should be noted that the section of line between Wellington and Shrewsbury was from the outset owned jointly by the Shropshire Union Railways and Canal Company and the Shrewsbury and Birmingham Railway. The latter company was absorbed by the Great Western Railway on 1 September 1854 and from that date the railway between Wellington and Shrewsbury was jointly owned and operated with the L&NWR.

Uttoxeter Canal

As previously mentioned the Trent and Mersey Canal opened throughout in 1777 and from that date provided a through means of communication between the River Trent and the River Mersey. An Act of Parliament which received the Royal Assent on 13 May 1776[10] enabled the Company of Proprietors of the Navigation to build a branch canal from its summit point at Etruria to Froghall in the Churnet Valley utilising parts of the River Churnet. This enabled it to tap the lucrative limestone traffic from the Caldon quarries as the same Act also provided for a railway to be built from Froghall to the quarries. The construction of the Caldon Canal, as the waterway soon became known, proceeded apace and it was opened at the end of 1778. Its provision was very fortuitous as it could also be used for feeding water into the summit level of the Trent & Mersey. An Act of Parliament which received the Royal Assent on 24 March 1797[11] authorised the construction of the Leek Branch and the provision of a large reservoir which became known as Rudyard Lake. This was engineered by John Rennie (1761-1821) and when full occupies 180 acres. Other well known reservoirs feeding into the Caldon Canal are Stanley Pool which was opened in 1786 and was extended to 33 acres in 1840 and the 40 acre Knypersley Pool, which was completed by Thomas Telford (1757-1834) in 1827.

The Leek Branch was opened for navigation in 1801. It is now necessary to retrace our steps in order to chronicle the history of the Uttoxeter Canal. On 6 June 1797 the Royal Assent was granted to another Act of Parliament[12] which authorised a 13¼ mile extension of the Caldon Canal from Froghall to Uttoxeter. The commercial interests in Uttoxeter had clearly seen the advantages of Leek being connected to the canal system and wanted to avail themselves of the same facility. However, Uttoxeter did not have the advantage of being on the route of an abundant supply of water. Indeed the route proposed would drain water from the canal reservoirs as it descended the Churnet Valley. For this reason the proprietors dragged their feet by proposing variations to the original scheme with the result that the first three and a half mile section from Froghall to Oakamoor was not opened

until August 1808; the next two mile section from Oakamoor to Alton took until by May 1809 with the final eight and a half mile section to Uttoxeter opening amid great pomp on 3 September 1811. The jollifications were not surprising as the inhabitants of Uttoxeter had endured some 14 years waiting before getting their canal!

After all this effort, Uttoxeter's canal was destined to be short lived. The promotion of the NSR presented the proprietors of the Trent & Mersey Canal with a formidable challenge and rather than oppose the new enterprise, they sought to be taken over by the new company. Extremely favourable terms were negotiated for the canal shareholders and this resulted in an agreement signed on 12 July 1845 between the railway promoters and the canal company. The NSR continued to invest in the majority of the canal system it had inherited but it had other ideas for the Uttoxeter Canal. The NSR's Churnet Valley line, authorised in 1846, superseded the route of part of the canal and it was proposed that the canal should be closed and parts of it filled in to accommodate the new railway. As the canal was not paying its way there was little opposition and so after a life of only 35 years the canal was closed to pave the way for the new railway era.

The 'Knotty' arrives at Uttoxeter

The North Staffordshire Railway, immortalised as the 'Knotty' through the use of the Staffordshire knot as its emblem, operated the first passenger train from Stoke-on-Trent to Uttoxeter on 7 August 1848 with three trains passing each way *conveying numerous parties of passengers, and as many of them were previously unacquainted with the luxury of railway travelling, much pleasurable excitement prevailed, especially amongst those who entered the trains from road-side stations. Although the speed seldom exceeded sixteen to twenty miles an hour, the honest yeomen exchanged significant glances of acknowledgement that steam was more than a match for horse-flesh, and that the pace of the fastest trotter that ever ran with market-cart would seem sluggish in comparison with the locomotive.* The new railway had obviously met with approval; Uttoxeter had joined the railway age. The inaugural train left Stoke at 9.40 a.m. and arrived at Uttoxeter at 10.40 a.m., having called at Longton, Blythe Bridge, Cresswell and Leigh.

The original lines of the North Staffordshire Railway were originally enshrined in three Acts of Parliament, all of which received the Royal Assent on 26 June 1846.[13] The line from Uttoxeter to Stoke was included as a 16½ mile branch in the North Staffordshire Railway (Churnet Valley Line) Act 1846 which authorised the line from Macclesfield via North Rode and Uttoxeter to a junction with the Midland Railway at Willington.[14] This was presumably an attempt to ensure that Stoke could be served if the proposed line through the Potteries failed. There had been strong opposition to the proposals by powerful industrialists and landowners in the Potteries and the NSR only got Parliamentary approval for all three Acts on the understanding that it came back to Parliament in the next session with a Bill that would satisfy the objectors. In the meantime steps were taken to form a statutory company, acquire the share capital of the Trent & Mersey Canal and exercise compulsory purchase powers to acquire land for the proposed railways.

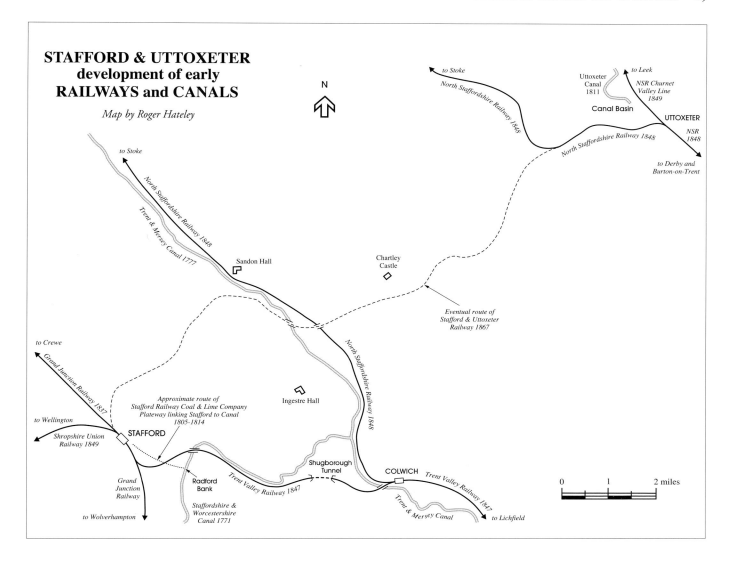

The North Staffordshire Railway (Alterations and Branches) Act 1847[15] which received the Royal Assent on 2 July 1847, authorised additional lines and variations to some of the lines already authorised in order to placate the objectors in accordance with the understanding reached the previous year. More importantly, it repealed the 1846 Acts, which contained enormous duplication, in their entirety while also making it clear that any actions already undertaken by the company, including its formation, were to be considered lawful. Part of the line from North Rode to Uttoxeter was built over the former Uttoxeter Canal, being a branch of the recently acquired Trent & Mersey Canal, but in spite of this possible advantage, priority was clearly given to the construction of the line from Uttoxeter to Stoke.

Railway development in the market town continued rapidly. The railway southwards to Burton-on-Trent came into operation on 11 September 1848 and the Churnet Valley line from North Rode to Uttoxeter opened on 13 July 1849 at the same time as the branch from Marston Junction to Willington Junction, where the NSR joined the Midland Railway, so giving access to Derby. The proposed Marston - Willington link of 4 miles 38 chains, included in the 1846 Bill, had been delayed through problems

with the landowner, Sir Henry Every, 9th Bart (1777-1855) and as a result required separate statutory powers in the form of the North Staffordshire Railway (Willington Deviation) Act 1848 which received the Royal Assent on 22 July 1848.[16] Trains calling at Uttoxeter served stations to Macclesfield, via the Churnet Valley and stations to Derby and Burton to the south and Stoke-on-Trent and Crewe to the north. Indeed the NSR regarded the line from Crewe to Derby as its second main line even though it started with statutory running powers over the L&NWR and ended in similar circumstances over the Midland! It became the practice to change at Tutbury for Burton-on-Trent. Uttoxeter's train services were further extended to Ashbourne on 31 May 1852 when a branch to that town was opened from the Churnet Valley line at Rocester.

Amazingly, Uttoxeter originally had three stations. Uttoxeter Bridge Street was opened on 7 August 1848 followed by Uttoxeter Junction station on 11 September 1848. The latter was intended to serve both the Crewe-Derby and Churnet Valley lines but it was not conveniently situated for the town. When the Churnet Valley line was opened on 13 July 1849 another new station was provided at Uttoxeter Dove Bank. Early in 1862 the Junction station was destroyed by fire but it was rebuilt by John Evans of Macclesfield for £760. All three stations were closed in 1881 when the present station was opened on 1 October and a new connection provided to link the Crewe-Derby line with the Churnet Valley line. Uttoxeter then had the benefit of a triangular junction arrangement whereby, if required, locomotives could be turned without the aid of a turntable (see Chapter Seven).

Consolidation

By the time the S&UR entered the scene rail services at Stafford and Uttoxeter were well established both for passenger and goods traffic. Stafford had the premier position on the L&NWR's West Coast Main Line but Uttoxeter was a very important junction. Operations at both locations took place around the clock throughout each day.

Notes

1   6 Geo III ch xcvi.
2   6 Geo III ch xcvii.
3   3-4 Wm IV ch xxxiv.
4   The six pottery towns of Burslem, Fenton, Hanley, Longton, Stoke and Tunstall, along with sixty villages, combined to form a single county borough of Stoke-on-Trent on 31 March 1910, later acquiring city status on 5 June 1925. The North Staffordshire pottery industry became world famous.
5   This description of the problem is taken from a contemporary report. As, strictly speaking, the axle-tree comprises the hub and spokes, it was probably the wheel rims or flanges that were scoring the undersides of the carriages.
6   8-9 Vic ch cxii.
7   9-10 Vic ch lxxxv. Very interestingly, and perhaps uniquely, this Act and the North Staffordshire Railway (Churnet Valley Line) Act 1846 (9-10 Vic ch lxxxvi) which received the Royal Assent on the same day, both authorised the same section of railway from an end on junction with the Manchester and Birmingham Railway at Macclesfield to North Rode and the proposed railway from there through the Churnet Valley to Willington Junction on the Midland Railway. The building of a railway does not normally involve two Acts!
8   9-10 Vic ch cccxxiii.
9   10-11 Vic ch cxxi.
10 16 Geo III ch xxxii.
11 37 Geo III ch xxxvi.
12 37 Geo III ch lxxiii.
13 The North Staffordshire Railway (Harecastle and Sanbach) Line Act 1846, 9-10 Vic ch lxxiv; The North Staffordshire Railway (Pottery Line) Act 1846, 9-10 Vic ch lxxv; The North Staffordshire Railway (Churnet Valley) Line Act 1846, 9-10 Vic ch lxxvi.
14 As previously mentioned, the section from Macclesfield to Willington was also duplicated in the North Staffordshire Railway (Pottery Line) Act 1846.
15 10-11 Vic ch cviii.
16 11-12 Vic ch lxiv.

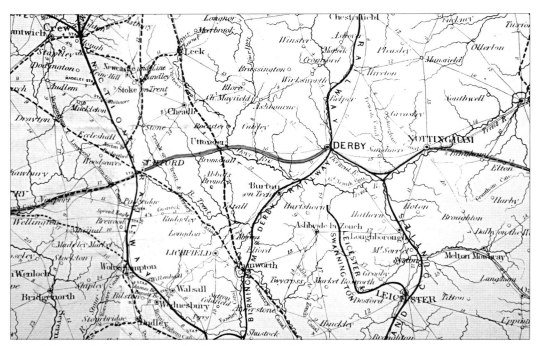

Map of the proposed route of the projected Derby, Uttoxeter & Stafford Railway of 1845, described in the next Chapter.

NA BT41/806/4505

CHAPTER TWO

Proposed East to West Links: Abortive Schemes

Preamble

Before delving into the enormously complicated plethora of schemes outlined in this chapter, it is worth informing readers that inevitably, reference has had to be made to the S&UR as eventually built. It might otherwise seem that the authors are putting the cart before the horse. Those readers wanting a full understanding of the complete picture will, therefore, have to cross reference between chapters. While craving readers' indulgence on this issue, no alternative or better way of presenting the information seemed appropriate.

Before the S&UR came to fruition there were no fewer than twelve railway schemes connecting Uttoxeter directly with Stafford, or at least serving much of the intervening area. In some cases the proposals had wider implications, spreading further east or west of the two towns or in some cases in both directions. Of the schemes five date from 1845, with one each from 1855, 1859, 1862, 1863, 1864 and 1865 and they are described in that order. The early part of the period under review is often colloquially

referred to as *The Railway Mania*, a period when literally hundreds of railway schemes were being promoted all over the country. The vast majority of them never came to fruition, while a good number of those that did, never made any commercial sense. To give an idea of the size of the issue, for the 1845-1846 Parliamentary session, almost 500 individual railway schemes were tabled, a figure which excludes a whole host of others that never got as far as having plans etc., deposited to meet the Parliamentary timescales. To enable Parliament to cope with this enormous workload, the various schemes were sorted into groups covering different parts of the country, or where they otherwise overlapped. This allowed the Select Committees to adjudicate, on hearing evidence for and against, as to which, if any, of the schemes should go forward. In that same year, 270 Railway Bills received the Royal Assent speculating in the construction of 4,540 route miles of new railway, involving the raising of £95,625,934 of capital (approximately a staggering £10bn at today's values), with borrowing powers for a further £36,087,272.[17] The multifarious

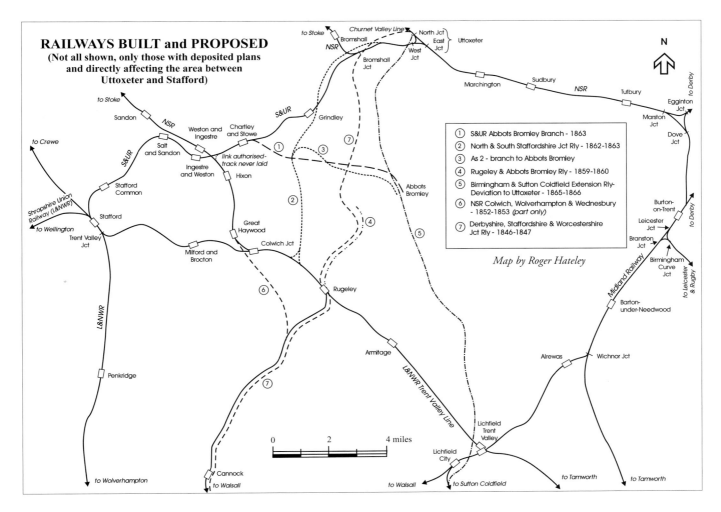

RAILWAYS BUILT and PROPOSED
(Not all shown, only those with deposited plans and directly affecting the area between Uttoxeter and Stafford)

① S&UR Abbots Bromley Branch - 1863
② North & South Staffordshire Jct Rly - 1862-1863
③ As 2 - branch to Abbots Bromley
④ Rugeley & Abbots Bromley Rly - 1859-1860
⑤ Birmingham & Sutton Coldfield Extension Rly - Deviation to Uttoxeter - 1865-1866
⑥ NSR Colwich, Wolverhampton & Wednesbury - 1852-1853 *(part only)*
⑦ Derbyshire, Staffordshire & Worcestershire Jct Rly - 1846-1847

Map by Roger Hateley

individuals involved in promoting all these railways and to a greater or lesser extent the folk who subscribed to them by taking shares, lost a great deal of money. This was despite the fact that in most cases the early calls on the share holdings were not to the full face value. A considerable number of the authorised railways were never built, such that even more of the money subscribed was lost.

The promoters of only five of the cases that concern us here got as far developing their schemes such that a Bill, along with all the necessary documents to comply with Parliamentary Standing Orders, could be lodged with Parliament as a start to the process of obtaining the necessary statutory powers to build a railway. In the case of the remaining six, provisional registration was under the Joint Stock Companies Registration Act 1841. This was quite a common method during the period in question, for aspiring promoters of railways to initially get their schemes established, thereby limiting individual's liability. Subsequently, enactment by Parliament of the Companies Clauses, Land Clauses and Railway Clauses Consolidation Acts in May 1845, while having far ranging consequences, generally steered embryo railway companies seeking statutory powers to adopt different methods of incorporation. There is one more issue before we move on and describe the individual schemes. For those of 1845 and to a lesser extent the later ones, it has to be remembered that few railways had been authorised by that date and even fewer completed and open to traffic. Therefore, projected railways often interfaced with other schemes, such that planned junctions between different proposals assumed that all would come to fruition. For example a proposed line of route for railway A, might be described and shown by overlaying it on a map as having junctions with railways B and C, while all three were proposals without any positive financial commitment that they would in fact be built.

Burton, Stafford, Shrewsbury & Newtown Railway

The first scheme was the Burton, Stafford, Shrewsbury & Newtown Railway Company, provisionally registered on 6 February 1845 by John Owens, a solicitor of Newtown with an office in London.[18] This is particularly interesting as support for a railway between Stafford and Uttoxeter from Shropshire and points further west into Wales is, as will be seen both in this chapter and later in the book, a recurrent theme in our story. The proposals in this case were for a railway from Burton-on-Trent (and the full title of this town was later included in the railway title) where the Midland Railway line from Birmingham to Derby already existed,[19] thence in a direct line to Stafford and onwards to Newport and Wellington. There it was intended to join either the projected Wolverhampton & Shrewsbury line or proceed on an independent course to Shrewsbury. From Shrewsbury westwards to Newtown, where it would join yet another projected line, that from Wolverhampton to Portdynllan [sic][20] which is on the west side of the Lleyn peninsular in Caernarvonshire and about five miles north-west of Pwllheli. Although no plan of the route appears to have survived, a direct line from Burton to Stafford, while requiring significant earth works, would have taken it just to the south of the town of Abbots Bromley, which was in the sights of the S&UR Directors when their line was later

promoted. The scheme had a proposed capital of £1,500,000, divided into 75,000 shares of £20 each with the first call of £2 2s 0d (£2 10p). It was reckoned the line would give a return on capital of 12%, which it has to be added, takes some believing. The provisional committee consisted of no fewer than 145 people, so one is left wondering quite how such a number could conduct any business at all! The list was headed by the Earl of Rossmore[21] and The Hon. Colonel Leicester Stanhope, with the vast majority being directors of one or more other railways, both actual and projected. Quite why an Irish Lord should involve himself has eluded the authors.

The principal engineer was no less than Sir John Rennie (1794-1874), assisted by George Remington, at which point it is perhaps worth saying a little about Remington. In the period under discussion there were two proposals for direct lines from Manchester to London, following dissatisfaction at what was seen as a circuitous route via Crewe of the Manchester & Birmingham Railway. One was promoted by George Remington[22] and known as *Remington's Direct Line*, while another by John Urpeth Rastrick[23] was, not surprisingly, known as *Rastrick's Line*. The former projected a route via Macclesfield, along the Churnet Valley via Leek and Uttoxeter, thence Burton, Leicester, Kettering and St Albans, to a terminus at Kings Cross. Part of the section from Manchester to Burton largely followed the route later adopted by the NSR, which opened between North Rode, south-west of Macclesfield, along the Churnet Valley to Uttoxeter in July 1849. On the other hand, Rastrick took his line from Stockport through the Derbyshire Peak via Buxton and Ashbourne to Leicester, onwards by a similar course to Remington's but to a different terminus in London, in this case at Farringdon. Although neither scheme came to fruition, both had a lot of support such that individuals were known to be *Remington's Direct Line* or *Rastrick's Line* supporters, but in no circumstances both! Colonel Stanhope by the way, mentioned in connection with the previous scheme, was the Chairman of *Remington's Direct Line*. Whatever the uptake of shares in the new company has gone unrecorded, although no fewer than 24 agents were appointed to whom subscribers could submit their applications with the required deposit. Although spread far and wide around the country, surprisingly there were no agents situated in Wales. In its last return of 21 November 1845, the company noted that two trustees had been appointed to represent the shareholders and that 11 of the promoters had agreed to take shares - only agreed and not yet taken - and that is the last to be heard of this scheme.

Derbyshire, Staffordshire & Worcestershire Junction Railway

The promoters of the Derbyshire, Staffordshire & Worcestershire Junction Railway (DS&WJR) of 1845-1846, also had rather grandiose ideas.[24] They planned a line from Uttoxeter, where it would have made connection with *Remington's Direct Line*, via Bramshall, Lea Fields, Grindley, Drointon, Colton and Rugeley, where it would have crossed the Grand Junction Railway (GJR). It ran thence via Hednesford, Little Bloxwich, Rycroft, Walsall, Wednesbury and Tipton Toll End to join the projected Oxford, Worcester & Wolverhampton Railway at Dudley. The section of this railway from Stourbridge Junction to Dudley did not open until 20 December 1852. The total length of the DS&WJR was 32 miles and approximately five chains, with a 711 yard tunnel at Moor's Gorse, just east of Hednesford; the estimated cost was £265,740. The engineers were once again, Sir John Rennie and George Remington. There was a lot of opposition to this railway at House of Commons Select Committee level, principally from the Birmingham Canal Company as it penetrated right into the heart of the Canal Company's system, as well as passing very close to a number of collieries on the Cannock Chase coalfield, many of which were served by various branch canals. Despite various amendments made to the Bill such that the Canal Company removed its opposition, it did not get beyond the Lords. Not daunted, the promoters came back the following year with a modified scheme, largely the same but not penetrating so far west and terminating at Cannock Mill, just west of Hednesford. The total length was now 18 miles and six furlongs, provision being made to connect with the L&NWR Trent Valley line at Rugeley. By this time the NSR had come into existence, such that the strategy regarding a line through the Churnet Valley to Uttoxeter was settled. There were clauses to accommodate a junction with the NSR at Uttoxeter, as well as protecting that company's interests in other areas. The South Staffordshire Railway Company (SSR) was also before Parliament in 1847, being empowered to build a line from Walsall to Cannock, effectively appropriating part of the earlier DS&WJR scheme and in this case, with branches to Norton and Wyrley.[25] Clauses were therefore, inserted in the DS&WJR Act to protect the SSR and on this occasion the promoters were successful, receiving the Royal Assent on 2 July 1847.[26] However, as events turned out, no progress was made in building the line although we will revert to the company again later, in its correct chronological order.

Macclesfield & Lichfield or Churnet & Blythe Junction Railway

Yet another scheme of 1845 got as far as the plans and sections, books of reference etc., being deposited with Parliament and with the Clerks of Peace of the counties through which it was to pass. The promoters however, seem to have been in some doubt as to what to call their railway and the plans carry the title, Macclesfield & Lichfield or Churnet & Blythe Junction Railway. This scheme, however, was the result of a joining of the ways by two of what might otherwise have been rivals. *The Manchester Times & Gazette* in its issue dated 3 January 1846, mentioned the possibility of the shareholders of the projected Manchester & Rugby Direct Railway joining forces with the Churnet & Blythe Valley Railway. The reasoning was that while the former scheme had not been in a position to have plans and sections etc., ready to meet the deadline for the Parliamentary deposit for the 1845-1846 Session, the latter scheme did. While the paper work had already been deposited, the financial commitment had not, as insufficient funds were available from the share options already taken. However, with the Manchester & Rugby shareholders on board, this was no longer an issue. A meeting of the shareholders from both projects held at the Albion Hotel in Leek on 16 January 1846, agreed to the amalgamation of the two schemes and the Bill was thus allowed to proceed through the Parliamentary stages.

Strangely the plans and other surviving documents[27] do not identify the engineer(s) involved which is surprising, as a lot of work had clearly been undertaken in surveying the land and establishing all the owners and leaseholders. As was the case with the previous scheme, the route initially followed that later adopted by the NSR Churnet Valley line. Starting at Macclesfield, where a junction was to have been made with the Manchester & Birmingham Railway branch to that town (opened 24 November 1845), the route was along the Churnet Valley as far as Kingsley, where with a grade of 1 in 100 for over a mile, it climbed out of the valley to pass just to the east of Cheadle, before descending to the valley of the Blithe at Upper Tean. It would then have proceeded via Lower Leigh, where a short spur of slightly over four furlongs and two chains long, was to make connection with the projected Derby to Crewe Railway. Continuing due south via Field, Gratwich and Grindley, where it would have crossed the route later adopted by the S&UR, then just to the west of Abbots Bromley, Hamstall Ridware, King's Bromley and Curborough to a terminus at Lichfield. There connection would have been made with the GJR Trent Valley line. Total length of the proposed line was 45 miles two furlongs and a little over two chains with one tunnel, 715 yards long, just north of Abbots Bromley. At the Select Committee stage of the House of Lords on 4 March 1846, despite no engineers having been mentioned on the plans, no lesser engineer than Joseph Locke appeared in support of the scheme, with George Parker Bidder against. Bidder was very soon to be engaged by the NSR as its Engineer and Manager and it may have been on behalf of the gentlemen plotting the embryonic NSR, that he gave evidence. The total cost quoted in evidence was an estimated £1,000,000. The committee discovered that on the plans there was no datum line referring to any fixed point marked on the sections and thus, they did not comply with Standing Orders. This leads one to question why so eminent an engineer as Locke was involved, as it would seem almost inconceivable that he would not have been aware that the surveys were incomplete. The House of Lords referred the Bill back to the Commons which, on 18 March, decided that Standing Orders should not be dispensed with[28] and therefore, the Bill failed at that point.

Derby, Uttoxeter & Stafford Railway

Next to be discussed is the Derby, Uttoxeter & Stafford Railway, another one provisionally registered under the 1841 Act; in this case on 23 May 1845.[29] The proposal was for a line from a junction with the Midland Railway at Stenson, about four miles south-west of Derby, via Uttoxeter to the GJR at Milford, a similar distance east of Stafford. The total length was quoted as approximately 33 miles with a capital of £500,000, divided into 20,000 shares of £25 each, the first call being £1 7s 6d (£1 37½p). The Engineer was William Millington Higgins, with a London address, who it was claimed had carefully surveyed the country and established that the line could be built at *exceedingly moderate cost*, no greater than £15,000 per mile. Great play was made in the prospectus that the line would provide a through connection between the eastern counties, north, central and south Wales to Birmingham and Manchester. Moreover, it was confidently (more likely optimistically) the view of the promoters that by this route, nearly all the through traffic from central parts of eastern England to central parts of western England and Wales, must pass over it. The original promoters were both employed by the Eastern Counties Railway (later part of the Great Eastern Railway) and by August 1845, the Provisional Committee consisted of no fewer than 45 people from a wide range of walks of life, including the Mayors of both Derby and Stafford, along with Aldermen of both towns. The Chairman was William Nash, described as Chairman of the Brighton, Lewes & Hastings Railway and late Chairman of the London & Brighton Railway – both later part of the London, Brighton & South Coast Railway. Because the number of committee members *had recently been considerably augmented*, alleged to be in view of an increasing local interest, the date for the allotment of shares was postponed from that originally set, to 25 August.

When notice was given to the public on 6 November 1845, that an application was to be made to Parliament for statutory authority to build the line, several branches had been added; the intended capital however, remained the same. Of the four branches one made a connection with the GJR nearer to Stafford station than Milford, while another served Burton-on-Trent. The other two were short lines near Derby, the exact purpose of which from the description is unclear, as no plans appear to have survived. The notice stated that plans and sections, books of reference (land ownership) etc., were being prepared and would be deposited with Parliament in accordance with Standing Orders on or before 31 December 1845. As no such plans were deposited, we can only assume that either none had been prepared, or they were insufficiently complete to meet the timescales. In any event, if little work had been done on them by 6 November, it would have been a tall order to have them ready in time. In fact, a newspaper report of 17 January 1847, mentions that the promoters had failed to make a Parliamentary deposit. We do not know what took place thereafter, other than on 10 March 1846 when at a General Meeting of the shareholders, the Committee of Management was requested to dissolve the Company, retaining a sum of £11,596 16s 11d (£11,596.85p) to meet outstanding liabilities and settle all claims. Presumably, for such an exact sum to be established, an accurate assessment of exactly what the liabilities etc., were, was available to the meeting. The minutes mention that the actual call on the shares had been £1 12s 6d (£1.62½p), slightly more than the original intention, the inference being that a significant number of shares had been taken up at this figure. Indeed, a notice dated 3 September 1845, would suggest that a complete allotment had taken place and may even have been over-subscribed. However, there is no mention of how much cash was returned to shareholders, other than it would be pro-rata to the number of shares held. Whatever the case, it would appear that a lot of people lost significant amounts of money on this abortive scheme.

Stafford, Uttoxeter & Mansfield Railway

Worth a brief mention is the projected Stafford, Uttoxeter & Mansfield Railway, yet another company preliminary registered under the 1841 Act[30], in this case on 4 October 1845. The proposal was for a line from Stafford via Uttoxeter, Ashbourne and Belper with a branch to Wirksworth. On 10 November the promoters wrote to the Company Registrar amending the title of the railway to the Ashbourne & Mansfield Junction Railway and at the same time abandoning plans for the section between Stafford and Ashbourne. In any event, nothing further appears to have materialised and as reported in the press on 17 January 1846, the promoters failed to make a Parliamentary deposit.

Staffordshire & North Midland Junction Railway

The next scheme to be discussed was an altogether more developed one, the Staffordshire & North Midland Junction Railway, for which a detailed survey was undertaken with plans, sections and books of reference being compiled and deposited with Parliament in 1846.[31] This company was also provisionally registered on 1 September 1845 under the 1841 Act, with a capital of £700,000, divided into 28,000 shares of £25 each for which a call of £2 12s 6d (£2.62½p) was made. Once again a sizeable Provisional Committee was formed, in this case 38 individuals, the majority of whom were already directors of other railway schemes, none of which, like this one, came to fruition. The engineer was William Millington Higgins, although he is only listed as in an acting capacity. The line would have left the GJR to the north of Stafford station, onwards to Uttoxeter following more or less the route as later adopted by the S&UR. However, the gradients were less severe, as on the 12 miles to Bromshall there were to be no fewer than three tunnels – 893, 972 and 550 yards long respectively. At Bromshall the line was projected to join the proposed Derby & Crewe Junction Railway, an 1845 scheme in connection with the Macclesfield & Lichfield or Churnet & Blythe Junction Railway (mentioned earlier), leaving it at Uttoxeter to head due east via Rocester and Ashbourne to Belper, a total length of 35 miles seven furlongs and four chains. At Belper it would have joined the Midland Railway line from Derby to Sheffield. Actually there was an alternative arrangement of the junction at Belper, the one mentioned above joined the Midland Railway line in the direction of Sheffield, while the alternative one faced Derby. There was also a branch to Wirksworth. Those readers familiar with the topography of the district between Ashbourne and Belper will not be surprised to learn that the section included four tunnels, one of which would have been 3,069 yards long and the others, 453, 1,738 and 1,705 yards. The engineering work would thus have been of some magnitude, hence the proposed capital, although the projected cost of the works is not recorded in the surviving papers. By the time the plans and sections etc., were deposited with Parliament, the Provisional Committee had increased to no fewer than 70 individuals, with a separate Committee of Management consisting of 15, led by the Hon. Rev. Augustus Duncombe of Calwich Abbey, Ashbourne. The consulting engineer appointed was the well established Joseph Locke and by the time of the deposit, Stourges Meeke is listed as the resident engineer. The trail goes cold with the Parliamentary deposit so we can only assume that the scheme failed to meet Standing Orders, certainly the deposit was incomplete which makes it once again quite surprising that such an eminent engineer as Locke was involved. A revised list of members of the Committee of Management was deposited with the Company

Registrar on 9 January 1846 adding, inter alia, Lord Viscount Ingestre (sic) to their number, followed on 16 January by a notice to the effect that an agreement had been reached with the embryo NSR, for friendly cooperation and use of a portion of its line. By this time the projected Derby & Crewe Junction Railway mentioned above, had amalgamated (November 1845) with the NSR, its intended route between Crewe and Derby becoming part of the NSR plans.

Birmingham, Lichfield & Uttoxeter Railway
The following scheme appears to have made little if any progress and no shares were issued. The Birmingham, Lichfield & Uttoxeter Railway was provisionally registered under the 1841 Act on 19 September 1845,[32] by Joseph Ludlow a surveyor from Birmingham. An announcement was made in local newspapers during October (submitted to the Company Registrar on 15 October) describing the project as a line from Birmingham, to join the projected NSR at Uttoxeter, passing through Sutton Coldfield, Lichfield and Abbots Bromley. The last return is dated 17 October 1846, noting that no shares had been issued. Despite the paucity of information, this scheme mentioned Abbots Bromley which was later in the sights of the S&UR as well as a number of other schemes.

North Stafford Aspirations and Politics
We must now return to the subject of the DS&WJR which we left in 1847, having got its Act to build a line from Cannock to Uttoxeter via Rugeley. However, first of all, it is opportune to mention briefly the NSR and its efforts to gain access to South Staffordshire. Almost from its inception the NSR had been in arguments with the L&NWR, largely but not exclusively, over its share of the Manchester to London traffic which could travel either via Crewe, or the NSR at Stoke. Suffice it to say, the L&NWR placed obstacles in the way of the smaller company with for example, insufficient facilities at Norton Bridge for the interchange of traffic and it was all clouded by several unsuccessful attempts for the two companies to amalgamate. Having concluded that the two companies were unlikely to come to an agreement on the financial aspects of an amalgamation, the NSR directors resolved at their meeting on 30 December 1851, to promote three Bills in Parliament in efforts to frustrate the L&NWR. Bills were formulated to build new lines from Sandbach to Warrington (to improve access to the Mersey ports) and of more interest to us, from Colwich to Wolverhampton and Wednesbury. Complete surveys of these two lines along with books of reference regarding land ownership etc., were undertaken in 1852 involving of course, considerable expense.[33] The scheme involved a main line a little over 17 miles long which would have left the Stone to Colwich route just before it joined the L&NWR Trent Valley line which it was proposed to cross on the level. This, of course, was guaranteed to upset its neighbour! It terminated in Wolverhampton by a junction with the Oxford, Worcester & Wolverhampton Railway (OW&WR), the section built under its 1848 Deviation Act, although this line was not opened from Tipton Junction through Priestfield to Cannock Road Junction at Wolverhampton until 1 July 1854.[34] The NSR

junction was a few yards short of a proposed station adjacent to the Cannock Road and to the north east of Wolverhampton town centre. There were three branches, two of which were quite short ones, seven and a half furlongs and almost three furlongs long at Wolverhampton connecting, respectively, with the original GJR[35] and the Birmingham, Wolverhampton & Stour Valley Railway, both just to the north of the town. The latter line had opened between Birmingham and Wolverhampton on 1 July 1852 and onwards to Bushbury Junction on 2 August; it was leased to the L&NWR from 1 January 1850. The third branch was much longer, a little over three and a half miles leaving the main line to the west of Bloxwich to serve Wednesbury, where it joined the Birmingham, Wolverhampton & Dudley Railway which did not open from Birmingham to Priestfield Junction until 14 November 1854.[36] As the OW&WR and the GWR lines involved were either broad gauge or mixed gauge, the NSR Bill also proposed some mixed gauge and while it is not clear exactly where this mixed gauge track would have been situated, it is presumed that at least the junction arrangements would have been involved. This was at the time of much controversy regarding the track gauge of railways following the Parliamentary Gauge Commission report of 1846 and the Gauge of Railway Act of the same year. We suspect, however, that the NSR was just hedging its bets! The Bill also outlined quite extensive running powers as part of the proposals.

A Special General meeting of the NSR shareholders was held at Stoke on 5 April 1852 when the sorry story of relationships with the L&NWR was outlined to the assembled company. According to the *Staffordshire Advertiser* in its issue of 10 April the NSR Chairman[37] along with seven fellow directors and the principal officers, were joined by a *tolerably numerous and very respectable attendance of the proprietary!* Despite the tolerance of the shareholders it was a somewhat stormy occasion; suffice to say however, for our purpose, the actions already taken by the directors of depositing Bills in Parliament for the line to Warrington and from Colwich to Wolverhampton, were approved and the directors were enjoined: *to obtain such an outlet for the traffic as will render them independent of the obstructions and impediments now thrown in the way by the L&NWR.*

The third Bill was to lease the NSR to the L&NWR and while the common seal of the Company was affixed to it, in the event it did not progress, rather the two companies eventually returned to the negotiating table, the larger company being particularly anxious to guard against its position at Liverpool. Later in April 1852 it was agreed to place the question of possible terms of an amalgamation with Robert Stephenson and Robert Hope to, in effect, act as arbitrators and at its meeting on 3 May, the NSR directors gave their Chairman authority to withdraw the leasing Bill if he felt it appropriate in the light of any progress made following the arbitrators' report. While this need not greatly concern us here, suffice to say, despite an agreement with the L&NWR, the Bill did not pass Parliament as the whole question of railway amalgamations was under consideration in the light of a much larger proposed amalgamation scheme, that of the L&NWR and the Midland Railway.

The DS&WJR applied to Parliament again in the 1854-1855

Session, as it needed to renew its powers as they had otherwise lapsed due to the lack of capital having prevented any work being undertaken; it also sought powers to abandon the section from Rugeley to Uttoxeter. The NSR directors at their meeting on 17 February 1854, elected to oppose the Bill while wanting to secure proper provision for protection of their *rights*. The *rights* they were referring to were of course, running powers over the line so as to gain access via Colwich, to South Staffordshire. The DS&WJR was again successful in getting its Act, the company also changing its name to the Cannock Mineral Railway (CMR), with Royal Assent on 14 August 1855.[38] Despite the fact that the Act gave powers for the line to be leased and or sold to the L&NWR, the NSR was able to reach an agreement in January 1856, to work the CMRs traffic. The arrangement was announced to shareholders at the NSR half-yearly meeting held on 30 January 1857, the terms being 50% of the gross receipts as well as sending annual traffic equal to 4½% of the capital, but not exceeding £116,000 (the capital was £160,000), a figure that could be increased to £280,000 should the CMR be successful in extending its line to Wolverhampton. This followed correspondence and meetings between John Addison, the line's Engineer and its Chairman, William Malins, resulting in a formal agreement in October 1856, with five NSR directors, including the Deputy Chairman[39], being appointed to the CMR Board. On this basis a Bill was formulated and presented to Parliament, although it was pointed out at an NSR directors meeting on 4 October 1856, that difficulty was being experienced in raising capital to build the line (as noted earlier this had already been the cause of delay).[40] It was then agreed that if it proved impossible to raise sufficient capital, the NSR would again go its own way and promote a Bill to build a line from Colwich to Wolverhampton. It then came to light that behind the backs of the NSR directors on the CMR Board and despite a Bill having been deposited with Parliament, discussions had been taking place with the L&NWR for that company to support the scheme and on better terms than those offered by the NSR. While it was not stated, doubtless help in finding the necessary capital was also involved. Not surprisingly, the NSR reacted to this very strongly, lodging a petition in Parliament arguing among other things, that the L&NWR was solely interested in keeping other companies out of an area that it was increasingly considering its own. The House of Commons Select Committee however, refused to hear this petition although one lodged by the SSR and citing almost identical issues, was heard. All was to no avail, as the Committee considered the Preamble proved.[41] To use a more modern term, to all intents and purposes, the NSR had been gazumped by the L&NWR, which offered 5%. News of this was conveyed to the NSR shareholders at their next half yearly meeting held on 28 July 1857. The NSR directors discussed at their meeting on 17 July 1857, a letter from Malins requesting that those members on the CMR Board should resign, which of course they did – doubtless being glad to do so! The NSR did get a clause in the CMR Act such that the latter company could not compulsory acquire any of its land. This came in useful in March the following year when it attempted to do so at Rugeley, where it crossed over the Trent & Mersey Canal which was NSR owned. One can be sure that

in recording their decision not to sell any land at their meeting on 4 March 1858, the assembled company were quite smug and that the issue engendered some lively discussion over lunch in the North Stafford Hotel that followed all Board meetings! [42]

To complete this sorry story, the NSR again proposed to build its own line from Colwich to the Wolverhampton district, but made absolutely no progress in doing so. It is assumed, however, that the 1852 plans would have been resurrected had this been the case. Neither did the CMR attempt to get powers to extend its line to either Wolverhampton or Colwich, as had originally been intended, opening between Cannock and Rugeley on 7 November 1859. Leased to the L&NWR from opening, the CMR was vested in that company by Act dated 12 July 1869.[43] The NSR soon made its peace with its larger neighbour and by an Act of 13 August 1859,[44] inter alia, the two companies agreed extensive running powers over each other's systems together with a procedure for the division of receipts in such cases, not least for the vexed Manchester to London traffic. Thereafter, the two companies lived happily ever after!

Rugeley & Abbots Bromley Railway

We now move on a few years to 1859, with Abbots Bromley once again the target. Plans and sections, books of reference etc., for the Rugeley & Abbots Bromley Railway were deposited with Parliament for the 1859-1860 Session.[45] The line would have left the L&NWR main line just north of Rugeley station and headed north-east and then north, to abut the Blithfield to Abbots Bromley road, now the B5013, at a place now subsumed by Blithfield reservoir and moreover, about a mile from the town. The route of the line and its terminus were doubtless selected in view of the high ground that would otherwise have had to be traversed to get closer to the town. In any event, there would have been a gradient of 1 in 80 for almost half a mile. The line would have been three miles five furlongs and five chains long at an estimated cost of £45,000, the Engineer being John Addison. Powers were intended for the L&NWR to work and maintain the line, although the deposited documents illustrate that in fact, the larger company had neither assented or dissented to the proposals. The scheme passed standing orders as the House of Lords Journal for 7 February 1860 mentions this, along with the fact that the Bill had been *laid on the table*. However, this is the last reference so we can only assume that the promoters, whoever they were and for whatever reason, lost interest. This was very much a local affair and the Solicitors for the railway were the Rugeley based, Landor, Gardner & Landor, who cannot have had much experience in such matters and it has not been possible to establish exactly who the promoters were and how much, if any, money was raised.

One does wonder however, how Addison came to be involved as although he had plenty of experience of surveying and building railways he was at the time (1858 through to 1885) Manager and Secretary and at one period the Engineer of the Maryport & Carlisle Railway.[46] A member of Joseph Locke's staff when Locke and John E. Errington were engineers of the Lancaster & Carlisle Railway, Addison was later involved with them on surveys around Shrewsbury, Stafford and the Black Country. He also did a lot of work in Scotland. What is more, we find him involved in the next scheme to be described, along with the same firm of solicitors, although on this occasion other solicitors were also involved, namely H. Herne of Newport in Shropshire.

North & South Staffordshire Junction Railway

The proposals in this case were for the North & South Staffordshire Junction Railway scheme of 1862-1863 . The statutory documents for this line were deposited with Parliament on 29 November 1862.[47] This is interesting as it post dates the Stafford & Uttoxeter Railway, which got its Act of Parliament on 29 July 1862, resulting in some interesting questioning at a House of Commons Select Committee. The plan was for a main line nine miles four furlongs, three chains and 95 links long, leaving the L&NWR main line just south of Colwich by a triangular junction, to join the NSR to the west of Uttoxeter. The junction connection there, however, was somewhat unconventional for instead of making connection at the point where the lines met, the new line was to pass over the NSR at Bromshall by a bridge with a 28ft span, giving the NSR a clearance of 14ft 6ins, then running parallel and on the north side of the NSR, to make a junction almost 1,400 yards further south-west and towards Uttoxeter. The line would have crossed under the authorised route of the S&UR at Grindley, the formation of that line having to be raised four feet as a consequence. A branch was planned to leave the main line at Drointon, three miles seven furlongs and three chains long, to serve Abbots Bromley. In this case the route approached the town from the north, rather than the south as in the previous scheme with, as a consequence, a terminus much closer to the town. There was also a proposed north facing connection to the L&NWR main line at Colwich four furlongs and seven chains long making, in effect, a triangular junction at that location. The estimated cost was £130,000 and the promoters sought powers to enter into agreements with the L&NWR, NSR and the CMR, or *either* of them, for the construction, working and maintenance of the line. It was in fact the CMR directors that were behind this scheme (for which Addison was also engineer). At the half-yearly meeting of NSR shareholders held on 21 February 1862, reflecting the previous half calendar year, it was noted that the scheme would be opposed by the NSR.

The Bill for the line having passed Standing Orders, a House of Commons Select Committee sat on 22-23 April 1863,[48] with Basil J. Wood MP in the chair. The NSR, L&NWR and not surprisingly the S&UR, had all lodged petitions against the Bill and were duly represented as, of course, were the promoters. The first witness was no lesser personage than the Earl of Lichfield[49] appearing in support of the scheme of which he was Chairman. In questioning he mentioned a long wanted communication between Uttoxeter and South Staffordshire, citing the mineral wealth of the Churnet Valley, both iron ore and limestone, along with timber from around Abbots Bromley and on Cannock Chase. Both this witness and others called later were strongly of the opinion that the proposed line would better serve the needs of communication between Uttoxeter and South Staffordshire. This included Wolverhampton, as it would be some 10 miles shorter from where the proposed line intersected with the authorised S&UR line at Grindley to Rugeley, than by the S&UR with its

proposed connection with the NSR line at Weston. When asked why he did not oppose the S&UR line the previous year, the Earl stated that while he was opposed to it, he was unable to be present as he had to attend the Staffordshire Quarter Sessions of which he was Chairman and they took place at the same time the Select Committee sat. Mention was then made of a Memorandum entered into by the NSR and L&NWR on 9 May 1862, as part of both companies' opposition to the S&UR scheme the previous year. It is summarised below:

The L&NWR and the NSR engage to apply for a line or lines of railway which may afford a good communication between Uttoxeter and Stafford and also a good communication in a southerly direction. In order to guard against any misapprehension as to the intention of the parties to the Memorandum, it is hereby declared and agreed on behalf of the L&NWR and NSR and that the line to be promoted shall be settled in concert with Lords Shrewsbury, Lichfield, Bagot, Harrowby, Ferrers, Anglesey and C.J.S. Kynnersely Esq. of Loxley Hall, as representing the general interests of the district and it is further agreed that in case of difference as to the course of the line to be adopted, the difference shall be left to the Board of Trade.

Richard Moon Chairman L&NWR
Thomas Brodrick Deputy Chairman NSR

This was of course, in the event that the S&UR Bill failed, although the Earl of Lichfield did not agree with this and felt the commitment was for a line, like the one now being proposed, from Uttoxeter, in the direction of Rugeley and Cannock Chase. He was quite emphatic about this and went on to say that all the noble Lords mentioned in the Memorandum, were in favour of the present proposal and of course, it would pass over much of their land. An interesting aside was in connection with some questioning regarding the traffic at Stafford station and the L&NWR allegation that even following recent enlargements, there was insufficient capacity there for the S&UR traffic. The Earl had found out at his cost that following the improvements, which included the construction of two through lines, not all trains stopped there anymore! We can perhaps visualize the fuming Earl, with his footman and luggage, seething as his train to London for some important Parliamentary business, went tearing through behind a Large Bloomer![50] In questioning, he did not think either the L&NWR or NSR Engineer had been consulted regarding the proposed junctions with their lines, although he did refer to two meetings that had taken place at Euston with the L&NWR regarding the proposed route. However, he only attended one, with Lord Shrewsbury and Talbot taking the lead in the discussions on behalf of the district interests.

A few other witnesses were then called in support and while the exact detail need not detain us, some of what was said is worth recounting. Details were given of both the output of limestone and ironstone from the Churnet Valley and the quantities going to South Staffordshire. The Consall Mining Company was sending the greater part of 500 tons a week of iron-ore to South Staffordshire. This all went via canal, a journey taking about a week and sometimes curtailed in the winter if the canal froze, as it sometimes did. The cartage price was 6s (30p) a ton to Netherton and while the NSR had quoted 5s 9d (29p) a ton, with a much shorter journey time, the cost would actually have been greater, in view of terminal charges at Netherton. The reason for this was that while all the relevant works were connected by branch canals, most of them had no direct rail access – this was of course, very soon to change. Mention was made of the proposed NSR line from Leek to Stoke which was also before Parliament in this same Session, as this would save the circuitous journey via either Burton-on-Trent or Macclesfield. It was pointed out that this line if authorised (it was), might in any event, result in some or all of the traffic transferring to rail. George Binns, a mine owner at Froghall had a similar story to tell, in his case sending around 1,500 tons a week of limestone and ironstone, all going to either Wednesbury or Great Bridge. He further stated that the demand was unlimited and with better transport more would be mined and dispatched. A South Staffordshire ironmaster was then called, William Haden. His evidence supported the view that because of the excellent quality of Froghall limestone, there was an insatiable demand that could only be satisfied by better transport links.

Lord Bagot's Estate Agent gave evidence in support of the scheme, mentioning timber traffic from the Lord's estates near Abbots Bromley for pit props in the Cannock Chase coalfield, along with coal traffic in the reverse direction. There was also mention of livestock traffic to and from Uttoxeter Market which was, apparently, one of the largest live stock markets for miles around. The evidence of John Addison, the Engineer for the line, came next. He mentioned that the reason the 1847 DS&WJR scheme was abandoned between Rugeley and Uttoxeter, was the heaviness of the civil engineering works which included two miles in a tunnel. However as we have seen, the section between Cannock and Rugeley, later constructed on a slightly different route, opened in November 1859. In the present proposal a much easier course to the west had been surveyed with a ruling gradient of 1 in 100, the total estimated cost, including the Abbots Bromley branch, being £124,487 (the £130,000 mentioned above had an allowance for contingences). The works were estimated to involve removal of 651,000 cubic yards of earth on the main line, 2,500 on the spur at the junction with the L&NWR and 116,000 on the Abbots Bromley branch. The earthworks and bridges would be made for a double track on the main line although only a single track would be laid, while the Abbots Bromley branch would be single in both respects. He then went on to mention why at the Uttoxeter end, it was proposed to pass over the authorised line of the NSR, rather than making a junction at Bromshall. The reasoning was to avoid the steep gradient that would otherwise be necessary at the junction, which was the case with the S&UR. He felt the Company would work the line independently although it would be better in his opinion, if either the NSR or L&NWR did so. In questioning on this issue and the proposed running powers in the Bill for the two existing companies, the S&UR counsel, Thomas Phillips, asked if the running powers being sought in the Bill were so that the line when built could be sold at a greater price, to which Addison answered that the reason was to cut operating costs. Phillips said that those he represented were of the view that

this was not the case, the actual reason was to cut their (S&UR) throats! Stations were proposed at Grindley, somewhere between there and Rugeley, as well as at Drointon, where the junction with the Abbots Bromley branch would be situated.

Thomas Brodrick the NSR Deputy Chairman was the next witness. He felt that the S&UR line was not one that would be very useful to the country it passed through and in his words, was very obnoxious to his company and the L&NWR. When questioned about the Memorandum outlined above, it was put to him by Mr. Dennison, also appearing in support of the S&UR, that the whole purpose of it (the Memorandum) was to defeat the S&UR and then forget about it! His answer to this was an emphatic *No*. John Curphey Forsyth, the NSR Engineer was then called and stated on cross examination, that the clause in the Memorandum relating to getting the consent of the various Lords regarding the actual route, was inserted by the L&NWR Solicitor in the period between the Select Committee hearings of the Commons and Lords. He went on to say that if that undertaking had been acted upon, it would have delivered a line on the route of the S&UR to Weston, with a south facing connection to the NSR, followed by a north facing connection with the L&NWR at Colwich, resulting in a triangular junction at that point. He felt strongly that a line from Weston to Stafford was both unnecessary and expensive to build. The Committee then interjected and said it would not agree to a line between Grindley Forge, where the projected line intersected the S&UR route and Uttoxeter, as duplication was not warranted under any circumstances. Dennison then said, on behalf of the S&UR, that if the present scheme was thrown out, his company would develop a scheme in the following year to build a branch from the S&UR to serve Abbots Bromley. The Chairman adjourned the hearing at this point. On reconvening Robert Daniel Newill, the S&UR Secretary was sworn. He was asked point blank, if the S&UR would definitely carry out the pledge made by Dennison to promote a Bill in the following year's Session, to build a branch to Abbots Bromley. He replied: *It will be carried out*. Following this, all the parties were again summoned and the Chairman stated that the Committee was of the opinion that the Preamble of the Bill had not been proved and that was the end of the scheme.

At the next half yearly meeting of the NSR shareholders held on 7 August 1863, mention was made that the scheme had been abandoned. Interestingly, at the following half-yearly meeting on 10 February 1864, it was stated that while the promoters had attempted to introduce their plans again in the following Parliamentary Session, the Bill had been withdrawn at an early stage. It has not, however, been possible to find any trace of this in the surviving records of Parliament. However, a copy of the Bill has been located in the papers of the Ferrers' Estate held in the Leicestershire and Rutland Archives.[51] The document is entitled *A Bill for making a railway from the Trent Valley Railway near Rugeley to the Potteries Line of the North Staffordshire Railway, near Uttoxeter*.[52] The promoters were listed as: the Earl of Lichfield, Earl of Harrowby, Lord Bagot and Henry Wyatt who would be the first Directors. The scheme was identical to the earlier one as was the proposed capital of £130,000. The S&UR did not honour its pledge to build a branch to Abbots Bromley.

Birmingham & Sutton Coldfield Extension Railway

We must now consider the Birmingham & Sutton Coldfield Extension Railway (B&SCER) which had been authorised by Parliament, receiving the Royal Assent on 21 July 1863.[53] The Company thus incorporated had powers to build a line, seven and three quarters of a mile long, from an end-on junction with the L&NWR Aston to Sutton Coldfield branch to a junction with the South Staffordshire Railway at Lichfield. The South Staffordshire line from Dudley to Wichnor via Lichfield, where it joined the Midland Railway line from Birmingham to Derby, had opened on 9 April 1849 and was worked by the L&NWR from July 1852. The L&NWR subsequently leased the line in January 1862 and then absorbed it in July 1867. The Aston to Sutton Coldfield branch had opened 2 June 1862. Some land would appear to have been acquired and construction work started as the balance sheet dated 30 June 1865[54] shows £3,384 as expended on the acquisition of land and no less than £45,200 on construction, out of an authorised capital of £100,000. Somebody with the name Greenhill is named as the contractor,[55] but we do not know exactly what was done. However, the B&SCER went to Parliament again in the 1865-1866 Session for further powers[56] as, among other issues, having not acquired all the land needed its powers to do so would lapse in June 1866. On this occasion it sought powers for four railways, one of which, railway number one, was almost the same at that authorised by the 1863 Act. This was a deviation line at Sutton Coldfield to replace and abandon part of the formation of railway number one, the inference being that some works had been undertaken although it is difficult to see how such a large sum as mentioned above, could have been spent. Railway number two, which is the one of most interest to us, was to make a junction with railway number one at Lichfield and proceed in a generally northerly direction, crossing over the L&NWR Trent Valley line, to join the NSR Churnet Valley line at Uttoxeter Dove Bank station. The route passed just to the east of Kings Bromley, Hamstall Ridware and Abbots Bromley, west of Bagots Park and east of Kingston to cross over the NSR Stoke to Derby line by Bridge Street station before joining the Churnet Valley line facing north at Dove Bank station. Total length was 18 miles four furlongs and three chains and the estimated cost £182,810. There were two short spurs at Lichfield, one of which, railway number three, would have connected with the SSR facing Birmingham, as opposed to the already authorised line which faced the other way. The second spur would have connected with the Trent Valley line and faced south. It can thus be seen, that direct connections were planned such that trains off the NSR Churnet Valley line could run directly to either Birmingham via the SSR, or onto the Trent Valley line heading south. Yet again, the promoters were after the limestone and ironstone traffic from Froghall for the Black Country ironmasters. The Bill also sought working agreements with the NSR along with running powers by both companies over their entire systems. The engineer was Julian Horn Tolmé who later became involved with the S&UR (see Chapter Five).

In the event the existing statutory powers were allowed to lapse and the Bill for the extension to Uttoxeter was withdrawn, for which we have no positive intelligence as to why this was so.

The Bill had its second reading in the House of Commons on 19 February when it was committed. However, on 12 June it was noted in Parliament that the parties stated: *not their intention to proceed with same.* The collapse of the merchant bank of Overend, Gurney in 1866, which cut short so many railway schemes and led to the bankruptcy of several contractors specialising in railway construction works, may well have had something to do with it. There was another later scheme to build a railway from Sutton Coldfield to Lichfield, the Birmingham & Lichfield Junction Railway of 1872,[57] but this too came to nought despite no fewer than three further Acts of Parliament and it was left to the L&NWR to eventually build the line under powers of its 1880 Act.[58] It opened on 1 September 1884.

Sheffield, Chesterfield & Staffordshire Railway

Another scheme requires a brief mention as while its promoters were not intending to cover the ground between Uttoxeter and Stafford, they were intending to make connection with the S&UR line at Bromshall. The Sheffield, Chesterfield & Staffordshire Railway emanating from the 1863-1864 Parliamentary Session, planned to use the NSR line by running powers from Ashbourne to Spath, just north of Uttoxeter on the Churnet Valley line.[59] From Spath a new line was projected, heading due west to cross over the NSR Stoke to Derby line at Bromshall and then join the S&UR. It was also proposed to provide a connection at Bromshall with the NSR line in the direction of Stoke. This was of course, before the triangular junction was constructed at Uttoxeter,[60] as at that time trains coming off the Churnet Valley line for Stoke had to reverse. While the rest of this ambitious scheme need not detain us long, suffice to say, it entailed some pretty massive engineering works on its route from Sheffield, via Bakewell, to join the NSR at Ashbourne, with several branches including two at Chesterfield from different directions. Powers were sought to run over parts of the NSR as well as the entire S&UR. John Fowler was the Engineer in Chief and the statutory Parliamentary deposit was made on 30 November 1863. At their meeting on 9 December 1863, the NSR directors elected to oppose this scheme in Parliament, which they did. However, prior to this the directors had suggested to the promoters that if the spur line at Uttoxeter to connect with the Churnet Valley line was left out, along with the running powers, they would not oppose the scheme. As agreement could not be reached on these and other issues, the Bill went forward only to be defeated at the committee stage. The principal reason for this was the formidable engineering work that would have been necessary and the lack of any firm indication as to where the capital would come from. It should be added that there were several other schemes around this time for railways to serve Sheffield, Chesterfield and surrounding area, such that there was a lot of competition, although most of them never saw the light of day. The Overend & Gurney bank collapse mentioned above may have had a bearing too.

Petition from Uttoxeter Parish Council

Last of all and from a much later period in 1895, Uttoxeter Parish Council submitted a petition to the L&NWR suggesting a line be built from Uttoxeter, via Abbots Bromley, Newborough,

Hoar Cross and Yoxall to Lichfield. Such a line followed a rather circuitous route between the two extremes. A public meeting was held in Lichfield on 22 March and correspondence entered into with the L&NWR and NSR; both companies indicating that while they would not be opposed to such a scheme, they would not support it either. Apparently the promoters also entered into discussions with potential financiers and appointed an engineer who did some very preliminary surveying. The Light Railways Act 1896 encouraged those involved that a financially viable way of making such a line might be available to them. However, by mid 1898 it had become only too apparent that there was nowhere near sufficient support to take the issue forward and it was quietly forgotten.[61]

It has been quite impossible to avoid the many references to the S&UR in this Chapter. However, it is now time to focus on its formation, construction, operation and subsequent history.

Notes

17 *The Railway Mania & Its Aftermath 1845-1852*, Henry Grote Lewin, *The Railway Gazette* 1936. In 1846, according to *Tuck's Railway Shareholders Guide for 1847*, no fewer than 1,118 new railway companies were provisionally registered under the Joint Stock Companies Registration Act 1841 (7-8 Vic ch cxx). Details of many of these can be found under the BT41 reference at the NA.

18 NA BT41/794/4350.

19 Birmingham & Derby Junction Railway opened 12 August 1839 became part of Midland Railway 1844.

20 Nowadays known as Porthdinllaen in Welsh and Porth Dinllaen in English.

21 Henry Robert (1792-1860) 3rd Baron.

22 George Remington (1821-1883) was born in Rotherhithe. His other accomplishments included surveys of the River Mersey and the Norfolk Estuary and being engaged by the Admiralty for several years as civil engineer at Bermuda Dockyard. In 1864 he published a project for a tunnel under the English Channel. Earlier on 9 June 1847 he married Harriet Arnold in Pimlico, London. She was born in Rocester, Staffordshire in 1820 and we suspect they met while he was surveying his proposed line through the Churnet Valley. By 1881 Remington was blind.

23 John Urpeth Rastrick (1780-1856), a civil and mechanical engineer, was involved with a number of railways and early locomotives, such that he was in some demand in connection with early railway Bills regarding the use of locomotives. His greatest work was for the original lines of the London & Brighton Railway in the period to 1841. He was also involved in the construction of the Liverpool & Manchester, London & Birmingham and Grand Junction Railways.

24 HLRO HL/PO/PB/plan 1846 D21; HL/PO/PB/plan 1847 D59.

25 10-11 Vic ch clxxxix - Royal Assent 9 July 1847. However, these powers were not exercised, although by later legislation, 17 Vic ch liii Royal Assent 2 June 1854, the line from Walsall Rycroft Junction to Cannock and the Norton branch were opened on 1 February 1858.

26 10-11 Vic ch cx - Derbyshire, Staffordshire & Worcestershire Junction Railway Act 1847.

27 HLRO HL/CL/PB/3/plan 1846 M1.

28 This is the standard Select Committee jargon of the period - in other words, ignored.

29 NA BT41/806/4505.

30 NA BT41/907.

31 NA BT41/907/5486. HLRO HL/PO/PB/3/plan S38.

32 NA BT41/788/4271.

33 CRO Q/Rum/233. NSR Colwich, Wolverhampton & Wednesbury Bill. The plans and sections were deposited on 29 November 1852.

34 The OW&WR was amalgamated with several other lines on 1 July 1860 to form the West Midland Railway. This line was absorbed by the GWR on 13 July 1863.

35 The junction was immediately prior to the original Wolverhampton station. This was renamed Wednesfield Heath for Wolverhampton in November 1852, four months after the station on the present site opened in July 1852.

36 The Birmingham, Wolverhampton & Dudley Railway was absorbed by the GWR on 31 August 1848.

37 This was John Lewis Ricardo (1812-1862).

38 18-19 Vic ch cxciv - The Cannock Mineral Railway Act 1855.

39 This was Thomas Brodrick (1796-1865) of Macclesfield. He was later NSR Chairman from 1862 until his death.

40 In 1853 of 20,000 shares of £20, only 11,500 had been issued and only £4 10s 0d (£4.50p) called up on each of them. No fewer than 7,666 shares had been forfeited when calls on them had not been fulfilled.

41 20-21 Vic ch lxiv - The Cannock Mineral Railway (Extension of Time) Act 1857, Royal Assent 27 July 1857.

42 In the event some land was sold: two plots under The Land Clauses Consolidation Act 1845. This, however, was not before the NSR had agreed a Bond with the CMR contractors, William Field and Thomas Brassey, dated 28 April 1848. NA RAIL 532/105.

43 32-33 Vic ch cxv - The London & North Western Railway (Additional Powers) Act 1869.

44 22-23 Vic ch cxxv - The North Staffordshire Railway Act 1859.

45 HLRO HL/PO/PB/3/ plan R1.

46 George Potter Neele (of the South Staffordshire Railway and later L&NWR), in his *Railway Reminiscences*, London 1904, mentions that Addison was *straightforward, clear and open* and may have been the originator of the red-cap as a distinguishing mark for Pilotmen conducting traffic of a double line of rails over a single line during repairs or obstruction. This was later replaced by an arm band with red letters on a white background.

47 HLRO HL/PO/PB/3/plan/1862 N6.

48 HLRO HL/CL/PB/2/31/25.

49 Thomas George Anson (1825-1892) 2nd Earl, of Shugborough Hall and at the time, Lord Lieutenant of Staffordshire.

50 These were the principal express passenger engines used on the L&NWR at the time. Designed by James Edward McConnell they were 2-2-2 inside cylinder, inside frame, tender engines built between 1851 and 1862. In view of their inside frames and straight running plate, they take their name from a ladies dress fashion of the period associated with American women's rights advocate Amelia Jenks Bloomer (1818-1894) - in other words a high skirt!

51 Leicestershire and Rutland Record Office 25D60/634.

52 27-28 Vic - Session 1864 - The North and South Staffordshire Junction Railway. It should be noted that, in the authors' experience, it is not unusual for Bills of railways not proceeded with, in cases where they were withdrawn before any Parliamentary proceedings had commenced, not to have survived in the Parliamentary archives.

53 26-27 Vic ch clxxiv The Birmingham & Sutton Coldfield Extension Railway Act 1863.

54 As recorded in *Bradshaw's Railway Manual, Shareholders Guide & Directory* for 1866.

55 *A Gazetteer of The Railway Contractors & Engineers of Central England 1830-1914*, Lawrence Popplewell, Melledgen Press 1986. ISBN 0-906637-09-0.

56 CRO Q/rum/ 372. HLRO HL/PO/PB/3/plan 1866 B42; House of Commons Journal 1866.

57 35-36 Vic ch clxx - The Birmingham & Lichfield Junction Railway Act 1872, Royal Assent 6 August 1872.

58 42-43 Vic ch x - The LNWR (Sutton Coldfield to Lichfield) Act 1880, Royal Assent 29 June 1880.

59 CRO Q/Rum/345.

60 43-44 Vic ch cxci - North Staffordshire Railway Act 1880, Royal Assent 26 August 1880. The curve opened in October 1881.

61 *The South Staffordshire Railway*, Bob Yate, Oakwood Press 2010 ISBN 978-0-85361-700-6.

CHAPTER THREE

The Stafford & Uttoxeter Railway

The Proposal

The proposal was extremely straightforward: to connect Stafford and Uttoxeter with a new railway. However, unlike previous schemes which had not come to fruition, the method chosen to achieve this scheme was unusual, if not unique. It involved obtaining statutory powers to enable the new line to access Stafford and Uttoxeter over the lines of two existing and well established railway companies, the L&NWR at Stafford and the NSR at Uttoxeter. Both these companies had invested significant capital expenditure in providing stations at these two towns and suddenly an interloper was on the scene seeking to take advantage of them. Clearly the S&UR would have to pay some sort of access fee but if the proposal were approved the new company would avoid investing in new terminal facilities at each end of its line. It was particularly galling for the L&NWR as that company had just invested in a brand new station at Stafford, the third station on the site, to cater for its own rapid expansion. The new station was built in Italianate style by John Parnell of Rugby to the designs of William Baker, the L&NWR Engineer.

The proposal was supported by the inhabitants of Stafford following a public meeting held on 31 March 1862 chaired by the Mayor of Stafford, William Buxton, who was one of the subscribers to the new enterprise. In business as a cheese factor, he mentioned that he often had to neglect such excellent markets as those at Uttoxeter and Derby on account of the inaccessibility of those places. There was definitely a good case for improving the communication between Stafford and Uttoxeter, that goes without question but there was also an underlying theme to improve communications between Wales and the east of England by means of the new railway. It is no coincidence that there was a linkage with the struggling Potteries Shrewsbury and North Wales Railway. Indeed, at one time both companies had a common general manager and at least three directors had an interest in both concerns. Access to Wales was to remain an unrealised ambition for the S&UR and its successor, the GNR.

The connection with the NSR was to be at Bromshall where the NSR had a station located 2 miles 62 chains to the west of Uttoxeter Bridge Street station. This station had opened on 7 August 1848 on inauguration of the line from Stoke to Uttoxeter but had a very short existence being closed on 1 January 1866, before the S&UR connection at Bromshall Junction had been completed and almost two years before the S&UR opened for

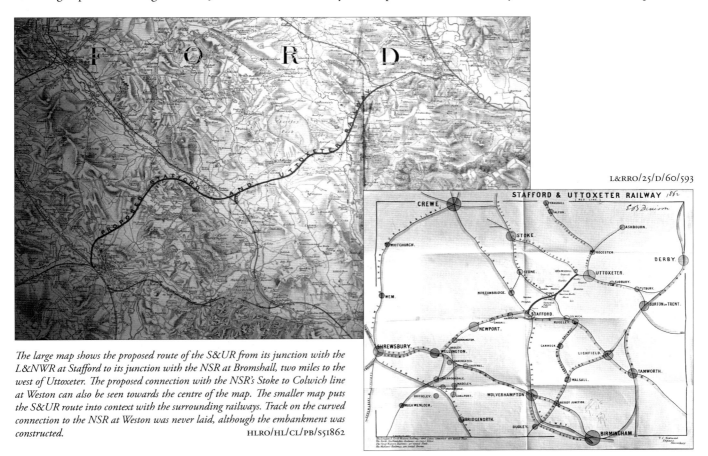

L&RRO/25/D/60/593

The large map shows the proposed route of the S&UR from its junction with the L&NWR at Stafford to its junction with the NSR at Bromshall, two miles to the west of Uttoxeter. The proposed connection with the NSR's Stoke to Colwich line at Weston can also be seen towards the centre of the map. The smaller map puts the S&UR route into context with the surrounding railways. Track on the curved connection to the NSR at Weston was never laid, although the embankment was constructed. HLRO/HL/CL/PB/S51862

Maker's photograph of an early design of the well-known Foden steam wagon, belonging to the Earl of Shrewsbury & Talbot's estate at Ingestre. As related in the text, the line passed over part of the Earl's land. The wagon is Foden number 534 of 1902 and one of the first half dozen built.

ROAD LOCOMOTIVE SOCIETY

traffic. It is interesting to note that on 9 April 1850 the NSR's Traffic Committee approved a proposal from Lord Willoughby de Broke[62] to find land at Bromshall and to construct a siding at his own expense (excepting points and crossings) and to allow a portion of the siding to be allocated for public use. We have been unable to ascertain whether the siding was actually constructed but clearly Bromshall was a notable location on the railway before the coming of the S&UR.

The Bill in Parliament

The inaugural Stafford and Uttoxeter Railway Act received the Royal Assent on 29 July 1862.[63] The Bill, which together with plans and sections, was deposited on 30 November 1861[64] had experienced a tortuous passage through Parliament: there was energetic opposition in the House Commons and even more vigorous opposition in the Lords. *The Derby Mercury* in its edition for 9 July 1862 reported on the success of the Bill and stated that it had been universally admitted that a necessity existed for more adequate accommodation for traffic between Stafford and Uttoxeter but there had been three main objections: first, that locally generated traffic alone would hardly warrant the construction of a new line; secondly, that if the line were made, it would be more advantageous to bring it into Colwich or Rugeley rather than form a junction at Stafford; thirdly, that to authorise the formation of such a small company with running powers over the L&NWR and NSR would be extremely annoying to those companies and most inconvenient in practice. The newspaper said the force of the three objections was well set forth by counsel representing the L&NWR and NSR and other influential witnesses. The Earl of Shrewsbury and Talbot[65] objected independently believing the scheme would injure his estate and that of his neighbour, Earl Harrowby.[66] However, all this well conducted opposition was to no avail as the Committee of Lords considered the provision of the new line of communication to be of paramount importance to the district concerned and unanimously gave the Bill its approval.

The evidence taken by the House of Lords Committee occupies some 900 pages of manuscript written in longhand as a verbatim report by a team of clerks.[67] As the S&UR owed its very existence to this Committee we now summarise the salient features of the evidence. The Committee was chaired by Lord Wodehouse[68] and met on consecutive days between 30 June and 3 July 1862. The S&UR subscribers were listed as William Buxton, Thomas Campbell Eyton, John Kenderdine, Richard Banner Oakeley, William Phillips and Sir Thomas Salt of whom Buxton, Eyton, Kenderdine and Oakeley subsequently became directors. Counsels for the Bill were Messrs. Davison and Harrison acting on behalf of the subscribers. Counsels against the Bill were Messrs. Hope-Scott, Merewether and W. Phinn jointly representing the L&NWR and the NSR. The Earl of Harrowby and the Earl of Shrewsbury and Talbot, both petitioners against the Bill, were not represented by counsel.

There was an almost farcical situation at the start of the proceedings. George Webb of Blythe Bridge and Joseph Wilkins of Uttoxeter, both landowners with property that would be required by the S&UR as originally laid out, were called before the Committee as they had signed petitions both in favour and against the Bill! They claimed to have been encouraged to do so by a firm of Uttoxeter auctioneers. The Committee decided not to recommend prosecution as there was insufficient evidence but demanded that their names should be struck off the petitions. This sort of shenanigans must have been commonplace.

This is the front elevation of Sandon Hall, seat of Earl Harrowby and from where attempts were made to see if the line of the proposed railway could be seen from rooms in the house. A series of 12 posts had been erected with flags atop, along the line of the proposed railway where it would have passed nearest to the Hall. Townsend, the S&UR engineer then accompanied Lord Sandon, son of the Earl, and it was only from two upstairs rooms that any of the flags could be seen.

FAR LEFT: *This rather unflattering caricature of the 2nd Earl of Harrowby appeared in* Vanity Fair *on 8 April 1871. It was by Italian artist Carlo Pellegrini (1839-1889) who used the pseudonym Ape and became* Vanity Fair'*s most influential caricaturist.*

LEFT: *This pencil sketch of Dudley Ryder, 2nd Earl of Harrowby, KG, PC, FRS is by Frederick Sargent (1837-1899). Dudley Ryder was born in London on 19 May 1798. He was styled Viscount Sandon between 1809 and 1847. He served as a Lord of the Admiralty in 1827 and became a Conservative Member of Parliament for Tiverton (1819-1831) and Liverpool (1832-1847). He was a Director of the North Staffordshire Railway from 1865 until 1872. He died at Sandon Hall, the family seat, on 19 November 1882 and is buried at All Saints Church, Sandon.*
© NATIONAL PORTRAIT GALLERY, LONDON

Several potential users of the new railway were called who all gave evidence in support of the new venture. These included a firm of boot and shoe makers in Stafford, a firm of *Coachmakers to Her Majesty* with works in Derby, a cattle dealer from Marchington, the Uttoxeter Brewery Company and the agent appointed by the Court of Chancery responsible for the salt works at Shirleywich (itself in liquidation). Also giving evidence in favour of the Bill were representatives from the Old Park Iron Company near Wellington, the Parkfield Iron Works of Wolverhampton and the Lilleshall Company of Oakengates. The latter company used 15,000 tons of limestone annually along with large quantities of hydrate of iron (iron ore heavily impregnated with water) from the quarries at Froghall in the Churnet valley owned by the NSR. The other two companies claimed that they would like to use Froghall limestone but that it was too expensive to obtain by existing routes. Colonel Gilbert Cogg, the Chief Constable for Staffordshire, said the proposed railway was needed by the public and would be a great advantage to the county.

Some four miles of the proposed route for the S&UR passed through land owned by the Earl of Shrewsbury and Talbot who was a director of the NSR and had been so since September 1858. We suspect a touch of bias! Earl Harrowby's land adjoined his and they had discussed what impact the S&UR might have on their interests. Indeed it was revealed that Earl Harrowby's son, Lord Sandon, had walked over the line of the railway with the Earl of Shrewsbury and Talbot in the company of Thomas Charles Townsend and William Field, the S&UR's engineer and contractor, respectively. As a result it was arranged for Charles Trubshaw, the County Surveyor of Stafford, to erect about twelve tall posts with flags atop on the proposed course of the line for about a mile. An attempt was then made to view these from each room on the ground floor of Sandon Hall but none were visible. The butler then accompanied the viewing party upstairs and two flags were sighted but only from one room with the aid of large field glasses. When giving his evidence before the Committee, Townsend pointed out that the NSR's main line from Stone

This stipple engraving by William Henry Mote (1803-1871) was originally published on 1 September 1860. It depicts Admiral Henry John Chetwynd-Talbot, 18th Earl of Shrewsbury, 3rd Earl Talbot, 11th Earl of Waterford CB, PC. He was styled Viscount Ingestre between 1826 and 1849 and was known as The Earl Talbot between 1849 and 1858. He was born at Ingestre Hall, the family seat, on 8 November 1803. He commanded HMS Philomel *in the Battle of Navarino in 1827 becoming a Rear Admiral in 1854 and Admiral in 1865. He was a Conservative politician representing Staffordshire South from 1837 until 1849 and a director of the North Staffordshire Railway from 1846 until 1847 and again between 1858 and his death. He died on 4 June 1868 at Newbattle Abbey, Renfrewshire, Scotland. His body was transferred to Ingestre Hall and laid in State before his burial in Ingestre churchyard.*
© NATIONAL PORTRAIT GALLERY, LONDON

to Colwich ran close by the hall as did the Trent and Mersey Canal and that the Earl's own estate gas works already blotted the landscape. In the light of this and further evidence extracted from the Earl of Shrewsbury and Talbot on 3 July, including mention of the fact that a stretch of line east of Salt would be in Hopton cutting, the petitions lodged against the Bill by the two Earls were ignored. By 1862 the economic benefit of railways to the well being of commerce and the general public was there for all to see and the power of the landed gentry to obstruct their progress had been weakened. The overall position with regard to landowners whose land was affected by the proposals was as follows:

	Owners	Lessees	Occupiers
Assenting	21	2	113
Dissenting	13	2	12
Neutral	15	2	15
No response	20	4	23

In mounting their opposition, the L&NWR and the NSR questioned the concept of the proposal in principle and then picked away at detailed engineering and operational concerns. For example, they queried the safety of the proposed junction at Bramshall [sic] and the operating difficulties that would be created by a small company using the existing stations at Stafford and Uttoxeter. They also threw up a smokescreen of proposing alternative routes to Rugeley or Colwich so avoiding any congestion at Stafford. They lined up an impressive array of witnesses to express their arguments, the most prestigious being George Parker Bidder (1806-1878) who by 1862 had achieved national prominence as an engineer and as a formidable witness before Parliamentary Committees. He had amazing powers of mental calculation and in his youth was known as *The Calculating Boy*. Moreover, he had been the consulting engineer for the overall construction of the NSR. He must have been able to demand a high price to appear as a witness for the opposition. During a question and answer session he referred to the many railways with which he had been professionally concerned including the NSR and said that he was well acquainted with the area through which the S&UR would pass. He said he would not have laid out the line as proposed in order to bring mineral traffic into the Stafford district. He felt that the line could not be worked independently with hostile companies at either end. In his opinion it needed to be worked by one of those companies and it was best dealt with on that basis. The promoters could not contemplate working it themselves and he did not think they had any intention of so doing. He was specifically asked if he felt the need for running powers was a means of selling the scheme to other companies and answered yes. He went on to say that great inconvenience would result if mineral traffic off the proposed line had to pass through Stafford station and thought that the L&NWR would have to spend further capital to accommodate S&UR traffic. He considered that there would be insufficient passenger traffic in the district for the line to pay its way and alluded to a similar situation on the NSR with regard to its main line through the Potteries, implying that it was freight not passengers that created the bulk of the NSR's revenue. However, he considered that the

proposed gradients on the S&UR would not favour the movement of mineral traffic from Froghall to Stafford. He reflected that in 1846 he had been over all North Staffordshire in order to establish the best routes for the NSR to serve the district but never saw a need to connect Stafford with Uttoxeter. He revealed that the NSR had been constructed for about £24,000 per mile whereas the comparable S&UR estimate was but £10,000 per mile.

The L&NWR fielded some of its own senior staff including William Baker, Engineer in charge of New Works, Charles Mason, General Goods Manager and Charles Edward Stewart, Secretary. The NSR fielded John Curphey Forsyth, Engineer and General Manager. As if this were not enough they were supported by a third party in the form of Thomas Elliot Harrison, Engineer-in-Chief, North Eastern Railway. Baker explained that for the past 12 months he had been involved in building the new station at Stafford at a cost of £18,000. He explained that there were only two lines through the old station but now there were four so that passenger trains were not interfered with by mineral and goods trains. He considered that S&UR traffic would cause inconvenience as it would have to pass through the station to get to the goods station which was at the south end and he would prefer the S&UR to join the L&NWR south of the passenger station, not to the north as proposed. He stated that there were 70 trains a day arriving at Stafford and that the four proposed off the S&UR would be a great inconvenience. He considered the proposals at Bramshall [sic] Junction to be a bad arrangement criticising the gradient, radius of the curve and the adjacent level crossing. Mason explained that he was very familiar with the workings at Stafford station such that he considered the proposed junction with the S&UR to be dangerous. Bad sighting for signalmen, would require an extra man in the signal box. He was also concerned about the proposed large amount of mineral traffic from Uttoxeter to Shrewsbury having to pass through the station in order to reach the goods station and then come back again in order to gain access to the line to Wellington and Shrewsbury. He added that if the Bill were approved the L&NWR would have to come to Parliament to enlarge Stafford station as there was no further company owned land to accommodate more expansion. Stewart then weighed in on the question of running powers saying that he thought the safety and efficiency of the L&NWR's operations at Stafford would be undermined. He thought that if the running powers were granted the L&NWR would end up buying the S&UR and that would be the better of two evils. However, he believed that the L&NWR would have to buy at a higher price than they paid their ordinary shareholders. This was because, in a public speech, Edward Banner Oakeley, one of the subscribers and the son-in-law of the S&UR's contractor, William Field, had proclaimed that: *The Directors have the up-most confidence in the scheme which would not pass out of their hands to any company or person at less than 6%.* Several years later Oakeley was jailed for five years for fraud in connection with another matter (see Chapter Four) which does perhaps bring his motives with regard to his S&UR involvement under question.

Forsyth had been associated with the NSR since the autumn of 1845 when he was engaged by George Parker Bidder to assist in the preparation of plans for the then new railway; he had been General

Manager and Engineer since 1853. In giving his evidence he agreed with the stance adopted by the L&NWR and considered that the S&UR would only pay its way if it attracted through traffic. He referred to two salt works at Weston saying that the NSR served one of them by a siding and that the Trent and Mersey Canal (owned by the NSR) passed between the two works, but the total amount of salt did not exceed 2,000 tons per annum. He said the NSR would have to enlarge Bridge Street station at Uttoxeter and would need to seek Parliamentary powers to acquire additional land. He then suggested that, jointly with the L&NWR, a scheme should be put forward in the next Parliamentary session involving a line from Uttoxeter to Weston and then by the NSR's existing line to Colwich where there would be a triangular junction enabling trains to run into Stafford without reversing. The Earl of Shrewsbury and Talbot in giving his evidence admitted that he was aware of such a scheme as, in his capacity as a NSR director, a resolution to this effect between the NSR and L&NWR dated 9 May 1862 had been read out at an NSR Board meeting (see Chapter Two). Several people were called with mining interests in the Churnet Valley and Cheadle but all stated that they would prefer the traffic for which they were responsible to be handled by one company and to pass via Rugeley, clearly all supporting the NSR in its opposition to the scheme.

With all this overwhelming opposition from the L&NWR and NSR it is amazing that those promoting the scheme were able to convince the Lords Committee that it should go ahead but this is exactly what they did. The engineering issues were handled by the S&UR's engineer, Thomas Charles Townsend along with the company's consulting engineer, John Robinson Maclean. They were supported by Joseph Cubitt (1811-1872), Civil Engineer for the Great Northern Railway and the London, Chatham and Dover Railway and by David Wylie, a civil engineer born in Dumfriesshire in Scotland in 1818 and residing in Shrewsbury. He had been involved with the Shrewsbury and Hereford Railway and various lines in Staffordshire and was familiar with the district to be served by the S&UR. All these engineers professed that the proposed line was well laid out and concurred that the estimates were realistic. Maclean said that the proposed junction at Bramshall [sic] had originally been surveyed at a gradient of 1 in 71 descending towards the NSR but had subsequently been altered to include a short level section. In response to questioning all the engineers considered there to be sufficient room at Stafford and Uttoxeter Bridge Street stations to accommodate the proposed S&UR traffic. Facilities at the latter location were said to include a double line of rails, two platforms (210ft long and 9ft wide), a large goods shed, sidings and an engine shed.

After four exhausting days of hearing evidence and cross examination, the Lords Committee concluded that the Bill should proceed. The promoters had won. The 1862 Act incorporated the Stafford and Uttoxeter Railway Company and authorised that company to construct and maintain a railway commencing at a junction with the L&NWR at or near the junction with the Shropshire Union Railway near Stafford and terminating by a junction with the NSR about two miles west of Uttoxeter. It also authorised a branch railway from the new line in the parish of Stone to connect with the Colwich branch of the NSR about 1,500

yards south of Weston station. The new lines had to be completed within four years from the passing of the Act. The Act laid down maximum charges for passengers, cattle and goods traffic and stipulated that the S&UR must repay the L&NWR for any loss, should its operations in any way delay the *Irish Mail* at Stafford![69]

The NSR took the S&UR's success in Parliament very badly. At the half-yearly shareholders' meeting held in the board room at Stoke on 8 August 1862 Thomas Brodrick, the Deputy Chairman, who presided, spoke at length on the matter. He said the *Stafford and Uttoxeter scheme was what was called an undertaker's line; and that undertakers, in times like the present, finding it difficult to give employment to their staff and rolling stock, took a glance at the map, and seeing two places between which there was no railway, took their ruler and drew a line, and then did their best to convince a number of persons that the line represented a railway which might be very advantageously constructed.* He went on to admit that the connections between certain parts of North Staffordshire and Stafford were circuitous but was of the view that the NSR/L&NWR proposal for an alternative line as mentioned in the Parliamentary proceedings would have been a better line in every respect. He said that the NSR had failed in its opposition to the S&UR but thought that Parliament had been lavish in granting permission for a number of lines to proceed in the last Session, including the S&UR. He went on to state that in his opinion *nothing was more injurious to railway property than the facility with which new lines had been granted. New schemes were originally started in the manner described, and then it often happened that they were brought up by adjacent Companies, or their existence might be accounted for by the fact that a third Company had its eye upon the district, and wanted to obtain a footing there. In that case other Companies already on the spot were compelled in self-defence to increase their capital for the purpose of taking lines which they thought would be comparatively unproductive.* The Earl of Shrewsbury and Talbot was present to hear the Deputy Chairman's words of wisdom. The NSR was clearly very hostile towards the newcomer and very suspicious of its motives. It was against this background, coupled with opposition from the L&NWR that the fledgling S&UR set about its task. As we shall see it was an uphill struggle.

The Ferrers' Estate
At the time the railway was being proposed and built, the Chartley estate and mansion, along with the remains of the ancient castle, were owned in trust for Sewallis Edward Shirley, the 10th Earl Ferrers, Viscount Tamworth (1847-1912). His father, the 9th Earl, had died on 13 March 1859 and as he was not 21 until 1868, under the law at that time, he was considered a *minor*. He was, therefore, represented by his uncle, Lord Adolphus John Spencer Churchill Chichester (1836-1901), at the time a Lieutenant in the 12th Lancers (later Lieutenant-Colonel 4th Battalion Royal Irish Rifles) and described in the legal terms of the day as his *next friend*. His trustee was Lord Edward Chichester, 4th Marquess of Donegal (1799-1899). The 10th Earl's mother, Augusta Anabella, was the eldest daughter of the Marquess. The Ferrers' family had two seats, Chartley and Staunton Harold Hall, three miles north-east of Ashby-de-la-Zouch in Leicestershire which is today in the care of The National Trust. The castle at Chartley dates back to

1220; it was abandoned after its owner, Walter Devereux (1431-1485), the 7th Baron Ferrers, was killed at the Battle of Bosworth on 22 August 1485. Chartley Manor, a moated and battlemented timber mansion was then built nearby. The original building was burnt down on two occasions, in 1781 and 1847. Prior to the second fire and since 1844, the family had used Chartley as its main seat while after its second rebuilding in 1848-1849, it was leased to Walter Lyndon, along with unfettered shooting rights over the entire estate. These rights were exercised to such an extent that much damage was done to tenanted farms on the estate and in 1862 Lyndon was given notice to quit. Henceforth shooting was confined to the Earl, his family and close friends, the family residing at Chartley for around three months each year. It is perhaps worth mentioning at this juncture that, after her removal from nearby Tutbury Castle, Mary, Queen of Scots (1542-1587), was imprisoned at Chartley between December 1585 and September the following year, without the knowledge and to the great annoyance of the 11th Baron Ferrers! She was removed from Chartley to Fotheringay Castle in Northamptonshire where she was beheaded on 8 February 1587.

Prior to the S&UR Bill being progressed through Parliament the Earl, through his uncle, raised a number of objections regarding the projected route of the railway. It was established that the line would pass through the estate for a distance of five miles and three furlongs. Entering the estate near Weston, on the Stafford side of the estate - actually about a quarter of a mile north-west of where the line would cross the River Trent - to a crossing of the River Blithe, some three quarters of a mile north-east of where Grindley station would be situated. In total the land area required was 54 acres two roods and 13 perches which included the bulk of the land required for the projected curve to join the NSR at Weston. It was established that the line would pass 682 yards from the gates to the old castle remains which were considered of great historical importance. Indeed, it was claimed that in recent times around £100 had been spent by the estate in stabilising the remains. The entrance gates to the manor house were 534 yards from where the line would pass and the house itself, a further 330 yards. Great play was made on the issues of locomotives whistling and making smoke, the latter drifting towards the house such that if the wind was blowing in that direction, the smoke would cause damage![70]

The Earl made a number of specific requirements as a condition of withdrawing his opposition in Parliament. He had already lodged a petition against the Bill for constructing the railway line. A survey and investigation had been commissioned for the Earl by Charles Lee, said to be a noted land surveyor from London with a Golden Square, Westminster address. In essence, the requirements were as summarised below - the numbers refer to the references on the deposited plans while the distances are similarly marked on the plans starting from Stafford.[71]

1. That the line where it passed by the castle remains and house at Stowe, be moved as far away as the proposed limits of deviation, as laid down on the deposited plans for the Bill, would allow.

2. Provide reasonable facilities for connecting sidings or branch railways from the salt works at Weston and the plaster works at Stowe, both belonging to the Earl, at S&UR cost, with facilities to carry traffic.

3. Erect and maintain a station at Stowe on the eastern boundary of the estate. No fewer than three passenger trains to stop in both directions on each weekday and one on Sundays, along with one goods train on weekdays.

4. Erect a bridge over road No. 5 in the Parish of Weston instead of a level crossing. Alternatively, the level crossing be provided with gates, manned at all times and a gatehouse be provided for the gateman at 5 miles, 1 furlong and 4 chains (this is the present A518 Weston to Stafford road) where in the event, an overbridge was constructed.

5. Archways to be provided at No. 17 over road No. 21 and at No. 43, both in the Parish of Weston (road No. 21 ran from Weston to the salt works where an underbridge was provided while No. 43 was just west of where the line was to cross the NSR at Weston where at 6 miles, 3 furlongs an underbridge was to be provided).

6. Provide level crossings in the Parish of Stowe (all the remaining physical issues are also in this Parish) at Nos. 13, 27 and 80 (at No. 13 an underbridge was provided at 6 miles 4 furlongs; at No. 27, which was the Amerton to Shirleywich road, an overbridge at 6 miles 6 furlongs and 2 chains, while at No. 80, at 8 miles 7 furlongs and 3 chains, it was an underbridge).

7. Provide a bridge between No. 72 and No. 73 and another at No. 89 (between No. 72 and No. 73, at 8 miles 3 furlongs, an underbridge was provided and at No. 89, 9 miles 3 furlongs, an overbridge).

8. Provide archways (cattle creeps) at Nos. 45 and 128 (No. 128 was an underbridge at 10 miles 2 furlongs and 5 chains).

9. Provide bridges and archways on the estate during the construction works as rendered necessary, so as not to interrupt the working of the estate – any differences to be settled by arbitration.

10. Pay for the land before taking possession and pay for severance and damage (during construction works) in accordance with the Land Clauses Consolidation Act 1845 (LCCA).[72]

11. That a sum of £250 be agreed to cover the Earl's costs. In the event the claim in this respect was considerably increased.

There were also concerns whether the line could be built for the projected sum of £130,000. Mention is made in the Earl's papers that Thomas Brassey had agreed he could build the line for £10,000 per mile, including the cost of the land and that he would take a quarter of his fees in S&UR bonds.[73] While on the face of it all these conditions requested by the Earl appear to present a rather tall order, in the event the issues between the parties boiled down to those covered by points 1, 3, 10 and 11. While agreement was reached for the Earl to offer no opposition, later on, when it came to agreeing a price for the land, arbitration was called for under the terms of the 1845 Act. Point 1 raised a number of issues in view of the close proximity of the projected route of the railway to the castle and manor house. Insofar as point 3 was concerned, the S&UR was only prepared to agree to a minimum of two passenger trains each way and none on Sundays. All these issues are dealt with in more detail below.

In the case of point 1, moving the course of the line south, further away from the castle and manor house involved both a deeper cutting in view of the terrain of the land and road Nos. 34 and 35 on the deposited plans, situated between seven and eight miles, being carried over the line rather than by less expensive level crossings – as per the deposited plans. These two roads are from Amerton to Hixon (No. 34) and Stowe to Hixon (No. 35), respectively, at seven miles one furlong and seven miles three furlongs and seven chains. There was much debate on this issue as it would have shifted the line very close to the extremity of the Earl's estate. It was even suggested that it might be less expensive to move the line completely off the Earl's property as in such a scenario, there would be no need to build the two bridges as level crossings would be acceptable. Eventually, on 31 October 1862 agreement was reached conceding all the Earl's issues except that the S&UR held out for the minimum of only two passenger trains per weekday, with none on Sundays.

It is worth mentioning that in raising the various issues, the Earl took into account points of concern regarding several of his neighbours. These included Samuel Plant, the Vicar of Weston, who was particularly annoyed regarding what he considered the damage to be done to the village, as he described it and not least, the close proximity of the proposed line to his vicarage![74]

On 16 September 1863 the S&UR gave notice to the Earl of its intention to take the lands required for the railway, in accordance with its Act, while *treating* with him regarding the price to be paid. As agreement was not reached on the price, each party, under the terms of the LCCA, appointed an arbitrator to establish its case. Insofar as the Earl was concerned Charles Lee was again appointed to act. For the S&UR, Samuel Girders, a surveyor of Ingestre with an office in Stafford,[75] acted, while also under the terms of the Act, an umpire had to be appointed and this role fell to John Clutton of Whitehall Place, Westminster in London. Lee's valuation at £11,834 is dated 7 October 1863 and while the records are silent on the figure Girders established, the umpire, on 13 June 1864, awarded a figure of £8,887 plus the Earl's expenses. In the event, as briefly alluded to above, the question of expenses was the subject of another dispute.[76] The position regarding the land did not end at this point either. As in any land purchase, the acquiring body is entitled to complete satisfaction that the vendor actually has title to the land to be acquired. At this point the S&UR solicitor, Robert Daniel Newill, was not satisfied and this issue dragged on for several years, made more complicated as by the time it was settled, the S&UR was in receivership. Insofar as construction of the railway was concerned, all was not lost as under the terms of the LCCA, such a situation

had been envisaged by whoever drafted the legislation. The Act made provision in such a circumstance for the purchase money to be paid to the Accountant General in the Court of Chancery and subsequently invested. Any interest accrued, along with the capital sum, eventually went to the account of whoever was finally established as having title to the land. The Act however, is silent as to what might be done if the investment was such that the capital figure reduced! We digress; the sum of £8,887 was invested by the Court in 3% annuities to the credit of the S&UR, until such times as title to the land be established.[77] In the meantime, the railway company was entitled to take possession of the land and commence construction works, which it did.

The Earl's estate was then put to a lot of trouble, via its solicitor, Henry Harris of 34 Moorgate Street in London, in establishing a lien on the land required by the railway under its Act. The land had been acquired over many years, some going back as far 1266,[78] in several lots such that it proved difficult to assemble an accurate Abstract of Title for each and every piece. As a consequence it was not until 1872, by which time the S&UR was insolvent, before a Rolls Court in Chancery was convened under Lord Romilly to establish a lien in the Earl's favour on the land required for the railway.[79] The Court sat on 12 March 1872. In the meantime three other issues arose. In the first instance, the question of the Earl's costs, as mentioned earlier, was the subject of a dispute, Lee and Gilders arbitrating again, with Clutton acting as umpire. This issue was finally settled on 15 April 1867, at the figure of £414 2s 4d (£414.12p). The second instance involved additional land required for the stations at Weston, Stowe and Grindley, where Lee, appointed yet again by the Earl, made a valuation of the land consisting of seven acres, one rood and 39 perches, at £1,624 10s od (£1,624.50p).[80] Not surprisingly the S&UR's representative, Gilders, did not agree; his valuation being £850. This brought Clutton into the fray again when in June 1865, a figure £1,350 was agreed.[81] The third and last issue involved two further plots of land following the agreement to divert the line as far away as possible from the castle and manor house at Stowe. This was not land required for the railway as such, rather land, that because of the revised position of the railway, was considered by the Earl to be of no further use to his estate. One of the pieces of land was claimed to be useless to the Earl, unless a bridge was built over the railway to give access to it. The S&UR was of the view that it would be cheaper to buy this particular plot of land rather than build a bridge. The total area of the two plots was seven acres, two roods and 19 perches for which the Estate, via the Earl's solicitor, Henry Harris, made a claim on 29 July 1865. The S&UR gave the Earl the statutory 10 days notice on 27 June 1866, that it intended to go to arbitration over the matter while, in the meantime, offering £850. In the event, after Lee and Gilders had gone about their valuations, Clutton awarded £1,000 for the larger section and £300 for the smaller. It was the smaller section where the S&UR considered that construction of a bridge, would have cost more than £300.[82]

What then was the overall result of all these negotiations? The Earl got his money for the land, which by the time it was paid had increased through interest on the investment of £8,887 to £9,985 7s 10d (£9,985 40p). It would appear from the surviving papers that he also received the agreed sum for the additional land required for the stations, along with that for the two plots at Stowe. However, in view of the fact that the S&UR was in receivership by the time the figure for his expenses were agreed, this account may never have been settled. Having said that, it could be argued that he was more than compensated by the interest that had accrued on the sum invested under the terms of the LCCA. We have taken the decision to explore in great detail the issues regarding the acquisition of the lands of Lord Ferrers as an example of the trials and tribulations that could face both aspiring railway companies and landowners when new railway lines were projected. In the authors' experience, it is a subject that hitherto has been given little exposure in railway histories and is thus one well worthy of this detailed investigation. We are, of course, fortunate that so many documents have survived to enable the story to be told.

The Prospectus

The S&UR's prospectus was published in the *The Times* on 21 March 1863. It was also published in other newspapers and circulated widely throughout Staffordshire and the neighbouring counties. It stated that the authorised capital was £130,000 in 13,000 shares of £10 each. In order to invest in the new enterprise a deposit of £2 per share was required and no call would be made on the shareholders until £50,000 had been expended on the new works and there would be an interval of three months between each call of £2.

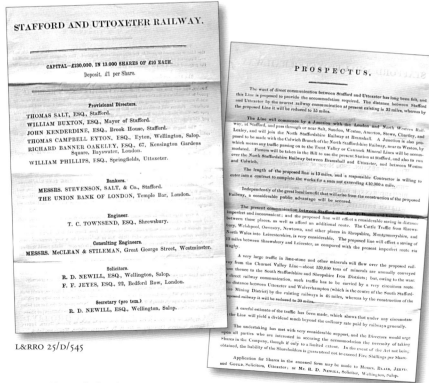

L&RRO 25/D/545

ABOVE: *The Stafford and Uttoxeter Railway Prospectus.*
RIGHT: *The S&UR Prospectus as published in* The Times, *21 March 1863.*

All the directors were listed together with the Engineer and the Secretary, the latter also acting as the company's Solicitor. The bankers were Messrs Hankey, Fenchurch Street, London; the Union Bank of London, Temple-bar Branch; Messrs Stevenson, Salt and Co., Stafford; the Manchester and Liverpool District Bank, Stafford; and the Burton, Uttoxeter and Ashbourne Union Bank. The brokers were John Pyemont of the London Stock Exchange and Thomas Warner of Stamp Office Buildings, Manchester.

The proposed railway was described with an explanation that it had been projected in the autumn of 1861 by a number of gentlemen, landowners and others interested in providing better railway communication between Staffordshire, Shropshire and the Welsh districts and that strenuous opposition by the L&NWR and NSR had been overcome. Great play was made of the existing communication between Stafford and Derby being *very imperfect and inconvenient* with claims that it was difficult to accomplish a journey there and back on the same day. The same inconvenience occurred when attempting to make a similar journey to Derby from Shrewsbury which was described as the terminal station for the Welsh system of railways. This inconvenience and the beneficial impact of the S&UR was analysed in a table which gave the following comparisons.

JOURNEY	DISTANCE BY		AVERAGE TIME		SAVING BY S&UR	
	Present miles	S&UR miles	Present hr min	S&UR hr min	Distance miles	Time hr min
Shrewsbury to Derby via Stafford and Stoke	82¼	64¼	5 09	2 30	18	2 39
Shrewsbury to Derby via Stafford and Lichfield	68¼	64¼	4 25	2 30	4	1 55
Shrewsbury to Derby via Birmingham and Tamworth	84	64¼	4 12	2 30	19¾	1 42
Shrewsbury to Derby via Crewe	83¾	64¼	4 03	2 30	19½	1 33
Stafford to Uttoxeter via Stoke	33	15	2 12	0 40	18	1 31
Stafford to Derby via Stoke	53	35	3 00	1 30	18	1 30
Stafford to Derby via Lichfield	39	35	2 44	1 30	4	1 14

Clearly this comparison was aimed at prospective passengers but the railway's freight potential was not neglected. The prospectus went on to point out that the neighbourhood of Uttoxeter abounded in rich mineral deposits and claimed that upwards of 200,000 tons of limestone and other minerals were annually conveyed from the NSR's Churnet Valley line into the South Staffordshire and Shropshire iron districts by the then circuitous routes. It was envisaged that a large proportion of this traffic would use the new railway. It was also claimed that cattle traffic from Shropshire, Montgomeryshire and North Wales to the neighbourhood of Uttoxeter, Derbyshire and Leicestershire would divert to the new railway especially as much of this traffic travelled by road with a great loss of time and a resultant depreciation in the value of the stock. It was explained that the proposed junction with the NSR at Weston would facilitate any traffic requiring to be conveyed over the Cannock Mineral Railway.

In forecasting future returns it had been calculated that a gross receipt of £2 per mile per week would yield a net divided of £5% per annum. Bearing this in mind and a comparison with other local lines built at a higher cost led the directors to claim that investment in the new railway would *yield to the shareholders a very handsome return on their capital*. Sadly, this was not to be.

A Proposed Deviation
On 30 June 1863 the NSR Traffic and Finance Committee received a deputation from the S&UR consisting of Robert Daniel Newill, Solicitor; Thomas Charles Townsend, Engineer; Thomas Wynne, director and two agents representing the Earls of Harrowby and Shrewsbury and Talbot. The agents explained that it was the earnest wish of their Lordships that the S&UR line be diverted at Salt to join the NSR Stone-Colwich line 7½ furlongs to the south of Sandon station, use then being made of the NSR line to Weston, before regaining the authorised route to Uttoxeter. The NSR Solicitors, Messrs Burchell & Co., of London had already been advised of the proposal which would require further Parliamentary powers. Amazingly the NSR personnel present (Lt. Col. Charles Pearson, Chairman; Jonathan Samuda, Secretary; and directors Frederick W. Tomlinson and William Brownfield) intimated on behalf of the NSR that there *was every disposition* to meet the wishes of their Lordships and that they would instruct the NSR Engineer, John Curphey Forsyth, to consider and report on the matter. The issue rumbled on until it appeared to come to a head at a meeting of the Traffic and Finance Committee held on 8 September 1863. William Field, the S&UR's contractor, was in attendance and the Earl of Shrewsbury and Talbot was present, presumably in his capacity as an NSR director and as an instigator of the proposed deviation. Forsyth had met with representatives of the S&UR at Stafford on 15 August and it was explained that the question of the deviation now rested with the S&UR who would need to promote another Bill in Parliament. After a lengthy discussion, Field said he thought it would be necessary to obtain the consent of the L&NWR to ensure that there was no opposition to the Bill. It was left with Field to contact the L&NWR but whether he did so was not recorded and the proposal was dropped. It seems quite amazing that the Earls of Harrowby and Shrewsbury and Talbot should attempt to divert the S&UR from the route authorised by Parliament just a few months earlier. We are convinced that Field was pleased to see the matter dropped and his suggestion of seeking L&NWR consent was perhaps a means of achieving this aim.

Construction and the Contractors

The prospectus explained that a contract for the construction and completion of the whole line within 18 months had been entered into with a responsible contractor for a guaranteed amount. It was claimed that possession of the land had been obtained and that the works would be commenced forthwith and prosecuted *with the utmost vigour*. While the famous railway contractor Thomas Brassey (1805-1870) gave evidence to a House of Commons Select Committee in favour of the S&UR, the contract to construct the railway primarily concerned William Field (1812-1894). Indeed there are two known Deeds of Contract with Field dated 17 June 1864 and 28 May 1866.[83] However, some form of contract was definitely in place much earlier as on 1 April 1862 the *Staffordshire Advertiser* contained a report which stated that William Field, at the request of the S&UR's Engineer, Thomas Charles Townsend, had gone over the ground to be occupied by the railway and had undertaken trial sections and borings of the only two significant hills on the proposed route at Hopton and near Loxley. The report went on to say that he had carefully examined Townsend's estimates and was so satisfied that he had entered into a provisional contract with the promoters to construct the works at a sum not exceeding £10,000 per mile, including the purchase of land, for the actual works would not exceed £8,000 per mile. The *Birmingham Daily Post* for 28 March 1863 reported that works had actually commenced at Loxley and Hopton Hill and on 10 April 1863[84] the contractor or his agent entered the Earl of Shrewsbury's land to take possession. On 24 February 1864 three cases were heard before the Master of the Rolls in the Court of Chancery concerning the S&UR and its contractors.[85] These were described as:

Finney v. S&UR, demurrer of defendant, Beattie
Finney v. S&UR, demurrer of defendants, Bateman and Harkey
Finney v. S&UR, demurrer of defendant, William Field

Each of the cases was heard separately. In the first, that of the defendant Beattie, the demurrer was disallowed. In the case of the second, that of defendants Bateman and Harkey, the demurrer was allowed; and in the third, that of the defendant Field, the demurrer was disallowed. Reporting on the matter the following day the *Birmingham Daily Post* said: *All the defendants were contractors, and there was such an admixture of contracts, and of accounts between them and the Company, as to render anything like an explanation of the cases extremely difficult.* The issue seemed to revolve around the S&UR borrowing money before the whole of the capital authorised by its 1862 Act had been subscribed and advancing the money so subscribed to promote a second Bill when not permitted to do so. What a rumpus. The second Bill eventually received the Royal Assent on 26 May 1865 and became the Stafford and Uttoxeter Railway Act 1865.[86] It authorised additional capital as costs were rising above the original estimates (see below). At this distance in time it is not possible to determine precisely what was at stake but the outcome no doubt resulted in Field entering into his 1864 contract and the other potential contractors probably disappearing from the scene.

William Field was christened at Pipe Ridware, Staffordshire on 6 September 1812. Pipe Ridware is on the north side of the River Trent some six miles to the north of Lichfield. The linkage between Field and Brassey was strengthened at St. Oswald's church in Chester on 30 August 1838 when Field married Brassey's sister-in-law, Christiana Harrison (1819-1885), the youngest daughter of Joseph Harrison of Birkenhead. The two men immediately struck up a rapport. Brassey had married Joseph's second daughter, Maria Farrington Harrison (1810-1877), on 27 December 1831. Field initially pursued a career as a surgeon and worked for Brassey in this capacity on the Trent Valley Railway contract which was let in 1845. Brassey had previously employed doctors on his French railway contracts. By 1851 Field, now of Rugeley, was recorded as a surgeon '*not practising*'.

Field was in partnership with Brassey for no less than 24 railway construction contracts, the first being for the Leominster and Kington Railway completed in 1857. The full list of these contracts is given below with the the year of completion and the mileages involved.

YEAR	RAILWAY	MILEAGE	
1857	Leominster & Kington	14	
1859	Cannock Mineral	10	
1860	Woofferton & Tenbury	5	
1860	Wenlock	4	
1861	Knighton	12	
1861	Nuneaton & Hinkley	5	
1861	Shrewsbury & Hereford	51	(widening)
1861	South Staffordshire	4	
1862	Cannock Chase	3	
1862	Coalbrookdale	5	
1862	Nantwich & Market Drayton	11	
1862	South Leicester	10	
1862	Tenbury & Bewdley	12	
1862	Wenlock & Craven Arms	14	
1862	Ludlow & Clee Hill	6	
1864	Wellington & Market Drayton	16	
1864	Enniskillen & Bundoran	36	
1865	Hull & Doncaster	16	
1865	Hereford Loop	2½	
1865	Hooton and Parkgate	5	
1865	Llangollen & Corwen	10	
1865	Nantwich & Market Drayton	11	(widening)
1866	Ebbw Vale	2	
1867	Sirhowy	2	

He was also in partnership with Brassey for three drainage schemes at Ludlow, Worm and Letton, works at Barrow Docks and reclamation works on the River Dee and so by the time he took on responsibility for the S&UR construction contract, he had acquired considerable experience in managing civil engineering works.

The 1871 census return describes Field as a railway contractor and records him living in Shrewsbury. In 1881 he was living at 13 Belmont, Shrewsbury and described as Retired Lieutenant Colonel, Volunteer Artillery. He had been the Commander of the 1st Shropshire Administrative Brigade Volunteer Artillery and was held in very high regard. In 1872 he was presented with a citation signed by the officers, non-commissioned officers and gunners under his command, together with a portrait showing him in uniform next to his charger. We are very fortunate in being able to reproduce that portrait which, as far as we are aware,

FAR LEFT: *Thomas Brassey (1805-1870) in a portrait by Frederick Piercy (1830-1891). Brassey gave evidence to a House of Commons Select Committee in favour of the Stafford and Uttoxeter Railway. His wife and the wife of the principal contractor, William Field, were sisters.*

LEFT: *Thomas Brassey as he appeared in 1862.*

William Field 1812-1894 was the principal contractor for the Stafford and Uttoxeter Railway. This painting was presented to him in 1872 and depicts him as Lt. Col. William Field, First Shropshire Administrative Brigade, Volunteer Artillery of which he was the commanding officer. The accompanying citation included the following words: 'The deep interest you display in all matters connected with the well-being of the Corps both as relates to its discipline and efficiency and the welfare of its members individually, would alone win the devotion of the officers and men and also endear you to the hearts of all who have the pleasure of your friendship or the honour of serving under your command'. This image is reproduced with the kind permission of the present owner Colonel William A. Oakeley (ret) US Army; William Field was his great, great grandfather.

is the only known image of William Field. By 1891 he had moved to Shelton Priory, Bicton, Shropshire and was '*living on own means*'. He died on 27 June 1894 leaving effects valued at £37,893 – £4.17m at today's values! His daughter, Mary Anne Field, had the unfortunate experience of marrying Richard Banner Oakeley, a onetime S&UR director who was subsequently jailed for five years on a fraud charge. (see Chapter Four).

Reverting to the construction of the S&UR, work was certainly underway again by 20 July 1864 as the *Derby Mercury* for that day reported that two navvies, James Hopwood and John Hudson, working on the S&UR near Bromshall cutting, had been charged at Uttoxeter Petty Sessions with trespassing on land in the possession of Mrs. Babb at Caverswall in search of rabbits. They admitted the offence and said that drink had led them to it. The bench fined each of them 5s 0d (25p) with 7s 9d costs (39p). On 7 September 1864 the same newspaper reported that Henry Lovatt, a workman on the new line, had been committed to the house of correction for one month, with hard labour, for snaring

rabbits on land belonging to the Earl of Shrewsbury and Talbot. Things were very different then!

On 14 February 1865 Samuel Ginders, acting on behalf of the Earl, entered into an agreement with the S&UR[87] setting out the terms and conditions for taking the Earl's land for the railway. Among the various undertakings given, were three which related to connections to the railway so enabling the Earl to take advantage of the new facility. The S&UR undertook to provide, at its expense, *a tramway sufficient to carry a locomotive engine and its tender at such proper and convenient point as may be agreed upon leading from their main line of railway to the vendor's salt works at Weston.* Moreover, the S&UR agreed to provide sidings at Hopton and Salt.

At the company's ordinary meeting held at the Swan Hotel, Stafford on 5 April 1865, the secretary said the new works had been proceeded with as rapidly as possible, but the severe weather had to some extent retarded them. The tunnel at Loxley and the cutting at Hopton were so far advanced as to enable those works to be completed simultaneously with the other portions of the line, which were being pushed forward with the utmost energy. Actual expenditure and liabilities at that stage amounted to £137,979. William Field said that the cost of land greatly exceeded anything contemplated citing that at Stafford Common an exorbitant £2,300 had been asked for 2¼ acres. Difficulty in getting possession of Lord Ferrer's land was the principal cause of delay. In answer to a shareholder, Field said he believed the line would be opened about the end of August or the beginning of September. What an optimist!

At the next ordinary meeting held at the Swan Hotel on 2 October 1865 the directors reported that during the last six months the works on the line had steadily progressed but not with the rapidity they could have wished. Delay had been caused by the very great difficulty in obtaining labour which it was hoped would shortly be remedied. The directors indicated that they were satisfied that the contractor had used every exertion in his power and that the delay had not been caused by any want of energy on his part, adding that the great interest he had in the line was the surest guarantee that the works would be completed as soon as possible. William Field stated that it had been extremely difficult to obtain sufficient labourers, notwithstanding the high wages which he offered. At two points of the line where large embankments were being made, the engines were only drawing five wagons instead of their proper compliment of fifteen. He claimed that if the present rate of progress were maintained the line would be opened by the beginning of March 1866 but if additional hands could be found it might be opened before Christmas 1865. Both prophecies proved incorrect.

Further delays were announced at the general meeting of shareholders held at Stafford on 12 March 1866. The report read by the secretary presents us with a conundrum as it said that William Field regretted the further delay which had arisen because of the death of his partner. Now this was certainly not his wife or Thomas Brassey as both were still very much alive. Clearly someone else was also involved with the construction of the line, perhaps a sub-contractor if the term 'partner' was not being used in a strictly legal sense. It was stated that the works were rapidly progressing towards completion with three locomotive engines at work and additional hands were now coming in daily for employment. Field said he thought that the line would be completed by the end of that half-year. Stations had been decided upon by the directors at Salt, Weston, Stowe and Loxley, the latter at the Stafford end of the tunnel, for passengers only. It had also been decided to have a station for picking up passengers and a coal wharf at Common Road, Stafford. At the conclusion of the meeting a special general meeting was held at which power was given to the directors to raise additional capital of £50,000. This was because the cost of the land, especially near Stafford, had exceeded the original calculations and because the Board of Trade had required greater protection for the public at certain level crossings that had not been anticipated.

On 27 August 1866 there was an accident on the line resulting in serious injuries to John Challinor aged 21 years. He was walking along the line near to Hopton cutting when he was caught by a passing horse drawn truck used for tipping spoil. He was dragged under the wheels of the truck which passed over his legs. He was rushed to the County Infirmary at Stafford and appears to have survived. The circumstances of this accident clearly indicate that construction works were still underway so it seems amazing that only one month earlier, it had been officially predicted that the new railway would by this time have been opened for traffic.

Contractors' Locomotives

Unfortunately, we know almost nothing about the locomotives used by William Field on the construction of the railway. In fact, the only information we have is a comment made at the ordinary meeting of the railway company on 2 October 1865, that two locomotives were in use and in the following year, 1866, at one point there were three. As the latter was towards the end of the construction period, doubtless they would have been involved in final ballasting work. We can, however, speculate on the likely identities of at least some of the locomotives that might have been used. This is because Field, along with his sometime partner Thomas Brassey, was involved in the construction of other railways in the locality at around the same period, on which locomotives are known to have been used. For example, between 1864 and 1866 with Brassey, Field was engaged in building the Wellington & Market Drayton Railway which opened on 16 October 1867, while at about the same time the partners widened the adjacent Nantwich & Market Drayton Railway from single to double track. One of the locomotives known to have been used on these jobs was *Christiand*,[88] a Manning Wardle 0-6-0 saddle tank of that manufacturer's Old I class with inside cylinders 11 × 17 inches, number 192, new to Brassey & Field at Market Drayton in March 1866. Another contender is Manning Wardle number 67 of February 1863, *Perserverance*, dispatched to Brassey & Field at Shrewsbury. Of the same Old I class, this one was probably used, initially at least, on one or both of the Llangollen & Corwen (opened between 1 December 1861 and 8 May 1865) and Corwen & Bala (opened between 16 July 1866 and 1 April 1868) Railways. The partners also built the Cannock Mineral Railway, briefly described in Chapter Two, which opened from Cannock to Rugeley on 7 November 1859. On their contract to widen the line from Shrewsbury to Hereford in 1861 - again from single to double track – they are known to have used *Perserverance*. Two other very interesting locomotives are thought to have been used on the Corwen to Bala job, one or both of which may have migrated to the S&UR. They were of the early design of Aveling & Porter four-wheel chain-drive traction engine type locomotives with a single cylinder engine mounted on top of the boiler. In the case of these engines, the drive was only on the rear wheels making them in effect 2-2-0s, while in a later design all four wheels were driven by a two cylinder compound engine with gear rather than chain drive. The locomotives in question were Aveling numbers 221 and 235 of 1866, although in fact, there were three of these locomotives, the other one being 220 of the same year. While the maker's records show 220 as being ordered by Brassey, the other two were ordered by Brassey & Lucas, Lucas being another one time partner with Brassey on various contracts.

Thomas Brassey and some of his other partners had a number of Manning Wardle locomotives in the early to mid 1860s of the same Old I class. It is, therefore, possible that one or more of these might have been loaned to William Field and used on the S&UR. For example, locomotives used with S Ballard, trading as Brassey & Ballard, were Manning Wardle numbers 83 *Colwall* of September 1863, 155 *Stoneyway* of February 1865, 174 *Cobden* of August 1865, 177 *Shakespeare* of November 1865 and 204 *Lincoln* of April 1866. With George Wythes, trading as Brassey & Wythes, there was also Manning 195 of October 1866 No 1, in this case a larger class M 0-6-0 saddle tank with inside cylinders 13 × 18 inches, along with 193 of March 1866. This latter was a class K, similar to the Old I class but with larger 12 inch diameter cylinders and in this case, working for Brassey & Ogilvie as *Cheshire* No 3. While all these locomotives were dispatched by the makers to locations other than the S&UR, once again it is quite possible Field borrowed one or more of them from his friend. Almost all the early railway contractors worked in partnerships rather than being registered as Companies under any of the Companies Acts, swapping and changing as opportunities arose. On occasions they often had more than one contract underway at the same time and with a different partner in each case. Sometimes a contractor would be awarded a contract to build a railway and then, after *shopping* round his contemporaries, form a partnership to undertake the work. Hence, locomotives were moved about and may only have spent short periods on particular jobs so that the maker's spares order records do not always help in identifying all the contracts on which individual locomotives were used.

As alluded to above, it is worth emphasising that the need for locomotives on the construction of railways was often quite spasmodic, depending on the type of work being undertaken at any one time. Obviously, for locomotives to be of any use, the works would need to have been in a state where at least temporary lines could be laid. In the case of the S&UR, as the construction works were so protracted, in view of financial and other problems, locomotives might have been brought to and from the site at various times, as Field may not have wanted to tie up expensive assets if, in fact, there was no use for them at any particular time.

Board of Trade Inspections

The official inspection of the railway by the Board of Trade Inspecting Officers did not go smoothly. Robert Daniel Newill (1826-1886) in his capacity as secretary first penned a formal letter to the Board of Trade (BoT) on 27 July 1866 stating that it was intended to open the railway *at the expiration of one calendar month from this date.*[89] It was a statutory requirement to give at least one month's notice. The notepaper was headed: Staffordshire and Uttoxeter Railway, Wellington, Salop, the company's registered office being located there. Following receipt of this letter nothing appears to have happened as the railway must have been far from complete. Some ten months later Newill tried again. He wrote on 16 May 1867 to say that in the opinion of the company the railway was *sufficiently completed for the safe conveyance of passengers and ready for inspection.* As a result Colonel William Yolland (1810-1885) accompanied by Major Charles Scrope Hutchinson (1827-1912) inspected the railway on 23 May 1867. All was not well.

This is what Colonel Yolland had to say about the railway in his inspection report.

I have inspected the Stafford and Uttoxeter Railway, which is a single line of 12 miles and 7½ chains in length, commencing at a Junction with the London and North Western Railway where the Shropshire Union Railway joins that line at Stafford Station and terminating at a Junction with the North Staffordshire Railway at Bramshall [sic] about 2 miles from Uttoxeter. These two Junctions are both double Junctions and there are Sidings at three of the four Stations on the Line, viz: Salt, Weston, Stowe and Grindley. The Branch to the North Staffordshire Railway in the Parish of Stowe is in an unfinished state and is not connected by Junction with either line of Railway at the present time.

Yolland went on to observe that he had not yet received details of the permanent way from the S&UR Engineer, Thomas Charles Townsend, but understood that the required information had been despatched. Indeed Townsend had written to the BoT on 21 May 1867 with the particulars required explaining that their late despatch was because he had been unwell and away from home.

Yolland had made his own observations about the permanent way and reported:

it consists of a double headed rail that weighs 75 lbs per linear yard, fixed in cast iron chairs that each weigh about 23 lbs by means of wooden keys placed outside the rails – these chairs are fastened on transverse sleepers by means of two iron spikes to each chair – the sleepers being placed about 3 feet apart on the average. The joints are fished. The gauge is 4 feet 8½ inches and the distance between the rails when there are two is 6 feet. Land has been purchased and the over bridges have been constructed for a double line, but the under bridges and the only tunnel on the line 320 yards in length have only been constructed for a single line of way.

There are 16 over and 22 under bridges and one tunnel with four viaducts – the bridges and viaducts with the exception of two small under bridges which are of wood, are all constructed either of stone or brick or with those materials combined with wrought or cast iron girders – the largest span is 47 feet on the skew. The iron girder bridges appear to be sufficiently strong by calculation and exhibited moderate deflections under load.

After this concise description Yolland went on to describe eight deficiencies:

1. He said the cast iron chairs in which the rails were fastened were very light and that they should be replaced by heavier chairs adjacent to the joints and one in the centre of each rail, not weighing less than 28 lbs per chair. This was a very onerous criticism. Each rail throughout the length of the new line, over 12 miles of it, would have to be lifted while three new heavier chairs were fitted under each single length of rail. It would be a very costly and time consuming exercise. This was a major blow and must have infuriated the contractor and the directors.

2. At Stafford North Junction the distant signal on the branch could not be seen from the signal box so that a repeating signal was required together with a new low level signal for a

siding lying north of the L&NWR up main line, interlocking with the other signals.

3. Because Salt station was constructed on a steep incline of 1 in 75 the siding already installed there needed to be altered into a loop siding with an indicator at the north end and an additional safety siding and stop block provided to arrest any carriage that might run back. A second platform at this station was also required.

4. The longitudinal beams that carried the chairs over the cast iron and wrought iron under bridges needed transoms and strap and tie bolts at about 11 foot intervals in order to preserve the gauge.

5. The sidings at Weston and Grindley were required to be controlled by low signals interlocked with the station and distant signals in each direction and linking, when at danger, to the facing points controlling newly constructed *blind* sidings that had to be constructed at these stations.

6. At some of the under bridges and cattle creeps the fencing adjacent to the wing walls needed raising and a temporary water tank at the Trent & Mersey canal bridge needed to be removed. This tank may have been used to supply the contractor's locomotives with water pumped from the canal.

7. Yolland observed that there were no engine turntables at either end of the line but he had been informed that the company had authority to use Stafford and Uttoxeter stations. There was an engine turntable at Stafford but only a 17 foot turntable at Uttoxeter which would not suffice to turn an engine and tender without uncoupling. He had no strict right to ask for a turntable beyond the limits of the line at Bromshall and commented that it was not yet known who was to work the line. However, an undertaking not to run trains with the engine tender foremost nor with the chimney of tank engines rearmost would be required from the S&UR and concurred in by any company which worked the line on its behalf. This was again a major setback to the fledgling S&UR and it is difficult to see the logic in requiring tank engines to be turned. Yolland's comments clearly indicate that the method of working the line had not yet been considered and clearly imply that the directors were contemplating another company doing this on their behalf.

8. The station clocks were required to be placed such that they could be seen from the platforms.

Yolland concluded his report by stating that the line could not be opened without danger to the public owing to the incompleteness of the works. As a result the company was instructed by the BoT to postpone the opening by one calendar month. This proved to be too short a timescale within which to rectify the deficiencies and so the process of inspection lingered on. It is interesting to note that Yolland did not comment on

Bromshall tunnel or the cutting at Hopton which, in spite of presenting construction difficulties, must have been satisfactory at the time of his initial inspection. However, Yolland did make a file note of a further improvement he required at Stafford. This is dated 11 September 1867 when he was about to go on holiday and stated as follows:

In the event of any other officer than myself being appointed to re-inspect the Stafford and Uttoxeter Railway, I beg to explain that there is a siding belonging to the London and North Western Railway Company at Stafford which crosses the incoming and joins the outgoing line of the Stafford and Uttoxeter Railway which I pointed out on the ground as objectionable, and which I have since my Inspection told the Engineer of the line must be altered.

Yolland must have heard that another request for inspection was imminent for on 18 September 1867 Newill wrote to the BoT stating that:

the Main Line of the Stafford & Uttoxeter Railway is now in the opinion of the Directors sufficiently completed for the safe conveyance of passengers and ready for Inspection.

Hutchinson (now promoted to Lieutenant-Colonel) undertook this second inspection on 25 September 1867. He reported that all the requests made by Yolland had been carried out except for the following:

1. The second platform at Salt station had been installed but required a second ramp at one end.

2. The transoms and tie bolts had not been added to the longitudinal timbers at the cast iron under bridges so as to preserve the gauge as the company had thought that Yolland was unaware of the existence of vertical bolts at four foot intervals connecting the longitudinal timbers with the cross girders. The company had, however, put them in as directed in the cast iron bridges where the vertical bolts were at 11 foot intervals. They were, of course, required at all the bridges.

A slight addition to the fencing was also required in two places. Hutchinson added a note to the effect that some arrangement was pending with regard to the siding at Stafford as the points connecting it with the outgoing S&UR line had been disconnected and a rail removed such that nothing could enter or leave the siding. He pointed out that if the siding were to be maintained it must be altered as pointed out by Yolland. As shall be revealed later the S&UR reneged on this understanding.

Hutchinson enclosed with his report an undertaking signed by the contractor, William Field, to the effect that the omissions would now be carried out. Field specifically referred to the fixing of transoms and tie bolts at the bridges across the canal, the turnpike roads and the NSR. Hutchinson concluded his report by recommending that the S&UR be opened for traffic on receipt of a satisfactory undertaking as to the mode of working the line. This was received by the BoT on 10 October 1867 and bore the company's seal and the signatures of the chairman and secretary.

Because of its interest it is worth quoting in full:

The Stafford and Uttoxeter Railway Company do hereby undertake that no Engine used on that Railway shall be run Tender foremost nor any Tank Engine with the Chimney rearmost and that this shall form part of the Agreement with any Company who may work the Line.

The Stafford and Uttoxeter Railway Company do hereby certify that the following mode of working the Line will be adopted viz:

That the Line shall be worked by Train Staff in the mode adopted on many of the leading Railways and described in the amended Regulations of the Board of Trade.

Dated this eighth day of October one thousand eight hundred and sixty seven.

Thos. Eyton, Chairman
Robert D. Newill, Secretary

Hutchinson endorsed the undertaking as satisfactory on 10 October 1867. That being so, it is something of a mystery as to why the first train in public service did not operate until 23 December 1867. It had been reported in the press[90] at the beginning of 1867 that negotiations were underway with the Midland Railway for that company to purchase the line, but obviously those negotiations proved unsuccessful as did a previous initiative for the L&NWR and NSR to work the line jointly. The NSR Traffic and Finance Committee first contemplated the matter on 6 February 1866 when a proposal by the S&UR contractor, William Field, was considered. The matter was clearly taken very seriously as evidenced by a top level meeting at Euston which took place several months later on 19 September 1866. The NSR Chairman, Lt. Col. Charles Pearson and the General Manager, Percy Morris, travelled south to meet a talented array of L&NWR personnel, including Richard Moon, Chairman; James Bancroft, a L&NWR Director who played a key part in many inter-company negotiations; George Findlay, General Goods Manager; Stephen Reay, Secretary; Francis Harley, Clerk (probably the committee secretary). The question of working the S&UR was referred to Percy Morris and Charles Mason, the L&NWR Assistant General Manager who had to report to William Cawkwell, the General Manager. The two companies were required to confer regarding the use of stations and lines at Stafford and Uttoxeter with a view to securing uniformity of terms. Neither company was to settle any terms with the S&UR without consulting the other company. Cawkwell and Morris were instructed to communicate with their GWR counterpart, James Grierson, who surprisingly had been appointed by the S&UR as their negotiator. Two months later he declined the terms proposed and so the negotiations came to nothing. Procrastination over who was to work the line clearly led to the final delay in opening the S&UR to traffic.

Description of the line
The best contemporary description of the line from a passenger viewpoint can be found in the *Staffordshire Advertiser* for 28 December 1867 which reported on the opening of the railway. This is how the newspaper described the new railway from west to east:

The line leaves the London and North Western Railway about half a mile from the Stafford station, passes over the Broad Eye Meadows, skirts the Stafford Cemetery and thence crosses Stafford Common to Hopton. From Hopton the line is carried to Salt – the first station, about 4½ miles from Stafford. Sandon Hall, the seat of the Earl of Harrowby and the Pitt monument in Sandon Park may be distinctly seen from this part of the line. Passing the pretty church at Salt, with its neat parsonage and schools, the line proceeds, for a short distance, along one of the most beautiful portions of the lovely valley of the Trent and thence by Weston and Shirleywich – the salt works at these places presenting singular appearances, situated as they are in what otherwise is purely an agricultural district – to Stowe. From the line at this spot a view is obtained of Chartley Castle and Park – the noble owner of which, Earl Ferrers, we may observe in passing, will obtain his majority next month. The next and last station on the line is Grindley, ten miles distant from Stafford; whence the line proceeds to Loxley – in the neighbourhood of which are Loxley Hall and the woods made famous by Robin Hood's exploits. Passing through a short tunnel the line joins the North Staffordshire Railway two miles from Uttoxeter, making the distance between the town and Stafford 15 miles.

A little flowery perhaps but indicative of what the potential traveller might expect to see from the carriage window.

The William Pitt monument in Sandon Park, a lofty Doric pillar surmounted by an urn, was erected in 1806. It was made of local grey stone and stands 75 feet high. The village church at Salt, built in 1843, is dedicated to St. James the Great and was built on land donated by the Earl of Shrewsbury and Talbot and was largely paid for by him. It has a distinctive open stone bell turret mounted at the east end of the church and is hung with two bells. The S&UR may have been a very short railway but it certainly traversed a part of Staffordshire which was steeped in tradition and history.

Principal Engineering Features
The newspaper went on to point out that the construction of the line had been a work of much difficulty explaining that there were several inclines and that at one part, Hopton, a hard rock of considerable length had to be penetrated. Moreover, the tunnel at Loxley [sic] though only 320 yards long, required much labour in its making. Potential travellers were thus made aware of the principal engineering features.

The profile of the line was something of a switchback with hardly any section of track being level. There was a gradual climb from Stafford after crossing the River Sow with little respite until the middle of Hopton cutting was breasted after over a mile at 1 in 70 and short stretches at 1 in 65 and 1 in 69. The line then fell at 1 in 75 towards Salt. At Ingestre the line began to climb again to Chartley after which there was another climb of over a mile at 1 in 79 and 1 in 80 before the line reached its summit level and started falling at 1 in 120 towards Grindley station. After Grindley the line undulated before falling sharply at 1 in 70 towards Bromshall Junction.

Hopton cutting and Bromshall tunnel, near Loxley, were obviously the principal engineering features of the line. The cutting was nearly half a mile in length and in places nearly 60ft in depth; the brick lined tunnel with an egg-shaped arch was actually 321 yards long and had a wall to wall span of 11ft 9½in with stone facings to the portals. The tunnel had four refuges on the up side and five on the down. The tunnel was built to placate opposition from Thomas Clement Sneyd Kynnersley (1803-1892) under whose land the tunnel passed. He was the son of Thomas Sneyd Kynnersley of Loxley Park and became the Stipendiary Magistrate for Birmingham (1856-1888), Recorder of Newcastle-under-Lyme (1858-1885) and Deputy Lieutenant for Warwickshire. In addition to the tunnel, there were 49 bridges on the line, some of minor significance but others demanding considerable skill in their design and erection. Amongst the latter, in sequence from Stafford, were the twin span bridge across the River Sow, the three span bridge across the River Trent near Ingestre, the bridge across the Trent and Mersey Canal and, shortly afterwards, the bridge across the NSR main line from Stoke to Colwich. All these bridges were constructed with iron girders, those across the waterways having the following dimensions:

	Span	Average height above water
River Sow	2 × 30ft 0in	3ft 6in
River Trent	3 × 30ft 0in	7ft 3in
Trent & Mersey Canal	1 × 50ft 5in	6ft 10in

The bridge across the NSR had a skew span of 34ft 4in[91] and a height above rail level of 14ft 0in. Shortly to the east of this bridge it was intended to put in a connection to the NSR in the direction of Hixon but although the embankment was constructed the track was never laid. The main girders of the bridge over the NSR were strengthened by the GNR in 1907. All the overbridges on the S&UR were constructed to accommodate a double line of railway but the underbridges and the tunnel at Bromshall were only built to accommodate a single line.

Stations

The original stations on the line were located at Salt (4 miles 59 chains from Stafford), Weston (6 miles 13 chains), Stowe (7 miles 79 chains) and Grindley (10 miles 33 chains). Weston was renamed Ingestre for Weston in December 1869 and Stowe was renamed Chartley and Stowe on 3 October 1874. Initially no station masters were appointed for the intermediate stations, tickets from those places being issued by a clerk who travelled on the trains. Stafford Common station, initially called simply Common, was not opened until 1 July 1874. Its full title was not adopted until 1 November 1881 and it was originally located to the west of Marston Road. At Stafford L&NWR station the S&UR trains initially shared platform facilities with L&NWR trains but from 1881 they were accommodated in a new bay platform constructed to the north east of the station. At Uttoxeter the trains terminated at the NSR's Bridge Street station. The NSR Traffic and Finance Committee at its meeting held on 7 July 1868 approved a tender of £260 15s 0d [£260.75p] from Thomas Crofts for additional accommodation at Uttoxeter Bridge Street, presumably to cater for the increased traffic.

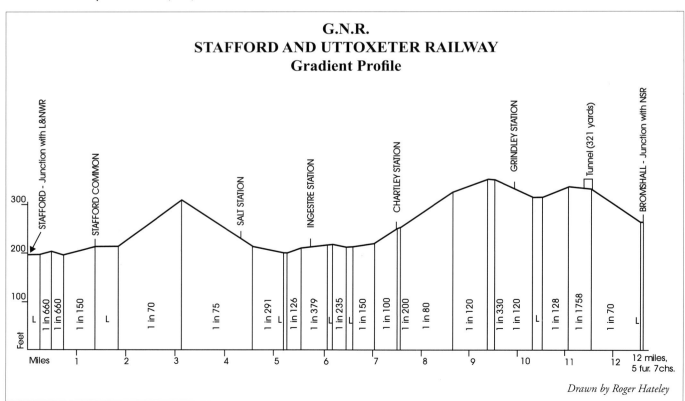

G.N.R.
STAFFORD AND UTTOXETER RAILWAY
Gradient Profile

Drawn by Roger Hateley

Abbots Bromley Branch

The S&UR deposited a Bill in the 1863-1864 Parliamentary Session for a branch to Abbots Bromley.[92] The proposed branch was five miles eight and a half chains in length and would have made a junction with the S&UR facing west at a point seven miles and 70 chains from Stafford near to the village of Stowe. The deposited plans and sections indicate that the surveyor was John Barber (1824-1881) of Wellington, Salop. Total expenditure was estimated at £50,000 including land and contingencies. The S&UR directors agreed to the scheme to facilitate the withdrawal of the rival North and South Staffordshire Junction Railway Bill (see Chapter Two). Initially the S&UR Bill did not comply with Parliamentary standing orders and had to be resubmitted but on 15 February 1864 the S&UR representatives *failed to appear before the Bill examiners* and that was the end of the matter. It is obvious that the fledgling company could not afford this extra commitment when it was struggling to secure sufficient funding to build its authorised main line.

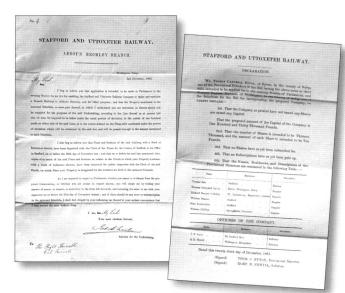

John Barber (1824-1881) of Wellington, Shropshire began his own business as a surveyor, valuer, estate agent and auctioneer in 1848. He undertook the survey for the abortive S&UR Abbots Bromley branch for which a Bill was deposited in the 1863-1864 Parliamentary Session. The deposited plans and sections bear his signature. (Image from The Story of the Barbers, established 1848 by Allan Frost).

Proposed Abbots Bromley branch superimposed on an early 1 inch OS map, submitted as part of the Parliamentary deposit.

HLRO HL/PO/OB/59/1864

A journey along the route

In order to help readers to become familiar with the line, the following pages present a photographic journey along the route, from Stafford travelling east to Uttoxeter. In deciding how best to present this information the authors have had to consider a number of difficulties. Whilst the Stafford to Uttoxeter direction may seem a logical way to explore the route, the company elected for official distances and bridge numbers to be measured from a datum at Bromshall Junction. It should therefore be borne in mind that bridge numbers and official distances diminish as we travel east from Stafford to Uttoxeter by way of photographs and captions. The majority of the bridge photographs which follow in this chapter can be found in a large album in the National Archive collection (NA/RAIL 532/49). The original pictures appear to have been taken around 1900 and judging by how they have been catalogued, appear to have come from NSR sources. A comprehensive list of official bridge numbers as recorded by the GNR Engineer's Department in April 1921 can be found in Appendix Nine. It will be seen that in some cases, there are very minor variations with the dimensions given in the captions applicable to the 1900 series of photographs, which are based on the official plans of the S&UR surveyed by Henry Fowler in 1903.

Stafford

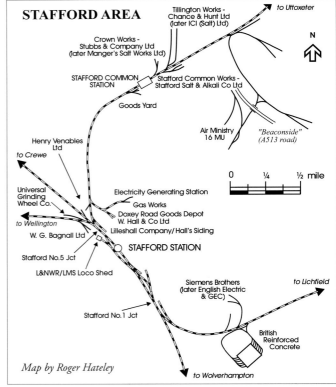

Map by Roger Hateley

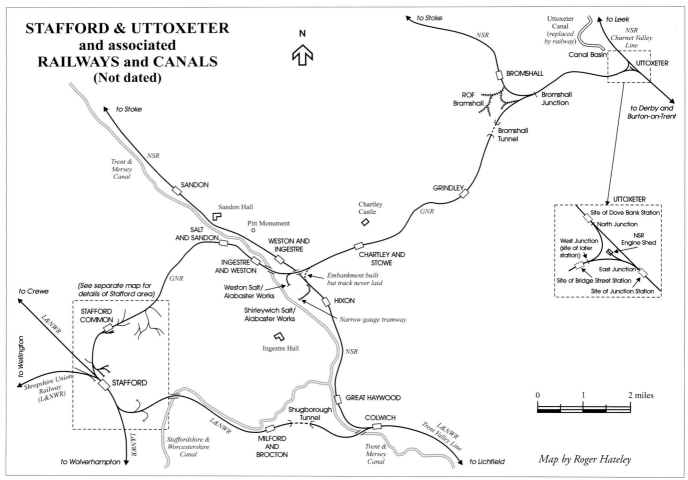

Map by Roger Hateley

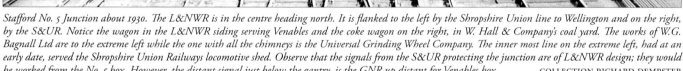

Stafford No. 5 Junction about 1930. The L&NWR is in the centre heading north. It is flanked to the left by the Shropshire Union line to Wellington and on the right, by the S&UR. Notice the wagon in the L&NWR siding serving Venables and the coke wagon on the right, in W. Hall & Company's coal yard. The works of W.G. Bagnall Ltd are to the extreme left while the one with all the chimneys is the Universal Grinding Wheel Company. The inner most line on the extreme left, had at an early date, served the Shropshire Union Railways locomotive shed. Observe that the signals from the S&UR protecting the junction are of L&NWR design; they would be worked from the No. 5 box. However, the distant signal just below the gantry, is the GNR up distant for Venables box. COLLECTION RICHARD DEMPSTER

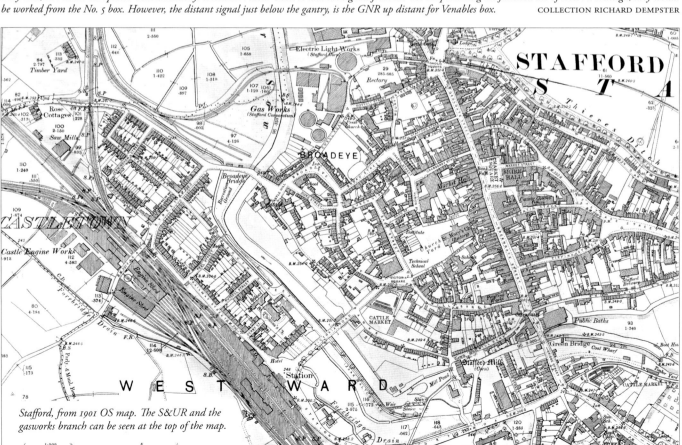

Stafford, from 1901 OS map. The S&UR and the gasworks branch can be seen at the top of the map.

One of three aerial views of Venables timber yard. This one looks due south with the former L&NWR main line to the right and the S&UR curving away from the main line top centre. The gas works branch can also be seen to the extreme top left. The three aerial views were all taken in the late 1950s.

VENABLES BROTHERS LTD

In this view, again with Venables timber yard prominent, the former L&NWR four-track main line heads north to the upper left, while the line to the bottom left is the former Shropshire Union Railways & Canal Company line to Wellington and Shrewsbury. The factory in the left-hand 'Y' is the Universal Grinding Wheel Company while to the extreme bottom left, is the top end of the yard of W.G. Bagnall Limited, locomotive manufacturers and railway engineers. The S&UR heads off to the top right with the Gas Works Branch curving off the picture to the right centre.

VENABLES BROTHERS LTD

Aerial view of Venables timber yard with the former L&NWR main line to the left and the S&UR in the foreground. The road crossing both railway lines is the Doxey Road and that is Venables signal box just to the right of where the road crosses the S&UR. Notice that as well as a connection into the timber yard from the S&UR, there is another to the bottom left, served by the L&NWR. Note too, that Doxey Road in effect, cuts the timber yard into two sections.   VENABLES BROTHERS LTD

Bridge No. 48 was on the Gas Works Branch at 12 miles and 50 chains from Bromshall Junction. It took a flood opening into one of several drains hereabouts that eventually found their way into the River Sow. The land around here is liable to flooding from the river and this was one of the reasons why construction of the railway took so long. This bridge was entirely of wooden construction with twin spans of 15ft 11ins and the height above the normal water flow, 4ft 4ins. The view looks north-north-west with the main line of the S&UR visible in the distance. The tall signal discernible above the bridge railings is the one controlling entry to the branch.

Venables signal box can be seen here through the arch of bridge No. 47, a view looking towards the Common. The bridge was at twelve miles and 47 chains and took the Doxey Road over the railway, with an elliptical arch having a span of 28ft. The siding leading off to the left served Venables timber yard while that on the right, served W. Hall & Company's coal yard.

Bridge No. 44 at twelve miles and 23 chains carried the railway over the River Sow and this is its south side. Construction consisted of brick abutments and piers, cast iron flat girders and a timber floor, with twin spans of 30ft. Built to suit a single line of railway, as this section originally was, only the overbridges were built to suit double track. The widened portion consisted of wrought iron plate girders and floor, with a span of 31ft.

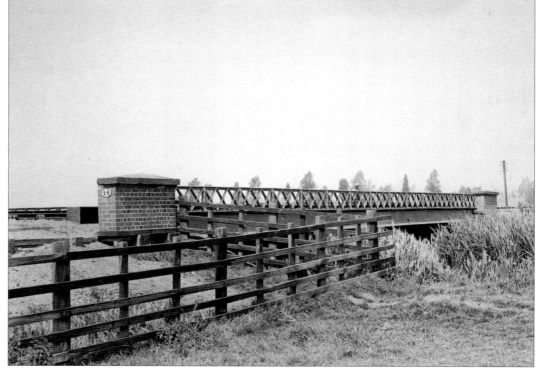

The line was later double track from Stafford as far as the Common as this photograph of bridge No. 42 illustrates. The bridge took the A34 Newcastle-under-Lyme to Stafford road over the railway at eleven miles and 68 chains. This is the west face looking towards the Common, another skew span of 26ft 9ins and 28ft 7ins consisting of cast iron flat girders.

ABOVE: The next sizeable bridge, No. 43, at twelve miles and 1 chain, was of similar construction, taking the Stafford to Eccleshall road, the present day A5013, over the railway. The skew arch had dimensions of 26ft 10ins and 28ft 7ins and this is the west face. The signal is the Venables down distant. The signal post on the up line discernible through the arch, is the Stafford Common up distant.

Stafford Common

The development of the station site at Stafford Common can be traced through this series of OS maps. Note the gradual expansion of the salt works

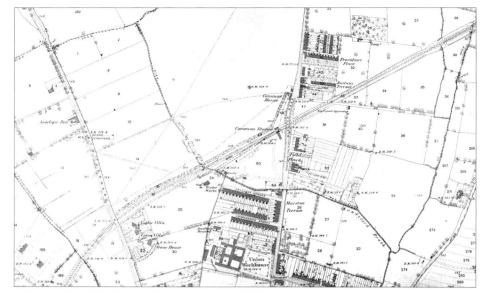

Stafford Common 1880.

Stafford Common 1901.

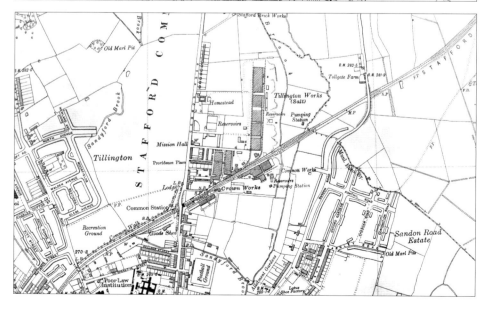

Stafford Common 1924.

Stafford Common Station, located at 11 miles and 42 chains, looking west towards Stafford. The bridge, No. 41, which also accommodated the booking office, took the Stafford to Marston road over the railway at this point. The bridge structure is described as brick with cast iron flat girders on a skew span of 26ft and 29ft 4ins. Notice Stafford Common Yard signal box (not a block post) through the arch and that the platforms are made of wood; they were later replaced by a more permanent arrangement. This was not one of the original stations on the line and dates from 1874.

Another, much later view of Stafford Common taken on 17 March 1957. The siding leading off in the centre foreground, served the Crown Salt Works. The terraced houses on the left are in Aston Terrace.

The road crossing the line at this point, ten miles and 74 chains, on bridge No. 38 is the present Stafford to Sandon B5066. The bridge has an elliptical arch on the skew, at 28ft and 32ft 3ins; this is the east face with the chimney and buildings of some of Stafford's salt works seen through the arch.

At ten miles and 15 chains the line crossed Hopton Road, which leaves the Stafford to Sandon road seen through the arch, serving Hopton Heath. This is the south face of bridge No. 35 and the span was 24ft 10ins.

Bridge No. 32 at nine miles and 19 chains was a brick arch occupation bridge with a nine foot span and known as Fenton's cattle arch. This is the south face and doubtless Fenton was the local farmer whose cattle needed to cross the line at this point. That will be his barn seen through the arch.

Bridge No. 29 was situated immediately on the Stafford side of Salt station at eight miles and 41 chains. It took Brook Lane under the railway by an 11ft 10ins span. This is the south face with part of the village discernible through the arch. The station approach road only used latterly for the surviving milk traffic is to the extreme right.

Salt

Salt from 1880 OS map.

Salt station looking towards Uttoxeter, a photograph dating from after the line lost its passenger traffic but was still in use for goods - probably taken in the late 1940s. There had originally been a loop here which also served the goods dock seen on the right, hence the signal box. This loop was removed in the period 1890-1895 when the station ceased handling goods traffic. The signal box was then replaced (although the building remained) by a ground frame to operate the remaining signals situated in the bay window of the office on the platform which can be clearly seen in this view. Milk traffic however, continued to be handled and that is the reason for the wooden extension outwards from the former goods dock. The station was situated at exactly eight and a half miles. In fact, that is the half-mile post to the extreme right foreground.

Another view taken about the same time as the previous one with more of the signal box visible. Although the signal box function had been replaced by the ground frame, its structure remained.

Bridge No. 27 was a cattle arch in this case at seven miles and 69 chains – the span was only six feet. This is the south face and the River Trent runs by those trees in the background while in the far distance are houses on the Uttoxeter to Stafford road – the present A518.

The very next bridge took the line over the River Trent at seven miles and 48 chains – bridge No. 26. Constructed of stone with cast iron semi-circular girders and a wooden floor, there were three spans each of 30ft.

Bridge No. 25, known as Weston Bridge, took the present A518 Uttoxeter to Stafford road over the railway at seven miles 42 chains. This is the east face looking towards Stafford and that is the Ingestre up distant signal rising above the parapet. This was another elliptical arch on a skew with spans of 27ft 10ins and 32ft 7ins.

Ingestre and Weston

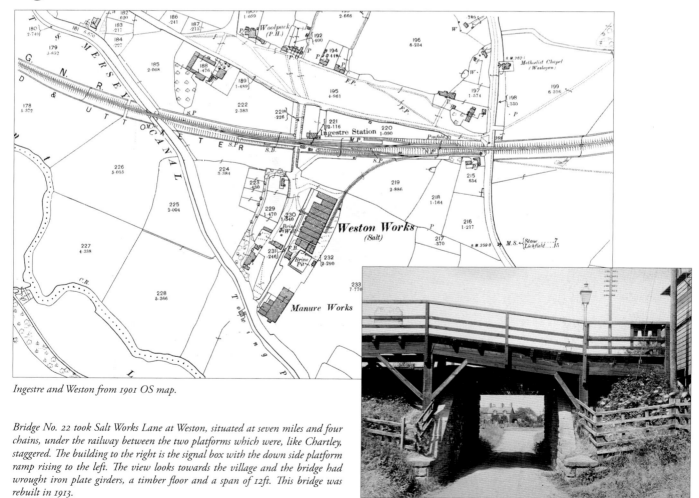

Ingestre and Weston from 1901 OS map.

Bridge No. 22 took Salt Works Lane at Weston, situated at seven miles and four chains, under the railway between the two platforms which were, like Chartley, staggered. The building to the right is the signal box with the down side platform ramp rising to the left. The view looks towards the village and the bridge had wrought iron plate girders, a timber floor and a span of 12ft. This bridge was rebuilt in 1913.

Ingestre and Weston station was located at exactly seven miles and note, like Chartley and Stowe, the signal box bears the singular name of Ingestre only. The station was plain Weston until December 1869. The view looks east towards Uttoxeter, the siding to the right forms a head-shunt for a siding to serve a salt works. The dairy for which Weston is better known, was on the other, up side, obscured in this view by the station buildings. There is a milk tank wagon standing in the siding to the left, beyond the platform. So as not to confuse the traveller, the NSR station nearby, was called Weston and Ingestre; it was closed for passenger traffic, along with the other intermediate stations between Stone and Colwich, on 6 January 1947. However, it survived for goods traffic until 2 September 1963.

Bridge No. 21 at six miles and 70 chains crossed what was then described as The Old Turnpike Road - it became a turnpike in 1728. Today this is the A51 from Stone to Lichfield. The bridge was constructed from stone with wrought iron plate girders and a timber floor - the span was 34ft 7ins and this is the south face. The authors well remember this bridge which was not removed until the early 1960s. It proved to be quite an obstacle for road traffic due to its limited height above the road.

Taking the S&UR over the NSR

This is bridge No. 20 at six miles and 49 chains taking the S&UR over the NSR. On a skew, the dimensions of the span were 29ft 9ins and 34ft 4ins. The girders were wrought iron, both the main ones and the cross ones. The main girders were strengthened in 1907. The photograph was taken on 24 March 1957 looking south.

Another view of the same date as the previous one but from the overbridge, looking north. The bridge in the distance is a farm occupation bridge. The former NSR line here is still in existence. It was electrified as part of the west coast main line electrification scheme of the early to mid 1960s. This section was inaugurated with electric traction on 6 March 1967 having been closed since 7 September 1964, during the electrification works. Today it carries the vast majority of the London-Manchester Virgin Pendolino trains. The route via Stoke including this line from Stone to Colwich where it joins the west coast main line Trent Valley route has, since it was opened in 1849, provided the shortest route between the two cities.

View taken on the same occasion as the previous one looking south along the NSR main line from the S&UR overbridge.

Proposed connecting curve

Just after the line crossed over the NSR main line from Stone to Colwich, at six miles and 20 chains, was the site of the intended spur to connect the two railways. As can be seen from these two photographs which look west towards Stafford and were taken on 24 March 1957, the embankment was constructed. Had the rails ever been laid, connection would have been with the up NSR line on the south side of the bridge carrying the S&UR over the NSR.

Weston proposed curve from 1901 OS map.

Bridge No. 18, at five miles and 73 chains, took the Amerton to Shirleywich road over the railway. This is the west face, another bridge built on a skew, the spans being 28ft and 32ft 5ins.

Bridge No. 17 taking the Amerton to Stowe road (Hamilton Road) over the railway at five miles and 45 chains. This is the west face and the structure is described as brick with cast iron girders and jack arches on a skew of 27ft 10ins and 28ft 10ins. Just discernible in the distance is the bridge on the west side of Chartley station along with the cattle pens which were situated on the opposite side of the bridge to the station. This photograph illustrates clearly the earthworks and bridges having been built to accommodate a double line of railway. Except that is, for the tunnel at Bromshall.

Chartley and Stowe

Chartley and Stowe station – five miles and 20 chains – although, as can be seen here, the signal box was plain Chartley. The photograph is undated although as the line is clearly out of use, but before the onset of dereliction, it probably dates from the early 1950s. The view looks east towards Uttoxeter. Notice the provision of a slip to allow up trains to access the down side siding which served cattle pens situated on the opposite side of the bridge that carried the Chartley to Stowe road over the railway. Notice too, that all the fixed signals except the shunting disc have been removed by this time.

Chartley and Stowe from 1901 OS map

LEFT: Just to the east of Chartley and Stowe Station was bridge No. 15, at four miles and 79 chains, carrying an occupation road and known as Chills – doubtless the local farmer's name once more. Of brick construction the three arches had spans of 24ft, 27ft 10ins and 23ft 9ins.

INSET: Through the arch Chartley and Stowe Station can be seen complete with GNR design somersault signals. The bridge visible behind the signal box is No. 16 (enlarged from photo left).

Another example of an occupation underbridge, in this case No. 13 at three miles and 70 chains, the south face with a nine foot span. This bridge was adjacent to Anglesea Coppice and known as Park Hill.

BELOW: Occupation overbridge No. 12 at three miles and 29 chains looking west, towards Stafford with the Grindley up distant signal visible through the arch. The three arches had spans, from left to right of 23ft 11ins, 28ft and 24ft 3ins. This bridge was known as Deville's.

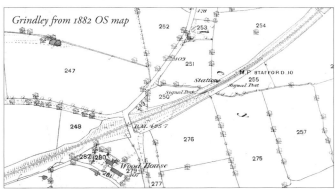

Grindley from 1882 OS map

Grindley

Grindley station looking east. Notice the signal box and staggered platforms. The bridge, No. 11, at two miles and 68 chains, takes the Grindley to Drointon road (Grindley Road) over the railway. It is described as of three spans, two at 24ft and the centre one at 27ft 10ins. The station master's house can just be seen above the bridge to the left.

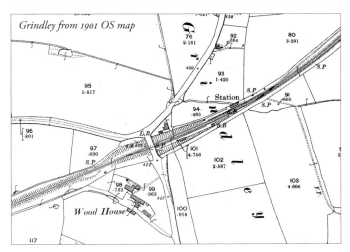

Grindley from 1901 OS map

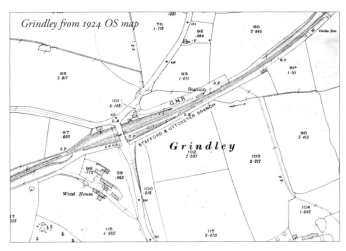

Grindley from 1924 OS map

Bridge No. 7 was at one mile and 70 chains, known as Lee's Hill. An occupation underbridge described as a cattle creep with twin semi-circular arches of 8ft 11ins span. This is the north face.

As we have seen, there were a large number of small occupation underbridges along the line to give access to farmers for lands otherwise severed by the railway. While most were part of the original S&UR plans, there were others built to forestall opposition to the line in Parliament. This is an example, the north face of bridge No. 5, at one mile and 47 chains, described as Durose's, a brick span of nine feet. Presumably Durose was the farmer whose land it served. Notice the cow visible through the arch.

Bromshall Tunnel

ABOVE: *The western portal of the 321 yard long Bromshall tunnel built to placate the opposition of Thomas Clement Sneyd Kynnersley (1803-1892), the owner of the land under which it passed. The present A518 Uttoxeter to Stafford road does however, pass over it. The distances between the portals were recorded as one mile and 21 chains to one mile seven chains. It contained five people refuges on the down side and four on the up.*

RIGHT: *The eastern portal.*

Occupation overbridge, bridge No. 3 at 47 chains which went under the name of Milnes, doubtless as that was the name of the farmer whose land it served. It led off the main Uttoxeter to Stafford road, the present A518, directly opposite Loxley Park. This is the west face of the 28ft elliptical span with the Bromshall West GNR up distant signal just visible through the arch.

Bridge No. 1 was an occupation underbridge at zero miles 16 chains called Statham's Cattle Creep. It had brick abutments with a segmental arch of 11ft 10in span.

The S&UR left the NSR main line at Bromshall Junction and this view looks south at that point with the connection still in situ although out of use by the time the photograph was taken on 23 March 1957. This was the occasion of the SLS special train hence all those folk milling around with one presumes, the permission of the signalman. Notice the high NSR McKenzie & Holland style signal box designed so as to give the signalman good visibility for both traffic off the S&UR and road vehicles. Beyond the signal box is the former crossing keeper's house dating from when the NSR line first opened, as there was no signal box at this point until the S&UR arrived. When the signal box and associated signals were abolished and replaced by automatic half barriers, the name of the crossing was changed from Bromshall to Bramshall.

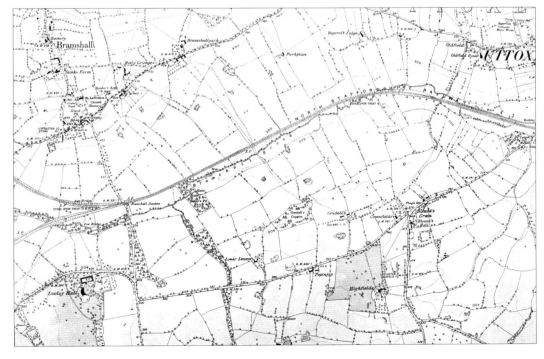

Bromshall Junction, from 1880 OS map.

Uttoxeter

BIRDSEYE VIEW OF UTTOXETER. EAST.3.

This elevated view of the NSR at Uttoxeter dates from around 1902; notice the new looking locomotive shed in the left far distance which opened that year. It was situated within the triangle formed by the Churnet Valley and Stoke to Derby and Burton lines. The station can be seen just below the shed along with the junction of the Churnet Valley line curving away to the left with the main line to Derby and Burton to the right. Goods yard to the right foreground with Bamford's agricultural machinery factory to the left.

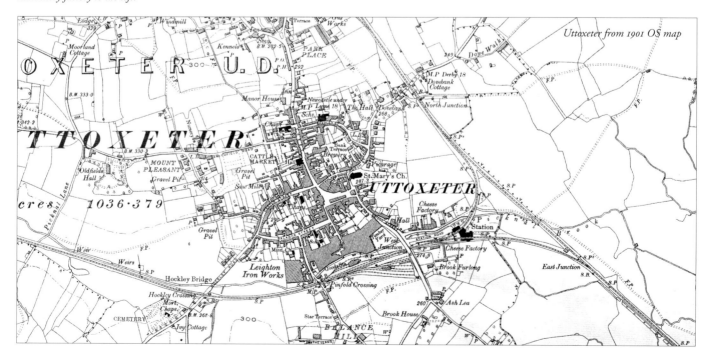

Uttoxeter from 1901 OS map

Uttoxeter from 1922 OS map

Aerial view of Uttoxeter, probably taken around 1930, looking west towards Stoke-on-Trent. The station can be seen to the bottom left with the Churnet Valley line curving away to the right and the direct Churnet line to the south, just visible to the extreme right hand bottom corner. Also to be seen at that point are the seven sidings that were situated within the triangle. Passenger trains are standing in both the down Churnet and Up Derby platforms and there is plenty of goods traffic in the various sidings, with an engine shunting just above the junction of the Churnet and Derby lines, along with a goods train departing towards Stoke at Pinfold Crossing. The buildings with the white roofs by the station are those of the United Dairy, while the large factory further towards the top of the photograph is Bamford's Leighton agricultural machinery factory. The other dairy, The Farmers & Cleveland Diaries, is the smaller building on the left hand side of the line by the station and just before the road bridge. The bridge took the main road from Stafford – the present A518 – to Uttoxeter over the railway. Originally there was a level crossing at that point. Compare this and the previous photograph with the accompanying OS maps.

COLLECTION BASIL JEUDA

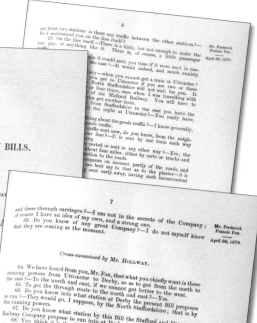

These few pages are an example of the form that evidence took when Parliamentary Select Committees were established in connection with Railway Bills. The House of Commons Select Committee in this case, hearing evidence in connection with the Stafford & Uttoxeter Railway Bill on 29 April 1879. In the vast majority of cases Select Committee records are in the form of hand written notes, difficult to translate in view of the contemporary hand writing, doubtless affected by the speed of the proceedings the clerks must have had to keep up with. However, in this particular case a printed copy was also made. To the authors' knowledge, as examples have rarely appeared in other railway histories, it has been felt appropriate to include these few pages to give a flavour of what took place. NA RAIL 1066/901

Notes

62 Henry Peyto-Verney, 16th Baron Willoughby de Broke (1773-1852), onetime owner of Bramshall [sic] Manor House.

63 25-26 Vic ch clxxv.

64 HLRO HL/PO/PB/3/plan 1862 – amended book of reference deposited 24 March 1862 HLRO HL/PO/PB/S5.

65 Admiral Henry John Chetwynd-Talbot, 18th Earl of Shrewsbury, 3rd Earl Talbot, 1803-1868.

66 Dudley Ryder, 2nd Earl of Harrowby, 1798-1882.

67 HLRO HL/PO/PB/5/28/16.

68 John Wodehouse, 1st Earl of Kimberley, 1826-1902.

69 Stafford and Uttoxeter Railway Act 1862, section 40. This was because the L&NWR was contracted by Act of Parliament to carry the Irish mails, under penalties for any delays.

70 L&RRO 25D60/569.

71 L&RRO 25D60/570, 572, 574 & 558.

72 The Land Clauses Consolidation Act 1845, 8 Vic ch xviii Royal Assent 8 May 1845. Following its enactment, an obligation to comply with the requirements was embodied in all Private Acts for railway companies. Without such, they would not comply with Parliamentary Standing Orders.

73 L&RRO 25D60/568.

74 L&RRO 25D60/568.

75 Gilders also acted as a surveyor for Lord Shrewsbury & Talbot, which might, therefore, appear to make him a strange appointment by the S&UR.

76 L&RRO 25D60/ 581, 596, 600, 619, 626.

77 L&RRO 25D60/346.

78 L&RRO 25D60/346, 581, 596.

79 L&RRO 25D60/626.

80 L&RRO 25D60/606.

81 L&RRO 25D60/625.

82 L&RRO 25D60/619.

83 NA RAIL 1007/583.

84 NA C16/824/S160.

85 NA RAIL 46/978.

86 28-29 Vic ch xlv.

87 NA C16/824/S160.

88 Some sources give this engine's name as *Christopher* or *Christiania*. However, two original copies of the maker's order books seen by the authors, quote the name as shown here.

89 NA MT6 193/8.

90 The *Derby Mercury* 27 February 1867.

91 The bridge dimensions given are taken from a GNR Engineers Department Report, revised and reprinted in April 1921 (See Appendix Nine, page 226). There are some slight variances with the official plans of the S&UR surveyed by Henry Fowler in 1903.

92 HLRO HL/PO/OB/S9 1864 - Bill deposited 31 December 1863.

CHAPTER FOUR
Directors 1862-1881

The Directors

The directors of the independent S&UR are listed below in alphabetical order with their period of office shown in brackets after their names. Five of their number acted as chairmen of the company for the periods indicated: Thomas Campbell Eyton (1862-1874); Michael Joseph Power (1875); John Edward Campbell Koch (1876-1878); Benjamin Bateman (1879) and Gerald Francis Talbot (1880-1881). The maximum number of directors permitted at any one time was six, the minimum number being three. A quorum was set at three or, if only the minimum number were appointed, two. Meetings were held in March and September. In order to qualify as a director it was necessary to hold shares in the company to the value of at least £250.

William Buxton, Eyton, John Kenderdine and Richard Banner Oakeley were described as subscribers in the inaugural 1862 Act. William Phillips and Thomas Salt were also so listed but they did not become directors. The extent of the biographical notes varies according to length of service, the interest and achievements of the particular individual and the amount of information available. The directors were an interesting group of individuals, two of them even achieving notoriety! There must have been a marked contrast between those based in London who saw their involvement as pure speculation against those based in Staffordshire and Shropshire who were keen to improve the local economy by forging cross country links. Whatever their motivation, it was the directors who were responsible for S&UR policy.

Benjamin Bateman
(1879)

Bateman was listed as a S&UR director in Bradshaw's Railway Manual, Shareholders' Guide and Directory (hereafter referred to as Bradshaw's Manual) for 1879 with an address of 9 Gracechurch Street, London. He gave evidence to the Committee of the House of Lords in 1879 concerning the company's Bill when he was described as chairman. In 1879 the company was in the hands of a receiver appointed by the Court of Chancery. Batemen appears to have served the company for this year only. He was also Deputy Chairman of the Mid Hants Railway.

John Winterbotham Batten
(1879-1881)

Batten was born on 3 June 1831 in Devonport, Devonshire being the son of John Batten and Mary Brend Batten (née Winterbotham). The 1851 census return describes him as an articled clerk. On 9 November 1854 he married Sarah Langstaff Derry in Plymouth and they had eight children. He then embarked on an interesting career: in 1861 he was described as a naval outfitter in Plymouth; by 1871 he was living at 35 Palace Gardens Terrace in Kensington and was a manager of a public company and landowner; by 1881, having by then been a director of the S&UR for three years, he was

described as a barrister in practice. According to Wrottesley[93] it was Batten who first approached the GNR about a possible acquisition in 1878 before he became a director. He then represented the London Financial Company which held the largest shareholding in the S&UR. At the time of his directorship with the S&UR, he was also a director of the Potteries, Shrewsbury & North Wales Railway. By 1884 he had greatly broadened his involvement with the railway industry being at that time a director of the following companies: the Brecon & Merthyr Tydfil Junction; Buckfastleigh, Totnes & South Devon; Central Wales & Carmarthen Junction; Devon & Cornwall; Harborne; Isle of Wight (Newport Junction); Kilkenny Junction; Louth & East Coast; Mid Wales; Plymouth & Dartmoor; Princetown; Sligo, Leitrim and Northern Counties and the Buenos Ayres & Ensenada Port! He died in 1901.

William Buxton
(1862-1878)

Buxton was Mayor of Stafford in 1860 and 1861, so who better to have on board as an initial subscriber and subsequent director. He was born in Sutton, Cheshire in 1816 and married Maria Timmis in Stafford in 1857. She was born in Darlaston, Staffordshire in 1829 and the couple had six children, all born in Stafford. In 1861 Buxton was described as Mayor of Stafford and hop merchant; in 1871 he was described as tea dealer and magistrate. He held these positions while continuing his civic duties as an Alderman. He died in 1878.

Charles Chandler
(1876-1881)

Chandler was christened in Brighton, Sussex on 7 May 1820 being the son of Charles Henry Chandler and his wife Mary. By the 1840s the family had moved to Ellesmere in Shropshire and at Wem in 1846 Chandler married Frances Jane Octavia Thomas who had been born in Shrewsbury in 1825. The 1851 census return describes him as a solicitor but the 1861 return records him as a solicitor and a farmer of 160 acres. His wife died without issue in 1862. In 1864 he was Registrar for the Provincial Grand Lodge of the Masonic District of North Wales and Shropshire. He was also Secretary of the Shrewsbury and North Wales Railway which in 1866 amalgamated with the Shrewsbury and Potteries Junction Railway to form the Potteries, Shrewsbury and North Wales Railway of which he became a director. In October 1867 he conducted a successful prosecution against the Rev. Edward Muckleston, vicar of Stavely, Warwickshire for an ingenious ticket fraud on the Great Western Railway (GWR). The 1871 census return describes him as an attorney whereas in the 1881 census his status reverts to that of solicitor. At that time he was living at Oakley Cottage in the parish of St. Julian and practising from the Talbot Chambers, Shrewsbury. He died at Atcham in 1867.

Thomas Campbell Eyton
(1862-1875)

Eyton was born at The Mansion House[94], Wellington, Shropshire on 10 September 1809 and, very unusually, he was baptised twice. The baptism register of All Saints Church, Wellington confirms that he was first baptised on 12 September 1809 and there is an additional note which says born 10 September 1809 and privately baptised by Revd Richard Littlehales, rector of Lopham in the County of Norfolk. The second baptism took place at St. George, Bloomsbury, Middlesex on 6 June 1810 and the record[95] again has an additional note saying Received into the Church 6 June 1810. He was the son of Thomas Eyton (1777-1855), recorder of Wenlock and later High Sheriff of Shropshire and his wife Elizabeth (c.1780-1817) who was the daughter of Major-General Donald Campbell. Eyton is mainly remembered as an ornithologist and agriculturist. He wrote books about birds, ducks, oysters and cattle and frequently corresponded with Charles Darwin, a contemporary and friend at St. John's College, Cambridge. On 13 May 1835 he married Elizabeth Frances Slaney (1813-1870) the daughter and co-heiress of Robert Aglionby Slaney (1792-1862) of Walford and Hatton who was Member of Parliament for Shrewsbury for 23 years. In 1836 he joined the Committee of the Shrewsbury Canal and, like his father and grandfather, played an active part in the management of the canal. In its last decade as an independent company, he occasionally chaired meetings and in July 1845 he was deputed to attend meetings of the Ellesmere & Chester Canal Company to discuss amalgamation and railway conversion. The Shropshire Union Railways & Canal Company was formed the following year with the Shrewsbury Canal as a constituent member.

Eyton and his wife had nine children. In 1841 they were living in Donnerville House, Wellington but by 1851 were recorded as living at The Vineyard. He succeeded to the family estate at Eyton Hall, Eyton upon the Weald Moors, in 1855. The hall had been in a ruinous state since at least 1763 but following a family scandal and the suicide of his grandfather in 1816, his father returned to the ancestral seat and set about its restoration. Thomas Campbell Eyton was instrumental in providing Wellington's public utilities, forming a company in 1851 to construct a reservoir at Ercall Pools to supply the town with drinking water and establishing another company to supply the town with gas. He was an original subscriber to the S&UR and held the office of chairman for 13 years, thereafter continuing as a director for one further year. He was also a director of the Wellington & Severn Junction and Shropshire Union Railways. He was Deputy Lieutenant for the County of Salop, an active magistrate, a keen sportsman, hunted with the Shropshire hounds and held a commission in the South Salopian Regiment of Yeomanry Cavalry. He entered as a Cornet in 1830 and progressed to the rank of Lieutenant. Against this virtuous background, it has to be said that his father-in-law insisted that Eyton made a promise to take steadily to water and leave off intoxicating liquors! He died at the family seat, Eyton Hall, on 25 October 1880 aged 71. He was buried with his wife, who predeceased him by ten years, at St. Catherine's Church, Eyton upon the Weald Moors. His will was proved at Shrewsbury on 17 December 1880 when his personal estate was valued at under £25,000. It was re-sworn in December 1881 at a value of under £30,000 which at today's prices is equivalent to £3.1m!

Francis Charles Hughes Hallett
(1879)

Bradshaw's Manual for 1879 listed Hallett as a S&UR director. He was described as Major Hughes Hallett, Jnr., United Service Club, St James's, London. Further research has shown him to be Francis Charles Hughes Hallett, who aspired to hold the rank of Colonel in the Royal Artillery with much service in India. He became the Member of Parliament for Rochester from 1885 to 1889 and got involved in a personal scandal that led to his being hounded by the media and shunned by his parliamentary colleagues such that he stood down from his seat. Hallett was extremely thin, always wore a white flower in his button hole and was an amateur actor of some note. He was the son of Charles Madras Hughes Hallett (1809-1843) and his wife Emma Mary (née Roberts) being born in 1838 in Canterbury, Kent. In 1871 he married Catherine Rosalie Selwyn (née Greene) the second wife and widow of Sir Charles Jasper Selwyn (1813-1869). It is now necessary to explain a little about Sir Charles who was a judge and Lord Justice of Appeal. His first wife was Hester Ravenshaw and they had three children, including Beatrice Eugénie Selwyn (1865-1898). After Hester's death, Sir Charles married Catherine on 2 April 1869 but their marriage was very short-lived as he died on 11 August 1869. Catherine died in 1875. In 1882 Hallett married his second wife, Emilie Page von Schaumberg from Philadelphia, USA who was the daughter of James von Schaumberg and Caroline Page. On 8 August 1887 whilst staying at Ellingham Hall, Bungay, Norfolk, the home of Henry Smith, he was caught red-handed in flagrante delicto with Beatrice Eugénie Selwyn his former wife's step daughter. Smith promptly booted the pair out of Ellingham Hall and related the events to Hallett's wife. The whole affair was exposed in public by Captain Charles William Selwyn (1858-1893), Member of Parliament for Wisbech and by Beatrice's sister. What a rumpus! There was more to come as in the following year Hallett became involved in expressing an opinion on the 1888 murder in Whitechapel of Martha Tabram, said to be an early victim of Jack the Ripper. Through having friends in the right places and political expediency, Hallett managed to hold on to his parliamentary seat for a while but the media attention became too much for him. His wife divorced him and moved to Dinard in France. The 1901 census shows Hallett living at 1 Edith Villas, Fulham with Annie Evelyn Hallett (née Gould 1868-1943) who was described as his wife. She was some 30 years his junior and had married George Alexander McCarthy (1859-1901) while living in Cawnpore, India on 20 December 1884. He was an army officer and much of their life together was spent in India before returning to England around 1898. Shortly afterwards McCarthy accused Hallett of having an affair with his wife and sought a divorce. There is some doubt about whether Hallett actually married Annie but they certainly had four children between 1898 and 1902. Hallett died in Kensington on 22 June 1903.

CHAPTER FOUR: DIRECTORS 1862-1891 · 73

Thomas Campbell Eyton was the S&UR's first Chairman and held the office for 13 years from 1862 until 1874, thereafter continuing as a director for one further year. He was born in Wellington on 10 September 1809 and became instrumental in providing the town's public utilities, especially water and gas supplies. He was an agriculturist and a famous ornithologist frequently corresponding with his friend Charles Darwin. He died at the family seat, Eyton Hall, on 25 October 1880 aged 71.

Major Francis Charles Hughes Hallett (1838-1903) was a S&UR director for one year only in 1879. He became the Member of Parliament for Rochester from 1885 to 1889 and got involved in a personal scandal that led to his being hounded by the media and shunned by his Parliamentary colleagues such that he stood down from his seat. Hallett was extremely thin, always wore a white flower in his button hole as seen here and was an amateur actor of some note.

Robert William Hand
(1862-1863)

Hand was born in Coventry, Warwickshire in 1810. On 29 August 1842 the Lord Bishop of Lichfield issued a notice saying that he had appointed Hand as solicitor, for his Lordship's secretary, steward and general agent and requested that all communications relative to the See of Lichfield be sent to Hand at his office in Stafford. In 1846 Hand married Fanny Keen at Stafford where she had been born in 1819 and they had five children. They lived at Rowley Hall, Castle Church. The 1868 Post Office Directory for Staffordshire shows that Hand also held the following public positions: Town Clerk, Clerk to the Lieutenancy, Clerk of the Peace and Deputy & Under Sheriff. He died at Upton-upon-Severn, Worcestershire in 1873.

John Kenderdine
(1862-1863)

Kenderdine was born at Brook House, Stafford on 8 June 1795 being the son of John Kenderdine (1741-1814) and Dorothy Kenderdine (née Titley). On 22 July 1808, at the age of 13, he joined the Royal Navy and on 7 March 1815 achieved the rank of Lieutenant. He married three times. His first wife was Hannah Ball (1802-1824) whom he married on 6 April 1822 in London. They had one child who died in infancy. He married Elizabeth Harriett Brutton (1803-1835) at St. Mary's, Stafford on 30 May 1827 and they had five children. By 1841 he had married Ann Dorothy Moore (1797-1874) from whom there was no issue. He died in Stafford on 30 December 1867. In the 1861 census, which took place in the year before his involvement with the S&UR, he is described as Lieutenant, Royal Navy on half pay.

John Edward Campbell Koch
(1876-1878)

Koch joined the S&UR in 1876 and was immediately elected chairman, a position he held until 1878. He was born at Streatham, Surrey on 31 March 1819 being the son of John Henry and Sarah Koch. He was baptised in Streatham on 18 June 1823. He married Ellen Sarah Palmer at Brighton in 1846 and they had three sons. He is described on the 1861 census return as an actuary. The S&UR recorded his address as South Frith, Tonbridge, Kent; this tallies with the 1871 census which shows him as having 'no profession'. However, he was also a director of the Mid Hants Railway, the Kilkenny Junction Railway and the Newry & Armagh Railway. In 1881 he was described as a merchant. He died in London in 1904 aged 85.

Paul Margetson
(1873-1878)

Bradshaw's Manual listed Margetson as a S&UR director in the issues for the years 1873-1878, inclusive, with an address of The Lawns, Clapham Common, London.

Richard Banner Oakeley
(1862-1863)

Oakeley[96] was one of the original subscribers. He was born in Norton, near Malton, Yorkshire being the son of Edward Banner Oakeley (1806-1841) and his wife Mary (née Kennett). He was baptised at Oswaldkirk, Yorkshire on 27 June 1834. In 1856-1857 he visited India where he photographed, quite spectacularly, one of the ruined Hoysala temples at Halebid, Karnataka following an arduous trek. His photographs based on paper negatives were published in 1859 and are now valuable. On 6 October 1859 in Shrewsbury he married Mary Anne Field who had been christened in Rugeley on 17 March 1841 and was the daughter of William Field (1812-1894), the S&UR's contractor.

In December 1859 the case of Oakeley v Ood-Deen was heard in the Court of Common Pleas. Mohammed Mussee Ood-Deen was the defendant and the case concerned a bill of exchange for £6,500. It was a complicated case and Oakeley appears to have acted in good faith but it was suggested that he had addicted himself to horse racing and as a result was not in good financial circumstances.

Worse was to come! Oakeley ceased to be a director of the S&UR after 1863 although he continued as a director of the South Leicestershire Railway (formerly the Nuneaton & Hinckley Railway) until 1866. Ten years later, after a foray in Scotland attempting to make money organising shooting parties for the gentry, he was sentenced on 12 August 1876 at the Central Criminal Court (the Old Bailey) to five years penal servitude. Oakeley, as founder of the Co-Operative Credit Bank was guilty of fraud. He was released from prison in July 1880 by which time his wife was living with her father back in Shrewsbury.

Thomas Brassey's sons, Thomas and Henry, were trustees of a Deed of Separation between Oakeley and his wife. This deed contained a covenant to give access to two of his children, Edward Banner Oakeley (born in Shrewsbury in 1860) and Edith Maud Oakeley (born in Oban on 13 August 1864). His other son, Richard Banner Field Oakeley (1861-1936) had already emigrated to the USA. In 1881 Oakeley claimed he was not being given access to his children living in England and applied for an order against the Brasseys in the Chancery Division of the High Court. The Master of Rolls in declining his application said that there was no evidence that the trustees had refused access. The daughter refused to see her father and the first son was now in Texas. The involvement of the Brasseys illustrates the closeness of the Brassey family with the Fields. Maria Farrington Harrison, the wife of the world famous contractor, Thomas Brassey, was (as previously mentioned) the sister of Christiana Harrison who was the wife of William Field. Mary Anne and her family must have experienced a very traumatic time when her husband was jailed.

The *New York Times* in its edition published on 17 August 1876 described him as 'An Aristocratic Swindler'. The *Pall Mall Gazette* for 21 January 1895 contained the following advertisement:

> THE TIMES,
> the ENGLISH CHURCH UNION
> and the
> CO-OPERATIVE CREDIT BANK
> By Richard Banner Oakely.
> Price 1d or post-free 1½d. 11 Queen Victoria Street E.C.
> A liberal reduction for quantities.

We wonder how many copies were sold! After Oakeley's release from prison he was described as an engineer variously concerned with ventilation, gas and electricity and in the 1901 census he was shown as a financial agent. His wife pre-deceased him on 15 November 1905 leaving an estate valued at £13,255 4s 5d (£13,255.22p) but not a penny of it went to her husband. The 1911 census records him living on Private Means at 1 Mount Prospect, Okehampton, Devon with widow Harriett Ball who was aged 50 and described as Partially Servant and Caretaker of Chapel.

In spite of his cavalier lifestyle and wrongdoings Oakeley lived to the ripe old age of 95 dying of broncho-pneumonia at the Cottage Hospital, Littleham, Exmouth, Devon on 16 December 1929. His death certificate described his occupation as Licensed Lay Reader of Independent Means.

James Heslop Powell
(1880-1881)

Bradshaw's Manual for 1880 listed Powell as a S&UR director with an address of Mayfield, Leigham Court Road, Streatham, Surrey. In 1866 a gentleman of this name was the Master of the Worshipful Company of Coachmakers and Coach Harness Makers of London. They may well have been one and the same. Powell was also a director of the Potteries, Shrewsbury and North Wales Railway.

Joseph Michael Power
(1873-1875)

Power was born in Tralee, Ireland in 1821. His main claim to fame was that he became Secretary to the London Office of the National Bank of Ireland where he was much respected. He was forced to resign through a heart condition on 1 October 1869.

He was a director of the Alexandra Palace Company Ltd and, as a trustee, had a stake in the Peruvian Railways Company over which there was a rumpus with the managing director of the National Bank over a share allocation.

Clearly Power's involvement with the S&UR occurred after his full-time employment had ceased. His final address was Stafford Terrace, 26 Phillimore Gardens, Kensington. He died on 6 September 1877.

Gerald Francis Thomas Talbot
(1879-1881)

Talbot joined the S&UR as chairman in 1879 and served in that capacity until the GNR takeover the following year. He was born in Stafford on 23 November 1848 being the son of William Whitworth Chetwynd-Talbot (1814-1888) and Eleanora Julia Coventry. He married Henrietta Clarissa Noyes Bradhurst (1850-1928) in Berlin on 1 June 1870 and they had six children, five sons and a daughter. Henrietta was born in New York and was an adopted daughter of Henry Maunsell Bradhurst (1822-1894) being an issue from his wife's first marriage.

Talbot pursued a career in the German army but soon after his marriage he met with an accident in the performance of his military duties and was disabled from active service. He had achieved the rank of Lieutenant in the 2nd Prussian Dragoon Guards and recorded his army experience in a book entitled *Analysis of the Organisation of the Prussian Army.* The book was published by W. Moeser, 34 & 35 Stallschreiberstrasse, Berlin, in 1871.

At the time of his involvement with the S&UR he was a Captain with the Royal Staffordshire Yeomanry and eventually rose to the rank of Lieutenant-Colonel. The S&UR recorded his address as Ingestre but the 1881 census records him living with his family and father-in-law at Greatwood House, Chislehurst, Kent. He died in London on 2 January 1904 aged 55.

John Taylor
(1864-1877)

Bradshaw's Manual listed Taylor as a S&UR director in the issues from 1864 until 1877, inclusive. He was recorded as being at the following addresses: Furnival's Inn, London (1864); 50 Gracechurch Street, London (1865); 27 Warwick Crescent, Kensington (1867). He was also a director of the Alton, Alresford and Winchester Railway.

Thomas Wynne
(1864-1881)

Wynne was the S&UR's longest serving director. He was born at Tenbury in Worcestershire on 7 February 1807 and was educated at Ledbury. Around 1836 he became the managing partner in the Mossfield Colliery Company at Longton, Staffordshire and at the same time became a partner in a pottery. His first two children were born in Longton by his first wife Sarah who died in 1840. By 1851 he was residing at Edensor Place, Longton and described as an earthenware manufacturer employing 34 men, 15 women, 18 boys and 16 girls.

In addition to his core business activity, he developed a practice as a valuer and arbitrator in railway and mining undertakings, especially in connection with the NSR, the Shropshire Union Railway and latterly the S&UR. He also became chairman of the Stone Gas Company. In 1855 he married Ellen Joule from Stone and they had six children. Back in January 1852, he had been appointed as one of H.M. Inspectors of Mines and investigated the tragic explosion at Talk o' th' Hill Colliery on 13 December 1866 which resulted in the death of 91 people. He resigned from his appointment of Inspector of Mines at the end of 1888 after 37 years' service.

By 1861 the family had moved to Field House in Stone and by 1881 they had moved to the Manor House in Gnosall where he passed away aged 84 on 4 June 1891 after suffering from a carriage fall.

For upwards of 36 years he was a member of the Institution of Civil Engineers whose Minutes of Proceedings recorded his obituary. This concluded by saying:

During a long and varied career he displayed much firmness of character, combined with great energy and excessive activity, almost to the end of his life. A man of powerful physique and hardy constitution, his genial disposition and kindly nature secured him many friends.

The S&UR needed such a man.

Board of Trade Inspecting Officers

Introductory Note

The Railway Regulation Act 1840 (3 & 4 Vic ch xcvii) received the Royal Assent on 10 August 1840. It brought regulation to a fast growing railway industry and provided for Inspectors to be appointed by the Board of Trade. Their prime purpose was to inspect and approve all new or modified railway works and to investigate railway accidents. Three Inspectors were concerned with the S&UR during its independent existence and they are all illustrated on this page. They were all recruited from the Royal Engineers which was the common practice at the time.

ABOVE: *William Yolland (1810-1885) was a military surveyor, astronomer and engineer. He was commissioned into the Royal Engineers in 1828. After service in Britain, Ireland and Canada he was posted to the Ordnance Survey in 1838 where he remained until 1854 when, although still an army officer, he joined the Railway Inspectorate of the Board of Trade. He retired from the army in 1863 with the rank of Lieutenant-Colonel retaining his position with the BoT. He was Chief Inspecting Officer of Railways from 1877 until his death in 1885. This was the man who undertook the initial inspection of the S&UR on 23 May 1867 and concluded that the line could not be opened without danger to the public owing to the incompleteness of the works. He also investigated the accident at Stafford station which occurred on 16 November 1877 (see page 101).* THE ROYAL SOCIETY

UPPER LEFT: *Sir Henry Whatley Tyler (1827-1908) entered the Royal Military Academy at Woolwich when he was aged 15 and just two years later obtained a commission in the Royal Engineers. He saw service in the West Indies and on return became involved with the Great Exhibition of 1851. He joined the Railway Inspectorate in 1853, by which time he had attained the rank of Captain. He remained in the army until 1867. He became Chief Inspector of Railways in 1870 and retained that position until his retirement in 1877 when he was knighted. Tyler reported on the accident at Hopton (see page 98) which occurred on 1 February 1873 causing the deaths of the driver and fireman of the Beyer Peacock tank engine* Shrewsbury and Talbot. *After his retirement he became President of the Grand Trunk Railway of Canada.*

LOWER LEFT: *Charles Scrope Hutchinson (1827-1912) obtained a commission in the Royal Engineers in 1843 becoming a Colonel in 1876 and retiring from the army later that year with the honorary rank of Major General. He joined the Railway Inspectorate in 1867 and was Chief Inspecting Officer from 1892 until 1895. He accompanied Yolland on the initial inspection of the S&UR on 23 May 1867 and after a further inspection which took place 25 September that year recommended that the railway could be opened for traffic on receipt of a satisfactory undertaking as to the mode of working the line.*

Notes

93 *The Great Northern Railway Vol. II* by John Wrottesley, Batsford 1979.
94 Later known as The Vineyard.
95 This record wrongly gives his birth date as 19 September 1809.
96 The name is spelt Oakeley on the S&UR prospectus, in the marriage records and this is how his surviving descendants spell their name. We have, therefore, adopted this version. However, surviving parish records show his father's name as Oakley and this is how his signature appeared on the 1911 census return. Various newspaper reports also spell his name as Oakley.

CHAPTER FIVE
The Officers 1862-1881

The Officers

During its short existence the S&UR had two secretaries, two solicitors, two engineers and three general managers. They are dealt with below in a similar manner to the directors. These individuals were, of course, paid a salary and were responsible for the day to day operation of the railway. It seems odd that the local focus for controlling the railway was from the registered office at Wellington; only one of the officers, John Henry Duffill, seems to have lived in Stafford. It is also interesting to note that some of the directors and officers were concerned with more than one railway of common interest.

James Brend Batten
(1869-1881)

Batten was a well-known solicitor and Parliamentary Agent of Great George Street Westminster, London who was prominently employed in railway work and acted as such for the S&UR from 1869. From 1879 he became responsible for all the S&UR's legal affairs following the departure of the local solicitor, Robert Daniel Newill (see below). He was an elder brother of John Winterbotham Batten who was a S&UR director from 1879 until 1881 (see above). He was born in Devonport, Devonshire on 17 May 1830 and was educated at Mill Hill School. He was articled to his uncle, a solicitor in Cheltenham and became manger of the firm Swift and Wagstaff of Liverpool and Westminster. He won a famous rating case in the House of Lords which resulted in the whole area of Liverpool Docks being brought into rating for the relief of the poor. On 2 May 1865 he was elected an Associate of the Institution of Civil Engineers. He was Deputy Chairman of the Plymouth & Dartmoor Railway and a director of the Sambre & Meuse Railway in Belgium. On 22 March 1881 he married Alice Mary Morris who had been born in Wrexham in 1855; there was no issue from this marriage. At the time of the 1892 general election he unsuccessfully contested Shrewsbury against the existing Member of Parliament. He died on 26 August 1897 at Homburg, Saarland, Germany at the age of 67.

Francis George Burton
(1875-1876)

This gentleman was shown as the S&UR's General Manager in *Bradshaw's Guide to the Railways of Great Britain and Ireland* for the months of December 1875 and January and February 1876. He held the position between the departure of John Bucknall Cooper and the arrival of John Henry Duffield. He was born in Preston, Lancashire in 1840. By 1871 he was living in lodgings at Pembroke in South Wales and was employed as a manager's clerk on the Pembroke and Tenby Railway. This railway company was incorporated in 1859 to build lines from Pembroke Dock to Tenby. The lines opened from Tenby to Pembroke on 30 July 1863 and to Pembroke Dock on 8 August 1864. On 30 July 1874 he

married Fanny Potter who was born at Pembroke Dock on 31 July 1850. They had a son and three daughters. After his brief flirtation with the S&UR from 1875 to 1876, he returned to Pembroke to establish his own business as a coal merchant/accountant. The 1881 census records him employing one man and 72 boys. In 1901 he was described as an incorporated accountant in Macclesfield and by 1911 was living at 1 Duncan Street, Higher Broughton, Lancashire engaged in a similar capacity. His death was registered at Barton upon Irwell, Lancashire in 1914.

John Bucknall Cooper
(1869-1875)

John Bucknall Cooper was the S&UR's first General Manager. He was also simultaneously the General Manager of the Potteries, Shrewsbury and North Wales Railway until October 1873 when he relinquished the latter position. He was christened on 8 July 1838 at St. Peter, Liverpool being the son of Charles and Margaret (née Partington) Cooper who were also born in Liverpool in 1816 and 1820, respectively, and were married in July 1837. His father and grandfather both worked for the Preston & Wyre Railway and so he was born into a railway family. In 1851 his father was employed by the NSR as a railway officer and the family was living in some style at Winton Square opposite Stoke station. By 1861 the younger Cooper had married his wife, Sarah Ann Slater, who had been born in Manchester in 1838. They were living at his father's house in Heaton Norris with their first child who had just been born. Cooper was described as a railway clerk whereas by this time his father had aspired to be a railway superintendent, both no doubt working for the L&NWR. By 1866 the younger Cooper had secured an appointment as General Manager of the Potteries, Shrewsbury & North Wales Railway which opened its line from Shrewsbury to Llanymynech on 13 August 1866. Whilst retaining this position he also became the General Manager of the S&UR and may have done so in time for its opening in December 1867. He was certainly there by the end of July 1868. It should be borne in mind that the S&UR also had Shropshire connections being managed from an office in Wellington. In 1871 the family was living at Belle Vue Gardens, St. Julian, Shrewsbury and Cooper was described as railway manager. He does not appear to have moved his home to Stafford obviously travelling there as required by means of the Shropshire Union Railway. In November 1873 he relinquished his post with the Potteries, Shrewsbury and North Wales Railway but retained his position with the S&UR until September 1875. He then became General Manager of the Belfast Central Railway (BCR) which had opened for goods traffic in 1874. The BCR soon succumbed to street tramway competition and in 1885 was acquired by the Great Northern Railway (Ireland) which promptly ended regular passenger working on 30 November 1885. Earlier that month Cooper had returned to England via Larne and Stranraer to take up an appointment in

Suffolk as Secretary to the Felixstowe Dock & Railway Company (FD&RC). In announcing his new appointment the *Liverpool Mercury* [97] stated *Mr. Cooper is a gentleman of much ability and experience, has been connected with English, Welsh and Irish railways, and he will bring into the management of the Felixstowe Railway and Dock much sound judgement, combined with great power of organisation.* The Felixstowe dock basin was opened on 7 April 1886. In 1890 he became a member of the new 'Felix' masonic lodge and by 1891 he and his family were recorded as living at South House, Felixstowe where, once again, he was described as railway manager. The house was built by Norwegian carpenters using Norwegian white pine, only the foundations and chimney stack were of brick. It replicated the style of the original FD&RC offices. Cooper and his wife had twelve children, the seventh, eighth and ninth boys being named Septimus, Octavius and Nonus! We have been unable to discover the date of Cooper's death but by 1907 he had returned to Belfast and was an Agent for the Broughton and Plas Power Coal Co. Ltd which mined coal near Wrexham in North Wales and exported its products to Ireland. Cooper operated from 93 Ann Street, Belfast and the phone book for 1910 confirms he was still working in that capacity at the same address.

John Henry Duffill
(1876-1881)

Duffill took over the General Manager's post in 1876 and remained with the S&UR until its acquisition by the GNR in 1881. He was born in Birmingham in 1839, the son of John Duffill, a coal dealer and his wife, Mary. His father was born in Birmingham in 1813 and his mother was born in Bridgnorth in 1816. In 1861 Duffill, then aged 22, was living with his mother and father at Aston, Birmingham and was employed as a railway clerk. Shortly afterwards he married his wife, Rhoda, who was also born in Birmingham in 1840. They had three children. In 1871 Duffill and his family were living at Bramhall, Hazel Grove, near Stockport and he was employed as a deputy railway superintendent. He was certainly on the S&UR's books by 11 February 1876 as a wages payment was made to him on that date. In 1881, just prior to the GNR takeover, the family were residing at 31 Friars Road, Castle Church, Stafford and Duffill was described as general manager, railway. After the takeover he continued as the local manager for the GNR but by 1891 he had found alternative employment as a tramway manager at Birmingham and was living at 81 Princes Road, Edgbaston. He died in 1896 at West Bromwich.

Charles James Hayter
(1878-1881)

Hayter was appointed Secretary in December 1878 and took over from the long serving Robert Daniel Newill but, unlike Newill, he did not undertake any legal work. Hayter was born on 16 April 1841 in Pentonville, London and was baptised in the Parish of St. Peter and St. Paul, Mitcham, Surrey on 30 November 1842. He was the seventh of eight children of George Smith Hayter (1794-1887), born in Surrey and Alice Stovin Hayter (née Lister 1802-1888) who was born in Whitgift, Yorkshire. He married Marion Climpson Bartholomew in Medway, Kent in 1860. She was born

John Bucknall Cooper, born in 1838, was the S&UR's first General Manager, a position he held from 1869 until 1875. He then became the General Manager of the Belfast Central Railway and this photograph depicts him in Belfast sometime between 1875 and 1885, after which he returned to England to take up an appointment with the Felixstowe Dock & Railway Company. JO PROBERT

in the East Indies. They had one child, a daughter, who was born at sea. Hayter was a professional company secretary and served several railway companies in this capacity, for example, in 1884 he was Secretary to the Central Wales & Carmarthen Junction Railway and the Kilkenny Junction Railway, operating from 1 Drapers' Gardens, Throgmorton Street, London – the same address as the S&UR's last registered office. He died in Brighton, Sussex on 17 October 1919 aged 78.

Robert Daniel Newill
(1862-1878)

Newill served the S&UR for 17 years, longer than any other officer. During this time he acted as both Secretary and Solicitor operating from the company's registered office in Wellington, Shropshire (or as the company's notepaper had it: Salop). He also acted as Receiver and Manager of the company pursuant to an Order made in the Court of Chancery dated 2 May 1868 until 4 February 1879 when he was replaced in that capacity by Henry Cecil Newton (see below). He was christened at Lydbury North, Shropshire on 29 May 1825. The 1851 census return describes him as solicitor and coroner. On 21 February 1860 he married Marianne Sarah Blase at Old Dalby, near Melton Mowbray, Leicestershire. She was born in London and was the only daughter of the then late Thomas Blase who was employed by H.M. Customs, London. Their marriage was announced in *The Illustrated London News*. They had eleven children. Over the census returns from 1861 to 1881 Newill was variously described as solicitor, registrar of county court, county coroner, clerk to the magistrates, a farmer of 10 acres and landowner. From 1879 all legal work for the S&UR was conducted from London and Charles James Hayter, also based in London, was appointed Secretary. At this time the company's registered office was changed from Wellington to 1 Drapers' Gardens, Throgmorton Street, London. Newill died in 1886.

Henry Cecil Newton
(1879-1881)
Newton replaced Newill as Receiver and Manager of the company pursuant to an Order made in the High Court of Justice, Chancery Division, dated 4 February 1879. He was born at St. Pancras, Middlesex on 5 February 1853 being the son of George Newton (b.1814) and Harriett H. Newton (b.1820). He was employed by the Great Western Railway (GWR) from 1869 until 1875, initially as a clerk in the office of the Goods Manager and latterly on the staff of the General Manager. From 1875 until 1881 he was based in Devonshire acting as Secretary and Manager of several small railways which were later absorbed by the GWR and the London & South Western Railway. It was during this period that he was appointed Receiver and Manager of the S&UR, no doubt because of his experience of small railway companies. In 1881 he became the Secretary and Accountant of the London, Tilbury & Southend Railway (LT&SR). He was also Secretary of the Tottenham & Forest Gate Railway which opened in 1894 and was operated jointly by the LT&SR and the Midland Railway; he was also appointed as Secretary of the Whitechapel & Bow Railway which opened in 1902 and was operated jointly by the LT&SR and the District Railway. His final set of accounts as Receiver and Manager of the S&UR covered the period from 14 July 1880 to 15 November 1881 - see Appendix Four. During his stay in Devon, he married Catherine Amelia Price at Ilfracombe parish church on 18 April 1876 and they had six children, three sons and three daughters. He died on 4 February 1915 leaving effects valued at £5,869 8s 7d (£5,869.43p).

Julian Horn Tolmé
(1875-1877)
Tolmé succeeded Townsend as Engineer. He was born on 28 January 1836 at Havana in Cuba being the son of Charles David Tolmé (1792-1872), merchant and British Consul in Havana from 1833 to 1840. His mother, Maria Eliza (née Peneke, 1796-1865) was born on the then Danish island of St. Thomas in the Caribbean. The marriage took place in Hamburg on 12 May 1824. The family returned to England about 1851 and Julian entered King's College, London where he studied geology, mineralogy and civil engineering. In 1855 he was articled for five years to Joseph Locke (1805-1860) and John Edward Errington (1806-1862) working chiefly under the latter who was Engineer to the London & South Western Railway. Following the deaths of his former masters he entered into partnership with William Robert Galbraith (1829-1914) with a view to continuing the practice. This partnership lasted until 1869. Tolmé then involved himself with a whole series of minor railways. For example, during his time with the S&UR he was also engineer to the following railways: the Birmingham & Sutton Coldfield Extension; Halesowen & Bromsgrove; Harborne; Mid Hants; Newport Pagnell; Poole & Bournemouth; Potteries, Shrewsbury & North Wales and the Whitby, Redcar & Middlesbrough Union. There were many other examples including railways in Sweden and Tunisia. He was very interested in the volunteer movement and took a leading part in the formation of the 3rd Middlesex Artillery achieving the rank of Lieutenant-Colonel. He did not marry and died aged 42 at his residence, Lindfield, Sussex on 25 December 1878. He was buried in the family vault at Highgate Cemetery, London. The Institution of Civil Engineers, of which he was a member, carried his obituary in its Minutes of Proceedings. He was said to be:

A man of extensive knowledge and experience, great amiability and social powers, and with a singularly winning manner, accompanied by a handsome presence.

The S&UR does not appear to have appointed a successor to Tolmé.

Thomas Charles Townsend
(1862-1874)
Townsend was the S&UR's first Engineer responsible for surveying the line, its specification and liaising with the contractor, William Field, with regard to its construction. He was born at King's Heath in Worcestershire in 1829 and in 1851 was lodging in Castle Street, Shrewsbury working as a civil engineer. In 1861 he was still lodging in Shrewsbury but at a different address. At this time he was described as a civil engineer & surveyor, no doubt being very much engaged in surveying the S&UR. In 1870 he married Alice Jobson in Kensington, London. She was born in Shrewsbury in 1846 and became the mother of their three children, all born in Shrewsbury. Amongst his many business activities, Townsend was the proprietor of a quarry trading as the Grinshill Free Stone Company which was located some 3½ miles south of Wem. This company failed and Townsend was declared bankrupt in April 1879. The bankruptcy was annulled in 1881 by which time the family was living at Wem. In 1891 they had moved to Richmond in Surrey and ten years later they were living in Chelsea. Townsend's notepaper bore the Latin motto Vita Posse Priore Frui which, rather strangely, means to be able to enjoy the recollections of a former life. He died in Wandsworth, London in 1918 aged 88.

Notes
97 *Liverpool Mercury* Thursday, 8 October 1885.

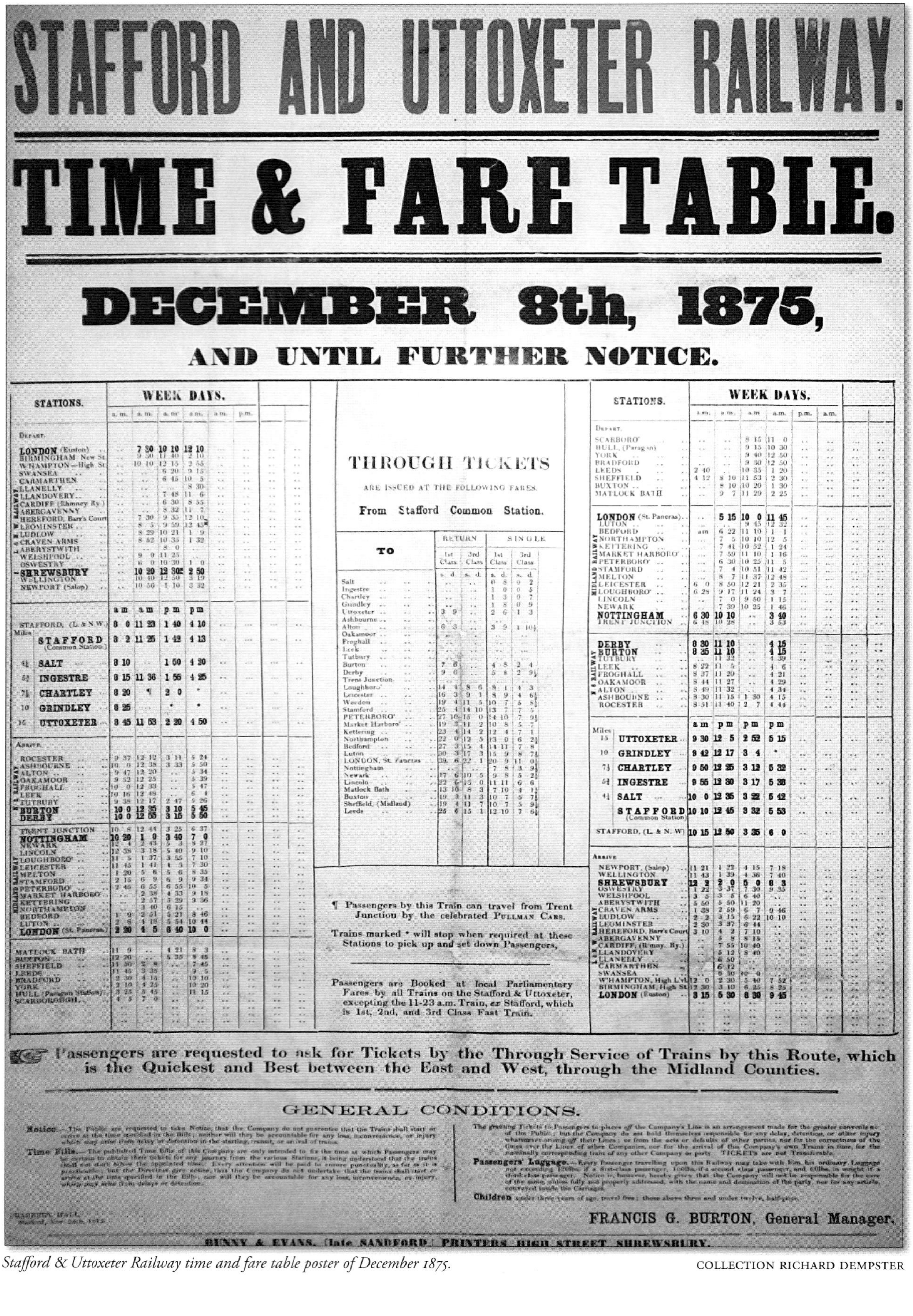

STAFFORD AND UTTOXETER RAILWAY.

TIME & FARE TABLE.

DECEMBER 8th, 1875,

AND UNTIL FURTHER NOTICE.

STATIONS.	WEEK DAYS. a.m.	a.m.	a.m.	a.m.
Depart.				
LONDON (Euston)	..	7 30	10 10	12 10
BIRMINGHAM New St.	..	9 50	11 40	2 10
W'HAMPTON—High St.	..	10 10	12 15	2 55
SWANSEA	..	..	6 20	9 15
CARMARTHEN	..	..	6 45	10 5
LLANELLY	..	..	..	8 30
LLANDOVERY	..	..	7 48	11 6
CARDIFF (Rhmney Ry.)	..	..	6 30	8 55
ABERGAVENNY	..	..	8 32	11 7
HEREFORD, Barr's Court	..	7 30	9 35	12 10
LEOMINSTER	..	8 5	9 59	12 45
LUDLOW	..	8 29	10 21	1 9
CRAVEN ARMS	..	8 52	10 35	1 32
ABERYSTWITH	..	..	8 0	..
WELSHPOOL	..	9 0	11 25	..
OSWESTRY	..	6 0	10 30	1 0
SHREWSBURY	..	10 20	12 30	2 50
WELLINGTON	..	10 10	12 50	3 19
NEWPORT (Salop)	..	10 56	1 10	3 32

(L. & N. W. Railway)

Miles		am	am	pm	pm
	STAFFORD, (L. & N.W.)	8 0	11 23	1 40	4 10
	STAFFORD (Common Station.)	8 2	11 25	1 42	4 13
4½	SALT	8 10	..	1 50	4 20
5¾	INGESTRE	8 15	11 36	1 55	4 25
7½	CHARTLEY	8 20	¶	2 0	*
10	GRINDLEY	8 25	..	*	*
15	UTTOXETER	8 45	11 53	2 20	4 50

Arrive.				
ROCESTER	9 37	12 12	3 11	5 24
ASHBOURNE	10 0	12 38	3 33	5 50
ALTON	9 47	12 20	..	5 34
OAKAMOOR	9 52	12 25	..	5 39
FROGHALL	10 0	12 33	..	5 47
LEEK	10 16	12 48	..	6 4
TUTBURY	9 38	12 17	2 47	5 26
BURTON	10 0	12 35	3 10	5 45
DERBY	10 0	12 55	3 15	5 50
TRENT JUNCTION	10 8	12 44	3 25	6 37
NOTTINGHAM	10 20	1 0	3 40	7 0
NEWARK	12 4	2 43	5 3	8 27
LINCOLN	12 38	3 18	5 40	9 10
LOUGHBORO'	11 5	1 37	3 55	7 10
LEICESTER	11 45	1 41	4 3	7 30
MELTON	1 20	5 6	5 6	8 35
STAMFORD	2 15	6 9	6 9	9 34
PETERBORO'	2 45	6 55	6 55	10 5
MARKET HARBORO'	..	2 38	4 33	9 18
KETTERING	..	2 57	5 29	9 36
NORTHAMPTON	..	3 40	6 15	..
BEDFORD	1 9	2 51	5 21	8 46
LUTON	2 8	4 18	5 54	10 44
LONDON (St. Pancras.)	2 20	4 5	6 40	10 0
MATLOCK BATH	11 9	..	4 21	8 3
BUXTON	12 20	..	5 35	8 45
SHEFFIELD	11 50	2 8	..	7 45
LEEDS	11 45	3 35	..	9 5
BRADFORD	2 30	4 15	..	10 10
YORK	2 10	4 25	..	10 20
HULL (Paragon Station)	3 25	5 45	..	11 15
SCARBOROUGH	4 5	7 0	..	..

(N. S. Railway; Midland Railway)

THROUGH TICKETS

ARE ISSUED AT THE FOLLOWING FARES.

From Stafford Common Station.

TO	RETURN 1st Class s. d.	RETURN 3rd Class s. d.	SINGLE 1st Class s. d.	SINGLE 3rd Class s. d.
Salt	..	..	0 8	0 2
Ingestre	..	..	1 0	0 5
Chartley	..	..	1 3	0 7
Grindley	..	..	1 8	0 9
Uttoxeter	3 9	..	2 6	1 3
Ashbourne	..	..	..	..
Alton	6 3	..	3 9	1 10½
Oakamoor	..	..	..	..
Froghall	..	..	..	..
Leek	..	..	..	..
Tutbury	..	..	..	..
Burton	7 6	..	4 8	2 4
Derby	9 6	..	5 8	2 9½
Trent Junction	..	..	..	..
Loughboro'	14 1	8 6	8 1	4 3
Leicester	16 3	9 1	8 9	4 6½
Weedon	19 4	11 5	10 7	5 8½
Stamford	25 4	14 10	13 7	7 5
PETERBORO'	27 10	15 0	14 10	7 9½
Market Harboro'	19 2	11 2	10 8	5 7
Kettering	23 4	14 2	12 4	7 1
Northampton	22 0	12 5	13 0	6 2½
Bedford	27 3	15 4	14 11	7 8
Luton	30 3	17 3	15 9	8 7½
LONDON, St. Pancras	39 6	22 1	20 9	11 0½
Nottingham	..	..	7 8	3 9½
Newark	17 6	10 5	9 8	5 2½
Lincoln	22 6	13 0	11 11	6 6
Matlock Bath	13 10	8 3	7 10	4 1½
Buxton	19 2	11 3	10 7	5 7½
Sheffield, (Midland)	19 4	11 7	10 7	5 9½
Leeds	25 6	15 1	12 10	7 6½

¶ Passengers by this Train can travel from Trent Junction by the celebrated PULLMAN CARS.

Trains marked * will stop when required at these Stations to pick up and set down Passengers.

Passengers are Booked at local Parliamentary Fares by all Trains on the Stafford & Uttoxeter, excepting the 11-23 a.m. Train, *ex* Stafford, which is 1st, 2nd, and 3rd Class Fast Train.

STATIONS.	WEEK DAYS. a.m.	a.m.	a.m.	a.m.
Depart.				
SCARBORO'	..	..	8 15	11 0
HULL, (Paragon)	..	..	9 15	10 30
YORK	..	..	9 40	12 50
BRADFORD	..	..	9 30	12 50
LEEDS	2 40	..	10 35	1 20
SHEFFIELD	4 12	8 10	11 53	2 30
BUXTON	..	8 10	10 20	1 30
MATLOCK BATH	..	9 7	11 29	2 25
LONDON (St. Pancras)	..	5 15	10 0	11 45
LUTON	..	..	9 45	12 32
BEDFORD	am	6 22	11 10	1 1
NORTHAMPTON	..	7 5	10 10	12 5
KETTERING	..	7 41	10 52	1 24
MARKET HARBORO'	..	7 59	11 10	1 16
PETERBORO'	..	6 30	10 25	11 5
STAMFORD	..	7 4	10 51	11 42
MELTON	..	8 7	11 37	12 48
LEICESTER	6 0	8 50	12 21	2 35
LOUGHBORO'	6 28	9 17	11 24	3 7
LINCOLN	..	7 0	9 50	1 15
NEWARK	..	7 39	10 25	1 46
NOTTINGHAM	6 30	10 10	..	3 40
TRENT JUNCTION	6 48	10 28	..	3 53
DERBY	8 30	11 10	..	4 15
BURTON	8 35	11 10	..	4 15
TUTBURY	..	11 32	..	4 39
LEEK	8 22	11 5	..	4 6
FROGHALL	8 37	11 20	..	4 21
OAKAMOOR	8 44	11 27	..	4 29
ALTON	8 49	11 32	..	4 34
ASHBOURNE	8 30	11 15	1 30	4 15
ROCESTER	8 51	11 40	2 7	4 44

(Midland Railway; N. S. Railway)

Miles		am	pm	pm	pm
15	UTTOXETER	9 30	12 5	2 52	5 15
10	GRINDLEY	9 42	12 17	3 4	*
7½	CHARTLEY	9 50	12 25	3 12	5 32
5¾	INGESTRE	9 55	12 30	3 17	5 38
4½	SALT	10 0	12 35	3 22	5 42
	STAFFORD (Common Station)	10 10	12 45	3 32	5 53
	STAFFORD, (L. & N. W)	10 15	12 50	3 35	6 0

Arrive				
NEWPORT, (Salop)	11 21	1 22	4 15	7 18
WELLINGTON	11 43	1 39	4 36	7 40
SHREWSBURY	12 2	2 0	5 0	8 3
OSWESTRY	1 22	3 37	7 30	9 35
WELSHPOOL	3 5	3 5	6 40	..
ABERYSTWITH	5 50	5 50	11 20	..
CRAVEN ARMS	1 38	2 59	6 7	9 46
LUDLOW	2 2	3 15	6 22	10 10
LEOMINSTER	2 30	3 37	6 44	..
HEREFORD, Barr's Court	3 10	4 2	7 10	..
ABERGAVENNY	..	5 8	8 15	..
CARDIFF, (Rmny. Ry.)	..	7 55	10 40	..
LLANDOVERY	..	5 12	8 40	..
LLANELLY	..	6 50	..	..
CARMARTHEN	..	6 12	..	..
SWANSEA	..	6 30	10 0	..
W'HAMPTON, High L'vl.	12 0	2 30	5 40	7 52
BIRMINGHAM, High St.	12 30	3 10	6 25	8 25
LONDON (Euston)	3 15	5 30	8 30	9 45

(L. & N. W. Railway)

☞ Passengers are requested to ask for Tickets by the Through Service of Trains by this Route, which is the Quickest and Best between the East and West, through the Midland Counties.

GENERAL CONDITIONS.

Notice.—The Public are requested to take Notice, that the Company do not guarantee that the Trains shall start or arrive at the time specified in the Bills; neither will they be accountable for any loss, inconvenience, or injury which may arise from delay or detention in the starting, transit, or arrival of trains.

Time Bills.—The published Time Bills of this Company are only intended to fix the time at which Passengers may be certain to obtain their tickets for any journey from the various Stations, it being understood that the trains shall not start *before* the appointed time. Every attention will be paid to ensure punctuality, as far as it is practicable; but the Directors give notice, that the Company do not undertake that the trains shall start or arrive at the time specified in the Bills, nor will they be accountable for any loss, inconvenience, or injury, which may arise from delays or detention.

The granting Tickets to Passengers to places *off* the Company's Line is an arrangement made for the greater convenience of the Public; but the Company do *not* hold themselves responsible for any delay, detention, or other injury whatsoever arising *off* their Lines; or from the acts or defaults of other parties, nor for the correctness of the times over the Lines of other Companies, nor for the arrival of this Company's own Trains in time, for the nominally corresponding train of any other Company or party. TICKETS are not Transferable.

Passengers' Luggage.—Every Passenger travelling upon this Railway may take with him his ordinary Luggage not exceeding 120lbs. if a first-class passenger, 100lbs. if a second class passenger, and 60lbs. in weight if a third class passenger. Notice is, however, hereby given that the Company will not be responsible for the care of the same, unless fully and properly addressed, with the name and destination of the party, nor for any article, conveyed inside the Carriages.

Children under three years of age, travel free; those above three and under twelve, half-price.

CRABBERY HALL,
Stafford, Nov. 24th, 1875.

FRANCIS G. BURTON, General Manager.

BUNNY & EVANS, [late SANDFORD] PRINTERS, HIGH STREET, SHREWSBURY.

Stafford & Uttoxeter Railway time and fare table poster of December 1875. COLLECTION RICHARD DEMPSTER

CHAPTER SIX

Operating the Railway 1867-1881

Motive Power

The first train in public service from Stafford to Uttoxeter ran on 23 December 1867 but the first of the S&UR's two locomotives, *Shrewsbury and Talbot*, was not delivered by Beyer Peacock of Manchester until 10 October 1868. This, of course, begs the question of what locomotive was used to haul the first train and subsequent trains until the arrival of the Beyer Peacock engine. William Field had approached the NSR on 1 December 1867 enquiring whether he could hire a locomotive and rolling stock but he was refused, although the NSR did offer to sell him an engine and three carriages - an offer which was declined. During the previous year, terms had been proposed for the NSR and L&NWR to work the line jointly but the idea was rejected. The S&UR did eventually hire locomotives on a regular basis from a variety of sources all of which is dealt with shortly but the first known hiring did not take place until June 1870, which leaves us with the possibility that the contractor's locomotives handled the trains from the opening of the line until October 1868,[98] or indeed beyond that date.

The Beyer Peacocks

The directors, having failed to secure the services of any other railway company to work their railway, placed an order in 1868 with Beyer Peacock & Company Limited, Gorton Works, Manchester, for a 2-4-0 side tank locomotive. The total cost of this locomotive was £2,687 14s 6d (£2,687.73) of which £400 was paid on delivery, followed by six instalments of £100 and a final payment of £1,687 14s 6d (£1,687.73), which was entered in the S&UR's books on 1 August 1872.[99] The works cost of this locomotive was £1,296 19s 7d (£1,296.98) including delivery[100] and so by spreading the payments over four years, Beyer Peacock made a huge profit of £1,390 14s 11d (£1,390.74) amounting to 107% of the total cost! The entry in the Beyer Peacock order book is dated 10 June 1868 and is recorded as No. 2264, maker's number 849. It says the order is to be precisely the same as *One Tank Engine No. 2017 July 11th 1866 with the exception that an additional weatherboard is to be fastened to the back of the Coaltank.* Order No. 2017 (maker's number 733) was for Boldemann & Co., for use on the Christianstad and Hässelholm Railway in Sweden. The entry also records that the locomotive was to be named *Shrewsbury and Talbot*. The brass nameplate, which was fitted at Gorton and placed in the centre of the side tanks, was 4ft 0in long and 5in wide with a raised border of ½in. The locomotive, which had a copper capped chimney, brass dome and safety valve covers, was painted green and was one of Beyer Peacock's standard classes, the first representative of which had been delivered to the West Midland Railway in 1861.

The S&UR locomotive was tried in steam at Gorton on 26 September 1868 and delivered via the L&NWR on 10 October 1868. Beyer Peacock records contain an entry for 'Carriage to

Stafford' at a cost of £9 13s 4d (£9.67) and their staff accompanied it, presumably to demonstrate the working of the locomotive and to lubricate the engine en-route as it probably made its way as part of a goods train.

At some later stage the locomotive was fitted with a roof covering the footplate which extended from the front to the back weather boards so giving extra protection to the enginemen. It was returned to Beyer Peacock in 1870 for repairs and again in 1872, being sent home in August of that year with a new firebox, new boiler tubes and with new steel tyres on the wheels. The locomotive was acquired by the GNR in September 1881 and allocated GNR running number 682; by the end of that year it had been broken up at Doncaster. Its scrap value of £500 was allocated to the GNR 'Repairs Account' for January and February of 1882.

Shrewsbury and Talbot was named after Charles Chetwynd-Talbot (1830-1877) who was the 19th Earl of Shrewsbury and 4th Earl Talbot. As we have seen in Chapter Three, his father, Admiral Henry John Chetwynd-Talbot (1803-1868) 18th Earl of Shrewsbury and 3rd Earl Talbot had strongly objected to the railway and died on 4 June 1868, shortly after it had opened. He never saw the *Shrewsbury and Talbot*.

The S&UR's second and only other locomotive was named *Ingestre* after Ingestre Hall, a 17th century Jacobean mansion and the family seat of the Earls of Shrewsbury and Talbot. It was acquired second-hand in May 1873 from Hendry & Co at a cost of £1,250, no doubt purchased in a hurry following the damage sustained to the *Shrewsbury and Talbot* in the fatal accident at Hopton on 1 February 1873 which rendered that engine inoperable. Like *Shrewsbury and Talbot*, it was built by Beyer Peacock being one of five 0-4-2 saddle tanks supplied to the North London Railway (NLR) in 1860.

The five locomotives were acquired primarily for working goods traffic. They were built to the Order No. 428, (maker's numbers 186-190) and became NLR numbers 38-42. As befitted their builder, the shareholders were told by the directors that they were *very superior engines*, doubtless to justify their cost, as Beyer's were by no means the least expensive locomotive builder. It may have been to improve their riding characteristics, or perhaps to increase the bunker capacity or even both, but in 1868 two of them, numbers 38 and 41, were rebuilt at the NLR Bow Works to an 0-4-4 wheel arrangement with a trailing bogie replacing the former radial axle.

The Locomotive Engineer of the NLR at the time was William Adams (1823-1904), the designer of the well-known, at least among railway engineers, *Adams Bogie*. This design was a considerable advancement on earlier types in better catering for both lateral and circular movement, resulting in improved control of locomotives so fitted, as they encountered track curvature. While it is generally regarded he first introduced this bogie on

This is the company's first locomotive, a 2-4-0 side tank built in 1868 by Beyer Peacock & Company of Gorton in Manchester, maker's number 849. Named Shrewsbury and Talbot, *the S&UR directors were obviously currying favour with the noble Earl!*
THE LOCOMOTIVE MAGAZINE

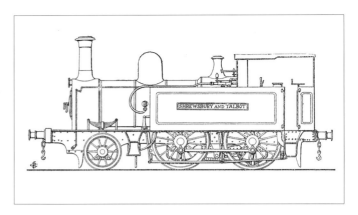

Unfortunately, the makers do not appear to have had an official photograph taken of the S&UR locomotive. However, there is one of an earlier engine built to an almost identical design and here it is. Order No. 2017 of 1866, maker's number 733, for the Swedish Christianstad-Hässelholm Railway as its number 3, with the name Christianstad.
MUSEUM OF SCIENCE & INDUSTRY IN MANCHESTER

RIGHT: *Beyer Peacock general arrangement drawing dated 19 July 1866, of its Order No. 2017, which was for maker's number 733, an identical engine to the Stafford & Uttoxeter Railway* Shrewsbury and Talbot. *In the case of 733, the customer was the Christianstad-Hässelholm Railway in Sweden. Similar engines went to the Isle of Wight Central Railway. Notice the engine had Allan straight link motion, a valve gear favoured by the makers over many years.*
MUSEUM OF SCIENCE & INDUSTRY IN MANCHESTER

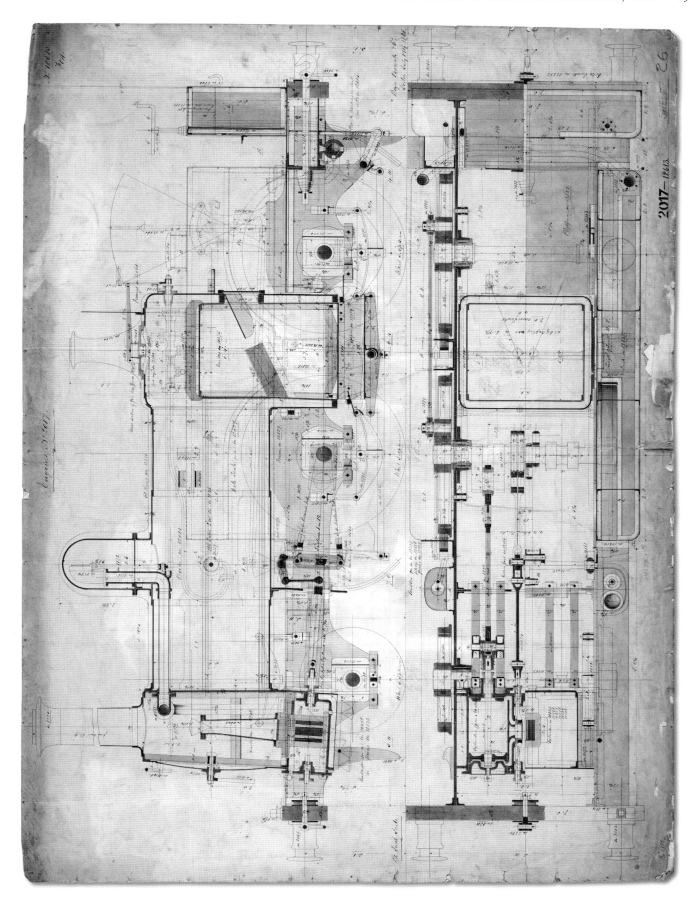

The second locomotive was of a quite different design, a relatively large 0-4-4 saddle tank, also built by Beyer Peacock, but in this case much earlier in 1860; the maker's number was 189. It had been new to the North London Railway (NLR) and acquired second-hand by the S&UR. In 1872 the North London Railway sold the locomotive to J. H. Johnson of Wigan for £1,000. Although he was the manager of a local colliery, on this occasion at least, he appears to have resold the engine to one of the NLR's regular dealer's for second-hand rolling stock, Messrs Hendry & Co., who promptly sold the engine to the S&UR. Arriving on the line by the following year, in all probability it went direct from the NLR to the S&UR. Originally built as an 0-4-2 saddle tank, it had been rebuilt to this configuration at the NLR Bow Works in 1868. As can be seen it was named Ingestre, yet another reference to the Earl as his seat was at Ingestre Hall!

THE LOCOMOTIVE MAGAZINE

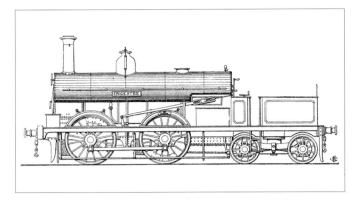

This is a stablemate of the second locomotive, Ingestre, in its original form as an 0-4-2 saddle tank as built by Beyer Peacock and delivered to the NLR as its number 38 in 1860; maker's number 186. The S&UR locomotive was originally NLR number 41.

MUSEUM OF SCIENCE & INDUSTRY IN MANCHESTER

RIGHT: Beyer Peacock general arrangement drawing dated March 27 1860, of Order No. 428, which covered maker's numbers 186-190, five locomotives for the NLR dispatched in 1860, one of which later became the Stafford & Uttoxeter Railway Ingestre as mentioned in the previous caption. As with the other Beyer Peacock drawing, it is a draughtsman's work of art with extensive use of colour on the original, to differentiate between the different materials used in construction.

MUSEUM OF SCIENCE & INDUSTRY IN MANCHESTER

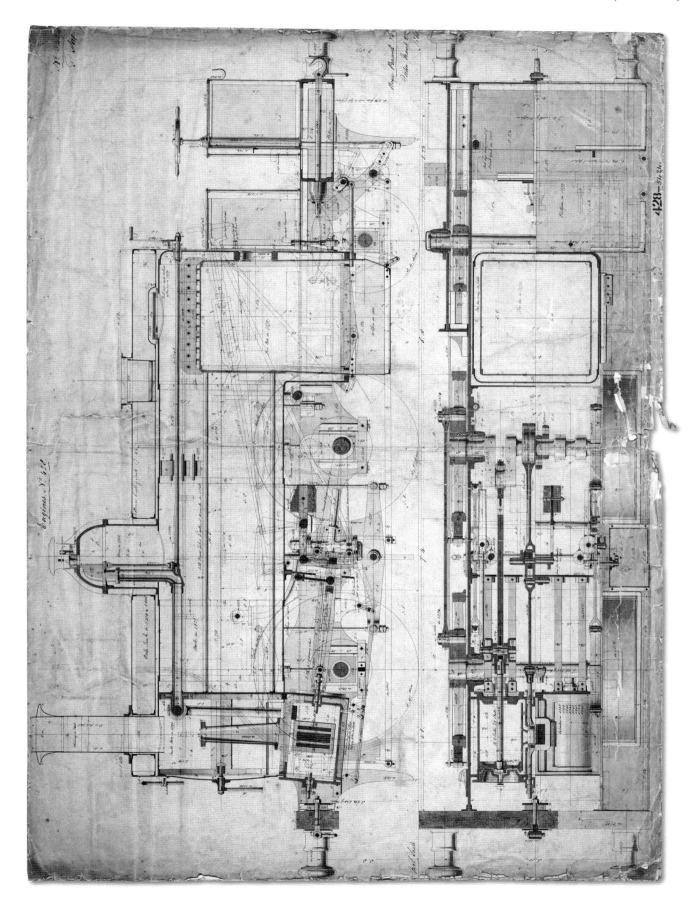

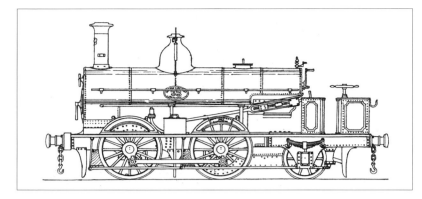

An outline drawing of NLR number 38 as built – the five in the series carried running numbers 38-42. THE LOCOMOTIVE MAGAZINE

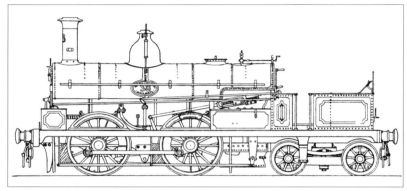

Here is an outline drawing of NLR number 38 again, after conversion to an 0-4-4 wheel arrangement by the addition of longer frames and a bogie, the latter to the NLR Locomotive Engineer, William Adams design. There is the possibility that the conversion of this locomotive and number 41, which became the S&UR engine, was to act as prototypes, allowing Adams to experiment with his new bogie design prior to more extensive use.
THE LOCOMOTIVE MAGAZINE

a new class of NLR 4-4-0 tank engines in 1868, later known as the 'No. 1 Class', there is evidence to suggest that the conversion of numbers 38 and 41, acted as the prototypes. The principles of this bogie design spread far and wide and locomotives so fitted remained in service in this country, almost to the end of BR steam working.

With new locomotive designs in hand and building, in 1872 the NLR decided to withdraw the five locomotives. Adams submitted a suggestion to the Locomotive, Stores & Traffic Committee on 4 June 1872,[101] that they be sold to Messrs Hendry & Co., numbers 38, 39 and 40 at £1,000 each and the other two, 41 and 42 at £900, although why the price difference has not been recorded. Although we have not been able to find out anything about Messrs Hendry & Co., it was one known to the NLR as they had previously been involved in the disposal of redundant rolling stock. Despite Adams' recommendation, presumably having been in touch with Hendry & Co., the members of the committee elected to advertise the locomotives in the hope of getting a better price. Such an advert appeared in *The Engineer*, for 21 June 1872. In the event all five locomotives were sold individually to various buyers over the period October 1872 and October the following year. A minute of 1 October 1872[102] tells us that number 41 (BP 189/1860), one of the two that had been converted with a trailing bogie, was sold to J.H. Johnson of Wigan for £1,000, subject to 2½% commission following the satisfactory completion and performance of a new outside cylinder engine constructed to replace it. The latter was one of the 4-4-0 side tanks of the 'No. 1 Class' referred to above. Johnson was a director of a number of collieries in the Wigan area coalfield as well as the West Lancashire Wagon Company Limited. There

is also a suggestion he acted independently as a dealer in second-hand locomotives. However, the accounts of the S&UR Receiver & Manager[103] record that a sum of £1,250 was paid to Hendry & Co. on 30 May 1873, for a locomotive. We are, therefore, left with somewhat of a conundrum. In the case of all five locomotive sales the NLR Locomotive, Stores & Traffic Committee minutes record commission being paid, sometimes 2½% as in the case of number 41 and sometimes as high as 5%. It may be that this commission was for Hendry & Co. acting as brokers in the various deals and in fact, for one of the locomotives, number 40, the sale was direct to Hendry & Co. In this case for £1,000 less 5% commission. Now we know that the S&UR was pretty desperate for a locomotive in 1873 and we can only assume that either via J.H. Johnson or Hendry & Co., the S&UR Receiver & Manager became aware of these NLR locomotives and their suitability for his purpose; Hendry & Co. subsequently brokering the sale on behalf of Johnson as doubtless the engine had not moved from London. We might also guess that the premium over the price paid by Johnson might have been split between the two parties!

Ingestre carried the usual Beyer Peacock copper capped chimney and brass dome but did not sport a cab or weather boards, the enginemen being completely exposed to the elements. The nameplate was fixed on the saddle tanks beneath the dome and under the hand rail. After acquisition by the GNR, *Ingestre* was allocated GNR running number 683 but instead became 683A. It was nominally replaced in June 1882 by a Stirling 0-4-4 tank engine but its actual withdrawal date is not known. The principal dimensions for *Ingestre* (as rebuilt) and *Shrewsbury and Talbot* are shown in Appendix One, together with a very detailed analysis about the actual identity of *Ingestre*.

Locomotive servicing and repairs

Until 1874 the S&UR locomotives were serviced at the L&NWR's Stafford locomotive shed and the NSR's engine shed at Pinfold, near to Uttoxeter. After Stafford Common station opened for traffic on 1 July 1874, a wooden locomotive shed was built nearby on a siding adjacent to the main line. Beyer Peacock undertook major repairs to *Shrewsbury and Talbot* after it sustained substantial damage in the fatal accident at Hopton on 1 February 1873. Those repairs cost £400 17s 1d (£400.85) and there is a relevant entry in the S&UR's books dated 11 May 1874 indicating that the engine had been away for some time. Beyer Peacock rendered two more significant bills for engine repairs costing £478 5s 11d (£478.30) and £162 11s 0d (£162.55) which are dated in the accounts as 22 September 1876 and 12 March 1877, respectively, with the latter shown as *in settlement of the a/c for repairs to engines* thereby implying that both engines were involved. It is interesting to note that the locomotives travelled to and from Beyer Peacock's Gorton Works at Manchester via Stoke-on-Trent and the NSR/ Manchester, Sheffield & Lincolnshire Railway (MS&LR) joint line line through Bollington. There is an entry in the S&UR accounts dated 30 June 1876 for a payment to the M&SLR for 7s 0d (£0.35) for piloting an engine on 9 October 1875 and another dated 11 October 1876 for a payment to the MS&LR for £2 12s 0d (£2.60) *for conveying engine from Gorton to Uttoxeter*. Beyer Peacock also undertook minor repairs as evidenced by a repair to a lubricator in April 1876 at a cost of one guinea (£1.05) and *engineering* in October 1880 at a cost of £14 10s 0d (£14.50).

Local firms were also involved in repairing the locomotives. For example, the Lilleshall Company of Oakengates in Shropshire rendered an account for repairing feed pipes in 1874; W.G. Bagnall Ltd, the Stafford locomotive builders, undertook repairs in 1876 and 1877; Hartley and Arnoux Brothers of Stoke-on-Trent supplied piston rings and repaired locomotive wheels in 1879. Even the NSR played its part, rendering an account for *trimming up wheels of engine* in October 1877 for the sum of £4 10s 0d (£4.50).

Locomotives on hire

The two Beyer Peacock locomotives could not cope with the sustained train mileage required which averaged nearly 46,000 miles per annum. Therefore, the hire of locomotives to cover for breakdowns, repairs and maintenance was inevitable. By studying the accounts prepared by the Receiver and Manager we know that locomotives were mainly hired from the L&NWR but they were also hired from Isaac Watt Boulton of Boulton's Siding in Ashton-under-Lyne, the East & West Junction Railway, the NSR, contractor William Moss who had a depot at Forebridge Wharf in Stafford and London based Firmin Hill & Company Limited. The accounts also attribute the hiring of locomotives to three employees: Charles Roden, Inspector of the Line; Francis George Burton who was briefly General Manager between 1875 and 1876 and John Henry Duffill who was General Manager from 1876 until 1881. These individuals obviously had the authority to hire locomotives but unfortunately where they obtained them from is not recorded, although we suspect it was largely from the L&NWR.

Appendix Two shows the known extent of locomotive hire from 1870 to 1881, the cost of which comes to an astonishing £3030. The breakdown for each year is shown below with the hire charges rounded to the nearest pound:

Year	Hire charge £	Year	Hire charge £
1870	10	1876	228
1871	100	1877	6
1872	772	1878	Nil
1873	370	1879	164
1874	Nil	1880	534
1875	53	1881	793

The large amount spent on hire in 1872 indicates that Beyer Peacock's *Shrewsbury and Talbot* may well have been inoperable for most of that year. The large amounts spent on hire in 1880 and 1881, the last years of the S&UR's independent existence, must demonstrate that by that time both Beyer Peacocks were in a very poor state.

As previously mentioned, the first recorded hiring shown in the accounts is dated June 1870 when an amount of ten guineas (£10.50) was payable to the L&NWR. The L&NWR Locomotive Committee minutes record that a locomotive was hired to the S&UR for the period 21-31 May 1870 which ties in nicely with that accounting record but this was an isolated instance as the next hiring did not take place until late in 1871 when Isaac Watt Boulton entered the scene.

The accounts feature the following entries in respect of Boulton:

1 November 1871	Hire of engine	£50 0s 0d
4 December 1871	Engine hire	£50 0s 0d
7 March 1872	Engine hire	£16 1s 5d
16 October 1872	Balance of engine hire	£16 10s 0d

The Locomotive for 14 March 1908 claims that the NSR at one period ran a through service between Stafford and Nottingham on the Midland Railway using outside cylindered 2-4-0 tender engines, outside cylindered tank engines and an old inside cylindered tender engine with a *Gothic* firebox. There may have been an element of truth in this but we suspect there was some confusion both with regard to the NSR's involvement and the engines used. However, it has been suggested that the locomotive with the *Gothic* firebox was the one hired by the S&UR from Boulton. If this was the case, then the engine in question was undoubtedly his *Cavendish*, originally a 2-4-0 tender engine with 14 × 20in inside cylinders and five foot diameter driving wheels. Boulton acquired this locomotive from the L&NWR in November 1871 and converted it into a 2-4-0 saddle tank. The locomotive started life with the Birkenhead, Lancashire & Cheshire Junction Railway. It was one of two 2-4-0 tender engines built in 1852 by Robert Stephenson & Company at Newcastle-on-Tyne (maker's numbers 820-821), the engine in question being 821 which took the running number 24 and the name *Majestic*. The railway changed its name to the Birkenhead Railway in 1859 and in November 1860 was vested jointly in the L&NWR and GWR.

The two locomotives found their way into the L&NWR fleet, *Majestic* becoming number 368; in May 1862 it was transferred to the duplicate list becoming 1140. The two locomotives were among the very few survivors with *hay-cock* fireboxes which *The Locomotive* almost certainly described as *Gothic*. We have a strong suspicion that Boulton hired this locomotive to the S&UR as soon as he acquired it from the L&NWR and again in 1872 after re-building. The engine was then hired to the Cowbridge Railway in Glamorgan and in August 1874 it went to contractors Griffiths & Thomas in connection with the construction of Alexandra North Dock at Newport, Monmouthshire which was opened on 13 April 1875. The same contractors were also responsible for an associated graving dock and a short canal from the North Dock to a timber float, both of which opened in 1878. *Cavendish* was broken up at Boulton's Siding around 1880.[104] As previously mentioned, the S&UR had undertaken only to run engines with the chimney foremost. This would present a problem when turning *Cavendish* as a tender engine at the Uttoxeter end of the journey where there was only a 17ft diameter turntable available at Pinfold, but the date of its acquisition by Boulton and the record of his hirings to the S&UR do coincide. Moreover, the S&UR did occasionally turn a blind eye to stipulations made by the BoT!

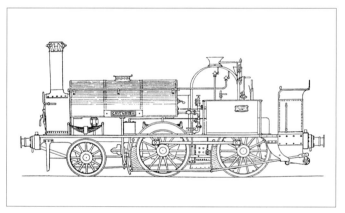

Isaac Watt Boulton's former L&NWR locomotive Cavendish, *thought to have worked on the S&UR, on hire from Boulton in the mid to late 1870s. Originally built in 1852 as a 2-4-0 tender engine by Robert Stephenson & Company, on acquisition by Boulton in about 1870, the engine was rebuilt to a saddle tank as illustrated here.* LOCOMOTIVE PUBLISHING COMPANY

We will now deal with locomotives hired from the L&NWR. The 1908 article in *The Locomotive* mentioned above records that old engines of the 'Trevithick' type were sometimes hired from the L&NWR and records that the L&NWR used to run frequent excursion trains over the line to Alton Towers on the NSR's Churnet Valley line. Yeomans[105] claims that 'Problem' Class 2-2-2s were used on these trains which is not surprising as in 1877 at least 21 members of the class were allocated to Stafford. The L&NWR Locomotive Committee minutes record four separate occasions when locomotives were hired to the S&UR, doubtless from Stafford shed. The periods covered, including that mentioned earlier, were from 21-31 May 1870, 2-22 January 1873 and two short periods in April and May 1875.[106] Unfortunately, no details were given of the individual locomotives concerned but the 1875 entries confirm that the fee was four guineas (£4.20)

per day paid daily in advance. In view of the limited turning facilities available at Uttoxeter, we assume that tank engines were the S&UR's preferred choice. Appendix Two shows the tally of entries specifically relating to the L&NWR. Locomotives from this company were hired in 1870, 1872, 1873 and 1879 and continually from October 1880 until the GNR takeover in August 1881. We suspect that most of the locomotives hired by Roden, Burton and Duffill were also obtained from the L&NWR. The practice of hiring locomotives from the L&NWR was, maybe, far more extensive than the entries in the Locomotive Committee minutes indicate.

The locomotives hired from the East and West Junction Railway (E&WJR) in 1873 were probably built by Beyer Peacock. Three 2-4-0 tank engines for that railway emerged from Gorton in February 1873 built to Order No. 2933. Similar but not identical to *Shrewsbury and Talbot*, they were allocated maker's numbers 1238-1240 and carried running numbers 4-6. It could well be that one of these engines was delivered direct to the S&UR prior to moving further south. All three were subsequently returned to the makers by the E&WJR due to lack of funds; they were resold to the Lancashire & Yorkshire Railway in 1875 becoming numbers 517-519 on that railway.

The NSR Traffic & Finance Committee minutes for the meeting held on 25 April 1876[107] record an authority being given to Charles Clare, Locomotive Superintendent, to hire an engine to the S&UR at £4 per day which was a better deal than that offered by the L&NWR earlier. Appendix Two shows only a single entry for locomotive hire from the NSR dated 1 July 1876 for an amount of £8 11s 2d (£8.56) but again we suspect that some of the locomotives hired by the various General Managers may have been from the NSR. There is a single entry for locomotive hire from William Moss dated 10 December 1877. William Moss & Son were contractors based at Stafford with an office at 56-57 Wolverhampton Road and a plant depot at Forebridge Wharf. There are a series of entries against Firmin & Hill & Co running from 25 October 1879 to 12 May 1880. This was a London based firm no doubt dealing with the hire of locomotives and other plant.

Rolling Stock

From the outset, the S&UR hired its carriages and wagons from the Midland Wagon Company but the Receiver's Accounts show that on 1 August 1872 it purchased a set of carriages from W.T. Endry & Co. for £510. We are convinced that this is a misspelling for W.T. Hendry & Co. which had dealings with the NLR and is one and the same as Hendry & Co. mentioned earlier. Indeed, the NLR Locomotive, Stores & Traffic Committee at its meeting held on 30 January 1872 (Minute 1424) confirmed a sale of 26 old passenger carriages to Messrs Hendry & Co. for a total price of £1,410. The carriages sold were as follows: six third class at £35 each; 16 second class at £50 each and four first class at £100 each. It was also agreed that any painting, varnishing, renumbering or renaming would be executed by the NLR at cost price of material and labour. We are convinced that the S&UR purchased up to ten of these vehicles. If so, they would all be four-wheelers. During 1873, 15 wagons and a brake van were purchased from the

Midland Railway at a cost of £1,500 in a deal financed with the London Financial Association. In 1875, four additional carriages were purchased from the Midland Wagon Company. In spite of these purchases, the S&UR continued to hire carriages and wagons from the Midland Wagon Company each year from 1872 until 1875. A hefty bill of £134 10s 8d (£135.53) was paid to that company in 1872 for repairs to the carriages on hire. Wooden brake blocks for the rolling stock were purchased from Henry Venables of Stafford. In 1876, the S&UR briefly hired wagons from the E&WJR at a cost of 11s 2d (56p) and the following year hired coaches from the NSR at a cost of £45. Through goods and mineral traffic was, of course, conveyed in other companies' rolling stock or in private owner wagons.

S&UR rolling stock totals for the years 1872 to 1877 and for 1879/1880 as shown in the Board of Trade Returns, submitted in accordance with the Regulation of Railways Act 1871, are summarised as follows:

	1872	1873	1874	1875	1876	1877	1879	1880
Passenger stock	10	9	9	8	8	8	8	11
Wagons	3	16	16	16	16	22	16	16
Other		1	1	1	1	2	1	1
Total	13	26	26	25	25	32	25	28

No returns were presented for the year 1878. The passenger stock included any vehicle of the description *other vehicles attached to passenger trains*. The wagons fell within the description of *all kinds used for the conveyance of livestock, minerals or general merchandise*.

The carriages hired from the Midland Wagon Company and used on the initial services were described as *roomy and comfortable* and there was *scarcely any jolting*. It is not known why there was a sudden increase in wagon stock in 1877 but there was a significant increase in traffic that year. The GNR inspected the S&UR rolling stock on 3 October 1881 when it was agreed that the price for 12 carriages, 16 wagons and one travelling crane would be £215, £164 and £10 respectively. It was estimated that the wagons would be fit for traffic for a further four or five years but that the carriages and the crane should be replaced immediately. They were obviously worn out and of no further use to the GNR. The maximum dimensions of a carriage or wagon load that could safely pass over the S&UR were: width of load – 9ft 0in; height in centre – 13ft 6in; height at side – 11ft 0in.

Supplies

The S&UR certainly shopped around for its supplies. Coal, for example, was purchased from various colliery companies based on the North and South Staffordshire coalfields and elsewhere. Supplies from North Staffordshire included coal from the Harecastle & Woodshutts Colliery Company at Kidsgrove and the Crewe, Coal & Iron Company which operated Leycett Colliery; those supplying the railway with coal from South Staffordshire included the Cannock Chase Colliery Company and the West Cannock Colliery Company. Supplies from further afield were sent by the Dowlais Iron Company and the Brynmawr Coal & Iron Company both located in South Wales. Coal was also purchased from local coal merchants including W. Hall

& Company Ltd which had a private siding connected to the S&UR at Stafford.

After 1872 the purchase of sleepers featured increasingly in the company's accounts indicating that those originally laid were quickly wearing out. As with coal, supplies were obtained from a variety of sources including Henry Venables of Stafford, Burt, Boulton & Haywood and even the NSR which supplied a batch in 1876 at a cost of £75. The latter may well have been second-hand. During the previous year, the NSR had also supplied stores at a cost of £280 17s 7d (£280.88) but we do not know the nature of these supplies. Water and gas was purchased from the L&NWR and gas was also taken from the Stafford Gas Company. Tickets were obtained from J.B. Edmondson[108] and from Waterlow & Sons. In 1873 the S&UR purchased a crane from J. Jevons at a cost of £150.

Running Powers

By virtue of its 1862 Act, the S&UR had statutory running powers into Stafford L&NWR station and into the NSR's Uttoxeter Bridge Street station which could be exercised continuously for all traffic. Indeed the S&UR could not have operated without these powers. The S&UR paid the L&NWR £600 per annum for services rendered at Stafford station under an agreement which was negotiated by the L&NWR's General Manager, William Cawkwell and the S&UR's contractor William Field.[109] Although it did not have statutory powers to do so, the L&NWR by agreement occasionally ran passenger trains over the S&UR during holiday times, particularly excursions to Alton Towers on the NSR's Churnet Valley line and, as previously mentioned, the NSR was reported to have operated a regular timetabled service from Stafford to Nottingham (Midland) station which ran via Tutbury, Castle Donington and Trent Junction. The latter, if correct, must have been very short lived.

The Stafford and Uttoxeter Railway Act 1879[110] which received the Royal Assent on 11 August 1879 gave the S&UR further extensive running powers as follows: over the NSR to the NSR, L&NWR and GNR goods depots at Burton-on-Trent; over the GNR curve between Egginton Junction and Dove Junction and over the GNR from Egginton Junction to Derby. Moreover, the S&UR was empowered to use the GNR's Derby Friargate station and all intermediate stations between there and Egginton for all classes of traffic. In return the 1879 Act granted running powers over the S&UR to the GNR and NSR for all types of traffic.

At the time these powers were granted the S&UR was not only in receivership, but also badly run down. Gaining additional running powers and especially attracting a larger company to operate over its line to Stafford might have been seen by the directors as the only hope of survival. For this reason, we have studied the passage of the Bill through the 1878-1879 Parliamentary Session in some detail.[111] The Bill was latterly supported by the GNR but strongly opposed throughout by the L&NWR, the NSR and the GWR. Initially the Bill was designed to give further running powers over the L&NWR and GWR between Stafford and Shrewsbury but that part of the Bill was abandoned in the House of Commons in an attempt to get rid of the opposition from those powerful companies. It was not that easy. We pick up the progress of the Bill in the House of Lords in July 1879 when those for and against the proposals were called before a Select Committee chaired by Lord Airlie.[112] Messrs Aspinall QC, Venables QC and John Winterbotham Batten appeared as Counsel for the S&UR. Sir Edmund Beckett QC represented the NSR and Messrs Pope QC and Littler QC the L&NWR. Battle commenced on 14 July and concluded on 17 July 1879.

The following list shows the witnesses brought before the Select Committee for examination in the order they appeared. The first group comprises customers of the S&UR; the second group comprises the railway officials who gave evidence for and against the proposals.

Frederick Francis Fox	Agent for Lord Ferrers
Henry George Bolam	Mineral and Estate Agent for the Earl of Shrewsbury and Talbot
John Tasker Evans	Provision Merchant, Auctioneer and a Member of Stafford Corporation and its Gas Committee
Henry Charles Webb	Secretary, Shrewsbury Estate Manure Company
Samuel Johnson	Shoe Manufacture
John Salkeld	Managing Partner in firm operating Chartley Cement and Plaster Works
John Henry Duffill	General Manager, S&UR
Henry Cecil Newton	Receiver, S&UR
Henry Oakley	General Manager, GNR
Benjaman Bateman	Chairman, S&UR
William Cawkwell	Director and former General Manager, L&NWR
James Grierson	General Manager, GWR

All the customers portrayed the S&UR as a small impoverished railway company constrained at one end by the L&NWR and at the other by the NSR and by a lack of investment in new and improved facilities. There were several examples quoted of S&UR passenger trains being held at Bromshall Junction while NSR trains bound for Derby were given the right of way. Upon arrival at Uttoxeter, the NSR Derby bound trains were found to have departed so breaking the connection and causing severe delay to S&UR passengers. There was overwhelming support for S&UR trains to run beyond Uttoxeter and for a larger company to take a positive interest in the local line. Fox said that some 4,000 tons of gypsum, brick and salt traffic was generated annually from Lord Ferrers' estate but insofar as the gypsum traffic was concerned it was more expeditious to send it to the NSR's station at Weston by carts drawn by horses and traction engines rather than use the much nearer S&UR station at Chartley and Stowe. There was much optimistic talk about attracting cattle and sheep traffic from Wales to the Uttoxeter markets, some of which was routed via Tamworth and Stoke-on-Trent. Fox also emphasised the potential for milk traffic to London to which Pope joked: *It would be butter by the time it arrived.* Evans was examined by Aspinall about a Petition in favour of the Bill from Stafford Corporation. Evans said there was no criticism about the facilities provided by the L&NWR for the S&UR at Stafford but the Corporation was highly critical of what was provided by the NSR at Uttoxeter, explaining that there were *difficulties thrown in the way of traffic going forward.* Using his experience as a member of the Gas Committee he said that 4,000 tons of gas coal sourced from Derbyshire was now routed circuitously by the Midland Railway

and the L&NWR to Wichnor Junction and then via Lichfield to Stafford. The other customers continued in the same vein.

Sir Edmund Beckett continually argued that the S&UR's 1862 Act gave powers for through carriages and through rates which had never been exercised. When questioned about this the customers were ignorant of these provisions which were cleverly, but rather naughtily, being used as a smokescreen in an attempt to demonstrate that the running powers then sought were, in fact, not required. Indeed at one stage in the proceedings there was great confusion between the concept of through carriages as opposed to running powers and through trains.

The S&UR's General Manager did not equip himself well. While being enthusiastic about having through trains he could not even attempt to quantify the additional traffic that would be generated if the powers sought after were granted. When pressed by Pope, he thought that 100 passengers per train would make a through service pay. He was right about that as the records demonstrate that the S&UR trains operating in 1879 only carried an average of 23 passengers per train! He said that he had on many occasions applied to the L&NWR and NSR for through carriages but had been refused, especially at busy times. Recent correspondence had indicated the NSR's willingness to provide better accommodation at Uttoxeter if the Bill were passed. This correspondence, which was conducted between S&UR Secretary, Charles James Hayter and NSR Secretary, Percy Morris, is

This is Baron Grimthorpe (1816-1905) as caricatured by SPY (Leslie Ward) in Vanity Fair on 2 February 1889. As Sir Edmund Beckett QC, he acted as Counsel for the NSR in the House of Lords in July 1879 by defending the company's interests against the S&UR Bill – the one that led to the S&UR acquiring extensive running powers over the NSR prior to the GNR takeover. He was an architect, horologist and a lawyer, became Queen's Counsel in 1854 and created 1st Baron Grimthorpe in 1886.

amusing in that there was also a request for the NSR to provide additional accommodation at Colwich. Percy Morris must have revelled in querying how the S&UR proposed to get access to Colwich, pointing out to the newly appointed Hayter that the proposed branch to connect the two railways in the Parish of Stowe had never been completed! Hayter was clearly office bound in London where he practised as a professional company secretary to several railway companies. The S&UR Receiver was quite blunt. He said that if the running powers sought after were not granted the S&UR would have to close.

Henry Oakley (1823-1914) in giving his evidence was very positive. It should be noted that having been employed by the GNR since 1849, becoming Secretary in 1858 and General Manager in 1870, Oakley's career was still in the ascendancy. He explained that the GNR originally objected to the Bill as first drafted as it gave the S&UR the right to run over the entire GNR system, which the GNR considered was unreasonable. The reciprocity of running powers now proposed was fair. Oakley said *Grantham is the Stafford of our main line* and foresaw a great interchange of traffic from west of Stafford to east of Grantham utilising the S&UR. He expressed surprise at the L&NWR opposition making the point that their route lay to the north and south whereas the GNR's current interest lay to the east and west. He said that the GNR Board's interest in the S&UR had first been aroused by Stafford Corporation which was most anxious to have some better form of communication with the east. Oakley went on to say that he thought the proposed running powers would do a great deal of good for the NSR and would certainly do no pecuniary injury to the L&NWR although some of the traffic currently exchanged with the L&NWR at Burton-on-Trent might in future be exchanged at Stafford. He said he would have no objection to the NSR having running powers over the S&UR and pointed out that the NSR already had running powers over the GNR from Egginton to Nottingham and Pinxton but these were not exercised because the NSR was happy to exchange traffic at Egginton. The question of amalgamation with the S&UR was touched upon by Sir Edmund Beckett to which Oakley responded, *we have not arrived at that stage yet.* Asked whether there was a station on the GNR where another competitive company was accommodated Oakley quoted the example of Peterborough where the Midland and the L&NWR were both admitted. Pope asked him whether he contemplated making Stafford station a main line terminus of the GNR to which Oakley replied *undoubtedly...because we should have no power to go beyond Stafford.* Re-examined by Venables he was asked whether calling Stafford a terminus of a main line in any way affected the proposals. Oakley retorted: *No, it is Mr. Pope's eloquent language – he always uses hyperbole whenever he can.* Oakley certainly had the measure of Pope!

Cawkwell then attempted to justify the L&NWR's position by stating that his company had spent vast sums of money in improving the facilities at Stafford station to which the GNR now wished to gain access. He said in all his experience he never knew of such a case where a large company like the GNR had attempted to force its way into a station belonging to a large rival company on the back of a small company like the S&UR. He considered the whole matter to be underhand. Littler put it to him that the GNR would in effect be using L&NWR capital expenditure at Stafford to steal L&NWR traffic to which Cawkwell replied: *That is so.* On re-examination Cawkwell said his greatest grievance was the GNR coming to Stafford without giving anything in return and openly said that he did not trust the GNR concluding by saying: *They will not stop at Stafford.* He was supported by the GWR's Grierson who repeated that it was wrong for the GNR to come to Stafford on the back of a smaller company. However, all this opposition was to no avail.

The audacity of Oakley's straightforward answers won the day and after a minor technical hiccough, Lord Airlie stated that the Committee was of the opinion that the Bill should proceed. It is just as well it did for it was very much a last ditch resort for the impoverished S&UR which simply could not have survived without the GNR's support. However, throughout the goings on in Parliament no one seems to have given any thought as to how the S&UR was going to secure adequate motive power to haul its trains beyond Uttoxeter. Clearly it was relying upon the GNR to take up this initiative with a new service of through trains.

Signalling

The Worcester based firm of McKenzie & Holland supplied the S&UR with signals and their patent junction locking apparatus. Apart from the junctions with the L&NWR at Stafford and the NSR at Bromshall, there was little need for signalling at the intermediate stations, especially when operating on the 'one engine in steam' principle. There were no telegraphic facilities or any provision for block working. However, it appears that signals were provided at some of the intermediate stations and operated from the station platforms. On 27 March 1873 the S&UR accounts record a payment of £162 3s 6d (£162.18) to the NSR for a *junction signal service* which must have referred to the facilities provided at Bromshall. Some five years later on 31 December 1878, the NSR Traffic & Finance Committee[113] agreed that an account for £624 13s 8d (£624.68) be rendered to the S&UR with a demand for immediate payment in respect of the renewal of signals at Bromshall Junction. The cost of the alteration had originally been estimated at £488[114] and so there was no doubt some reluctance to pay.

Train Services

As previously indicated the S&UR initially provided four intermediate stations between Stafford and Uttoxeter Bridge Street. These were Salt, Weston, Stowe and Grindley sited at 4¼, 5¾, 7½ and 10 miles from Stafford, respectively. Salt and Weston were described as *neat and substantial buildings.* However, no station masters were appointed for the intermediate stations, tickets for those stations being issued by a clerk who travelled with the train. Weston was renamed Ingestre for Weston in December 1869 and Stowe was renamed Chartley and Stowe with effect from 3 October 1874. All these stations were served by passenger trains and they had siding accommodation for goods traffic. A new station at Stafford Common was opened on 1 July 1874 to serve the north end of the town which was steadily expanding in that direction. The station was provided with a goods yard

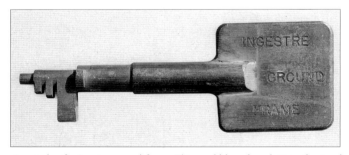

Single line electric token for the section Ingestre to Stafford Common that was in use until the line closed. The second illustration shows the instrument in one of the leather pouches that would have been used to ease its collection and delivery between signalmen and engine crews. RICHARD DEMPSTER

Block instrument from Venables signal box for communication over the double track section from that box to Stafford Common.
RICHARD DEMPSTER

Annetts key for Ingestre ground frame. This would have been kept in the signal box, normally locked in the lever frame such that it could only be released to be used to unlock the ground frame, provided no other signals were cleared that would have allowed conflicting moves. RICHARD DEMPSTER

Les Davis (Big Les), was conductor guard on that last train to traverse the S&UR – the SLS Special on 23 March 1957. By that time he was one of but a few who knew the complete route. Here he is on 23 March 2011, sitting outside his cottage in Hopton Heath, just outside Stafford and very near the route of the old railway. Les holds the Ingestre to Stafford Common single line electric token complete with a pouch.

which was also expanded and became increasingly important. It was equipped with a weighbridge, goods shed, transhipment shed and a five ton capacity crane. Stafford Common became the S&UR's headquarters thus reducing its dependence on the facilities provided by the L&NWR at Stafford.

The initial service provided for three trains a day on weekdays in each direction. Departures from Uttoxeter were at 9am, 2pm and 5pm, the corresponding return trains leaving Stafford at 10.15am, 4pm and 6.30pm. On Sundays a train left Uttoxeter at 10am returning from Stafford at 5pm. Journey time was about 45 minutes. This pattern of working seems to indicate that the S&UR locomotive working the service was stabled overnight at the NSR's locomotive shed at Pinfold, Uttoxeter. From April 1868, the first departure was changed to Stafford with trains

leaving at 7.45am, 11.23am, 4.25pm and 6.40pm with return workings from Uttoxeter at 9am, 2.30pm, 5.15pm and 7.40pm. Extra trains at cheap fares were run on market days. Following a memorial from the Earl of Shrewsbury and Talbot and others, the NSR's Traffic and Finance Committee at its meeting held on 10 November 1868[115] resolved that the last train of the day from Stafford be allowed to run forward to Uttoxeter Junction station when it contained passengers for the Churnet Valley line. On Sundays trains left Stafford at 9.0am and 2.55pm, returning from Uttoxeter at 10.15am and 6.30pm. This pattern of working would require the S&UR's engine to be stabled overnight at the L&NWR shed at Stafford.

A detailed study of the weekday train service offered throughout 1869 has shown a basic frame work of five trains in each direction starting with the 7.45am from Stafford. That train ran throughout the year, however, between January and June, some of the trains ran on Wednesdays and Saturdays only and in August one of the trains ran on Thursdays only. There was a constant tinkering with the timing of some of the trains but by September 1869, there were only four trains in each direction. Throughout the year (excepting in April and May) the 11.25 from Stafford to Uttoxeter ran as an express running none stop or, from June onwards, calling only at Weston if required to take up passengers. This practice had commenced in May 1868 and the journey time allowed was 30 minutes. From August 1869 the 12.5pm from Uttoxeter was given similar status and advertised to complete the journey in 25 minutes. It was this timing that was much criticised by the Board of Trade inspector following the fatal accident at Hopton on 1 February 1873 (see below). A Sunday service of one train in each direction ran from August until October 1869 and a similar service operated the following year commencing in May.

Throughout 1875 five trains ran in each direction on weekdays and the practice of running the 11.25am train from Stafford as an express continued. However, following the Hopton accident, the corresponding return train now ran as a stopping train. In May 1875 two trains ran in each direction on Sundays but the experiment was not a success as the Sunday trains were withdrawn the following month. From June to November 1875 an additional up train ran from Chartley starting at 9.30am arriving at Stafford at 10am. In 1876 four trains ran in each direction between January and May, increasing to five between June and December. In some cases Chartley and Grindley were conditional stops. There was no Sunday service and we doubt that the S&UR as an independent concern ever reintroduced one. On 23 December 1878 the S&UR wrote to the NSR asking for accommodation at Uttoxeter Bridge Street station for booking clerks with a request for the through booking of passengers and the introduction of through carriages. The matter was discussed at the NSR Traffic & Finance Committee[116] meeting held on 31 December and the Secretary was instructed to reply. Unfortunately, the Committee's decision was not recorded. The pattern of running four or five trains on weekdays in each direction continued until the GNR acquired the line and we give below a typical example for the months of June to September 1880.

	am	am	pm	pm	pm
Stafford	8.00	11.23	1.50	4.30	6.45
Stafford Common	8.05			4.35	6.50
Salt	8.15		2.02	4.46	7.02
Ingestre for Weston	8.21	11.35	2.07	4.51	7.07
Chartley	8.25		2.12	4.56	7.12
Grindley	8.33			5.03	
Uttoxeter	8.45	11.50	2.25	5.15	7.25

	am	pm	pm	pm	pm
Uttoxeter	9.35	12.05	2.50	5.30	7.35
Grindley	9.50		3.02	5.42	
Chartley	9.58	12.19	3.08	5.48	8.00
Ingestre for Weston	10.05	12.24	3.14	5.53	8.05
Salt	10.11	12.29	3.19	5.58	8.10
Stafford Common	10.22		3.28	6.08	8.20
Stafford	10.30	12.40	3.35	6.15	8.25

Excursions

In addition to the scheduled passenger services we know that there were frequent excursion trains especially during the summer months. For example, on Tuesday, 2 June 1868 there was a day excursion to Alton Towers and Rudyard Lake on the NSR's Churnet Valley Line. The train departed from Stafford at 7.45am, Salt at 8.00am, Ingestre at 8.05am, Stowe at 8.10am and Grindley at 8.18am. The return train left Rudyard at 7.30pm and Alton Towers at 8.00pm arriving back at Stafford at 9.30pm. No luggage was allowed! Presumably this excursion was operated either by the L&NWR or NSR. Alton Towers and Rudyard were very popular destinations for excursionists from the West Midlands.

On Wednesday, 30 July 1879 a special train left Stafford for Salt conveying 83 inmates, including 54 children, from the Stafford Workhouse together with at least 180 visitors, including the mayor, for a picnic at Sandon Park through the courtesy of the Earl of Harrowby who had made his facilities available to the promoters of this annual event. A bountiful supply of tea, plum cake and sandwiches was available together with a distribution of tobacco and snuff to the males and packets of tea and sugar to the females. For the non-smokers and children a quantity of handsome neckties was provided. A contemporary report advised that the infirm inmates and imbeciles were left behind at the workhouse. A similar excursion took place the following year on Wednesday, 23 June 1880. On Tuesday, 13 July 1880 a special train conveyed a party of scholars from the Christ Church Sunday Schools to Ingestre for their annual festival, Lady Shrewsbury having made available the use of the Ingestre deer park for the day.

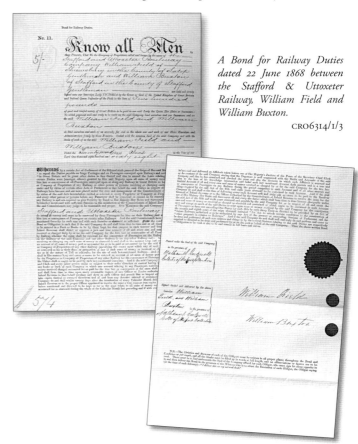

A Bond for Railway Duties dated 22 June 1868 between the Stafford & Uttoxeter Railway, William Field and William Buxton.

CRO6314/1/3

Passenger Traffic

On 22 June 1868 the company's common seal was applied to a Bond in connection with the payment of railway duties on passenger carryings to the Commissioners of Inland Revenue. William Field, Contractor and William Buxton, Director acted as sureties in the sum of £200 and also applied their seals in the presence of Nathaniel Cresswell, Collector of Inland Revenue, Stafford.[117] The fact that sureties were required was undoubtedly an indicator of the company's dire financial position.

An insight into passenger carryings during 1868 can be gleaned from NSR records which reveal that during January that year passenger bookings for the S&UR at Uttoxeter Bridge Street station totalled 826, producing revenue of £55 19s 2d (£55.96p). By June this had increased to £91 4s 10½d (£91.24p). From the Board of Trade returns we have extracted the following information covering the miles travelled by passenger trains and the number of passengers carried between 1872 and 1880.

	1872	1873	1874	1875	1876	1877	1879	1880
Miles travelled	44,790	46,500	46,800	40,430	39,885	38,462	37,560	39,340
Passengers conveyed:								
1st class	4,692	4,285	4,212	5,311	3,749	3,037	3,423	4,720
2nd class	8,111	6,970	6,145	8,240	5,155	5,207	5,111	5,388
3rd class	58,395	52,393	57,024	62,114	63,173	58,679	62,004	77,366
Total	71,198	63,648	67,381	75,665	72,077	66,923	70,538	87,474

The number of season ticket holders, not included in the above figures, was miniscule: five in 1872, four in 1873, two in 1875, four in 1879, nine in 1880 and nil in the other years covered.

Goods and Mineral Traffic

From the same source the following information is applicable to goods and mineral traffic.

	1872	1873	1874	1875	1876	1877	1879	1880
Miles travelled	nil	nil	nil	540	6,753	6,759	9,390	9,360
Tons conveyed:								
Minerals	330	nil	5,970	5,235	5,205	5,841	4,004	5,268
General merchandise	751	2,061	2,852	3,752	6,179	6,781	4,815	7,646
Total	1,081	2,061	8,822	8,987	11,384	12,622	8,819	12,914

From these statistics we can perhaps deduce that until 1875 whatever goods and mineral traffic on offer was conveyed by the scheduled passenger trains which on those occasions became mixed trains. The NSR working time table for November 1879 records a S&UR mixed train working on Saturdays only between Bromshall Junction and Uttoxeter Bridge Street leaving the junction at 8.25pm and arriving at Uttoxeter at 8.30pm. From this timetable we can deduce that on weekdays a S&UR goods train ran in each direction being the last train of the day to travel the branch. It left Bromshall Junction at 8.55pm, arriving at Uttoxeter Bridge Street at 9.5pm. It returned from there at 9.30pm passing Bromshall Junction at 9.38pm on its return to Stafford. The carriage of so little mineral traffic over the S&UR must have been extremely disappointing, in fact, in terms of receipts it was always surpassed by the general merchandise traffic. The mineral traffic that was carried during this period was from the Weston Salt Works which was rail connected to the S&UR in 1873. A bill for £524 4s 6d

(£524.23) was presented in July of that year by Edward Cory for the new rails for the siding. It was left to the GNR to take advantage of the salt traffic from the deposits at Stafford Common and the traffic to and from Stafford gas works as these developments took place after the S&UR was sold – see Chapter Seven. However, the general merchandise figures above did include live stock which was carried in all the years under review but again it proved to be but a shadow of what had been predicted.

Railway Clearing House

The S&UR had a somewhat chequered relationship with the Railway Clearing House (RCH). This body was formed in January 1842, when it became apparent with the burgeoning expansion of railways in this country that some form of through booking was required and if so, a method of apportioning costs between respective owning companies over whose lines the traffic passed. This was the case for all forms of traffic and not just passengers. Indeed, by far the bulk of its work was associated with non passenger traffic.[118] Despite being a company run by the railway companies for railway companies, membership was optional and of course, came at a cost.[119] However, for those railways that were not members, unless they had local arrangements with adjacent railways, there was no method by which they could book either passengers or merchandise to other parts of the country, or equally, receive them. In these situations, passengers and consignees of merchandise would have had to make their own arrangements at terminal points of non-member railways, for onward movement. Likewise, for traffic arriving at terminal points from railways that were members, local arrangements would also have to be made for onward movement. Obviously, all the larger companies were members, as indeed were the vast majority of the smaller ones. There were, however, some that were not, while several others, like the S&UR, found the financial burdens of membership not always commensurate with income gained from through traffic, not to mention individual cash flow problems! Some companies flirted in and out of membership, presumably under varying management appointments and assessments of income and expenditure on through traffic. Membership was by application and there was a vetting process to ensure budding applicants had the financial wherewithal to manage the process and pay their dues. All member companies were entitled to send representatives to the committee meetings although, apart from the larger ones, few did. By and large the running of the organisation was left to the officers, appointed from the member companies, along with the permanent staff. By 1900 there were over 2,000 employed.

Membership by the S&UR was first discussed at the committee meeting on 10 June 1868 when, in accordance with established practice, it was referred to the superintending committee. This was the vetting process. The application must have been considered appropriate as at the next committee meeting on 9 September 1868, it was agreed to admit the S&UR as members on the recommendation of the superintending committee. Between joining and acquisition by the GNR in 1881, the S&UR was only represented at committee meetings on three occasions, 11 June and 10 September 1879, along with 10 March the following year; in each case the representative was Henry Cecil Newton. At that time the company was in receivership and his attendance was doubtless due to problems the S&UR was having in paying its dues. At the 12 June 1878 meeting it was minuted that the S&UR was in arrears to the tune of £868 10s 4d (£868.52p) and that unless this was paid within seven days of the meeting, the secretary was authorised to take the necessary legal proceedings to recover the money. Similarly, on 11 September the same year a figure of £163 15s 4d (£163.77p) was owing and on this occasion, a calendar month was allowed for payment prior to legal proceedings. Lastly, on 9 March 1881, there was a sum of £317 outstanding with 14 days being allowed to pay. This money would almost certainly be in respect of cash received by the S&UR for through passengers and merchandise, doubtless more of the latter, which had started with journeys over the S&UR. In such cases while the S&UR would have received the total carriage costs, as some of the distance travelled would have been on different railway systems, other companies would have been entitled to a proportion of the money and it was the job of the RCH to make the appropriations.

We are left to conclude that on all the occasions mentioned above, the money owing was paid and it may have been to placate the committee that the S&UR felt motivated to send Newton to some of the meetings. In May 1879 the NSR Traffic and Finance Committee was under the impression that the S&UR had ceased membership of the RCH as it had previously stopped the through booking of passengers to the S&UR and proposed that they should only be resumed when the S&UR was re-admitted to the RCH.[120] Our researches have proved that this was wrong but the committee members would have known that there were outstanding financial issues between the two parties. The RCH committee minutes are quite perfunctory, only noting resolutions passed, so we are left wondering what was actually said in what were doubtless, lively discussions. At the 14 September 1881 committee meeting the S&UR gave notice of its intention to withdraw from membership, with one month's notice, which was accepted, subject to any remaining liabilities. The liabilities included an obligation under a 9 March 1881 binding agreement on all members, to spend £25,000 on office extensions, although the S&UR's contribution is not mentioned. However, to give an idea of scale, when in September 1874 it was agreed to spend no less than £250,000 on building extensions, the S&UR contribution was but £30, as compared with, for example, the NSR figure of £1,652. What the outcome of this September 1881 resolution was has gone unrecorded, but as at that time the S&UR was being taken over by the GNR, it is rather academic. The GNR was, of course, a RCH member and had been for all its existence.[121]

Finances

Appendices Five and Six show the company's capital, revenue and expenditure situation for the years 1872 to 1880. An initial glance will reveal that the S&UR was a financial disaster; it never paid a dividend to its shareholders and only produced a tiny profit in the year 1872. There were two fundamental reasons for this: first, the cost of constructing the railway was under-estimated and so the return on capital expended never met projections; secondly, the traffic forecasts were too optimistic.

The Stafford and Uttoxeter Railway Act 1862, provided for the

capital of the company to be £130,000 divided into 13,000 shares of £10 each and permitted the company to borrow on mortgage up to £43,300, but not until the entire share capital had been subscribed. By 1865 it had become apparent that it would be necessary to raise further capital in order to complete the railway and this was done by means of the Stafford and Uttoxeter Railway Act 1865[122] which received the Royal Assent on 26 May 1865. This Act authorised the company to raise an additional £50,000 by the creation of new ordinary shares and to borrow an additional sum on mortgage up to £16,600. Within months of the line opening to traffic there was further trouble. On 2 May 1868 by an Order of the Court of Chancery, Robert Daniel Newill, the Company Secretary was appointed manager and receiver of the general undertaking of the company. From that point onwards the company remained in receivership throughout its independent existence.

Interestingly, the petition brought before the Court of Chancery that resulted in receivership was by George Harrison (1815-1875) and Thomas Brassey.[123] George Harrison was a civil engineer and brother-in-law both to Thomas Brassey and William Field. His early career was spent in France where he was Locomotive Superintendent of the Paris & Rouen Railway which opened in 1843; he then became Locomotive Carriage and Wagon Superintendent of the Orleans & Bordeaux Railway before the revolution of 1848 compelled him to return to England. He was then appointed Locomotive Superintendent of the Scottish Central Railway whose line from Perth to Lambert had opened that year. In 1853 he was approached by Brassey with reference to the construction of locomotives for the Grand Trunk Railway in Canada following which he visited that country. His report resulted in establishing the Canada Works at Birkenhead which constructed not only locomotives but also wrought iron bridges, including the Victoria Bridge over the St. Lawrence River at Montreal. It is this work for which he is most famous, but he clearly also had the time to become involved with the S&UR and many other railway projects both at home and abroad.

The fundamental problem of the sad state of affairs on the S&UR was that the company could not pay the contractor, William Field and other creditors, monies due to them. There were insufficient funds from which to make the payments. Debentures had been issued to the contractor for the full sum of £59,900 authorised to be borrowed under the 1862 and 1865 Acts with interest set at 5% per annum and £56,300 was overdue. Moreover, during the course of the company's contracts with William Field, certificates of indebtedness had been issued to him in the form of Lloyd's bonds for sums amounting to £70,000 which, with unpaid interest, amounted to £85,364. By agreement, this sum had been fixed at £72,580 as at 31 December 1869 with interest accruing thereafter at 5% per annum. Of the 13,000 shares into which the capital authorised by the 1862 Act was divided, 5,869 shares were registered in the name of William Field. Of these shares 1,200 were fully paid up, the remainder having £8 per share outstanding. The entire share capital authorised by the 1865 Act had also been issued to the contractor in 5,000 shares of £10 each with £5 per share paid up. Between 1864 and 1872 four Bills of Complaint were filed in Chancery all concerning

IN THE MATTER OF
"THE RAILWAYS COMPANIES ACT, 1867,"
AND
IN THE MATTER OF
THE STAFFORD AND UTTOXETER RAILWAY COMPANY.

SCHEME OF ARRANGEMENT.
(Confirmed by an Order made by his Honour the Vice-Chancellor Sir James Bacon, on the 16th day of July, 1872, and enrolled in the High Court of Chancery on the 6th day of November, 1872.)

SHARP & ULLITHORNE,
Gray's Inn,
Agents for
R. D. NEWILL,
Wellington, Salop,
Solicitor for the
Stafford and Uttoxeter Railway Company.

IN THE MATTER OF "THE RAILWAYS COMPANIES ACT, 1867,"
AND
IN THE MATTER OF THE STAFFORD AND UTTOXETER RAILWAY COMPANY.

SCHEME OF ARRANGEMENT

BETWEEN

THE STAFFORD AND UTTOXETER RAILWAY COMPANY
(HEREINAFTER REFERRED TO AS "THE COMPANY")
AND THEIR CREDITORS,

PREPARED BY THE DIRECTORS UNDER THE RAILWAYS COMPANIES ACT, 1867.

Confirmed by an Order made by his Honour the Vice-Chancellor Sir James Bacon, on the 16th day of July, 1872, and enrolled in the High Court of Chancery, on the 6th day of November, 1872.

WHEREAS the Company were incorporated by "The Stafford and Uttoxeter Railway Act 1862" (hereinafter referred to as "the Act of 1862") as the Stafford and Uttoxeter Railway Company, for the purpose of making and maintaining the Railway and works following, with all proper approaches, stations, works, and conveniences connected therewith (that is to say) :

1. A Railway commencing by a junction with the London and North Western Railway at or near the junction of the Shropshire Union Railway with that Railway near Stafford, and terminating by a junction with the North Staffordshire Railway, about two miles west of Uttoxeter, all in the county of Stafford :

2. A branch Railway commencing by a junction with the said Railway No. 1 in the parish of Stowe, and terminating by a junction with the Colwich branch of the North Staffordshire Railway about 1,500 yards south of the Western station on that Railway, all in the county of Stafford :

And it was thereby provided (Sections 5 and 6) that the capital of the Company should be £130,000 divided into 13,000 shares of £10 each, and (Section 8) that the Company might borrow on mortgage any sums not exceeding in the whole £43,300 :

And whereas by "The Stafford and Uttoxeter Railway Act, 1865" (hereinafter referred to as "the Act of 1865") the Company were authorised (Section 3) to raise additional capital to the amount of £50,000 by the creation of new ordinary shares to form part of the general capital of the Company, and (Section 5) to borrow on mortgage any additional sum of money not exceeding £16,600 ; and it was enacted (Section 6) that all mortgages granted by the Company before the passing of that Act, and which should be subsisting at the time of the passing thereof should during the continuance of such mortgages have priority over any mortgages to be created by virtue of that Act :

And whereas the Railway and works of the Company have to a certain extent been constructed by William Field, as their contractor, under the provisions of two Deeds of Contract dated respectively 17th June, 1864, and the 28th May, 1866, and by virtue of those contracts and arrangements from time to time made between the said William Field and the directors of the Company there have been issued to the said William Field, or to other persons by his direction, mortgages in the form provided by "The Companies Clauses Consolidation Act 1845" (which mortgages are hereinafter referred to as debentures), for the full sum of £59,900, authorised to be borrowed by the said Acts of 1862 and 1865, with interest at the rate of 5 per cent. per annum, and £56,300 of the said debentures are now overdue and unpaid, and there is also due to the holders thereof in arrear of interest on the principal sums secured thereby ;

And whereas from time to time during the progress of the works comprised in the said contracts there have been issued to the said William Field certificates of indebtedness under the common seal of the Company, in the form generally known as Lloyd's Bonds, for sums amounting in the whole to £70,000, and the interest in arrear on this sum, computed according to the terms of the bonds,

---

amounted on the 31st day of December 1869 to £15,363 14s., and it has been agreed between the holders of these bonds and the Company that the total claim against the Company thereunder, both for principal and interest, shall be fixed at £72,580 as on the 31st day of December, 1869, and that interest shall accrue on the said sum of £72,580, as from that date at the rate of £5 per cent. per annum.

And whereas the present position of the Company as regards its share-capital is as follows : The whole of the share-capital of £130,000 authorised by the Act of 1862 has been created and issued, and, out of the 13,000 shares into which such capital was by the same Act divided, 5,869 shares stand registered in the name of the said William Field, of which 1,200 are registered as fully paid up, and the others as having £2 per share only paid thereon. The residue of the shares in the said capital stand registered in the names of persons other than the said William Field, and with the exception of 678 shares have been fully paid up. Sums varying from £1 to £8 per share have been paid up on the said shares, and £5,380 now remains due with respect to them. The entire share capital of £50,000 authorised by the Act of 1865 has been issued to and stands registered in the name of the said William Field, in 5,000 shares of £10 each, with £5 per share paid up thereon :

And whereas by an Order of the Court of Chancery, dated the 2nd May, 1868, made by the Vice-Chancellor Sir George Markham Giffard, on the Petition of a Judgment Creditor of the Company, Robert Daniel Newill, the Secretary of the Company, was appointed manager and receiver of the general undertaking of the Company, as defined and referred to in the Act of 1862 and the Act of 1865, and the works and property comprised therein or connected therewith and to receive the tolls and sums of money arising upon or out of the said general undertaking, and inquiries were directed for the purpose of ascertaining what were the debts of the Company, and the incumbrances or charges on the undertaking, and the rights and priorities of the persons interested therein :

And whereas the income of the Company, since the said appointment of a receiver, owing to the imperfect equipment of the line, has not been sufficient to meet the expenses by the said Order directed to be paid thereout, and the several other payments which have been sanctioned by the Court, and it is anticipated that when the receiver passes his final accounts, and is discharged, which is intended to be done forthwith, there will be a balance due to him : and he has incurred liabilities in respect of the undertaking, against which he is entitled to be indemnified.

And whereas the Company are indebted to several persons, firms, and companies other than and besides the holders of the said debentures and Lloyd's Bonds in a sum amounting to £18,000 or thereabouts, due to owners of land purchased and taken by the Company for purchase-money, compensation, interest, and costs and to the local solicitor of the Company for his costs in connection with land purchased and taken by the Company, for principal, interest and costs on account of claims for compensation for land injuriously affected by the Railway and works of the Company, and in a sum amounting to £5000 for debts incurred by the Company in the ordinary course of business, making a total sum of £23,000 :

And whereas the Company are unable to meet their engagements with their creditors :

Therefore this Scheme of Arrangement has been prepared pursuant to the provisions of "The Railway Companies Act 1867," and is intended to be submitted to the Court of Chancery for confirmation according to the same Act.

Article 1. The Company may create and issue a Capital Stock, to be called Debenture Stock A, bearing interest at the rate of £5 per cent. per annum and of such a nominal amount as shall be required for the following purposes, that is to say : first, to satisfy the balance found due to the receiver on passing his final account, as also all liabilities properly incurred by him and not discharged at the time of passing such account, and all moneys advanced by the London Financial Association, Limited, for working and keeping open the line, and paying vendors of land, and costs of litigation with vendors, together with interest thereon ; secondly, all claims, whether for principal or interest, against the Company for purchase-

---

money and compensation for land purchased and taken by the Company, and the costs incurred by vendors or by the Company in connection with purchasing and taking land ; thirdly, to pay the costs of and incidental to the said Order of the 2nd May, 1868, and the proceedings thereunder, and of, and incidental to, the preparation of this scheme, and the confirmation thereof ; and all costs incurred by and due from the Company up to the date of such confirmation ; and, fourthly, to provide funds for the erection of stations and sidings, the purchase of rolling stock, and the general repair and equipment of the line. The Debenture Stock A issued under the authority of this Article, and the cash received by means of the issue thereof, shall be applied exclusively to the purposes in this Article mentioned, and the interest on such stock shall be payable in priority to the interest upon stock issued under Articles 3 and 4.

Article 2. It shall be lawful for the Company to agree with the vendor of any land purchased by them for the grant to him of an annuity or rent-charge charged on the tolls and rates of the Railway, in lieu of payment of the amount due to him for purchase-money and compensation, interest, and costs, or any portion thereof, and to grant such rent-charge accordingly, and such rent-charge shall be payable *pari passu* on the Debenture Stock A, issued under Article 1, and shall have priority over the interest payable on that issued under Articles 3 and 4.

Article 3. The Debentures issued by the Company under the said Act of 1862 prior to the passing of the Act of 1865, shall, as from the 1st January, 1872, be converted into a Capital Stock to be called Debenture Stock B, bearing interest at the rate of 5 per cent. per annum, and the Company shall on that day issue to holders of such debentures, and they shall be entitled and bound to receive in exchange for their debentures, Debenture Stock B, of a nominal value equal to the aggregate sum of the principal moneys secured by their respective debentures, and the interest in arrear thereon according to the terms of such debentures calculated up to the 31st December, 1871, inclusive, and such

The 1872 Scheme of Arrangement between the Stafford & Uttoxeter Railway Company and its creditors.

NA RAIL 1007/583

alleged irregularities in taking land for the railway and the non payment of sums owed and interest. The landowners concerned with the dates when their complaints were filed were: Humphrey Downes Lawrence of Lees Hill (7 June 1864),[124] William Lycett of Marston Villa, Stafford (13 January 1870),[125] Earl Ferrers (13 March 1871)[126] and the Earl of Shrewsbury (6 June 1872).[127] The way out of this mess was enshrined in a Scheme of Arrangement between the S&UR and its creditors. The scheme was confirmed on 16 July 1872 and enrolled in the Court of Chancery on 6 November 1872.[128] It provided for a capital restructuring by the creation of debenture and preference stocks so enabling the company to:

1. Satisfy the balance due to the Receiver on passing his final account and all monies advanced by the London Financial Association Ltd for keeping open and working the line.

2. Settle all claims against the company for purchase money and compensation for lands taken by the company with associated costs.

3. Settle costs associated with and incidental to the Order dated 2 May 1868 appointing Robert Daniel Newill as Receiver and Manager.

4. Provide funds for the erection of stations and sidings, the purchase of rolling stock and the general repair and equipment of the line.

On 13 July 1878 an official receiver, Henry Cecil Newton, was appointed for the second time. He inherited a deficit of about £7,000 and discovered that gross receipts were averaging from £8 to £9 per mile per week which fell far short of meeting working expenses. The S&UR was to remain in receivership until purchased by the GNR two years later for £100,000 *free and discharged from pecuniary liabilities*. In June 1880 the NSR's Secretary was instructed to decline the S&UR's offer to settle the debt owing to the NSR in debenture stock.[129]

With regard to revenue and expenditure the sums showing receipts and costs in Appendix Six well illustrate the company's misfortune: except in the year 1872, the receipts simply did not cover the outgoings. There are one or two items of particular interest. For example in 1873 there is a huge increase in miscellaneous working expenditure from £100 in the previous year to £1,100. This undoubtedly covers the purchase of the second locomotive which was not charged to capital. In 1874 there is a sum of £230 for compensation for personal injury, this being an outcome of the accident at Hopton the previous year. The increased expenditure on locomotive power in 1876 probably indicates a major overhaul of one of the locomotives. Insofar as passenger fares are concerned it is interesting to note the fare structure which in August 1875 was as follows for journeys from Stafford:

Destination	1st Class		3rd Class	
Salt	8d	(3p)	4d	(2p)
Ingestre for Weston	1s 0d	(5p)	5½d	(2p)
Chartley	1s 3d	(6p)	9½d	(4p)
Grindley	1s 8d	(8p)	10d	(4p)
Uttoxeter	2s 6d	(12.5p)	1s 3d	(6p)

The fares to Uttoxeter had not altered since 1869. In an endeavour to encourage more traffic the third class fares were reduced in December 1875 as follows: Salt 2d (1p), Ingestre for Weston 5d (2p), Chartley 7d (3p), Grindley 9d (4p). The fare to Uttoxeter remained the same but a 1st Class day return could be purchased for 3s 9d (19p). The change made no difference to the S&UR's fortunes; passenger carryings actually reduced in 1876 and total passenger receipts were down on the previous year. From January 1880 the fare structure from Stafford was as follows:

Destination	1st Class	2nd Class	3rd Class
Stafford Common	4d (2p)	3d (1p)	2d (1p)
Salt	8d (3p)	6d (2.5p)	4d (2p)
Ingestre for Weston	1s 0d (5p)	9d (4p)	5d (2p)
Chartley	1s 3d (6p)	1s 0d (5p)	7d (3p)
Grindley	1s 8d (8p)	1s 3d (6p)	10d (4p)
Uttoxeter	2s 0d (10p)	1s 6d (7.5p)	1s 0d (5p)

with the following fares applying from Uttoxeter:

Destination	1st Class	2nd Class	3rd Class
Grindley	10d (4p)	7½d (3p)	5d (2p)
Chartley	1s 3d (6p)	1s 0d (5p)	7½d (3p)
Ingestre for Weston	1s 7d (8p)	1s 2½d (6p)	9½d (4p)
Salt	1s 10d (9p)	1s 4½d (7p)	11d (5p)
Stafford Common	2s 0d (10p)	1s 6d (7.5p)	1s 0d (5p)
Stafford	2s 0d (10p)	1s 6d (7.5p)	1s 0d (5p)

The 1880 exercise was obviously geared to improve passenger carryings prior to acquisition of the railway by the GNR and that it certainly did as the number of passengers using the railway increased from 70,538 in 1879 to 87,474 which was the highest number ever carried by the independent company. However, receipts from passenger traffic reduced from £2,414 to £2,373 which made the exercise somewhat futile.

The sets of accounts prepared by the two official Receivers and Managers are summarised in Appendix Four. They cover the period from 2 May 1868 to 15 November 1881 and paint an overall picture very similar to that portrayed in the returns made to the BoT. Straight comparisons are not possible because the accounting periods adopted stem from the dates the Receivers and Managers were appointed rather than follow calendar years. The sums shown have been rounded to the nearest pound. Robert Daniel Newill was appointed Receiver and Manager on 2 May 1868, his successor, Henry Cecil Newton, was appointed on 4 February 1879.

Accident at Hopton – 1 February 1873

During the S&UR's independent existence there were two serious accidents both requiring investigation by Board of Trade inspectors. The first occurred on Saturday, 1 February 1873 at Hopton. The *Birmingham Daily Post* reported the accident the following Monday under the following heading: *FATAL ACCIDENT ON THE STAFFORD AND UTTOXETER RAILWAY – THE DRIVER AND FIREMAN KILLED*. The report was prefaced with the following remarks: *Familiar as the public are with the oft-recurring story of railway accidents, surprise must yet be felt at the peculiar character of the disaster which happened near Stafford on Saturday. The 'new and direct route' from the West of England to Derby – as the Stafford and Uttoxeter Railway is styled – is a single line of rails between Stafford and Bramshall Junction, near Uttoxeter, and as there is but one engine and train at work upon the line, except during the excursion season, when the thousands of South Staffordshire pass over it to Alton Towers, a feeling of comparative safety is apt to be induced in the mind of the traveller between the two towns. No luggage trains before, nor expresses behind; no runaway trucks in front, nor treacherous sidings with open points through which the train could glide to swift ruin. Surely, here is no peril. Such might have been the reasoning of the passengers by the mid-day train from Uttoxeter to Stafford last Saturday.* The report went on to describe the accident, gave rather gory details of the injuries to the deceased enginemen and hinted at reckless driving.

The Board of Trade requested Captain Henry Whatley Tyler (1827-1908) to report on the accident which he did on 18 February 1873.[130] The following summary is largely based on his findings. He said the accident happened at Hopton bank when the 12.10pm train from Uttoxeter for Stafford left the rails while running at high speed about two miles from Stafford. The engine driver, John Powell (32), and the fireman, Andrew Richard Buxton (24) were both killed, a booking clerk and the guard were injured and six passengers had complained of injury.

Tyler went on to describe the line which he confirmed had been open since December 1867. He said it was laid with double-headed rails weighing 72lbs to the yard, fished at the joints, with suspended wrought-iron plates and four screw bolts and nuts to each joint. The chairs were of cast-iron and were of two types: heavier chairs, on either side of the joints and under the middles of the rails weighed 28lbs each while the other chairs, four in number under each rail, weighed 21½lbs each. The keys were partly of elm and partly of oak and were driven into the outside of the chairs. The rails were 21ft long and there were seven sleepers under each rail. The sleepers were partly half round and partly squared. Tyler explained that the sleepers were originally half round red Baltic, 9ft long by 10in by 5in in section. However, the sleepers in use at the time of the accident were either rectangular, 9ft long by 10in by 5in in section, or half round English larch of the same dimensions. The ballast was broken sandstone taken from a nearby cutting. There was a falling gradient of 1 in 70 for rather more than a mile from the direction of Uttoxeter up to and beyond the point of the accident and there was a curve of from 40 to 60 chains where the accident occurred. The curve was to the right in the direction of travel and the engine left the rails to the left or on the outside of the curve. The guard, Adam Roden, stated that he was looking to the front just before the accident when he saw the engine apparently give a sudden jump. He was then thrown down in his van and remembered nothing further until, on recovering himself, he found that his van had fallen on its side.

The train was hauled by *Shrewsbury and Talbot* and consisted of a L&NWR brake van occupied by the guard, a second class carriage, a first class carriage and two third class carriages. The marks found on the permanent way after the accident appeared to show that at a point 32 yards east of an occupation crossing to Mr. Sayers's farm, the flange of the left leading wheel of the engine mounted the outside rail of the curve and after running along the top of the rail for 29ft 7in dropped off on the outside of the rail. Further marks showed that the corresponding wheel on the off side had derailed 20ft beyond this point and the coupled wheels of the engine appeared to have left the rails very shortly afterwards. The two rails on the near side, between the above point and the occupation crossing, were more or less bent and bulged outward between the joints, eight chairs under those rails being fractured and four sleepers damaged. At 56 yards from the point at which the near leading wheel first mounted a rail, the off wheels of the engine crossed another rail on the near side and the steel tyres of the engine made severe indentations in that rail in so doing. There were three distinct marks showing the rail was struck by the off leading wheel, the off middle wheel and the off trailing wheel, respectively. Having got clear of both rails, the engine ran off at an angle of about twenty degrees towards the left for a distance of about 30 yards until it partly embedded itself in the slope of the cutting, leaning over on its right side as it did so. The dirt was thrown up from the slope of the cutting into a field beyond with so much force as to break through the post and rail fence. The engine then turned over and lay finally on its left side in an oblique position across the space left for a second line of rails with the detached chimney to the front. In the words of the *Birmingham Daily Post* it *lay like a crippled gladiator.*

The brake van and part of the second class carriage became uncoupled and had almost overtaken the engine before it fell over smashing the last two compartments of the carriage to pieces. The brake van turned over and came to rest on the slope of the cutting. The two leading compartments of the first class carriage were destroyed as it hit the overturned locomotive but the next third class carriage remained upright although derailed. The last carriage remained on the rails.

Tyler proceeded to describe the locomotive quoting its leading dimensions as we have previously described and mentioning the engine's return to Beyer Peacock in 1870 and 1872 for repairs. In his description there were two minor discrepancies: the diameter of the wheels was ½in less than the official specification which could be due to tyre wear or the recent fitting of new tyres and the distance between the middle and trailing wheels was given as 6ft 3¾in making a total wheelbase of 13ft 3¾in against the official figure of 13ft 4in. Maybe the official tape measure was more elastic!

Tyler went on to explain that the locomotive had six springs, the leading springs being above the framing and so placed as to bear upon the axle-boxes inside the leading wheels and the framing. The middle and trailing springs were also inside the wheels but below the axles and there were compensating bars between them. After the accident, the engine's regulator was found to be shut and the reversing lever was in middle gear. The buffer plank and one of the life guards was broken off. The locomotive was said to have run 170,000 miles throughout its history with 25,000 miles run since its last overhaul in August 1872.

Tyler then went into great detail about the springs. He said the leading and driving springs were original having been in use since 1868; the trailing springs were renewed in October or November 1872. He insisted that all springs were removed from the engine so that he could examine them plate by plate after the buckles had been removed. The leading springs were 31⅜in long and were composed of ten plates each 4in wide by ½in thick. The off leading spring was in perfect condition but the near leading spring had a piece 4¼in long broken off from the third plate which was an old fracture. The driving and trailing springs were 31¼in long and were composed of 15 plates, each 4in wide by ½in thick. The buckle of the off driving spring had shifted to the extent of ⅞in and that of the near driving spring by 1½in. In the off driving spring the 14th plate was cracked and the 15th plate was broken. Moreover, the 15th plate of the near driving spring was also broken. The trailing springs were both in perfect condition. The fractures exposed had occurred some time ago and were thus present at the time of the accident but Tyler concluded that they were not sufficient to account for the accident. He reported that the engine was generally in good order and emphasised that the tyres had been renewed in August 1872. He added that the leading brasses which he had removed from the axle boxes were wearing fairly and concluded that there was no defect apparent in the engine to cause the accident.

At the time of the accident the track was in a frozen and rigid condition and it had been so for about three days. The foreman ganger in charge of the length of track concerned stated that about a week before the accident he had repaired the line, picking up the joints and putting in six new sleepers between the point at which the engine first left the rails and where it then lay but he had not opened up the portion of line on the Uttoxeter side of where the

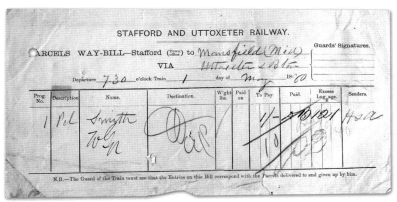

COLLECTION ARMAND CHATFIELD

engine left the rails for two or three months previously. He added that he had a good deal of trouble during the wet weather of the past winter in keeping the joints up at the site of the accident and had put ashes in from time to time to assist in keeping the ballast dry. The cant or super-elevation of the outer rail of the curve at the spot where the flange of the engine wheel first mounted the near rail was fractionally under 2½in and the line was stated to have been undisturbed at that spot since the accident although there had been a thaw. The gauge was a little tight.

Tyler then focused on the speed of the train. He said the train in question was timed to leave Uttoxeter at 12.10pm and to reach Stafford at 12.35pm thus allowing 25 minutes for 15 miles with a stop at Ingestre. He deduced that in order to keep to the timetable, the engine driver would have to run the 15 miles in 20 minutes allowing for the station stop and the checks for the junctions at Bromshall and Stafford. This would give an average running speed of 45mph but the driver would be unable to keep up this speed on the rising gradients, especially on 1 in 75 for three quarters of a mile in two places, thus requiring the driver to exceed 45mph on the falling gradients.

The General Manager, John Bucknall Cooper, explained that when this particular train left Uttoxeter on time it had in fact more time than was allowed in the timetable to catch the 12.42 train from Stafford to Shrewsbury and that there was half an hour in which to connect with the London train. When there were passengers for Shrewsbury he explained that the great object of the engine driver was to arrive in Stafford for the 12.42pm connection. The General Manager had supplied Tyler with a table showing the performance of the train in question during January 1873. It was annexed to Tyler's report and revealed the following information.

DATE January 1873	UTTOXETER Departure	STAFFORD Arrival	JOURNEY TIME In minutes
1	12.23	12.55	32
2	12.20	12.55	35
3	12.15	12.43	28
4	12.15	12.45	30
6	12.10	12.40	30
7	12.13	12.42	29
8	12.14	12.42	28
9	12.17	12.45	28
10	12.12	12.40	28
11	12.10	12.40	30
13	12.13	12.40	27
14	12.13	12.43	30
15	12.16	12.45	29
16	12.15	12.40	25
17	12.15	12.42	27
18	12.12	12.45	33
20	12.20	12.50	30
21	12.40	1.15	35
22	12.12	12.40	28
23	12.10	12.40	30
24	12.10	12.45	35
25	12.23	12.50	27
27	12.12	12.40	28
28	12.21	12.50	29
29	12.18	12.50	32
30	12.12	12.40	28
31	12.10	12.38	28

Obviously the train did not run on Sundays. Amazingly the train only left on time on five occasions and never arrived on time! If the Shrewsbury connection left on time it was missed on at least 16 occasions! Tyler concentrated on the running times the fastest of which, 25 minutes, was performed on only one occasion. He remarked that John Powell, the engine driver, *had been employed by the general manager of the Stafford and Uttoxeter line for about six years on that line and the Potteries line, and he had been running since August last* [i.e. August 1872] *with the same engine on the Uttoxeter line.* This comment maybe indicates that John Bucknall Cooper left the Potteries, Shrewsbury and North Wales Railway in August 1872 and brought John Powell with him. The 1871 census shows John Powell living with his wife, Elizabeth, and his three young sons at St. Julian, Shrewsbury where he was duly described on the return as railway engine driver. He was born at Crewe in 1840. Tyler comments that Powell was represented to have been a sober, intelligent man. However, he went on to say that the General Manager had warned Powell on the Wednesday previous to the accident to equalise his running – to run well up banks and to run steadily down the banks. The Inspector of the line, Charles Roden, had apparently also warned Powell on three previous occasions against running too fast down the banks. He went on to say that about a fortnight before the accident the engine driver, while smiling, said that the General Manager had given him the same warning. Roden said that he had explained to Powell that although 12.35pm was the time mentioned in the timetable, the object to be attained when the train left Uttoxeter at its proper time was to reach Stafford at 12.40pm so as to catch the 12.42pm train for Shrewsbury. Roden considered it to be the understanding that when the train was late starting from Uttoxeter, time should not be made up with a view to catching the Shrewsbury train.

Tyler was not entirely convinced by these explanations. Looking at all the circumstances he attributed the accident to imprudent speed down a gradient of 1 in 70 and round a curve at the bottom with a light tank engine at a time when the line may have been out of adjustment through frost. The frost, which was stated to have lasted for about three days, after much rain, would no doubt have caused not only rigidity but inequality of levels in the permanent way. A high rate of speed which under normal circumstances could have been accommodated with less risk led to the mounting of the near rail by the flange of the near leading wheel. The fact that the flange, after mounting, ran for nearly 30ft along the top of the rail before the wheel fell to the outside negates the idea of violent oscillation or disturbance of the engine in the first instance and was a further confirmation of the absence of any serious defect in the engine or in the permanent way. There appeared to have been just enough want of adjustment in the latter to admit of the engine wheel mounting the outer rail of the curve at the speed at which the engine was travelling and with the super-elevation of the outer rail which existed in the permanent way. He went on to say that it was possible and even probable that the accident might not have happened if the engine had been constructed with a little more weight on its leading wheels. However, he accepted that the engine, apart from one minor incident in Stafford yard, had not previously left the rails.

He finished his report by stating that it was apparent from the warnings given to the engine driver that the locomotive had been frequently driven at excessive speeds on falling gradients. The speed on the occasion of the accident may not have been greater than on previous occasions but the rails may have been a little more out of adjustment and the absence of more weight on the leading wheels would then have made just the difference as to whether the flange of the leading wheels would mount the outside curve of the rails or not. He then added that, in his opinion, an engine was not in the safest condition for running chimney foremost when there was a considerable preponderance of weight on the trailing as compared with the leading wheels. In other words if the S&UR had broken its undertaking always to run tank engines chimney foremost, it might have operated more safely! What a contradiction.

There was then a reprimand for the company. Tyler said he was compelled to observe that the system of advertising departure and arrival times in the public timetables which, if adhered to, would require excessive speed on certain parts of the line was, in spite of the warnings given, objectionable and unfair on the deceased engine driver. After the accident the 12.10pm from Uttoxeter was retimed to call at all stations covering the journey in 45 minutes. A Shrewsbury connection ceased to be advertised until August 1875 by which time the train departed from Uttoxeter at 12.15pm and was taking one hour for the journey to Stafford.

The accident was widely reported and the railway company suffered a lot of criticism from the media, including an unfair suggestion that the *Shrewsbury and Talbot* was *an old and used-up affair* – an accusation strongly and rightly refuted by the general manager. Hermann Jaeger, who had been employed by Beyer Peacock since 1861, had strongly defended his firm's product at the Coroner's inquest. The Coroner's jury was critical of the line been repaired immediately and at the delay in sending the Board of Trade Inspector to the scene of the accident through Captain Tyler having to attend a trial at Westminster.

Only one passenger was seriously injured, Dennison Waddington, a reporter on the staff of the *Staffordshire Sentinel*. He subsequently received a sum of £50 by way of compensation. The S&UR also paid out £165 compensation to a Colonel Fortesque who was travelling with his lady, her maid and valet even though they were able to leave for Shrewsbury during the evening following the accident. Like those in the Fortescue party, several other passengers suffered cuts and bruises and other compensation payments were made to a Mr. Brown, £65 15s 0d (£65.75) and Emanuel Noakes, £15 15s 0d (£15.75). Beyer Peacock rendered a bill for £400 17s 1d (£400.85) for repairs to the engine. The bill was entered into the S&UR accounts on 11 May 1874 and so the locomotive was clearly away for some considerable time.

Accident at Stafford – 16 November 1877

The second accident was less serious and fortunately did not involve any loss of life or injury. Nevertheless it did warrant the attention of the Board of Trade as it concerned the part derailment of a passenger train on the approach to Stafford station.[131] Colonel Yolland was sent to investigate. Readers will recall that it was Colonel Yolland who first inspected the S&UR in 1867 and refused to recommend its opening to the public unless remedial works were undertaken. His report into the Stafford accident is dated 4 December 1877, printed copies of which were sent to the S&UR and the L&NWR on 22 December 1877.

The accident happened to the 9.35am up passenger train from Uttoxeter to Stafford on 16 November 1877 when the tank engine hauling it and the leading wheels of a horse box behind the locomotive were derailed at facing points on the approach to Stafford station. Yolland described the precise location as the facing points at the commencement of the loop which was about 380 yards in length from the L&NWR junction. The train consisted of the horse box, three carriages and a brake van. The engine, which was running chimney leading, was completely derailed at the facing points running on for some 40 yards. The carriages and brake van remained on the track. The life guards and the rear buffer casting of the locomotive were knocked off and the coal bunker was stove in. The heel chair on the left side of the points was broken as were other chairs and one rail was bent and had to be replaced.

After describing the accident Yolland proceeded to explain the working of the facing points. He said that at the time the line was opened it was customary to weight the facing points at the end of loop lines and thus make them self-acting and lie open for the road on which the trains were to travel. Indicators were usually attached to the facing points to show engine drivers how the points were set and whether it was safe to pass over them. However, in this case, a low semaphore signal had been attached to the points. When the points were right for an up train to run on towards Stafford station this signal showed a white light at night and the semaphore arm fell entirely into a slot on the signal post. If the points were not quite close to the stock rail, the semaphore arm stood out from the post showing that the facing points were not properly closed or in a fit state for a train to pass safely over them.

Yolland interviewed the following staff: John Dickenson, engine driver, Samuel Hinton, fireman, Samuel Hodson, guard, James Kershaw, inspector of permanent way and John Henry Duffill, general manager. Dickenson, who had been in the service of the S&UR for about 18 months, said the low semaphore signal seemed to be all right but admitted that the arm was just visible and not lying in the socket of the post in which it was usually found. As he got closer to the points he could see that they were not quite half open. He then shut off steam and applied the brakes. Hinton, who had been a fireman for about six years but had only been in the employ of the S&UR for eight days, was entirely ignorant of the existence of the low signal. Hodson contradicted the driver and said the arm was not standing partly outside of the post. Both Hinton and Kershaw claimed there was a hard pebble near the facing points which could have been the reason for them not closing properly and although Duffill disagreed with this observation Yolland was shown such a pebble.

After ascertaining that the points had not been repaired or altered in any way since the accident, Yolland tested them in conjunction with the low semaphore signal. He said that no facing points could be better set than those at Stafford and that the right facing points could not be moved from the right stock rail until the bottom of the arm of the low semaphore signal was from 10 to 14 inches from the side of the signal post. He then had the pebble placed between the facing point and right stock rail. The bottom of the arm of the signal then stood 18 inches from the side of the signal post. He then arrived at the conclusion that the points were not properly closed at the time of the accident and that the accident was caused by the negligence of the driver not obeying the indication of the signal. He went on to say that it was likely that a pebble or stone was preventing the points from closing properly but that it was dislodged by the engine after which the points at once closed and enabled the latter part of the train to travel on the rails of the up loop line.

Yolland had not quite finished. He also observed that the recommendation he made about a L&NWR siding at Stafford when he had inspected the line during the summer of 1867 had not been complied with. As explained in Chapter Three, this siding crossed the incoming S&UR line at Stafford and joined the outgoing line. When Major Hutchinson re-inspected the line in September 1867 he observed that a point and a rail had been removed such that the siding was inoperable. Yolland now discovered that the point and rail previously taken out had been replaced and the siding was in use. His suggested alterations had been completely ignored! He told the Board of Trade who again drew the matter to the S&UR's attention. Whether any action was taken is unrecorded but the blatant disregard of a recommendation, especially one concerning the safety of operating the railway, must not have endeared the S&UR to Yolland or the Board of Trade.

An Extraordinary Story – 7 October 1879
The *Staffordshire Sentinel* ran a short feature with the above heading on the date shown which read as follows: *A goods train proceeding along the Stafford and Uttoxeter line, near the Common Station, one night last week, ran over a cow which suddenly came out from behind a bush by the side of the line and got upon the track just as the engine was getting to the spot. The cow was literally cut to pieces, but strange to state, the animal being very heavy in calf at the time, on the railway servants going back to the spot where the accident occurred found a newly born calf alive by the mangled remains of the cow. The calf was removed to the goods shed, where it was fed and is now doing well.* Such was life (and death) on the Stafford & Uttoxeter!

Accident at Stafford Common – 27 August 1880
A tragic fatal accident of a more serious kind occurred at Stafford Common on 27 August 1880 as evidenced by this report which was printed in *The Staffordshire Advertiser* for the following day. *Yesterday morning Jacob Godridge of Weston aged 45, a platelayer on the Stafford and Uttoxeter Railway, was killed while at work on the line. Shortly before 8 o'clock a train was shunting at the Common Station, Stafford. The deceased uncoupled a wagon next to the engine and as he stooped to get between the engine and the train the former caught him and carried him several yards. He was picked up and at once taken to the infirmary but died before he reached the institution. An inquest was held last evening before Mr. W. Morgan, Coroner, when a verdict of accidental death was returned.* Jacob Godridge was baptised on 11 December 1836 at Nuneaton in Warwickshire and so the newspaper report may have been a little inaccurate insofar as his age was concerned. He married Elizabeth Hudson in Nuneaton on 1 March 1857 and by 1871 they were living with their family in Weston. Jacob was described as a platelayer and so he must have joined the S&UR at an early date in its existence. They had four daughters and three sons, one of whom, John Godridge (1863-1947) was for many years the signalman at Weston on the NSR's Stoke to Colwich line.

Notes
98   This view was also expressed by G.A. Yeomans in *Great Northern to Burton and Stafford*, published privately in 1977.

99   Receiver and Manager's Accounts, NA C30/2545.

100 *The Stafford & Uttoxeter Railway*, P. Jones, Oakwood Press 1981.

101 NA RAIL 529/45 NLR Locomotive, Stores & Traffic Committee minute 1524, 4 June 1872.

102 NA RAIL 529/46 NLR Locomotive, Stores & Traffic Committee 1595, 1 October 1872.

103 NA C30/2545.

104 *The Chronicles of Boulton's Siding* by Alfred Rosling Bennett, Locomotive Publishing Company, 1927 and *British Locomotive Catalogue 1825-1923 Volume 2A* by Bertram Baxter, Moorland Publishing Company, 1978.

105 *Great Northern to Burton and Stafford* by G.A. Yeomans, private paper 1977.

106 These dates are out of kilter with the Receiver and Manager's accounts but the L&NWR may have been somewhat tardy in submitting its bills.

107 NA RAIL 532/19 NSR Traffic & Finance Committee minute 9051, 25 April 1876.

108 John Beeby Edmondson (1831-1887) was the inventor of the railway ticketing system using his patented presses to date the small cardboard tickets.

109 NA RAIL 1066/901, Minute 348 of evidence given in House of Lords on 14 July 1879.

110 42-45 Vic ch ccii.

111 HLRO HL/PB/5/45/13.

112 David Stanley William Ogilvy, 6th Earl of Airlie, 1856-1900.

113 NA RAIL 532/19 Traffic & Finance Committee minute 10237, 31 December 1878.

114 NA RAIL 532/19 Traffic & Finance Committee minute 10115, 13 August 1878.

115 NA 532/18 NSR Traffic & Finance Committee minute 6141, 10 November 1868.

116 NA RAIL 532/19 NSR Traffic & Finance Committee minute 10236, 31 December 1878.

117 CRO 6314/1/3.

118 In later years the RCH got involved in a number of other areas of railway working, including some technical issues - standards for private owner wagons for example.

119 Although the RCH came into existence in 1842 as described above, which allowed certain railway companies to exchange traffic, The Railway Clearing Act (13-14 Vic ch xxxiii) was not enacted until 25 June 1850. This Act conferred on the RCH statutory obligations for the apportionment of fees and charges for through traffic between member railway companies.

120 NA RAIL 532/19 NSR Traffic & Finance Committee minute 10361, 5 May 1879.

121 NA RAIL 1081/100; RAIL 1081/101.

122 28-29 Vic ch xlv.

123 NA C30/2545.

124 NA C16/216/L83.

125 NA C16/653/L3.

126 NA C16/712/F34.

127 NA C16/824/S160.

128 NA RAIL 1007/583.

129 NA RAIL 532/19 NSR Traffic & Finance Committee minute 10685, 1 June 1880.

130 NRM Board of Trade Accident Reports.

131 NRM Board of Trade Accident Reports.

CHAPTER SEVEN

Great Northern Railway 1881-1922

Acquisition of the S&UR

The GNR directors first seriously considered the purchase of the S&UR in 1880. At their meeting on 16 January that year they decided to defer exercising the company's newly acquired running powers over the S&UR until the directors had visited the line. At their meeting on 4 June a report was received from Richard Johnson, the GNR's Engineer. It explained that expenditure of about £40,000 would be required in order to bring the line up to the standard of modern requirements. At the same meeting it was resolved to make an offer of £80,000 to the S&UR for the outright purchase of the line in its present state. John Winterbotham Batten replied on behalf of the S&UR rejecting the offer but suggesting that the GNR purchase the line on the basis of £10,000 per mile. This equated to £127,500 for the 12¾ miles with an alternative proposal of £13,000 per mile, if the S&UR put the line in first rate order. By July Batten had backed down suggesting that if the GNR increased its offer to £103,000, the S&UR would accept. At their meeting on 6 August 1880

the GNR directors resolved that Henry Oakley be authorised to offer to purchase the S&UR for a sum not exceeding £100,000, subject to Parliamentary approval. The offer was quickly accepted in principle and no doubt the rather beleaguered S&UR directors breathed a sigh of relief that there was now a clear way out of receivership.[132] The purchase price did not include the rolling stock and other moveable assets which were subsequently valued at £1,449 15s 5d (£1,449.77½p) as follows: two locomotives – £800; furniture and stores at stations – £114 15s 7d (£114.78p); permanent way tools and scrap – £69 13s 9d (£69.69p); lamps – £14 7s 2d (£14.36p); blacksmith's tools – £71 18s 7d (£71.93p). There was also an interim arrangement whereby the GNR in return for a modest rental could gain immediate access to the line to update it with a guarantee that all such expenditure would be recovered if Parliamentary approval were not forthcoming. It is not known whether this arrangement was implemented. A Bill to secure the acquisition of the S&UR, amongst other matters, was deposited by the GNR in the 1880-1881 Parliamentary Session.

Down GNR train arriving at Stafford and signalled into what was known locally as the GNR bay platform, on the up side of the L&NWR main line. Originally S&UR trains in this direction were designated 'up' while after the GNR take-over, the designation was reversed. The locomotive is one of the Stirling 6ft 6in 2-4-0 tender engines number 868 built at Doncaster in 1892, rebuilt by Ivatt with a larger boiler in 1902 and scrapped in June 1925. Notice the coal piled up high on the tender – the crew was clearly not intended to need any at Stafford before the return journey! The photograph is undated but about 1920. The building on the left is the erecting shop of the locomotive builders and railway engineers W.G. Bagnall Ltd. L&GRP NO. 16607

Agreement dated 23 February 1881 between the S&UR and GNR   THE NATIONAL ARCHIVES RAIL 236/1133

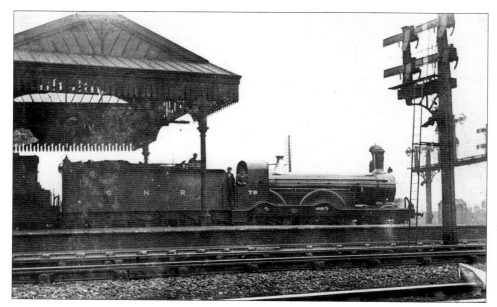

Another of the Stirling 2-4-0 tender engines at Stafford although in this case, in one of the L&NWR down platforms and not the GNR bay. The engine is number 78 of 1882 and not one of those rebuilt by Ivatt. As it was scrapped in December 1910, the photograph must have been taken some time earlier.

GNR enginemen caught by the camera while engaged in shunting at Stafford Common. Unfortunately, we do not have any identification of who they are.

In January 1881 concern was expressed that the L&NWR and Midland Railway might petition against the Bill and so it was agreed that Henry Oakley and the GNR Solicitor, Henry Nelson, should meet with representatives of both companies to ascertain what could be agreed to avoid any opposition. This they did by agreeing to grant running powers to the L&NWR over the S&UR and similar powers to the Midland Railway, but the latter were only to be effected if the line from Stafford to Bromshall Junction were doubled throughout, which never happened. Other concessions were made to these two companies in order to expedite the movement of their traffic routed via the S&UR.

The Bill was enacted on 18 July 1881 as the Great Northern Railway Act 1881,[133] and the GNR took possession of the S&UR on 1 August 1881. The Act provided for the GNR to pay £75,000 within three months of taking possession, with the balance of £25,000 payable on 1 August 1882. There was a minor setback when it was discovered that some of the land used by the S&UR had not been properly conveyed and so under a Memorandum of Agreement dated 1 November 1881, the GNR retained £6,000[134] of the purchase money until the title deeds to this land had been handed over. This final amount together with an interest payment of £425 14s 4d (£425.72p) was paid on 29 November 1883. The Act stipulated where all the purchase money was to be applied and specified the following pecking order: unpaid purchase money for land taken compulsorily; any balance due to the receivers; payments to holders of debenture stocks; payments to creditors; payments to holders of preference stocks; and, finally, the balance to be distributed to shareholders in proportion to their interest in the undertaking. The Act also stipulated that all minute books must be delivered to the GNR for preservation.[135]

As an amusing aside, it is interesting to note that late in 1879 the S&UR secretary approached the GNR requesting a pass for the Chairman, Gerald Francis Thomas Talbot, to travel over the line free of charge. Consideration was deferred by the directors in December 1879, reconsidered in June 1880 but deemed *undesirable* at that time and only to be conceded after the takeover in August 1881, along with passes for two other S&UR directors but for one year only.

Re-equipping the line
Richard Johnson was given the task of re-equipping the line. In order to put it in good condition he had previously estimated that expenditure amounting to £40,216 would be required. Separate estimates have survived for improvements to the stations at Stafford Common (£10,452), Salt (£805), Ingestre (£1,128), Chartley (£1,592) and Grindley (£954) and these are shown in Appendix Seven. We have assumed that these estimates, totalling £14,931, were included in Johnson's overall estimate for re-equipping the line. Late in 1881 he arranged for the line to be re-laid with steel rails to replace the original wrought iron ones. Passing places with additional platforms were provided at Grindley, Chartley and Ingestre. The platforms at Grindley and Ingestre were staggered which gave those stations a very distinctive appearance. The re-signalling work was undertaken by McKenzie & Holland which provided new signal boxes at

Bromshall West, Grindley, Chartley, Ingestre, and Salt. The new boxes were unusual in that they did not sport decorative barge boards, a common GNR feature. Moreover, the traditional porch over the entrance to the boxes was moved to cover the hut for the earth closet. Previously there were no signal boxes, the signals being worked from lever frames located on the station platforms. On 8 April 1882 the GNR's Assistant Secretary, William Latta, wrote to the BoT stating that the works in connection with the re-signalling of the S&UR were approaching completion and requesting an early inspection. Irish born Colonel Frederick Henry Rich (1824-1904) undertook the inspection on 27 April 1882.[136] His report recorded that about one third of a mile of track had been doubled at the junction with the NSR at Bromshall and that loop lines had been constructed at the stations. This seems to imply that there were no such loops before but we know from the BoT inspection carried out in 1867, that a loop siding was constructed at Salt along with a second platform. Rich reported that the arrangements at Salt, Ingestre and Grindley stations were satisfactory, but he required an alteration to a siding connection at Chartley with the provision of a catch point to improve operating safety on the 1 in 75 gradient. Rich also inspected a new under-bridge of increased width at Ingestre necessary to accommodate the new loop line and concluded that the iron girders were sufficiently strong. At Bromshall he recommended that the down distant signal should be moved a little further from the NSR junction signal box so that it would be better seen by drivers approaching the junction. It was repositioned at 714 yards from Bromshall Junction home signal. He also considered that the double track at Bromshall should be extended a little further to the west. Drawings of the new works were made available for the inspection and copies sent to the BoT. Those showing the new arrangements at the stations and the junction were dated 20 April 1882 and signed by Richard Johnson. Details were given of the lever frames at the new signal boxes as follows:

Salt	10 working, 5 spare
Ingestre	17 working, 8 spare
Chartley	16 working, 3 spare
Grindley	16 working
GNR Bromshall	6 working, 9 spare

The capital cost of the new NSR box at Bromshall Junction was paid for by the GNR which also met the operating costs – an arrangement presumably inherited from the S&UR and subsequently passed on to the L&NER. There were four ground signals controlling access to the sidings at Ingestre, one of which served Weston Salt Works. Interestingly, the drawings gave the station names as shown above and this is the way the stations were described in Bradshaw and in GNR and L&NER public and working timetables. The extended names, Salt and Sandon, Ingestre for Weston and Chartley and Stowe, only seem to have been displayed on the station name-boards. They do not appear on the limited number of tickets that we have been able to examine. A set of well executed and extremely detailed coloured plans of the S&UR was drawn for the GNR in 1903 by Henry Fowler, surveyor and Lithographer from Manchester. They show identical layouts for all the stations excepting Salt and use the

CONTINUED ON PAGE 113

The 1882 GNR re-signalling

Grindley signalbox with a smart and proud looking signalman posing for the photographer. Notice his water supply and what, we presume, is the toilet.

COLLECTION JIM FOLEY

The re-signalling work was undertaken by McKenzie & Holland which provided new signal boxes at Bromshall West, Grindley, Chartley, Ingestre, and Salt. The new boxes were unusual in that they did not sport decorative barge boards, a common GNR feature. Moreover, the traditional porch over the entrance to the boxes was moved to cover the hut for the earth closet. Previously there were no signal boxes, the signals being worked from lever frames located on the station platforms. Drawings of the new works were made available for the inspection on 27 April 1882 by Colonel Frederick Henry Rich and copies were sent to the BoT. Those showing the new arrangements at the stations and the junction were dated 20 April 1882 and signed by Richard Johnson.

Note: The original scales shown on these plans are not valid for this reproduction.

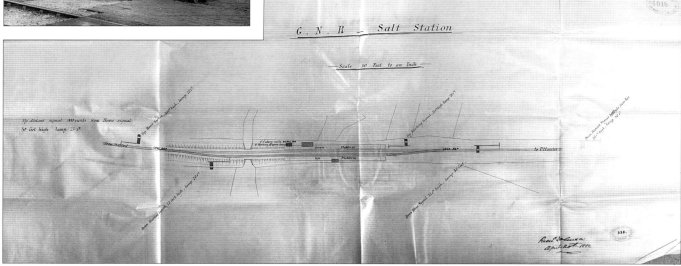

GNR drawing dated April 20 1882 showing signalling alterations at Salt Station.   NATIONAL ARCHIVES MT6/306/6

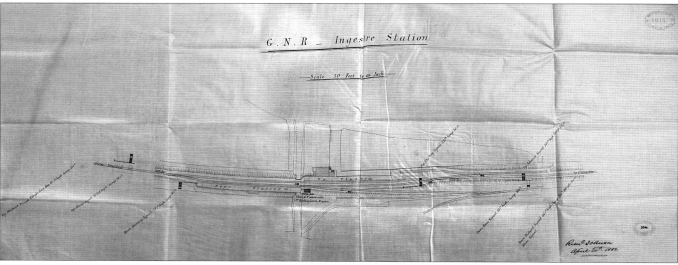

GNR drawing dated April 20 1882 showing signalling alterations at Ingestre Station.   NATIONAL ARCHIVES MT6/306/6

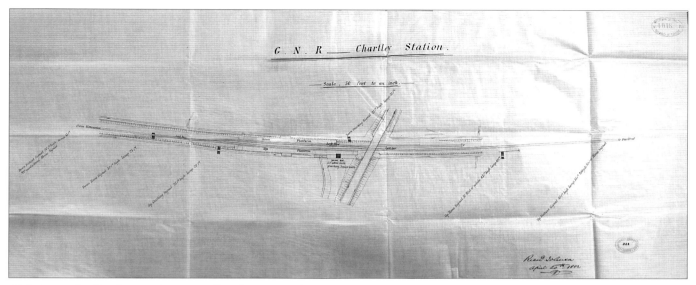

GNR drawing dated April 20 1882 showing signalling alterations at Chartley Station. NATIONAL ARCHIVES MT6/306/6

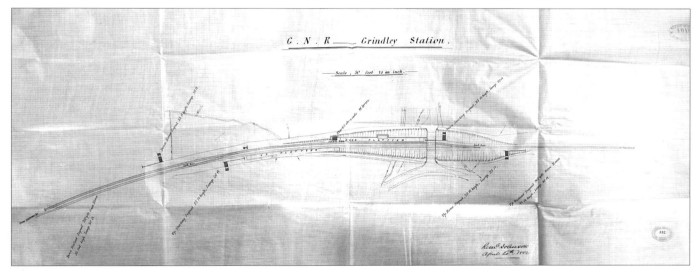

GNR drawing dated April 20 1882 showing signalling alterations at Grindley Station. NATIONAL ARCHIVES MT6/306/6

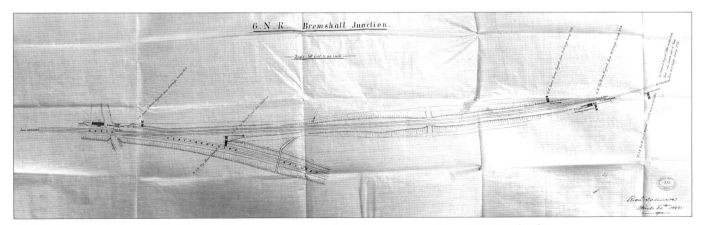

GNR drawing dated April 20 1882 showing signalling alterations at Bromshall Junction. NATIONAL ARCHIVES MT6/306/6

Henry Fowler GNR plans of 1903

A set of well executed and extremely detailed coloured plans of the S&UR were drawn for the GNR in 1903 by Henry Fowler, Surveyor and Lithographer from Manchester. They show identical layouts for all the stations excepting Salt and use the extended names for Ingestre and (not 'for') Weston and Chartley & Stowe. At Salt the plans indicate that the loop and the up platform have been removed but show that a stage for loading milk churns has been erected opposite the remaining platform. It appears that the station was renamed Salt and Sandon sometime during the following year. Just to add a little confusion, the 1903 plan book describes the line as running from Bramshall (not Bromshall) to Stafford.
NA RAIL 236/470

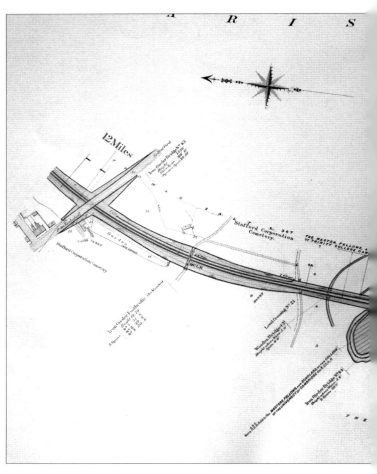

RIGHT
Plan from milepost 12 to the junction with the L&NWR station at Stafford. The plan tells us that the total length of the line from Bromshall Junction to the termination at Stafford is 12 miles 5 furlongs 9 chains 60 links. Note the iron footbridge giving access to Stafford Corporation Cemetery. Near to milepost 12½ is the commencement of the gasworks branch.

BELOW
Plan from milepost 11 to milepost 12 showing Stafford Common Station. Note the salt works of Stafford Salt & Alkali and Stubbs & Co. to the east of the passenger station. Note original scale shown is not valid for this reproduction.

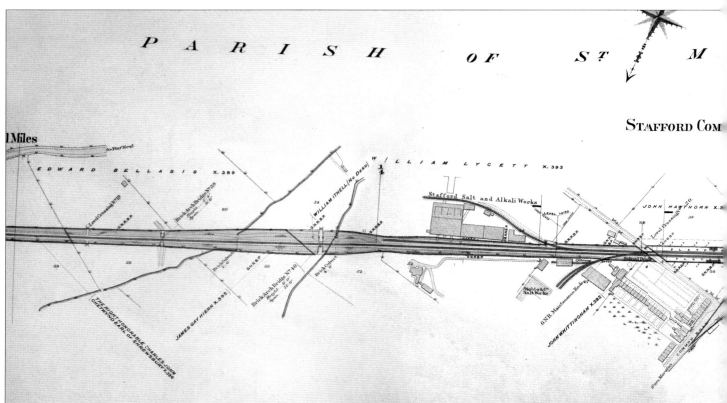

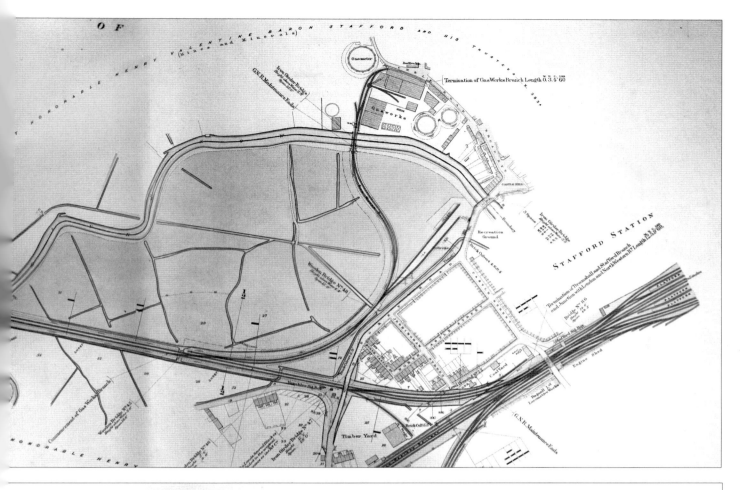

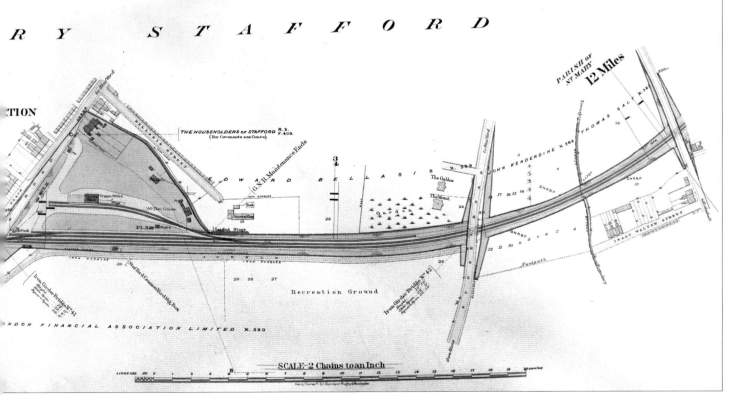

SCALE-2 Chains to an Inch

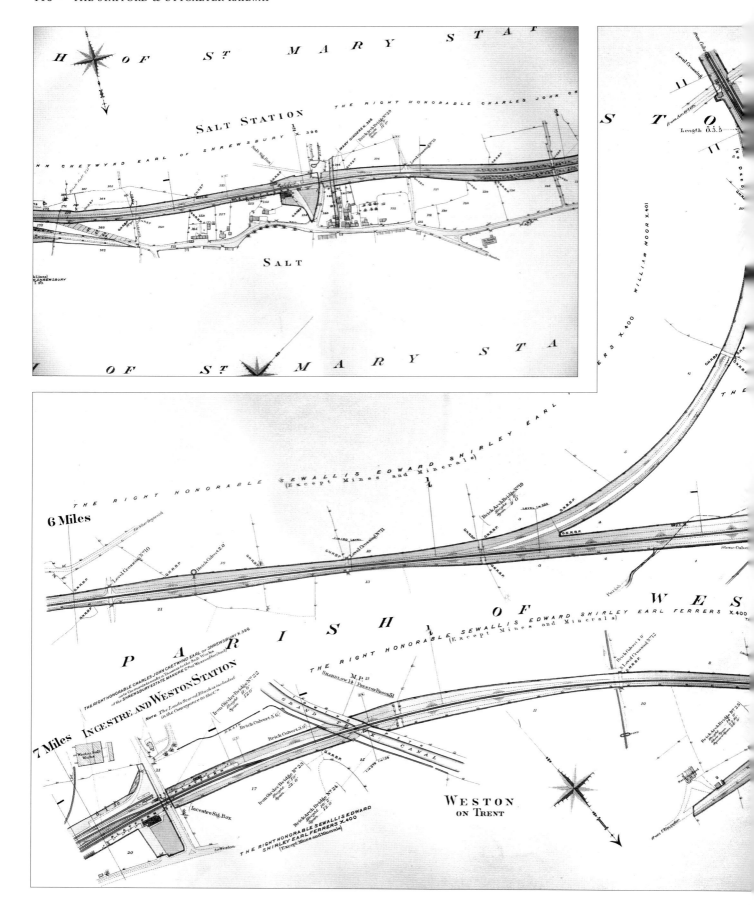

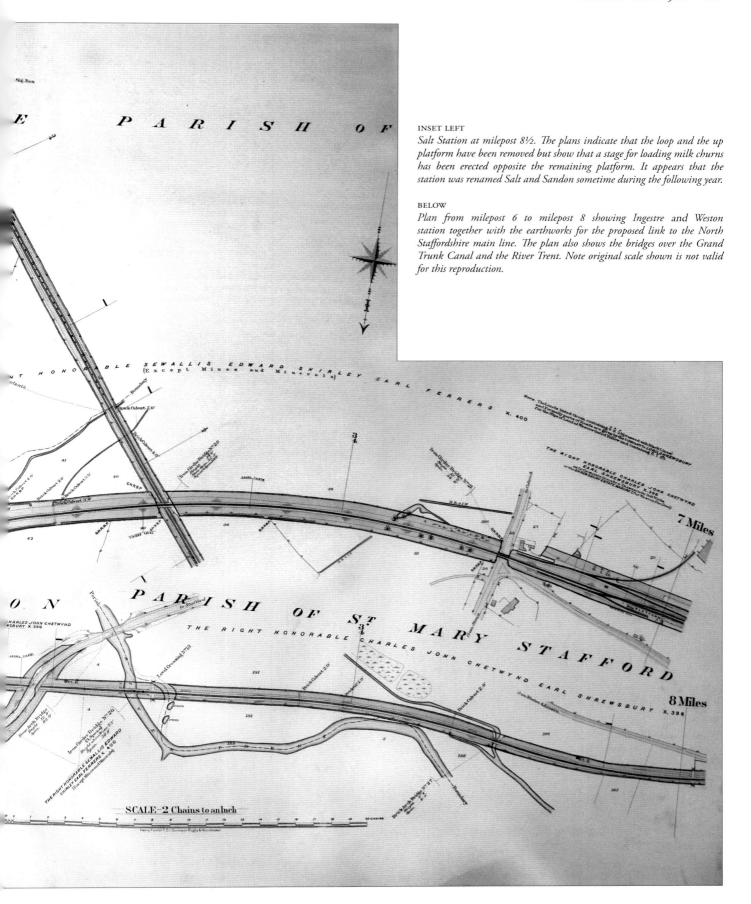

INSET LEFT

Salt Station at milepost 8½. The plans indicate that the loop and the up platform have been removed but show that a stage for loading milk churns has been erected opposite the remaining platform. It appears that the station was renamed Salt and Sandon sometime during the following year.

BELOW

Plan from milepost 6 to milepost 8 showing Ingestre and Weston station together with the earthworks for the proposed link to the North Staffordshire main line. The plan also shows the bridges over the Grand Trunk Canal and the River Trent. Note original scale shown is not valid for this reproduction.

SCALE—2 Chains to an Inch

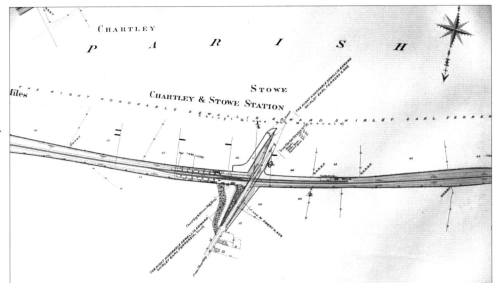

Chartley & Stowe Station and bridge number 16 at milepost 5¼.

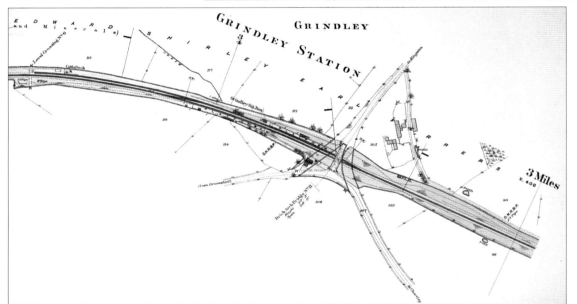

Grindley Station, between mileposts 2¾ and 3.

Bromshall Junction (here spelt Bramshall) milepost 0 to milepost ½.

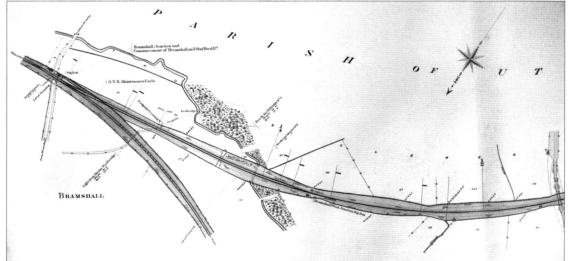

extended names for Ingestre and (not 'for') Weston and Chartley & Stowe. At Salt the plans indicate that the loop and the up platform have been removed but show that a stage for loading milk churns has been erected opposite the remaining platform. It appears that the station was renamed Salt and Sandon sometime during the following year. Just to add a little confusion, the 1903 plan book describes the line as running from Bramshall (not Bromshall) to Stafford. The GNR continued to maintain the line to a high standard and the permanent way was kept in excellent condition. Granite ballast was purchased from the Mountsorrel Granite Company in Leicestershire. All the intermediate stations were repainted in 1913 under a contract let to A.A. McDermott for £257 2s 5d (£257.12p).

The Great Northern Railway Act 1882 (see below) gave powers, inter alia, for a branch railway of three furlongs, 8.45 chains in length from an intended junction about 520 yards east of the bridge over the line at Chartley station, terminating about 100 yards north of the road from Stowe to Drointon. Nothing was done and the powers were allowed to lapse. In March 1885 a contract was let to E. Wood of Derby for the provision of two improved waiting sheds at Grindley and Chartley for the total sum of £300 and in February 1888 expenditure of £300 was approved for the provision of a station master's house at Grindley and by virtue of the Great Northern Railway Act 1903, which received the Royal Assent on 5 May that year, the company obtained statutory authority to acquire three parcels of land at Grindley station. Back in 1892 the GNR sanctioned expenditure of £200 for a coal weighbridge at Ingestre, subject to the Cannock & District Coal Co. paying a minimum charge of £6 per annum for the use of the machine. Moving forward to 1920 a 10 ton road weighbridge was installed at Grindley at a cost of £148 which included the charge for its transfer from Bawtry.

Signalling changes

By 18 January 1892[137] Salt and Chartley signal boxes had ceased to become block posts. The single line between Stafford Common and Bromshall Junction was now worked with three block sections under the absolute block telegraph system with train staff and paper tickets, the sections being: Stafford Common and Ingestre; Ingestre and Grindley; Grindley and Bromshall Junction. Details of the head of the train staff and colour of the tickets were as follows:

Train Staff Station	Head of Train Staff	Colour of Train Ticket
Stafford Common and Ingestre	Oblong	Yellow (Down) Green (Up)
Ingestre and Grindley	Diamond	Red (Down) Orange (Up)
Grindley and Bromshall West	Circular	Blue (Down) White with blue letters (Up)

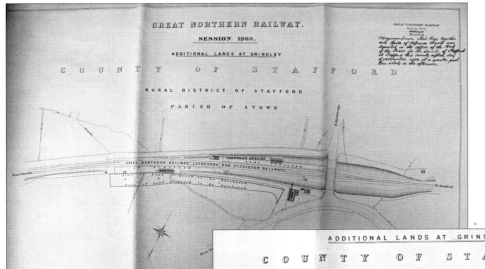

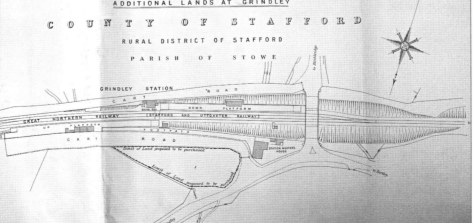

LEFT: The GNR Act of 1903, which received the Royal Assent on 5 May, included powers to purchase three parcels of land at Grindley, to allow for expansion and improved facilities. This is the plan that accompanied the railway company's submission to Parliament.
SCRO QRUM/777

RIGHT: A later 1913 plan of Grindley illustrating the proposed purchase of another parcel of land.
CRO QRUM/748

GREAT NORTHERN RAILWAY.

Circular No. 12,453a.

REGULATIONS FOR WORKING THE SINGLE LINE

BETWEEN

BROMSHALL JUNCTION AND GRINDLEY

BETWEEN

GRINDLEY AND INGESTRE

AND BETWEEN

INGESTRE AND STAFFORD COMMON.

This branch is worked under the instructions in Appendix I. of the general rules and regulations.

DESCRIPTION OF TRAIN STAFF.		COLOUR OF TRAIN TICKET.

Lettered on one side :— · Lettered on the other side :—

BROMSHALL JUNCTION AND GRINDLEY. ○ GRINDLEY AND BROMSHALL JUNCTION.

Down—Bromshall west jun. to Grindley **blue.**

Up—Grindley to Bromshall west jun. **white**
(*blue letters*)

GRINDLEY AND INGESTRE. ◇ INGESTRE AND GRINDLEY.

Down—Grindley to Ingestre ... **red.**

Up—Ingestre to Grindley ... ... **orange.**

GO TO STAFFORD COMMON. ▭ GO TO INGESTRE.

Down—Ingestre to Stafford Common **yellow.**

Up—Stafford Common to Ingestre... **green.**

DESCRIPTION OF TRAIN TICKET.

No._____

Great Northern Railway.

TRAIN STAFF TICKET.

STAFFORD & UTTOXETER LINE.

Train No._____ (**UP** or **DOWN**
as the case may be).

To the Engine-driver.

You are hereby authorised, after seeing the train staff for the section, to proceed from _____ to _____ and the train staff will follow.

*Signature of person in charge*_____

Date _____ [OVER.]

(*Back of ticket.*)

This ticket must be given up by the Engine-driver, immediately on arrival, to the person in charge of the staff working at the place to which he is authorised to proceed, to be cancelled. At the end of the day the tickets must be sent to the Great Northern Company's Agent's office, Stafford.

In force from 6.0 a.m. on Monday, May 9th, 1898.

J. ALEXANDER,
Superintendent of the line.
(37,359.)

KING'S CROSS,
May 2nd, 1898.

Circular 8,352a is cancelled.

GNR circular No. 12,453a – Regulations for working the single line, issued on 2 May 1898. RICHARD DEMPSTER COLLECTION

The engine drivers were responsible for giving up the tickets on arrival at the next block station and at the end of each day the tickets had to be sent to the GNR Agent's Office at Stafford. On 2 May 1898[138] fresh regulations were issued for working the line which introduced new descriptions on the train staffs but the shape of the heads and the colour of the train tickets remained exactly the same. This method of working continued until the end of the GNR's existence and was inherited by the L&NER.

Bromshall tunnel, along with four other tunnels, was specifically mentioned in the GNR General Regulations for train signalling on single lines in the context of platelayers' lorries going through tunnels. Regulation 9 stipulated that when it

was necessary for a platelayers' lorry to go through the tunnel *it must be signalled on the block instrument in accordance with the authorised code, and the signalman at the box in advance must, if the line be clear to the home signal, give permission for the lorry to approach his box in accordance with regulation 5. No train must be allowed to enter the section at either end until the lorry has left the tunnel and has passed the next block signal-box, or until the signalman at either end of the section has been advised by the ganger that the lorry has been taken off the rails. Should the lorry, after passing through the tunnel, be removed from the rails before reaching the next signal-box, the ganger must go forward and inform the signalman that the lorry is clear of the line. If, however, time would*

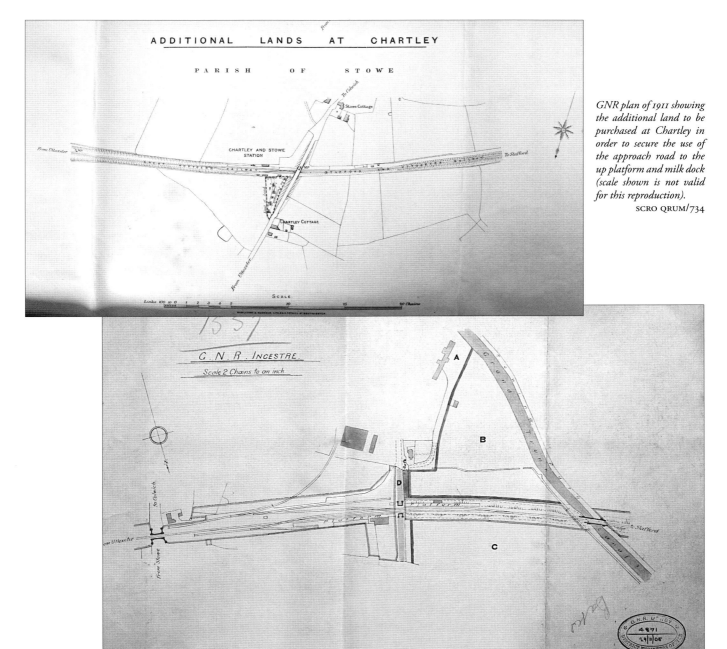

GNR plan of 1911 showing the additional land to be purchased at Chartley in order to secure the use of the approach road to the up platform and milk dock (scale shown is not valid for this reproduction).

SCRO QRUM/734

Plan of Ingestre station dated 29 November 1905 (scale shown is not valid for this reproduction).

NATIONAL ARCHIVES - RAIL 1189/1487

*be saved, the ganger must return to the signal-box in the rear and inform the signalman that the lorry is clear of the line; the signalman must then send the **Cancelling** signal to the signal-box in advance.* The L&NER perpetuated this rule but with effect from 1 January 1923 amended the description of a platelayers' *lorry* to *trolley*.

A problem at Chartley

In 1907 a problem arose with regard to the approach road to the up platform at Chartley. This was used by passengers and, more importantly, by farmers despatching milk from the milk dock which was located on the up platform. At that time the value of the milk traffic at Chartley produced revenue for the GNR of about £1,000 per annum. The land occupied by the approach road was owned by Earl Ferrers. His agent had advised that the Earl had recently sold all his property around Chartley and that very shortly the road would be closed permanently. However, the land which comprised an area of one rood and twenty poles (1,815 sq yds) could be purchased for £100. Apparently the GNR District Engineer had made a verbal agreement in 1896 whereby the railway company would undertake to maintain the road in return for its use. This agreement had been honoured but there was no legal right to access the land. The station master pointed out that the down platform was constructed of timber and would soon have to be rebuilt if used continually for milk cans. The up platform was much more durable as it was made of stone. After some haggling, the land area subject to purchase was increased to 2 roods and 12 poles for the same consideration in order to provide sufficient land to erect a house for the station master at some future date. The GNR Board approved the expenditure at its meeting held on 26 July 1907.[139] A cottage for the station master was eventually provided in 1911 at a cost of £200. The company then acquired further land in the vicinity of Chartley station under the Great Northern Railway Act 1911[140] which received the Royal Assent on 18 August 1911.

A dispute at Ingestre

Towards the end of 1905 a protracted dispute arose between the Earl of Shrewsbury and Talbot and the GNR over the access road to and from Ingestre station and goods yard. Originally the road led to Weston Salt Works opened in 1821 on the Earl of Shrewsbury's estate and closed in 1901 following the development of salt workings at Stafford Common. Since 1874 the works at Weston had been connected to the S&UR by a siding at Ingestre station. The dispute lasted for over two years and became very acrimonious. Access to the station and goods yard was subject to an agreement dated 10 August 1882 whereby the Earl of Shrewsbury granted permission to the GNR to use the access road *with and without vehicles and horses* for 1s 0d (5p) per annum. The agreement was terminable by either party giving 30 days written notice. A second agreement dated 16 July 1886 enabled the GNR to lease a parcel of land on the west side of the private road leading to the salt works to provide a means of access to Earl Ferrers' land which was severed by the coming of the railway. For this the GNR was charged an additional rental of 5s 0d (25p) per annum. The predicament of the severed land was considered by the GNR Way and Works Committee on 1

April 1886 which authorised the construction of a level crossing to connect the severed sites at an estimated cost of £127 if the railway company was ever requested to do so. Such a request was never made as the 1886 agreement provided for an alternative means of access.[141]

The dispute arose following the sale by Earl Ferrers of the parcel of land to the north west of Ingestre station and a disagreement with the Earl of Shrewsbury and Talbot over the use of the remaining portion on the south side of the line which could only be accessed under the 1882 and 1886 agreements. This was a plot of just over three acres and was known as Bastard's Flatt; its western boundary bordered the Trent and Mersey Canal. The disagreement had reached a pitch whereby the Earl of Shrewsbury and Talbot was threatening to terminate the agreements which enabled Earl Ferrers to gain access to his severed land. Such action would, of course, also deny the GNR access to Ingestre station and goods yard. The matter was handled by their Lordships land agents who entered a battle royal with the GNR with a series of meetings and a terse exchange of correspondence. It was suggested that the level crossing idea muted in 1886 but not pursued should be resurrected but the GNR argued that this solution could not apply as the northern parcel of land was no longer owned by Lord Ferrers which negated the original understanding. Ferrers' agent suggested that a way out of the problem would be for the GNR to buy Bastard's Flatt and then sell it to the Earl of Shrewsbury and Talbot, suggesting a price of £230. The dispute reached fever pitch when the agent for the Earl of Shrewsbury and Talbot gave notice for the GNR to stop using the access road with effect from 16 July 1907. The GNR sought help from their solicitor but received no comfort, his advice being that the Earl Shrewsbury and Talbot had every right to give notice. Pressure mounted on 22 July 1907 when a letter was sent to the GNR by the Earl of Shrewsbury and Talbot's agent stating that the notice to terminate the agreement had not been complied with; both the GNR and Earl Ferrers were still using the road. This resulted in a proposal for the GNR to buy the land for £200, which it did and then resell it to the Earl of Shrewsbury and Talbot so that access to the station and goods yard could be maintained. When the land was offered, the Earl of Shrewsbury and Talbot's agent replied that £200 was too much and suggested a lower price of £120. Reluctantly the battered GNR acquiesced, losing £80 in the process, but suggesting that the new agreement should grant access in perpetuity. Recognising their dominant position the agent wrote on 31 December 1907 in very strong terms demanding an instant settlement on the basis of £120 with a reinstatement of the original agreement but for a period of 21 years, i.e. the payment of 1s 0d (5p) per annum for the longer period. Having ascertained that the construction of a new road would cost £285, the GNR gave in and the new agreement was signed on 31 October 1908. There was, of course, no need to renew the 1886 agreement as its sole purpose was to give access to Earl Ferrers' severed land.

During this saga it is interesting to note that the GNR did consider the possibility of closing Ingestre station and goods yard and sought the advice of the District Manager at Nottingham. His report dated 13 January 1908 is most illuminating. He predicted that if the station were closed the whole of the goods traffic would be diverted to the NSR's station at Weston but he considered that this would not be a serious matter as goods traffic was comparatively small. However, he was most concerned about the serious loss of milk and other traffic carried by passenger trains. The receipts for this traffic amounted to £2,097 for 1907 with an additional £356 for actual passenger traffic. Ingestre also handled 1,423 head of livestock. If closure took place it was predicted that the milk traffic which was all destined for London would be lost to the L&NWR, collection being switched to the NSR's Weston station.

Developments at Stafford

The GNR was considerably better at negotiating with the L&NWR than its predecessor as from 1 August 1881, the rent for the use of the L&NWR's Stafford Town station was reduced to £450 per annum, plus £15 for the use of a booking office.[142] The principal fee covered rates and taxes, porters, signalmen and maintenance expenses but the GNR remained responsible for cleaning and lamping its own carriages. From 1 January 1889 the main fee was increased to £500 per annum having regard to the expenditure incurred by the L&NWR in covering in the bay platform used by the GNR passenger trains. The platform became known as *The Great Northern Bay* and the GNR regulations stipulated that trains running into the bay platform must not exceed 11 vehicles some of which would, of course, be four-wheeled carriages. Improved office accommodation provided by the L&NWR in 1896, resulted in the total fee increasing to £528 14s 7d (£528.72½p) per annum.

The GNR inherited two private siding agreements at Stafford. The Lilleshall Company's siding was located to the north east of the L&NWR passenger station. In Chapter Three we explained how Colonel Yolland was critical of the way in which this siding was connected to the S&UR when he undertook his inspection of the line in May 1867. The siding had been disconnected when Major Hutchinson undertook the second inspection in September 1867. However, when Colonel Yolland again had cause to visit Stafford in order to investigate the accident to a passenger train which occurred just outside the station on 16 November 1877, he found that the siding connection had been reinstated without his recommended improvements. The company was again reminded of the requirements but they never seem to have complied with the request. It is interesting to note that when Colonel Yolland first inspected the line he recorded that the siding belonged to the L&NWR. It served a coal yard which accommodated coal mined in the Lilleshall Company's Shropshire pits. Section 34(4) of the Great Northern Railway Act 1881 specifically mentioned this siding in the context of giving access free of charge to the L&NWR and also referred to it as Hall's siding. William Hall was a coal factor. In later years the site sported a large sign with the legend W. Hall & Co. Ltd and so that firm which also had a siding at Doxey Road (see below) must have obtained an agreement to use it. The other private siding inherited by the GNR served Venables timber yard. This firm was also served by a siding off the L&NWR main line which abutted the western boundary of the site while the S&UR siding ran right into the yard and was controlled from Venables signal box (known by railwaymen as Blackberry Lane). This was the first GNR box after the junction at Stafford, being located just to the east of Doxey Road Bridge.

The GNR was quick to exploit all possible opportunities at Stafford and by November 1881 the Way and Works Committee authorised the inclusion of provisions to provide new facilities at Stafford in the company's omnibus Bill for the 1881-1882

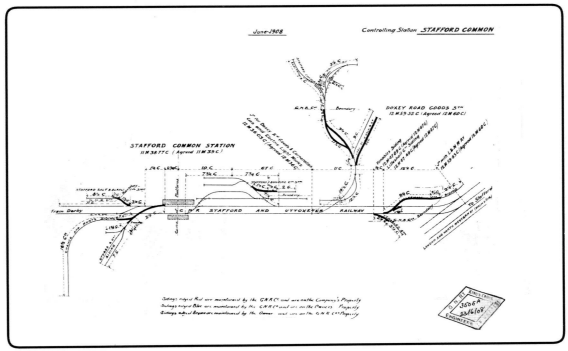

Details of sidings at Stafford and Stafford Common, June 1908.

NETWORK RAIL ARCHIVES

GREAT NORTHERN RAILWAY USE OF STAFFORD STATION.

Memorandum of Meeting at King's Cross. 31/10/1881.

Stafford Station Rent.

It was agreed that from the 1st August 1881,
on which date the G.N. Co. commenced to use Stafford
Station, for 12 months and thereafter subject to
6 months notice, the rent payable by the G.N. Co. for
the use of the Station including rates and taxes,
staff, signalling and maintenance expenses be fixed at
£450 per annum. The G.N. Co. to clean and lamp their
own carriages.

Mr. Findlay intimated that it was proposed to
cover over the G.N. Bay in the Stafford station in
respect of which a certain outlay will be required, upon
which the G.N. Co. would be required to pay interest.

Minute 35,221 Traffic Committee (L.N.W.) 17/6/1882.

Booking office for G.N. Co. = £15.

Memorandum of Meeting held at Euston. 21/2/1889.

Stafford Station Rent.

It was agreed to recommend having regard to the
expenditure incurred by the L.N.W. Co. in covering the
platform used by the G.N. Co's trains at the Stafford
Station, that from the 1st January 1889 the amount
payable by the G.N. Co. for rent and services at the
Station be increased from £450 to £500 per annum, subject
to 6 months notice.

Passenger Traffic Committee (L.N.W.). 13/1/1897.

Improved office accommodation costing £212
(estimated) G.N. to pay 6% per annum of cost.

Memorandum of meeting at King's Cross on 31 October 1881
relating to station rents at Stafford.   NA RAIL/1007/281

ABOVE
*Aerial view of Stafford
Gas Works with the River
Sow to the left; the view
looks north-east. At the
extreme left the bridge
carrying the GNR siding
into the gas works can just
be seen and there is a rail
tank wagon on the siding.
Beyond is the electricity
sub-station.   Sainsbury's
supermarket now occupies
this site!*

STAFFORDSHIRE ARTS &
MUSEUM SERVICE

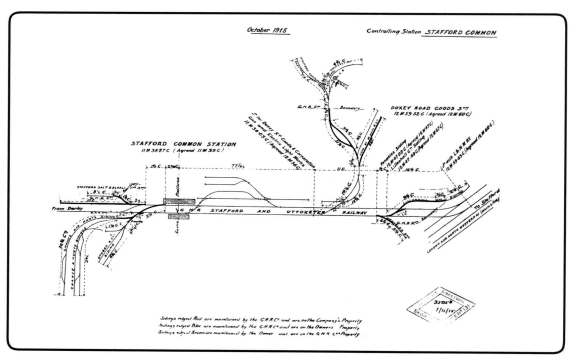

Details of sidings at Stafford and Stafford Common, October 1915.

NETWORK RAIL ARCHIVES

Parliamentary Session.[143] These included a new goods station in a more central position connected by a new branch railway which would also serve Stafford gas works. Gas had been supplied in Stafford since 1831; initially in private hands, the enterprise was acquired by Stafford Corporation in 1876. The new railway was four furlongs 3.65 chains in length from a junction with the existing line in the Parish of Saint Mary at Stafford and terminating in a field adjoining the gas works. A siding off the new line, one furlong 0.4 chains in length, was to terminate at the northern boundary of the gas works. The Bill was enacted as the Great Northern Railway Act 1882,[144] receiving the Royal Assent on 10 August that year. However, there had been a major problem in that the Staffordshire General Infirmary had petitioned against the Bill on the grounds of noise and disruption. In order to placate the infirmary trustees and ensure the smooth passage of the Bill, which included many provisions in addition to those which affected Stafford, the GNR had agreed to find an alternative site for the new goods yard. A formal agreement with the trustees had been sealed in May 1882 after which their petition was withdrawn. Shortly afterwards Shelford Bidwell (1851-1903), a land agent and surveyor appointed by the GNR, was instructed to ascertain what terms would be required for the purchase of land on the south-west side of the River Sow which could be used as an alternative site.

The GNR chairman and deputy visited Stafford on 17 October 1882 to inspect the site following which the engineer was instructed to examine its suitability for a goods station to be located to the south of the position previously proposed. The inspection and examination proved favourable and Bidwell was asked to negotiate with Lord Stafford's agent to purchase the land. In the meantime a fresh Bill had been deposited in the 1882-1883 Parliamentary session which included a provision for an alternative scheme.[145] Negotiations for the land purchase continued but by April 1883 Lord Stafford had declined to quote a price for the 10 acres required as the whole frontage of his property would be taken leaving no access to the 19 acres of land to the rear. However, he was prepared to sell the total area of just over 29 acres at £300 per acre or £8,550, including one half of the river bed. On 6 April 1883 it was resolved that all the land should be purchased at £250 per acre, including that comprising half of the river bed and the mineral rights. By the following month a deal had been struck and Lord Stafford had withdrawn his opposition to the Bill. This became the Great Northern Railway Act 1883[146] which received the Royal Assent on 2 August 1883. It enabled the GNR to abandon the previous proposal and establish a new goods station on the north side of Doxey Road with a link to the gas works. The new facilities were to be connected to a new branch line of three furlongs 4.6 chains in length which joined with the former S&UR in the Parish of Castlechurch. On 1 December 1883 the GNR agreed to pay an annual donation of £3 per annum to the infirmary, doubtless in the interests of securing a future good relationship. The new branch and goods yard were eventually completed but it was not until 1891 that the gas works was connected. The gas works connection, including the permanent way, cost £2,072 in return for a guaranteed payment of £100 per annum but reducing by 5% per annum for every £100 paid by way of freight charges on

traffic to and from the gas works. The bridge across the River Sow was erected by Stafford Corporation which was responsible for its maintenance. A condition fundamental to the agreement with the owners of the gas works was the new connection also being used by the L&NWR. Indeed the L&NWR became a party to the siding agreement. No doubt the gas works sourced its coal from the South Staffordshire coalfield and required the L&NWR to bring this direct rather than pay GNR trip charges. The GNR imposed a speed restriction of six mph over the gas works branch and engines were not permitted to proceed beyond the weighbridge in the gas works yard. Quite how the drivers judged their speed to be below the precise maximum limit allowed is not known but exactly the same ruling was imposed by the GNR's successors. The branch crossed the River Sow on an iron bridge which had a span of 55ft and an average height above water level of 3ft 8in. The GNR was not responsible for its maintenance or the maintenance of the sidings beyond it within the gas works. There was a smaller timber bridge (No. 48) over a water course just before the entrance to the new goods yard. This had two spans each of 16ft and a height above water level of 4ft 4in. On 1 December 1893 the GNR Way and Works Committee authorised expenditure of £250 for the construction of a loop on the gas works branch between the link to Doxey Road goods yard and the crossing of the River Sow with ballast provided by Stafford Corporation which, as mentioned earlier, owned the gas works. This loop was designed to hold 20 wagons. The new arrangement was encompassed in an agreement dated 27 January 1894. Drivers of trains propelling from the up main line onto the gas works branch were required to give one long blast on the whistle before commencing the movement. In March 1914 the GNR directors approved expenditure of £160 on the provision of a goods shed at Doxey Road. Developments at the gas works continued apace with a new retort house, washers and purification plant being installed in 1900, followed by further extensions in 1919 and 1920. Coke and tar were produced as by-products and sent away by rail. It became common practice to use cinder ash from the works to ballast the gas works branch.

The Stafford Corporation Electricity Department was founded in 1895 with works located immediately to the east of the gas works and served by a siding leading from the branch just after the crossing of the River Sow. By 1900 the generating station contained three 125hp reciprocating steam engines each driving a continuous dynamo with an output at full load of 300 amps at 220 volts. The method of generation remained in service until 1955 when the original DC system was changed to AC. The generating station with new plant survived until 1959, when connection was made with the national grid.

On 23 May 1895 the GNR entered into a five-year agreement[147] with William Hall, a coal factor, to construct and maintain an additional siding at Doxey Road goods yard (the one to the west) to hold 25 wagons with hard standing for the stacking of coal. Under the agreement, William Hall agreed to pay 6d (2.5p) per ton for the carriage of all coal passing over the new siding from the L&NWR at Stafford with a guaranteed minimum payment based on an annual throughput of 15,000 tons, even if that amount was not actually carried. In addition, Hall agreed to pay a rental of £30

CRO QRUM 522

This plan is part of the GNR submission to Parliament which included the branch from the S&UR to serve both the gas and electricity works at Stafford. The works were authorised as part of the GNR 1882 Act, referred to in the text, but were substituted by an alternative scheme authorised in 1883.

per annum. He was entitled to use the GNR's weighbridge free of charge but the GNR reserved the right to use the new siding if it was not required for Hall's traffic.

The agreement was renewed for a further five years effective from 1 July 1900[148] but with Luther William Potts, William Francis Fowke and Herbert Tyler trading together in partnership under the name W. Hall & Co. The renewal terms were similar to those in the original agreement except that the minimum annual guaranteed tonnage was reduced to 13,000 tons, including coal and coke traffic passing to and from Stafford Common station, but the annual rental was increased to £50 with a rebate of £20 if the guaranteed minimum throughput was actually achieved. The new agreement was not signed and sealed until 18 October 1901.

The partnership was dissolved and the firm became a limited liability company, W. Hall & Co Ltd, which had its registered office at Doxey Road. The agreement was formally assigned to the new organisation on 5 February 1904. Shortly afterwards the new company indicated that it would it would welcome a renewal of its lease for another five years, but at a reduced rental.

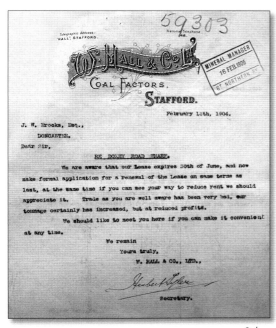

NA RAIL 783/517

This request prompted a review of the terms and it was discovered that the figures used to calculate the guaranteed annual throughput also took into account coal delivered to the Stafford Salt & Alkali Company and the salt works owned by Stubbs & Co., at Stafford Common (see below). Moreover, this traffic was already rebated in its own right and the railway company was no longer prepared to pay a rebate twice on the same traffic. W. Hall & Co. Ltd stated that it no longer supplied coal to the Stafford Salt & Alkali Company but admitted that it did supply 5,000 tons of coal annually to Stubbs & Co. The outcome was that the agreement was renewed for a further five years until 30 June 1910 at the same rental, but the tonnage threshold used to trigger the rebate was reduced to 8,000 tons per annum and the new agreement, which was signed and sealed on 12 October 1905,

contained a clause specifically stating that traffic to Stubbs & Co. should not be taken into account in calculating the minimum tonnage. It is interesting to note that this negotiation was led by the GNR's mineral manager, J.W. Brooks, who was based at Doncaster. He made recommendations to William James Grinling, the Chief Traffic Manager at King's Cross, who had to seek the approval of the directors before the new agreement could be implemented. When considering the renewal it was borne in mind that the traders had to pay 3d (1½p) per ton more on the coal delivered to Doxey Road than would apply if they used the L&NWR facilities. It was also noted that the members of the firm were tradesmen in the town, including drapers (Potts), boot makers (Tyler), chemists (Fowke) and other prominent citizens. The GNR clearly cared about its customers at Stafford and was ever conscious of the L&NWR competition.

There was another tussle when the agreement was again due for renewal in 1910.[149] During the previous year only 7,851 tons of coal and coke passed through the wharf at Doxey Road and so the GNR argued that a rent reduction should not apply. However, W. Hall and Co. Ltd drew attention to an understanding that had been made with the GNR's mineral manager from the outset to the effect that timber routed via Stafford from the north east coast ports for the Cannock and Rugeley Colliery Co. Ltd at Hednesford should be taken into account on the basis that one ton of timber equated to two tons of coal even though none of the timber was handled at Doxey Road. The colliery company's general manager added weight to the argument stating that the equivalent of 1,045 tons of timber had passed over the GNR's route to Stafford in 1909 threatening to divert this traffic if the GNR did not play ball! The point was conceded but the timber concession was withdrawn. The next agreement, which was signed and sealed on 27 March 1911, ran for another five years commencing 1 July 1910 with a rental of £30 per annum with the tonnage threshold reduced to 7,000 tons per annum. If the firm failed to make this target it was obliged to pay extra rent on the basis of 3d per ton on the shortfall below 7,000 tons. For example, if the throughput were only 6,000 tons the rental would be £42 10s 0d (£42.50p). In reaching this agreement the traders stressed that the development of Littleton Colliery, Huntington had distorted the market following the introduction of preferential rates for coal delivered to Stafford. The representatives of W. Hall & Co. Ltd were tough negotiators relying heavily on their Manager, George Walter Wheat (1865-1929) to look after day to day operations. The firm remained at Doxey Road and continued to have an interest in the Lilleshall siding throughout the lifetime of the GNR and continued to trade with its successors, the L&NER. The sidings were sometimes referred to as Wheat's sidings after the firm's long serving manager. The L&NWR exercised its running powers to the Lilleshall siding and to Doxey Road, the powers continuing under the LM&SR.

Stafford Common

The line from Stafford Common to Stafford was doubled in 1882, requiring an additional wrought iron girder bridge over the River Sow. On 11 July 1883 Stafford Corporation was granted an easement to construct and maintain a footbridge across the

Another group of GNR staff during shunting operations at Stafford Common. Once again, unfortunately, we do not have any identification but the fellow on the left is clearly a loco man while the one on the right is a shunter. The more senior looking fellow in the centre could perhaps be the local yard foreman. The engine providing the backcloth, number 1095, is one of the Stirling design six-coupled goods tender engines although in this case, built in Ivatt's time as Locomotive Engineer of the GNR. It was one of those built by Dübs & Company of Glasgow in 1898 and lasted into L&NER days. It was not withdrawn until April 1934 and was in fact, rebuilt with a larger boiler as late as 1924.

View looking towards Stafford Common with the goods yard on the right. The Stafford Common Yard signal box, which was never a block post, can just be discerned on the left opposite the goods yard.

The Stafford Common goods yard from the opposite direction to the previous view with a locomotive shunting in the background. Notice the Stafford Common Yard signal box again on the right, by this time boarded up and no longer in use.

Another view of Stafford Common goods yard with one of the GNR Stirling 0-4-2 mixed traffic tender engines shunting after it had been rebuilt with a domed boiler and an Ivatt cab. Notice the presence in the yard of coaching stock vehicles and some of the distinctive hip-roofed salt vans. More of these vans are included in the formation of the train on the down main line.

Another of the Stirling 0-4-2 tender engines, in this case number 357 of 1893. This locomotive was rebuilt in 1910 with a domed boiler and an Ivatt cab so this photograph at Stafford Common, must have been taken at an earlier date. In its rebuilt form, it lasted until March 1921 although in November 1910, it was fitted with a domeless boiler once again while retaining the Ivatt cab. It was a long term resident of Colwick shed. The driver is George Simpson (1849-1927), probably one of the first GNR drivers on the former independent S&UR and the firemen, Dodson, is his son-in-law. The gent standing on the framing with the uniform cap is we suspect, the Stafford Common Station Master and that will be one of the salt works' chimneys behind.

Yet another of the Stirling 0-4-2 tender engines which were popular on the line in the GNR period. This one is number 599 of 1876 seen here at Stafford Common. As the engine was withdrawn in June 1919, never having been rebuilt with a domed boiler and Ivatt cab, the photograph must be earlier than that.

Stafford Common again and one of the Stirling 2-4-0 passenger tender engines, in this case umber 202 of 1882, which was never fitted with the larger boiler and withdrawn in October 1911. The device at the front alongside the smokebox is the vacuum ejector for the brake system, modified to work the automatic, rather than the simple vacuum system as described in this Chapter. The photograph is said to date from 1897; the fellow on the left is Driver George Simpson while Fireman Dodson, his son-in-law, is on the right.

Not a very good photograph we fear, but one that illustrates through running of L&NWR engines and trains over the S&UR. This is an L&NWR Precursor class 4-4-0 express engine with a Stour Valley Excursion to Uttoxeter Races, calling at all stations from Stafford to Uttoxeter, in about 1910. It is about to leave Stafford Common Station and the engine is blowing off furiously.

double tracks to provide safer access to Stafford Cemetery, which was located on both sides of the line. The bridge had brick abutments and piers with steel girders and concrete flooring. In spite of the footbridge the cemetery occupation crossing continued in use and presented a possible danger to users. Therefore, a board bearing the legend *whistle* was fixed on the down side of the line 400 yards before the crossing and the drivers of down trains were required to sound the engine whistle on passing the board and continue to do so until they saw that the crossing was clear. On 4 May 1882 a contract in connection with a new station located to the east of Marston Road, together with other buildings, was awarded to Edward Wood for £2,121. The new station, which was opened later that year, was of all timber construction with a booking office astride the Marston Road over-bridge. The roof of the booking office sported a large and very distinctive notice board bearing the legend *Great Northern Railway*. Gated stairways connected with the booking office and Marston Road. In 1884 the GNR obtained powers[150] to abandon an occupation crossing which ran over its tracks and the throat of the goods yard to the south west of Stafford Common station.[151] This was a prelude to further expansion. On 6 March 1885 the

GNR entered into an agreement with Alfred Wilson, a Stafford engineer, for a siding just completed by the railway company, *a little to the east* of Stafford Common station for the purpose of carrying goods and material to and from Wilson's premises which adjoined the railway.[152] There was a charge of £10 per annum for the new connection which had been approved at a GNR directors' meeting held on 31 December 1884 at a cost of £122. In 1889 Wilson sold his works to Sampson Fox, an engineer from Leeds and on 19 July 1889 the siding agreement was transferred to the British Water Gas Syndicate Limited as Fox's nominee.[153] We suspect that the site for this activity was later occupied by the Stafford Salt & Alkali Company (see below).

Stafford Common goods yard became quite extensive with seven sidings, two of which had run around facilities for incoming and outgoing trains. The yard included a goods shed, weighbridge, cattle dock and a crane with a lifting capacity of 10 tons. The crane was actually transferred from Finsbury Park in 1903 at a cost of £120. Many of these items were covered in the estimates for improvements detailed in Appendix Seven but the proposal to build an engine shed to house four locomotives was not pursued. This may be because the original S&UR wooden locomotive shed at Stafford Common had burnt down in November 1881, causing the GNR to make alternative arrangements with the L&NWR at Stafford. All types of traffic could be handled at the goods yard, parcels being dealt with at the station. The GNR rented a four-stalled stable and loft on Bellasis Street which adjoined the southern boundary of the goods yard site. A rental of £18 per annum, including rates, taxes, gas and water was paid to the owner, Thomas Nixon, with effect from 15 September 1881 but he had the right to collect the manure from the horses. The horses were no doubt used for cartage and shunting within the goods yard.[154] This arrangement continued until 1904 by which time the GNR directors approved the provision of new stables at a cost of £460.

On 29 June 1909 the GNR's Chief Traffic Manager recommended to the directors that expenditure of £1,900 should be incurred on improving facilities at Stafford Common. Trade had been growing rapidly following an expansion in salt traffic (see below) such that the gross tonnage in goods and coal had increased from 54,621 tons in 1905 to 102,889 tons in 1908. Serious delays to traffic were being incurred and many complaints had been received from customers. There was also a waste of engine power in that the shunting engines had to run 1¼ miles to the L&NWR yard to take water. The Chief Traffic Manager reported that he had recently visited Stafford in order to see the difficulties and decide how they could best be met with the minimum outlay. This was how he costed his proposals:

£195 - Additional facing slip in main line to facilitate working and avoid delays to shunting engines.

£995 - Additional siding in goods yard to provide for sorting of traffic.

£275 - Provision of additional siding for dealing with wagons in and out of Chance and Hunt's works.

£215 - Proposed alterations to the existing sidings into Chance and Hunt's works.

£220 - Provision of water crane.

On 6 April 1910 Lt. Col. Edward Druitt (1859-1922) of the Railway Department of the Board of Trade inspected the new facilities.[155] He reported that Stafford Common yard box had been closed and that an old trailing connection to the down line formerly worked from that box was now worked from a new two-lever ground frame which was bolt locked from Stafford Common signal box. The new facing connection laid in the up line leading to new goods yard sidings was inspected and found satisfactory as was a replacement locking frame that had been installed in Stafford Common box. The new frame had 28 levers, including four spare. The new water crane was installed at the west end of the down platform.[156] A wagon re-railing ramp was made available at Stafford Common on the strict understanding that it was not used for re-railing engines or tenders as it was of insufficient strength. For more serious incidents the steam breakdown crane had to be summoned from Colwick.

The GNR in the 1910-1911 Parliamentary Session included provisions in its omnibus Bill[157] to abolish the occupation crossing at Blakeford Lane at the east end of Stafford Common station. In 1909 problems had arisen following the death of a horse which had strayed onto the line. Following this incident the 11ft wide gates protecting the crossing had been locked.[158] This action had created a furore of objections from the owner of a local field, two of the three salt companies and the owner of some nearby houses who claimed that the railway company's action had devalued his property. The field owner was placated by being given a key but Stubbs & Co. and the Stafford Salt & Alkali Co. Ltd initially refused to take a key arguing that the GNR should

man the crossing. Thomas Gibson, the manager of the latter company, had actually threatened to pull the gates down! Prior to the gates being locked, difficulties were also being encountered with children continually running over the line and women using the crossing to gain access to a public house. On several occasions they had been seen clambering under the wagons of goods trains standing in the station. George Shaw, GNR Goods Manager, went to Stafford on 10 November 1909 and visited both the salt companies who had objected to the closure. He pointed out to both of them that if the occupation crossing were made a public crossing, as suggested by some of their directors, the shunting operations to and from their private sidings would be greatly impeded as each movement to and fro would foul the crossing and cause delays through stricter controls. This rather obvious point had the desired effect and they backed down. Shaw also observed that the nearby houses built parallel to the railway on the south side of the station could be accessed by a private road connecting directly with the public road at the west end. In view of this he surmised that the owner could not possibly have a grievance. The private road was actually owned by the Stafford Salt & Alkali Co. Ltd.

In December 1910, the Station Master at Stafford Common, John Milburn Foster (see Chapter Ten) drew attention to yet another problem. On Saturday afternoons and Wednesday nights, the crossing was used by the local football team with their supporters causing great inconvenience to shunting operations. The landlord of the Volunteer Inn had a key to the gate but this had not been granted by the GNR. However, the field on

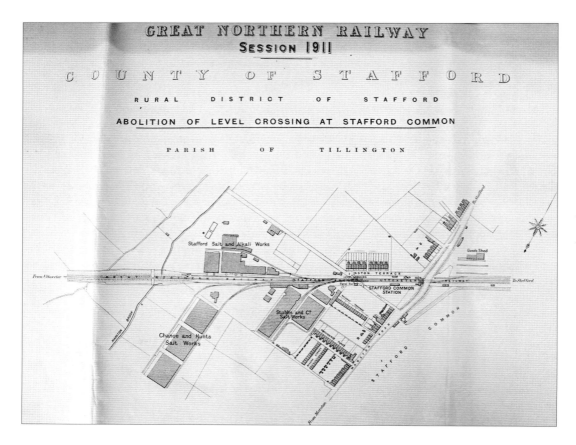

Proposed abolition of level crossing at Stafford Common, 1911. CRO Q/RUM/734

This is a particularly interesting photograph at Stafford Common as it shows the prototype of the Ivatt 4-4-0 passenger tender engines, later L&NER class D2, number 400. This engine was built at Doncaster in 1896 and was the first design credited to H.A. Ivatt when he became Locomotive Engineer of the GNR, a position he reached in 1895. It was rebuilt with a larger boiler to L&NER class D3 in September 1920, in which condition it is seen here so the photograph dates from between that date and the L&NER renumbering some time after January 1923. When it was new this engine was allocated to Retford and by November 1905 it had migrated to Grantham. However, by December 1922 it was at Colwick, hence its appearance at Stafford. It was withdrawn in September 1947.

which the team played was owned by Stubbs & Co., who had no doubt made their key available. In the days of the S&UR, the Blakeford Lane crossing was used solely for agricultural purposes and did not present a problem. It was now in the midst of three salt works, straddled a very busy station area, was used by the occupants of an increasing number of new houses and was clearly impeding the smooth flow of railway traffic. Something had to be done and the GNR took legal advice. Unfortunately the railway company's solicitor did not entirely give the advice hoped for. He said that the obligation imposed by section 75 of the Railways Clauses Consolidation Act 1845 [159] was to *shut and fasten gates* with a penalty in default. He did not consider that fastening necessarily meant locking and did not think that the railway company could compel the people concerned to use keys. The GNR ate humble pie and went begging to the Stafford Salt and Alkali Company with a proposal that the company's private road, known as Aston Terrace, should become a substitute for the access currently provided by the occupation crossing. The salt company said it would entertain the proposal but wanted the GNR to undertake not to build a siding into the land on the south side of the station owned by their rival, Stubbs & Co., i.e. the land used as the football field. Clearly the competition between the salt companies was at fever pitch and there was a fear that Stubbs and Co. could develop the football field for further salt extraction. The result of all this was that the GNR resorted to Parliament and was eventually granted the necessary statutory powers to abolish the crossing. The effort required to achieve this was quite amazing and one can only sympathise with the station master, the man on the spot, who must have had a nigh on impossible task in weighing up the interests of the safe and efficient working of the railway against upsetting two of his major customers and making himself very unpopular with the locals. He must have been a tough character and it is not surprising that John Milburn Foster's stint at Stafford Common lasted for 25 years. However, he must have been extremely frustrated when the crossing was subsequently reinstated!

Salt traffic

As mentioned in our Introduction, the accidental finding of a substantial salt deposit in Stafford in 1892 during attempts to secure a new fresh water supply for the town resulted in the establishment of three salt manufacturing firms at Stafford Common. This was a great and unexpected bonus for the GNR's freight carryings. All three firms used the open pan method whereby brine was pumped from underground into large iron pans and heated at normal atmospheric pressure. As the heat was applied salt crystals began to form and these were manually removed for processing.

The first firm on the scene was the Stafford Salt & Alkali Company which established a salt works to the east of Stafford Common station on the south side of the line. An agreement made between the GNR and the salt company on 20 February 1893 provided for the GNR to construct at its cost and maintain a siding connection to the new works and extend an existing siding to serve the firm's new store houses. The cost of this work amounted to £187. The salt company, under the agreement, had to complete the siding from the new connection to serve its coal holes and salt pans. In addition, it had to erect and maintain a gate across the GNR boundary and keep it locked except for the passage of traffic. The GNR required a rental of £18 4s 0d

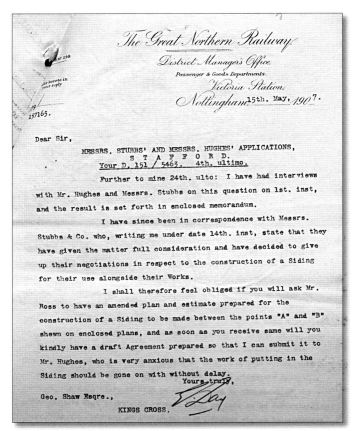

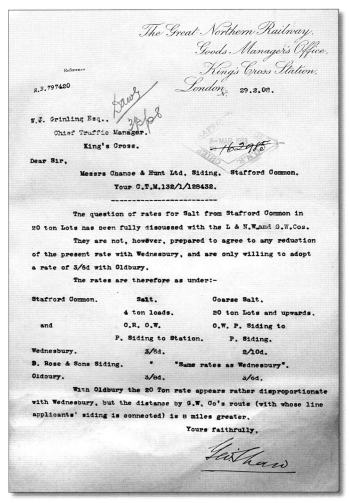

Official GNR correspondence relating to the arrival of the third company to establish a salt works at Stafford Common – Chance & Hunt of Oldbury, which conflicted with Stubbs & Co's interests. NA RAIL 783/516

(£18.20) per annum for not less than 14 years for providing and maintaining the new facilities with an annual rebate of £5 per cent on the gross amount received for the carriage of traffic with a limit on the maximum rebate equivalent to the annual rental.

With effect from 1 July 1913 the initial agreement was amended for the GNR to provide additional siding accommodation. It also clarified the position with regard to six loading stages previously erected by the salt company partly on its own land and partly on land owned by the GNR. The additional siding accommodation amounted to an extension of the existing siding which paralleled the main line. The traders undertook to pay a yearly sum equivalent to 10% on the cost of the siding extension in addition to the payments provided for in the principal agreement. In addition, the traders also had to pay a fee of 1s 0d (5p) in respect of each loading stage effective from 31 December 1913. This fee enabled the salt company to maintain and use the existing and erect any further loading stages whilst acknowledging that the firm had no right or title to the facilities they had provided! The new agreement was for a period of 14 years and also extended the principal agreement for a similar period.

The second development involving the Crown Salt Works, was undertaken by Stubbs & Co. Frederick Stubbs concluded a siding agreement with the GNR on 31 May 1895, but this was superseded

by a second agreement which came into effect on 1 January 1898, formally signed and sealed by no less than nine members of the Stubbs family, including Frederick, on 3 June 1898. The family hailed from Winsford in Cheshire where those involved with the Stafford venture had already been engaged in the salt trade in one form or another. The siding agreement required the firm to pay £10 per annum for the connection with provision for a rebate based on the amount of traffic carried over the siding. It left the down line at Stafford Common by a trailing connection at the east end of the station platform, crossed the up line by a diamond crossing and then entered the firm's premises. At this point GNR maintenance for the siding ended and a gate was placed across the siding which Stubbs & Co. were required to keep locked at all times except for the passage of traffic. Drivers of trains moving from the down main into the salt works were required to give one long blast on the engine's whistle before starting. Salt traffic from the Crown Salt Works amounted to 12,209 tons in 1904; 11,760 tons in 1905 and 17,092 tons in 1906. On 30 November 1906 Stubbs requested additional siding accommodation in order to cope with increasing demands for their salt.[160] In subsequent exchanges they argued that there was considerable delay to their outwards traffic as there was only standing room for three wagons loading bulk salt. During the spring when there was an increased demand for salt for agricultural purposes, they often received orders for 17 wagon loads resulting in sales being turned down. The congestion experienced at these times created additional work for GNR shunting engines. Stubbs pointed out that, at its own expense, the firm had provided an additional siding some seven years ago and now required siding accommodation for 24 wagons alongside its site similar to the arrangement prevailing for the Stafford Salt & Alkali Company on the opposite side of the line. The proposal, estimated to cost £365, was well received by the GNR but there was a problem.

Whilst negotiations for the new siding were continuing, the railway company was approached by John Hughes, representing a syndicate whose identity had to be kept secret. Hughes explained that he had been the Chief Mining Engineer to Lord Dudley for some 52 years and was the Chairman of Sandwell Park Colliery, West Bromwich. The GNR recognised him as a man of means and excellent standing and proceeded to negotiate with him in respect of a siding to a new 50 acre site at Stafford Common where the syndicate was proposing to invest upwards of £40,000 in a third salt works. On 3 May 1907 Hughes revealed in strict confidence that he was representing Chance and Hunt Ltd which had been registered in 1898 following the merger of the Oldbury Alkali Company Ltd and William Hunt & Sons of Wednesbury. There was a problem in that the siding connection to the new site would cut across that currently proposed by Stubbs & Co. The latter did not take kindly to the proposal especially when the GNR suggested that the company pay two thirds of the revised cost of £370 with only one third being paid by the newcomers. Moreover, Stubbs were somewhat staggered when it was pointed out that, under clause four of their agreement, the GNR was entitled to connect the firm's siding with any other that the railway company chose to provide for any other company. The upshot of all this was that Stubbs withdrew from the negotiations and a new arrangement was agreed with Hughes at a revised cost

of £330. In July 1907 Chance and Hunt revealed their identity and the new siding opened later that year on 25 September. By 17 May 1908 just over 15,600 tons of inward traffic had been received over the siding, mainly comprising bricks, lime and other construction materials but also including 3,605 tons of coal; 2,075 tons of salt had been forwarded.

The official siding agreement between the GNR and Chance and Hunt Ltd (referred to as 'the traders') was dated 21 May 1908. It provided for the railway company to lay in the connection from the lead into Stubbs' siding and provide a gate across the new link where it entered the traders' premises. From that point, Chance and Hunt was responsible for extending the siding into the company's premises to the satisfaction of the GNR's Engineer. The GNR was responsible for maintaining the siding up to the gate. The traders were responsible for locking the gate when no traffic was passing and for maintaining the siding beyond that point. The agreed annual payment for the use of the new connection was based on 10% of the cost of providing the siding and the gate, including labour and materials. The GNR allowed the traders a yearly credit of 5% on traffic carried, provided that the total credit allowed did not exceed the fixed annual payment. The traders were required to send a reasonable amount of traffic over the new siding with 'reasonable' being described as traffic producing £750 of revenue every six months.

In December 1909 Stubbs & Co. were relieved of their obligation to keep the gate across their siding closed as the new arrangements for Chance and Hunt had necessitated its removal and the GNR no longer considered a gate necessary.[161] In July 1911 Stubbs had another attempt at persuading the GNR to improve their siding accommodation but the proposal proved impracticable through the proposed curves being too tight. In 1913 the output from all three firms totalled 81,000 tons; the salt was used for agricultural purposes and in the chemical, tanning, food and fishing industries, some finding its way to the east coast

Stafford Common was well known for its salt works of which there were three separate establishments. The Chance & Hunt works was on the north side of the line and this is one of its private owner wagons, number 321 built by Charles Roberts of Wakefield, a 12-ton seven plank open wagon, probably used for bringing coal to the site.

COLLECTION KEITH TURTON

ports of Hull and Grimsby. The Stafford salt firms continued to provide a useful source of traffic to the GNR until it ceased to exist on the grouping of the railways which took place with effect from 1 January 1923. Thereafter they dealt with the L&NER which, of course, inherited all three siding agreements.

The Stafford Salt & Alkali Company used a powered capstan and wire ropes to shunt the wagons and vans whereas Chance and Hunt employed four shire horses. The latter's salt loading and coal bay sidings were both protected with semaphore home signals owned and worked by the salt company. The agreement dated 3 June 1898 with Stubbs & Co. was replaced with a new agreement dated 20 May 1920. The new agreement reflected two significant changes. First, it was made with Stubbs and Co. Ltd to reflect the change in the firm's previous status as a partnership and, secondly, it provided for the GNR to shunt the firm's siding once a day. If the shunting requirement became more onerous, the agreement provided for additional charges to be levied.

One characteristic of the salt trade was the development of distinctive hip-roofed vans specifically designed to disperse rain water quickly and protect the goods carried from water seepage. Most of these vans had rain strips above the side doors. All three

Stafford firms adopted this design for the carriage of some of their products and examples were built by the Birmingham Railway Carriage & Wagon Company, Charles Roberts of Wakefield and Hurst, Nelson of Motherwell. These private owner vehicles bore colourful liveries displaying their owners' names and sometimes the trade names for their products. The records for Charles Roberts reveal that vehicles built to the following specifications were delivered to Chance & Hunt Ltd at Stafford Common for the carriage of salt shortly after the opening of the new works.

14 April 1908 – 6 × 10 ton salt wagons 15' 6" × 7' 4" × 4' c"; side doors; Nos. 140-145; registered GWR; deliver to Stafford Common GNR. Fit Williams' patent sheet supports and sheet string fasteners. Paint red, yellow letters shaded: CHANCE AND HUNT LIMITED, OLDBURY WEDNESBURY & STAFFORD.

29 July 1908 – 6 × 10 ton salt wagons 15' 6" × 7' 0" × 4' 0"; 7" × 7" planks; side doors; Nos. 148-153; registered GWR; deliver to Stafford Common GNR. Fit Williams' patent sheet support and sheet string fasteners. Top of underframe to be well tarred before frame fitted; floor to be of 2½" tongue and groove longitudinal battens; underframe to be well coated with tar. Paint red with yellow letters as before.

For the salt traffic itself, special vans were used like the one illustrated here, with hip-roofs. Although bearing a later number (333) than the wagon in the previous view, this one is actually of an earlier build date as it has grease rather than oil axle boxes. Built by the Birmingham Railway Carriage & Wagon Company at its Smethwick works in 1913.

COLLECTION HISTORICAL MODEL RAILWAY SOCIETY

2 January 1909 – 12 × salt vans to specifications; Nos. 169-179; registered GNR; deliver to Stafford Common GNR; paint red: CHANCE AND HUNT LTD. OLDBURY WEDNESBURY & STAFFORD. This is a sample order in competition with another firm and further orders may depend on it. A FIRST CLASS JOB MUST BE MADE OF THE TRUCKS.

8 February 1909 – 10 × covered salt vans ; Nos. 180-189; North Central plates 63429-63438; registered GNR; deliver to Stafford Common GNR. Exactly the same as previous order.

6 April 1909 – 6 × 10 ton salt wagons 15' 6"× 7' 0" × 4' 0"; 7"× 7" planks; side doors; ends rising 11"; Nos. 211-215; North Central plates 64225-64320; registered GNR; deliver to Stafford Common GNR. No Williams' poles. To be fitted with Williams' sheet string fasteners. Inside ironwork to be covered with wood; floor 2½" tongue and groove sloping to middle of floor and laid longitudinally; tops of underframes to be well tarred and ironwork in underframe to be well coated with tar. Paint as before.

6 April 1909 – 6 × covered salt vans as previously; Nos. 205-210; North Central plates 64219-64224; registered GNR; deliver to Stafford Common GNR.

20 May 1909 – 15 × 10 ton salt wagons 15' 6"× 7' 0" × 4' 0"; 7"× 7" planks; side doors; ends rising 11"; sheet pole not required; specifications as previous order; Nos. 234-248; North Central plates 65618-65632; registered GNR; deliver to Stafford Common.

20 May 1909 – 15 × covered salt vans to specifications; Nos. 219-233; North Central plates 65603-65617; registered GNR; deliver to Stafford Common GNR.

Thus, in just over a year, the new works took delivery of 33 seven-plank wagons and 43 covered vans which demonstrated the strength of the new business. Some of these vehicles were leased from the North Central Wagon Company of Rotherham which was founded in 1861, becoming a joint stock company with limited liability in 1894. Because of the corrosive nature of the salt, the vans and wagons proved difficult to maintain requiring frequent attention to paintwork and axle boxes.

In 1926 Chance & Hunt became part of the Imperial Chemical Industries empire and this is one of the salt vans in ICI ownership – number 185.

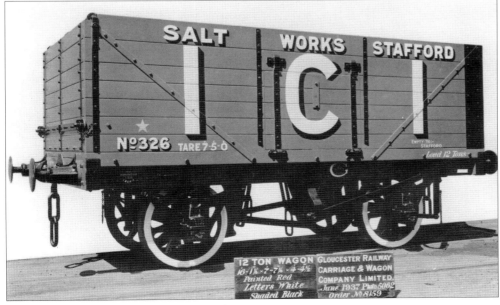

In 1937 the Gloucester Railway Carriage & Wagon Company supplied this wagon, fleet number 326, to ICI for use at the Stafford Works. Although not a salt carrying wagon, it was presumably used for the disposal of waste products from the works as it is marked 'EMPTY TO:-STAFFORD'. COLLECTION PHIL JONES

The oldest of the salt companies was the Stafford Salt & Alkali Company which had its works on the south side of the line, opposite Chance & Hunt. This is one of its wagons bearing the trade name "SNOWDRIFT" SALT. Although it might not be discernible in the photograph as reproduced here, the lettering to the left reads 'Home for repairs or advise W.E. Dinham & Son, Wagon Works, Stafford'. Dinham's had a workshop to the south of Stafford Station on the up side opposite Trent Valley Junction.

COLLECTION KEITH TURTON

Stubbs & Co's Salt Works was like Chance & Hunt, on the north side of the line at Stafford Common. This is one of its special wagons designed for carrying salt, number 111 built by the Birmingham Carriage & Wagon Company at Smethwick. It is an early design with grease axle boxes.

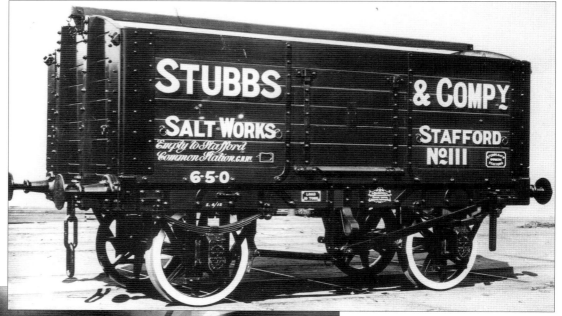

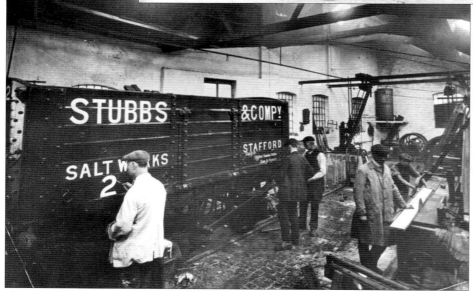

Stubbs & Co. had its own wagon repairing facilities seen here with a newly repaired six plank wagon number 2; a signwriter is busy completing the final touches.

COLLECTION PHIL JONES

In 1930 Stubbs & Co. Salt Works was acquired by Manger's and here is some of its rolling stock, although the location is not recorded. Two vans of the special and distinctive design and one open wagon behind the one lettered LMS.

COLLECTION HISTORICAL
MODEL RAILWAY SOCIETY

This photograph of Manger's No. 116 was taken at Berkhamsted on 6 October 1946. In a census of private owner wagons undertaken by the British Transport Commission in May 1950, Manger's still had a fleet of 113 hip-roofed covered 10-ton vans built between 1891 and 1916 and Stafford Salt & Alkali had five 8-ton and 48 10-ton examples. The vehicle illustrated was one of a batch built in 1896 and registered by the GNR as No. 5155. It has a wood frame, grease axle boxes and split spoke wheels, all indicative of its age. The lettering on the far right lower planking reads 'Empty to Stafford Common'.

H.C. CASSERLEY NO. 47565

This is Manger's No. 121, a vehicle with a similar specification to No. 116 but with a much more attractive livery. Photograph taken at Berkhamsted on 21 July 1946.

H.C. CASSERLEY NO. 47506

Stafford was also well known for its brine baths due to the salt-bearing strata of the ground. Here is one of the tank wagons used by the Corporation in connection with the baths. It was built by Hurst, Nelson & Company of Motherwell.

Developments at Uttoxeter

Almost coincidental with the GNR's acquisition of the S&UR there was a major improvement in facilities offered by the NSR at Uttoxeter which included the construction of a new double-tracked curve of 28 chains in length to connect the Churnet Valley line to the Stoke-Derby line with a new junction facing Stoke, new signalling and a new four-platform station. The new facilities were inspected by Major General Charles Scrope Hutchinson and in his report dated 1 June 1881, he approved the new arrangements with the exception of the station itself which was not ready.[162] The new station was subject to a second positive report dated 20 September and opened on 1 October 1881. It had a long lattice girder inter-connecting footbridge which later became even more distinctive when it acquired a roof during the spring of 1895. The new station replaced Uttoxeter Bridge Street, Uttoxeter Junction and Uttoxeter Dove Bank stations. These stations had opened on 7 August 1848, 11 September 1848 [163] and 13 July 1849 respectively and had been a recipe for confusion and inconvenience. The new station was managed by Station Master Thomas Mellor (1842-1921) who had previously been the station master at Uttoxeter Bridge Street and had also been responsible for Dove Bank and the Junction stations which did not have separate station masters. The Junction station was merely an exchange point for passengers switching trains; it had neither road nor pedestrian access to the town. Thomas Mellor would often travel from Bridge Street to the Junction station to superintend the transfer of passengers and then travel back to Dove Bank on a Churnet Valley line or Ashbourne train, walking from there back to Bridge Street. The new station eliminated the need for this palaver. The new connection to the Churnet Valley line enabled a train from Macclesfield or Ashbourne to run directly to Stoke or vice versa. In practice such movements were rare and usually involved excursion trains but the new station provided a much improved connection for Churnet Valley line passengers wishing to interchange with Crewe-Derby line trains at Uttoxeter. On opening, the new station immediately became a station of significant importance on the NSR network, even sporting a W.H. Smith newspaper and book stall. With effect from 1 November 1881, all trains running between Stafford and Derby in accordance with the GNR's revised timetable called at the new station thereby enhancing its importance.

From the outset of S&UR operations in 1867 the company's locomotives had used the single road NSR locomotive shed situated to the south of Pinfold West Crossing and Uttoxeter West Junction. This shed, which could accommodate two locomotives under cover, had a coaling platform at the rear and a small 17ft diameter turntable. In 1873 a new 45ft diameter turntable was installed at Uttoxeter East Junction and all S&UR locomotives would have used this turntable until 1881 when it was transferred to Stoke. Thereafter, all locomotives requiring turning at Uttoxeter used the triangle created by the newly opened curve to the Churnet Valley line but this facility was not normally required by the GNR as its trains now ran through to Derby and beyond. In 1901[164] the NSR provided a new three road locomotive shed at Uttoxeter capable of holding twelve locomotives at a cost of £4,054 plus an extra £240 for a culvert to collect water and, in July 1903, a further cost of £550 for a Worlaston water softening plant to treat the hard water supplied. An original estimate of £8,000 was approved by the NSR directors at their meeting on 27 March 1900, but this included a turntable and carriage washing shed which were subsequently cancelled because of increased costs. No doubt GNR locomotives used this facility in an emergency but such occasions were rare as the crews of any ailing locomotives would be encouraged to struggle on until repairs could be carried out at the GNR's Derby Friargate locomotive shed. Uttoxeter shed passed into the LM&SR and BR eras and finally closed on 7 December 1964. The shed code 5F was adopted in 1935 and this remained in use until the end. It was always a sub-shed of Stoke.

Passenger services to Derby and beyond

The GNR's first passenger timetable was introduced with effect from 1 September 1881 and operated until 31 October that year. It provided for four trains each way between Stafford and Uttoxeter on weekdays with an additional train from Stafford to Uttoxeter on Saturdays; no trains ran on Sundays. Departures from Stafford L&NWR were at 8am, 11.5am, 1.40pm and 4.10pm, arriving at Uttoxeter at 8.45am, 11.50am, 2.25pm and 4.55pm, respectively. The extra train on Saturdays left Stafford at 7.30pm arriving at Uttoxeter at 8.30pm. Departures from Uttoxeter were at 9.35am, 12 noon, 2.50pm and 5.20pm with corresponding arrivals at Stafford at 10.20am, 12.40pm, 3.35pm and 6.5pm. All these trains called at all the intermediate stations, excepting the 11.5am from Stafford and the 12 noon from Uttoxeter which only called at Grindley to set down passengers on notice being given to the guard or to pick up passengers when required by signal. The extra train from Stafford on Saturdays was introduced for the benefit of passengers wishing to attend the Stafford market. Cheap market tickets were available for use on the 9.35am train from Uttoxeter for return by the 4.10pm and 7.30pm trains from Stafford. Return fares from Stafford to Uttoxeter were 3s 9d (19p) first class, 3s 0d (15p) second class and 2s 6d (12½p) third class. For the first two months the GNR did little more than carry on the existing service with the former S&UR staff while their capability was tested.

Importantly, the purchase of the S&UR enabled the GNR to reorganise its Nottingham to Burton timetable and work the S&UR as an integral part of its Western Division from the District Office at Nottingham. The railway from Grantham to Burton was always regarded as the main line of the GNR's Derbyshire and Staffordshire extension with the S&UR treated separately as the Derby and Stafford line. With effect from 1 November 1881, the timetable was reorganised such that six passenger trains ran in each direction between Stafford and Derby on weekdays and one train in each direction on Sundays.

Down trains or light engines were restricted to 10mph when passing over facing points or running through the intermediate stations. A similar restriction applied to up trains but in this case the limit was increased to 15mph when passing through stations. In April 1884 trains left Stafford L&NWR at 6.20am, 9.0am, 11.23am, 2.32pm, 4.30pm and 7.25pm. Arrival times at Derby Friargate were 7.51am, 10.23am, 12.56pm, 3.53pm, 6.11pm and 8.52pm. In the reverse direction, trains left Derby at 6.42am, 8.43am, 10.55am, 1.16pm, 4.13pm and 6.31pm with arrivals in Stafford at 7.58am, 10.15am, 12.37am, 2.32pm, 5.45pm, and 8.4pm. On Sundays a train left Derby at 4pm, arriving at Stafford at 5.35pm. It returned at 6.10pm, arriving in Derby at 7.42pm. Obviously a Sunday return day trip would serve no useful purpose but presumably the trains enabled people to return home on Sundays following a weekend or a longer period away. The weekday and Sunday trains called at all stations on the branch. The GNR encouraged excursion traffic, especially to the east coast resorts of Skegness and Cleethorpes and so it is of no surprise to discover that on Whit Monday 1883 the Stafford Wesleyan Mutual Improvement Society took advantage of a special train to Great Grimsby and Cleethorpes for its annual outing. The train left Stafford at 5.30am, arriving at Cleethorpes shortly before 11am. Second class accommodation on all trains to and from Stafford was abolished with effect from 1 May 1885.

The GNR working timetable (WTT) effective from 1 July 1895 shows a similar pattern of trains in each direction but with the through service on weekdays being extended to and from the GNR's Nottingham London Road station. The second train of the day from Nottingham ran as a mixed train from Egginton Junction to Stafford. Most of the trains destined for Stafford were permitted to take cattle from Uttoxeter to Stafford providing the cattle vans were fitted with brake pipes. The Sunday train still commenced from Derby at 4pm but ran as a mixed train from Egginton Junction to Stafford. It returned from Stafford at 7.20pm as a passenger and milk train but only ran as far as Egginton.

With the opening of the GNR and Great Central Railway (GCR) joint station at Nottingham Victoria on 24 May 1900, the GNR's Burton and Stafford trains, which had previously terminated at Derby and Nottingham, were extended to Newark and Grantham thereby providing a very competitive cross country service which lasted until 31 December 1916, the one exception being the withdrawal of the Stafford Sunday service from 1 October 1908. The new extended service reflected the zenith of passenger operation on the former S&UR. Taking the April 1912 timetable as a typical example we find the following departures and arrivals at Stafford.

DEPARTURES	ARRIVALS
6.20am to Grantham	7.55am from Grantham
8.55am to Derby	10.42am from Nottingham
11.30am to Newark	12.41pm from Derby
2.15pm to Derby	2.49pm from Grantham
4.30pm to Derby	6.18pm from Newark
7.25pm to Derby	9.1pm from Nottingham

There were excellent connections at Derby Friargate with the GNR's Burton trains. The outbreak of the First World War on 4 August 1914 had no immediate impact on the country's passenger services. It was not until 1 January 1917 that the GNR along with other railway companies drastically reduced the services offered. Insofar as the S&UR was concerned the cuts eliminated the 6.20am and 11.30am departures from Stafford with their corresponding return trains. As a result the GNR no longer needed to stable a locomotive overnight at the L&NWR's Stafford running shed.

The GNR's separate booking facility at Stafford station ceased with effect from 1 August 1915, the L&NWR staff taking over the issue of tickets and the booking of parcel traffic for the duration of the war. The reduced service of four trains in each direction continued until grouping. The WTT effective from 2 October 1922, one of the last to be issued by the GNR, provided for the following departures from Stafford: 8.55pm, 2.15pm, 4.40pm and 7.25pm. All these trains terminated at Derby except the 4.40pm departure which ran through to Ilkeston except on Saturdays or Bank holidays. In the opposite direction there were four arrivals from Derby.

In summary, there were four distinct phases of passenger services over the S&UR prior to grouping:

1. The purely local service offered by the independent company between Stafford and Uttoxeter between 1867 and the GNR takeover in 1881.

2. The GNR's initial extended service to Derby Friargate and Nottingham London Road with six trains in each direction which sufficed until 1900.

3. The GNR's enhanced service introduced following the opening of Nottingham Victoria station on 24 May 1900 which provided for certain trains to run through to Grantham and Newark.

4. The GNR's final phase of four trains in each direction to Derby operated from 1 January 1917 until grouping.

The Sunday service was at best meagre and ceased to exist completely in 1908.

Horses and carriages
Horses and carriages could be handled at Stafford and Uttoxeter. They could also be handled by GNR staff at all the intermediate stations except Salt and Grindley. However, at Grindley horses could be loaded and unloaded when in charge of their owners or servants. At Chartley it was only possible for light carriages to be handled if they could be man-handled over the side of an open carriage truck. Whenever horse boxes were ordered for horses going to a meet of hounds, for example, the Meynell hunt, an advice had to be sent by the station master to the divisional superintendent's office the previous day, either by an urgent train message or by telegraph stating how many boxes were required and indicating where they would be loaded and by which train the vehicles would travel.

The racecourse at Uttoxeter opened in May 1907 and stimulated more traffic on and around race days. However, Uttoxeter had always been something of an equestrian centre and horse shows at the town were fairly common as evidenced by the show held between 25 and 31 August 1901 when special instructions were given to add additional carriages to the workings between Stafford and Uttoxeter. A fare concession was also granted for this event whereby tickets equivalent to a single fare and a quarter could be issued for the double journey.

Milk traffic

The GNR was very successful in developing milk traffic from the stations between Stafford and Derby. Readers will recall that counsel for the L&NWR when supporting the L&NWR's petition against the Stafford and Uttoxeter Railway Bill in the House of Lords in 1879, said that milk using the GNR route to London *would be butter by the time it arrived*. As events transpired nothing could be further from the truth. The milk was carried in 17 gallon galvanised iron conical churns; the cylindrical type with the mushroom shaped lid carrying 10 gallons not being introduced until the 1930s. A four-wheeled milk van could hold 40 × 17 gallon churns whereas a six-wheeled van could accommodate 50 churns. Each churn carried a brass plate near the top to identify its owner and when full carried a white label tied to the handle which was used for accounting purposes by the creamery or dairy. The churns were very heavy and the usual practice was to tilt them on one side and roll them along. By 1900 the GNR was operating two express milk trains from Egginton to London on each night of the week. The first departed at 8.45pm and the second at 9.30pm. Both trains ran non-stop from Grantham to Finsbury Park. On Sundays the workings were similar with a 9.0pm departure from Egginton but the second train started from Stafford at 7.0pm, stopping at all intermediate stations to Uttoxeter, departing Egginton at 9.10pm. On weekdays milk from the intermediate stations on the S&UR was carried in vans on the scheduled passenger

services and transferred at Egginton. It later became the practice to start one of the weekday trains from Stafford Common. In December 1902 the GNR Directors approved expenditure of £222 to provide a road to the rear of the up platform at Grindley for better accommodation of the milk traffic for which Grindley had become a significant concentration point.

Dairies were located at Ingestre, Uttoxeter and Egginton, the Egginton Dairy Company being incorporated on 3 October 1887. In 1901 the Nestlé Anglo-Swiss Condensed Milk Company opened its factory at Tutbury and from 1911 condensed milk was consigned via the GNR from the Tutbury factory to London's Poplar Dock. The NSR conveyed the condensed milk traffic to Egginton on weekday afternoons in time to catch the GNR's 4.45pm Burton-Colwick goods train. On 23 November 1911, the GNR entered into an agreement with Great Western and Metropolitan Dairies Ltd whose new dairy was adjacent to the up line at Ingestre and Weston station. Under this agreement the GNR undertook to build a loading stage for milk traffic on the strip of railway owned land between the railway and the dairy. In 1920, the GNR agreed to extend the loading stage further to the west at a cost of £418. The dairy at Ingestre did not have its own siding until 1928 (see Chapter Nine).

The Sunday milk train from Stafford became something of an institution especially after all other Sunday services ceased in 1908. The silence at the country stations would be rudely interrupted by the incoming train and the unloading of the

These two photographs taken at Ingestre and Weston though not particularly good, do show the United Diaries milk traffic. In the first view the tank wagons are being loaded while in the second, they are in the process of being attached to a passenger train. At least some of the wagons in this view, the ones with the larger tanks, are high capacity six-wheelers.

This is the dairy adjacent to Ingestre and Weston Station with the down side station platform building to the right. Undated but about 1900.
COLLECTION PHIL JONES

A rather nice photograph of a Wilts United Dairies Ltd of Uttoxeter, motor milk lorry registration number MW 7788 (Swindon registered) doubtless engaged in either collecting full or delivering empty milk churns at local farms. The cylindrical churns each held ten gallons.
STAFFORDSHIRE ARTS & MUSEUM SERVICE

empty churns and then again later in the day as the London bound train called to take on the loaded churns. The bustle and noise and the interaction between the railway staff and farmers must have created a very animated scene. In order to discharge milk churns and save delay, special instructions allowed the down milk train to be turned on to the up platform lines at Grindley, Chartley and Ingestre stations. The Appendix to the GNR rules and regulations and working time tables issued from King's Cross in May 1912 allowed this practice and stipulated the following. *After the facing points have been securely set for the up line, and the train has been nearly stopped at the respective home signals, a hand caution signal must be shown from the signal box to the driver as authority to pass the signal at danger and proceed along the up road to the up platform for the purpose of unloading. The driver must not start his train again after the churns have been unloaded without first obtaining permission from the signalman.* By this time Chartley signal box was not worked as a block box but only as required when it was operated by a porter. At Chartley all up and down trains usually used the down loop and so the milk train was very much an exception to the general rule. The arrangements for the down Sunday milk train were perpetuated by the L&NER.

Accident at Chartley – 30 March 1882

On Thursday morning an alarming accident occurred on the Stafford and Uttoxeter branch of the Great Northern Railway to a special train which was being run from Derby to Ingestre for the convenience of the Meynell Hunt, whose fixture for the day was at Stafford Lodge, Shugborough. This report under the heading *'Disastrous Accident'* was carried by *The Derby Mercury* on Wednesday, 5 April 1882. The accident concerned a serious derailment at Chartley and it was indeed a disaster both for the GNR less than a year after it had acquired the line and for the Meynell Hunt who had to abandon its meeting following the death of one horse and one hound and injuries to the other animals. Fortunately, none of the passengers which included some 20 gentlemen and two ladies, was seriously injured neither were any of the staff. The Board of Trade sent Colonel Frederick Henry Rich (1824-1904) to investigate. What follows is based on his report which was written on 29 April 1882, printed copies being sent to the GNR on the following 17 May.[165]

The special train ran as follows:

Derby Friargate	dep.	8.58am
Mickleover	arr.	9.04
Mickleover	dep.	9.08
Egginton	pass	9.16
Tutbury	arr.	9.22
Tutbury	dep.	9.26
Sudbury	arr.	9.33
Sudbury	dep.	9.40
Uttoxeter	arr.	9.48
Uttoxeter	dep.	9.59
Bromshall Junction	pass	10.07
Off the road at Chartley		10.20

The train called at Mickleover to collect Reginald Walkelyne Chandos-Pole (1853-1930) who was master of the hunt. With him was a party from his home at nearby Radbourne Hall. At Sudbury the train called to pick up the hounds from the Meynell Hunt kennels, huntsmen and more passengers with their horses and servants. The train was hauled, chimney leading, by Stirling 0-4-2 No. 569 built by Sharp Stewart & Co. (maker's number 2591) in November 1876. It was fitted with Smith's non-automatic vacuum brake and as far as Sudbury the whole train was so braked. At Sudbury several non-vacuum fitted NSR horse boxes were added to the formation. Six of these were marshalled behind a GNR 3rd class brake which was next to the engine's tender and so when the train left Sudbury only the locomotive, its tender and the first vehicle of the train had the benefit of the vacuum brake. The exact make up of the train behind the engine after leaving Sudbury was as follows:

GNR 3rd class brake	No. 1483
NSR horse box	No. 2
NSR horse box	No. 14
NSR horse box	No. 12
NSR horse box	No. 1
NSR horse box	No. 30
NSR horse box	No. 22
GNR horse box	No. 1253
MS&LR horse box	No. 608
GNR horse box	No. 1158
GNR horse box	No. 1206
GNR 1st class coach	No. 1370
GNR 1st class coach	No. 39
GNR 2nd class brake	No. 1752
NSR horse box	No. 13

Evidence was taken from eleven GNR employees, ten of whom experienced or witnessed the derailment. Those who gave evidence were: Samuel Austin, signalman at Chartley; George Culpin, signalman, acting porter at Chartley; John Curtis, passenger guard, acting station master at Chartley; George Dickinson, engine driver; John Drury, foreman at Derby, riding in the rear GNR 2nd class brake to assist in unloading horses at Ingestre; John Greasley, fireman also acting as pilotman; Hook, goods guard, riding in the front GNR 3rd class brake to assist in

The Meynell Hunt assembling at Grindley with the station to the top right. No sign of the hounds.

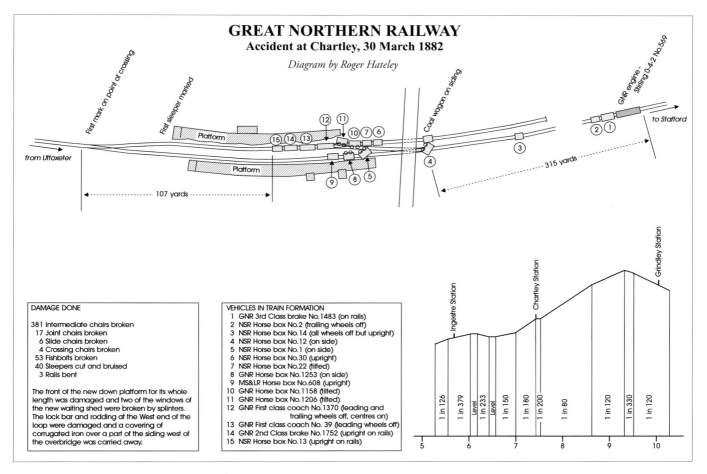

GREAT NORTHERN RAILWAY
Accident at Chartley, 30 March 1882
Diagram by Roger Hateley

DAMAGE DONE

381 Intermediate chairs broken
17 Joint chairs broken
6 Slide chairs broken
4 Crossing chairs broken
53 Fishbolts broken
40 Sleepers cut and bruised
3 Rails bent

The front of the new down platform for its whole length was damaged and two of the windows of the new waiting shed were broken by splinters. The lock bar and rodding at the West end of the loop were damaged and a covering of corrugated iron over a part of the siding west of the overbridge was carried away.

VEHICLES IN TRAIN FORMATION
1 GNR 3rd Class brake No.1483 (on rails)
2 NSR Horse box No.2 (trailing wheels off)
3 NSR Horse box No.14 (all wheels off but upright)
4 NSR Horse box No.12 (on side)
5 NSR Horse box No.1 (on side)
6 NSR Horse box No.30 (upright)
7 NSR Horse box No.22 (tilted)
8 GNR Horse box No.1253 (on side)
9 MS&LR Horse box No.608 (upright)
10 GNR Horse box No.1158 (tilted)
11 GNR Horse box No.1206 (tilted)
12 GNR First class coach No.1370 (leading and trailing wheels off, centres on)
13 GNR First class coach No. 39 (leading wheels off)
14 GNR 2nd Class brake No.1752 (upright on rails)
15 NSR Horse box No.13 (upright on rails)

unloading horses; Henry Mady, guard, riding in the front GNR 3rd class brake; Thomas Sibthorpe, guard, riding in the rear GNR 2nd class brake; George Wilson, inspector, riding in the rear GNR 2nd class brake; Wilson, district locomotive superintendent at Colwick who was not on the train. The attention given to this special train was quite amazing.

The engine driver stated that he had been a driver for nearly seven years and drove passenger and goods trains in the Nottinghamshire district but had not previously travelled over the S&UR. The fireman had been employed in that capacity for two years and had been kept on duty at Colwick specially to act as pilotman on the S&UR as he was well acquainted with the line having worked on it *some scores of times* before the accident. The driver recalled that when leaving Sudbury superintendent Wilson told him to be aware that he only had the vacuum brake on the van next to the tender. All went well until the approach to Chartley which was not a booked calling point. We will now let the driver tell his own story: *I shut off steam about three quarters of a mile before reaching Chartley. As soon as I saw the points open for the left-hand line I applied the vacuum break [sic] to the engine, and this was connected with the front carriage break [sic] only. The pilotman who was with me was experienced and knew the road; he was acting as fireman. I noticed the gradient board to be 1 in 80, and asked the fireman how far it was like that? He said it was a falling gradient all the way to Ingestre, but it was not 1 in 80 all the way. I knew that we were approaching Chartley by having passed*

the distant signal, and by approaching the down home signal, which was at all-right, but I did not know that we should have to pass over a sharp curve such as that which leads to the down platform. The reverse curve on entering the loop was the nub of the problem. While the fireman had worked the line scores of times before the accident, he said that when he last passed through Chartley there was only one line of rails and admitted that he did not know it had been doubled through the station. Indeed the new arrangement had only been brought into use on 21 March, nine days before the accident.

Colonel Rich observed that the driver, on becoming aware that he would have to enter the 'S' curve on entering the loop, applied the vacuum brake which was fitted to the engine, tender and the 3rd class brake next to it. He did his best to check the speed of his train, which ran safely through the facing points, but the leading brake van appeared to have struck the crossing point about 36 yards inside the facing points and jumped off the rails. All the horse boxes, except the one immediately behind the brake van and the one at the tail of the train, were then thrown off the rails to the right and left as they reached the station platform. The down line platform was considerably damaged for the whole of its length and there was some damage to the up platform. The engine and the 3rd class brake (which had somehow re-railed itself) and NSR horse box No. 2, which had lost its trailing wheels, stopped some distance from the station. The driver and fireman were unhurt and later drove the engine on to Ingestre. Twelve vehicles in the train were damaged, the only vehicles surviving unscathed being GNR 1st class coach No. 39, GNR 2nd class brake No. 1752 and NSR horse box No. 13, which formed the last three vehicles of the train. Colonel Rich concluded that the accident was caused by the engine driver approaching Chartley station at such a speed that his train could not run round the 'S' curve at the west end of the loop and that he certainly paid no attention to the orders of the inspector to *run cautiously through stations*. The evidence showed that the train was running at about 30 mph at the time of entering the loop but he thought it may have been higher. He added a note to his report saying that the GNR had since issued instructions that the speed through the stations where there were loop lines should not exceed 10 mph which, if adhered to, would prevent a recurrence. Insofar as Chartley was concerned, this restriction remained in force throughout the line's existence but at the other stations and when passing over any facing points it was relaxed to 15 mph.[166] Surprisingly, there was no criticism of the pilotman also acting as the fireman.

The Colonel noted that the line had recently been re-laid with strong permanent way which was generally in use on the GNR. He also observed that since the GNR had acquired the line, all the stations had been re-arranged, re-signalled with the points and signals interlocked and worked from raised cabins. This was clearly a vast improvement to what had prevailed hitherto. However, he did conclude that it was desirable for the loop lines at the S&UR stations to be constructed so that the run through on the facing-points should always be on the *straight* and that the S curves should be at the opposite end where the trains run out on to the single line. This practice was subsequently followed.

Immediately after the accident the line was cleared with remarkable rapidity using the GNR breakdown crane from Nottingham, such that by 6pm the same evening the line was open for through traffic. This must have been by using the up line through the station as the permanent way on the down line was extensively damaged: 408 chairs and 53 fish bolts were broken, three rails bent and 40 sleepers cut and bruised. Amazingly, prior to through traffic being restored, passenger services had continued to operate with separate trains running to Chartley from Stafford and from Uttoxeter with passengers walking the short length of impassable line!

Smith's non-automatic vacuum brake

The GNR's Locomotive Superintendent, Patrick Stirling (1820-1895), favoured Smith's non-automatic vacuum brake and first adopted it in 1875. John Y. Smith was born in Cumberland and emigrated to America. In 1866 he went into partnership with Henry Kirke Porter to form the locomotive building firm of Smith and Porter in Pittsburgh, Pennsylvania. Smith's apparatus worked by ejecting air from the brake pipe in order to apply the brakes; the automatic system did just the opposite - a vacuum was created to release the brakes by trapping a vacuum on one side of the brake pistons and introducing atmospheric air into the pipe in order to apply them. At the beginning of 1888, the GNR decided to abandon Smith's system in favour of the automatic system as it had transpired that several accidents might have been averted or minimised had the automatic system been applied from the

outset. With Smith's system it took time to exhaust the air from the brake pipe before the brakes could be applied whereas with the automatic system braking was almost instantaneous with the admission of air. The term automatic complied exactly with the terms of the Oxford English Dictionary – if for any reason a train so fitted became divided, the brakes applied automatically on both sections without human intervention. This braking system is still in use in many parts of the world. We just wonder whether the accident at Chartley could have been prevented had the engine, tender and first vehicle of the train been controlled by the automatic system.

Near miss at Uttoxeter – 11 October 1890

At 8.20pm on Saturday, 11 October 1890, Thomas Mellor, the station master at Uttoxeter was engaged with the GNR's last passenger train of the day from Stafford to Derby. It was running late and should have left at 8.10pm and he and Inspector Poole had been supervising the attachment of a milk van. A series of whistles was then heard *three sharp pops several times repeated*. Mellor called out *send the driver ahead at once* following which someone went to the GNR driver with the intention of telling him to go ahead even though the signal was not off. The signal came off as the man arrived at the engine but before the train moved no more than three or four yards there was a great crash in the Churnet Valley line platforms. The crowded GNR train was unscathed and continued on its way but the story might have been very different had it not been for the quick thinking of NSR signalman William Beaman, aged 37, who manned Uttoxeter West Junction signal box. Just after the GNR train had arrived, Beaman had placed NSR 2-4-0 No. 14 (Dübs 859/1875) as a light engine in the down Churnet Valley line platform. Behind this engine there stood an uncoupled Midland Railway milk van and four NSR carriages forming the next train to Ashbourne. Beaman then faced a dire emergency as a very late running coal train consisting of 36 loaded wagons and brake van (422 tons gross) was running out of control towards Uttoxeter on the up main line behind NSR double-framed 0-6-0 No. 86 (Neilson 1147/1865). The engine did not have a steam brake but the driver had applied the tender brake and reversed the engine before Pinfold distant signal 1,100 yards from Uttoxeter. However, this action was having no effect, neither was the frantic attempt to get the guard to apply his brake by blowing the engine's whistle. The runaway train continued with the speed unchecked at about 15 mph. Signalman Beaman then decided to protect the lives of the passengers in the crowded GNR train, which he had seen pass his box only minutes earlier, by allowing the coal train onto the down Churnet line for which the points were already set following the light engine movement. He knew it would hit the light engine and cause damage to the vehicles behind and possibly cause injuries to passengers in the stationary Ashbourne train but it was the lesser of the two evils and subsequently the Inspecting Officer concurred that it was the right decision. The two locomotives were severely damaged, the milk van was demolished and the four NSR carriages were damaged, the one next to the milk van very badly. Nineteen passengers in the Ashbourne train were injured but there were no fatalities.[167] Colonel Rich, mentioned earlier in this chapter, investigated the accident and concluded that the collisions were a result of the driver of the coal train losing all control of his train while descending the long incline to the west of Uttoxeter, although he acknowledged that there was a dense fog at the time and that the rails were greasy making it difficult for the driver to judge at what speed the train was running. He also sanctioned the guard concluding that he must have been asleep and was only roused when the train reached Uttoxeter West Junction. It was noted that both men had been on duty for about 12 hours when the collision occurred. The NSR did not escape unscathed as Rich expressed the view that all engines should be braked and that the rules should provide for there to be at least a 10 ton brake van for every 20 wagons or parts of 20. Rich praised Beaman and the driver and fireman of the light engine for acting with *coolness and judgement*. Rich's praise for the signalman was somewhat dampened by a report which appeared in *The Derby Mercury* on 29 October 1890. It said following the inquiry, the Colonel went by special train to Leigh to collect on the way all possible evidence from the signalmen and gate-keepers on duty on the night of the catastrophe. It went on to say: *It is now stated that the fact of the goods train finding its way to the Ashbourne platform was not due in any way to the pointsman* [sic] *but to the fact that the points were set for those lines, having been used but a few minutes before and not reversed.* The newspaper had previously implied that Beaman had acted heroically, now it was suggesting that he did nothing but watch the accident happen. We hope that he at least received a letter of thanks from the GNR for his actions which avoided severe damage to the GNR train and its passengers at the expense of damaging his employer's assets and injuring the passengers in the NSR train. He continued to be signalman at Uttoxeter until he died somewhat prematurely, aged 50, in 1903.

GNR Locomotives

As previously mentioned, the GNR's inaugural time table effective from 1 September to 1 November 1881 was identical to that operated by the S&UR and no doubt for this short period the trains continued to be operated by the newly acquired 2-4-0T *Shrewsbury and Talbot* and the 0-4-4ST *Ingestre*. Thereafter, all the former S&UR rolling stock was condemned and replaced with GNR locomotives, carriages and wagons. The cost of renewal was estimated at £9,000 made up as follows: two engines - £3,000; 12 carriages - £4,500; 16 wagons - £1,200; 1 crane - £300. This total of £9,000 was offset by £1,189 being the estimated capital value of the stock taken over. From this analysis it appears that the S&UR must have owned a rail crane. The first GNR engine recorded on the branch was Class J6 0-6-0 No. 651 which on Friday, 16 September 1881 worked an excursion train for the Stafford Agricultural Show, departing from Derby Friargate at 8.48am. The locomotive, which was built at Doncaster in April of that year, was in the charge of Driver Simon and Fireman Charlton. The GNR engines were stabled at Stafford L&NWR shed under the care of a chargeman, supervised by the district locomotive superintendent at Colwick, Nottingham. Class E2 2-4-0s Nos. 201 and 202 were initially stationed at Stafford before being replaced by Class E2 2-4-0 No. 204 and Class J7 0-6-0 No.

369 in 1908. All GNR locomotives known to have worked on the branch are listed below in numerical order of their running numbers. For ease of reference the class designations used in this section and in the list are those used by the GNR's successor, the L&NER. The list has been compiled from photographic evidence and contemporary reports.

GNR No.	TYPE	CLASS	DESIGNER	BUILT
78	2-4-0	E2	Stirling	Doncaster 338/1882
197	0-6-0	J7	Stirling	Doncaster 88/1872
201	2-4-0	E2	Stirling	Doncaster 343/1882
202	2-4-0	E2	Stirling	Doncaster 344/1882
204	2-4-0	E2	Stirling	Doncaster 472/1888
357	0-4-2	F2	Stirling	Doncaster 611/1893
369	0-6-0	J7	Stirling	Doncaster 29/1869
400	4-4-0	D2	Ivatt	Doncaster 712/1896
523	0-6-0	J22	Ivatt/Gresley	Doncaster 1313/1911
564	0-6-0	J22	Ivatt/Gresley	Doncaster 1399/1913
569	0-4-2	F2	Stirling	Sharp Stewart 2591/1876
577	0-4-2	F2	Stirling	Sharp Stewart 2650/1877
599	0-4-2	F2	Stirling	Kitson 2077/1876
600	0-4-2	F2	Stirling	Kitson 2078/1876
651	0-6-0	J6	Stirling	Doncaster 308/1881
818	2-4-0	E2	Stirling	Doncaster 490/1889
868	2-4-0	E2	Stirling	Doncaster 579/1892
882	2-4-0	E2	Stirling	Doncaster 584/1892
1095	0-6-0	J5	Stirling/Ivatt	Dübs 3550/1898
1111	0-6-0	J5	Stirling/Ivatt	Dübs 3705/1899
1350	4-4-0	D2	Ivatt	Doncaster 811/1898

Tank engines are notable by their absence and it is clear that after the departure of *Shrewsbury and Talbot* and *Ingestre*, the former S&UR became a tender engine line with the engines being turned on completion of their journeys at Stafford and Derby. The Stirling 2-4-0s and 0-4-2s were gradually replaced by more modern motive power with 0-6-0s handling the freight trains while the passenger trains were subsequently handled by the class D2 4-4-0s.

There is a notable exception to our list as recorded rather famously in the *The Locomotive* for 14 March 1908: *On a certain Monday morning, about eight years since, the officials at Stafford had a surprise, the large Atlantic locomotive No. 990 of the GNR, now named* Henry Oakley *making its appearance there.* During the early part of his career, the GNR's locomotive superintendent, Henry Alfred Ivatt (1851-1923), had held the position of L&NWR district locomotive superintendent at Stafford and it was said that he wanted to create an impression or perhaps a little mischief at his former workplace by showing off the first British 4-4-2 tender engine. We are certain that his mission was accomplished with aplomb! Ivatt Atlantic No. 990 was built at Doncaster and put into traffic on 17 May 1898. By the following July it was shedded at Grantham and completed twelve months regular service from there, returning to Doncaster on 13 June 1899. It was named in June 1900 and so its visit to Stafford must have taken place during the early part of that year.

As previously mentioned, the reduction in passenger services which took place from 1 January 1917, avoided the need to keep a GNR locomotive overnight at Stafford and so the locomotive stabling arrangement with the L&NWR was cancelled with effect from that date.

First World War

On 4 August 1914 the government took operational control of the GNR and the other railways of this country under the Regulation of Forces Act 1871. They were administered by a Railway Executive Committee which was composed of the President of the Board of Trade and ten leading general managers, including the general manager of the GNR, Charles Basil Demetrius Hastings Dent (1865-1956).[168] A total of 10,038 GNR employees served in the forces of which 980 were killed in action or died subsequently as a result of their wounds or sickness. Men from the S&UR joined the forces, including some who were drafted to the Longmoor Military Railway for training by the Royal Engineers, but we know of only one local GNR employee who was killed in action. This was Private Frederick Devenport (service number 12597), a porter at Salt station, who was born at The Barracks, Dunston in Staffordshire on 3 April 1896. His father was William Devenport (1859-1939), a domestic gardener, and his mother was Sarah Ann Devenport, née Addison (1864-1949). He served with the 8th Battalion King's Shropshire Light Infantry and was killed in action aged 22 on 18 September 1918 in Salonika (now Thessalonica) during the first day of the third battle of Doiran. He is commemorated on a Roll of Honour which used to hang in the Station Master's Office at Salt but, unfortunately, his name is spelt incorrectly. It is also wrongly spelt on the war memorial at King's Cross station in London which was unveiled by Field Marshal the Earl Haig on 10 June 1920. This wall mounted memorial,[169] which contains 938 names of former GNR employees etched into white marble, has recently been re-fixed following the alterations at the station and the

creation of a new booking hall. The original marble tablets have been reset inside eleven individual steel frames aiming to echo each of the soldiers depicted in the famous 1919 painting *Gassed* by John Singer Sargent (1856-1925). The redesigned memorial, which is mounted in the concourse opposite Platforms 4 and 5, was unveiled on Sunday 27 October 2013. Unfortunately, his name is yet again misspelt on the Moreton Corbet war memorial in Shropshire, as is that of his elder brother, Thomas, who fell in France on 26 September 1916. The final resting place of Private Frederick Devenport is not known but his name can be found on the spectacular Doiran war memorial in Greece, which stands close to where the battle was fought on Colonial Hill. We hope that there his name is rendered correctly.

The maintenance standard on the GNR and other railways fell significantly during WW1 but the former S&UR seems to have fared quite well insofar as its permanent way was concerned. A notebook issued by the GNR Engineer's Office at Stafford and used by T. Horley, who was responsible for maintaining the line between Stafford and Uttoxeter, has survived in a private collection. It covers the period from 6 February to 18 July 1917 and records references to ballasting, re-sleepering, new drainage works, renewal of switches and crossings at Venables and Stafford Common and a proposal to relay the line from mileposts 9¼ to 10¾ in 1918. Another feature of the period under review was the leasing of gardens ground on either side of the line to railway employees, no doubt for the growing of vegetables for the family cooking pot. Following the armistice signed on 11 November 1918, the government's Railway Executive Committee handed back control of the railways to the owning companies.

GNR Great War Roll of Honour from the Station Master's Office at Salt. It should have read **F. DEVENPORT.** COLLECTION ARMAND CHATFIELD

GNR staff circa 1920

RIGHT
This is possibly a Permanent Way Foreman alongside the single main line circa 1920. Note the bull-head rail and the wooden keys and cast iron chairs. The double chair in the left foreground is particularly interesting in that it supports a fishplate and rail joint. This track probably dated from 1881 when the GNR re-equipped the line.

BELOW LEFT
The Stafford Common signalman by the steps to his box circa 1920. Note in the background the sign for Stubbs & Co. Ltd which operated the Crown Salt Works.

BELOW CENTRE
Another signalman outside the box at Stafford Common circa 1920.

BELOW RIGHT
We assume this to be the Booking Clerk outside the booking office on the road bridge at Stafford Common Station.

Notes

132 NA RAIL 236/1133 - agreement dated 23 February 1881.

133 44-45 Vic ch clvi.

134 NA RAIL 236/1134.

135 Despite an extensive search in the surviving GNR records at the National Archives, the minute books have not been located. Either they were not, in fact, handed over or they have subsequently been lost or destroyed.

136 NA MT6/306/6 and MT6/307/15.

137 GNR Circular No. 8352a issued by Francis P. Cockshott, Superintendent of the Line.

138 GNR Circular No. 12,453a issued by J. Alexander, Superintendent of the Line.

139 NA RAIL 1189/1525.

140 1-2 Geo V ch clxxix.

141 NA RAIL 1189/1487.

142 NA RAIL 1007/281.

143 CRO Q/Rum/522 - Bill deposited on 30 November 1881.

144 45-46 Vic ch cxci.

145 CRO Q/RUM/526 - Bill deposited on 13 November 1882.

146 46-47 Vic ch lxxv.

147 GNR Register of Private Siding Agreements, Network Rail Archive.

148 NA RAIL 783/517.

149 NA RAIL 783/518.

150 47-48 V ch xxxvi - Royal assent 19 May 1884.

151 HLRO HL/PO/PB/plan 1883 G18. CRO Q/Rum 548.

152 NA RAIL 236/1173.

153 NA RAIL 236/1075.

154 NA RAIL 236/1100.

155 NA MT6/1885/1.

156 Strangely, the L&NER Appendix to the WTT effective from 17 October 1927 does not mention this facility but there is a reference to the water column in the L&NER Appendix effective from 1 November 1947.

157 CRO Q/Rum/734 - Bill deposited 28 November 1910. Great Northern Railway Act 1911, 1-2 Geo V ch lxxix.

158 NA RAIL 783/516.

159 8-9 Vic ch xx - Royal Assent 8 May 1845.

160 NA RAIL 236/1143.

161 NA RAIL 783/515 and 783/576.

162 NA MT6/287/4.

163 The original station buildings at Uttoxeter Junction were destroyed by fire in March 1862 and replaced the following year, the contract being awarded to John Evans of Macclesfield in the sum of £760 on 21 October 1862. NA RAIL 532/17 NSR Traffic Committee minute 3818.

164 NA MT6 1011/17.

165 NRM Board of Trade Accident Reports.

166 GNR WTT Appendix 1912, L&NER WTT Appendix 1927 and 1947.

167 North Staffordshire Railway Study Group, Newsletter No. 2, June 1996 also NRM Board of Trade Accident Reports.

168 His father was Admiral Charles Bayley Calmady Dent, the L&NWR's former Marine Superintendent and his brother was Sir Francis Henry Dent, General Manager, South Eastern & Chatham Railway.

169 UKNIWN Ref. No. 2776.

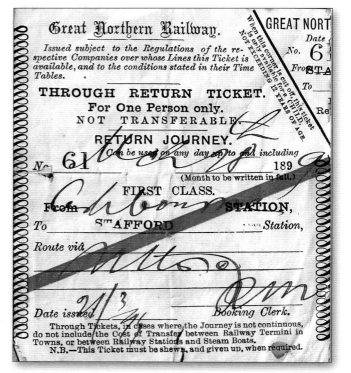

Extract from Allbut & Daniel's Penny Pocket Time Table - April 1884.

GNR through return first class ticket 1899. COLLECTION ARMAND CHATFIELD

CHAPTER EIGHT

GNR Relationships with the North Stafford

Aspirations westwards

The GNR's aspirations westwards were only realised by running over the NSR. This was the case prior to the GNR's involvement with the S&UR as NSR metals were already used to gain access to Burton-on-Trent. However, the relationship between the two companies intensified after the GNR gained access to Stafford. For this reason we have decided in this chapter to explore this relationship in some depth even though it takes us beyond the strict domain of the S&UR.[170]

Into Derbyshire and Staffordshire

The GNR's line from Colwick near Nottingham via Ilkeston and Derby to a projected junction with the NSR at Egginton, including a branch from Awsworth Junction to Pinxton, was authorised by the Great Northern Railway (Derbyshire and Staffordshire) Act 1872 which received the Royal Assent on 25 July 1872.[171] By 24 January 1878 work was sufficiently advanced for a preliminary special train from Grantham hauled by a GNR locomotive to work over the new line to Egginton. Goods and mineral traffic commenced four days later on 28 January but for the first two weeks goods traffic for Burton-on-Trent and beyond was worked over the NSR to Tutbury and thence by the NSR into Burton. On 11 February 1878 the new GNR curve from Egginton to Dove Junction was brought into use, access being controlled by new NSR signal boxes at Egginton Junction and Dove Junction; the former had a 47 lever McKenzie & Holland six-inch frame. Traffic for Burton was then directed over the new curve although it was still worked by the NSR for several weeks until the GNR began operating through goods trains to Burton on 1 May 1878.

Earlier, on 27 March 1878, the Board of Trade's Inspector, Major Francis Arthur Marindin (1838-1900) had approved the GNR's new line for passenger traffic even though the stations at Derby Friargate and Mickleover were incomplete and building work for a new joint station at Egginton Junction had not started. The first GNR passenger trains ran on 1 April but westbound trains, like the goods trains, terminated at Tutbury. Through passenger workings to Burton utilising the new curve to Dove Junction and the NSR branch from Marston Junction did not commence until 1 July 1878 when the new station at Egginton Junction was opened. From this date the NSR's original station at Egginton, which was sited ½ mile to the east, was closed to passengers but remained open for goods traffic.[172]

Although authorised under the 1872 Act, the triangular junction at Egginton was never built as the north to east curve was not laid. The origin of this curve stemmed from the fact that when the GNR was promoting its new way westwards there was no proper agreement with the NSR to run over its tracks or for a new station at Egginton Junction. Needing the NSR as an ally, the GNR decided not to risk alienating a potential friend by applying for statutory running powers. However, in order to make its tactics seem plausible to the Parliamentary committees, it was obliged to include a line giving access to the NSR's original station at Egginton so that GNR passengers could change into NSR trains to and from Stoke. A formal approach to the NSR for running powers was made in November 1873 and these became enshrined in the Great Northern Railway (Further Powers) Act 1874.[173] This Act gave the NSR reciprocal running powers to Nottingham and Pinxton. Once these running powers had been granted and the proposals for the new joint station agreed, the north to east curve was rendered unnecessary. The station buildings at Egginton Junction housed the facilities for both the GNR and NSR with the staff being paid jointly. The NSR side of the four-platform station comprised a pair of rather bleak platforms with an open-fronted timber waiting shelter on the down side, but no cover whatsoever for passengers travelling in the up direction. Initially, the NSR made very little use of its newly acquired running powers over the GNR and continued to run passenger trains into the Midland Railway's station at Derby until the end of its existence.

In order for the GNR to reach Burton-on-Trent station the existing running powers which took the NSR from North Stafford Junction on the Midland Railway main line ¾ mile into the Midland station at Burton were made joint with the GNR so enabling it to run into the premises of its rival. Red rag to a bull! As a result the station soon became inadequate to cope with the increased traffic and it was rebuilt in 1883. The GNR Hawkins Lane Goods Depot at Burton and the line serving it were authorised under the 1874 Act but it did not come into use until 1 July 1878. It was reached from a connection with the NSR's high level goods line at Burton North Junction.

On 24 February 1882 the NSR entered into an agreement with the GNR for a telegraph wire between Egginton and Bromshall Junction. The NSR agreed to erect and maintain the wire for the GNR's exclusive use for an annual wayleave charge of £14 5s 0d (£15.25p) plus a similar annual amount for maintenance. The signatories to the agreement were Percy Morris, Secretary, NSR and Henry Oakley, General Manager, GNR.[174] The NSR Appendix to the Working Time Book for January 1893 until further notice contained the following entry in respect of GNR passenger trains:

When the Line between Bromshall Junction and Egginton is obstructed, and there is a probability of Up G.N. Passenger Trains being seriously delayed, the Station Master in whose district the block has occurred must immediately advise by wire the Egginton and the Derby G.N. Station Masters, and also telegraph the G.N. District Superintendent, Nottingham, so that any special arrangements necessary may be made.

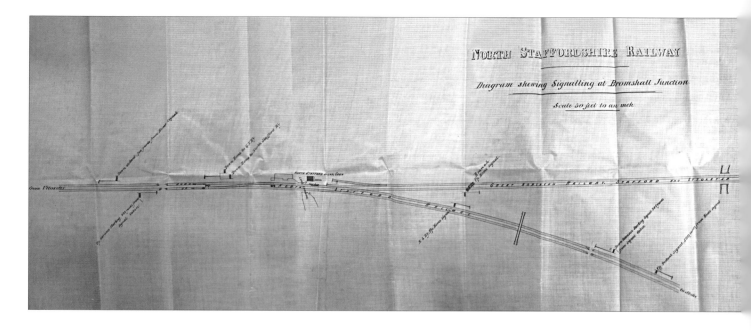

All this was a far cry from what prevailed when the S&UR was an independent concern.

The GNR's service to and from Burton became such a success that the NSR eventually opened three new stations on the stretch of line between North Stafford Junction on the Midland main line and Dove Junction which were used by NSR and GNR trains. These were: Horninglow, opened on 1 August 1883; Rolleston-on-Dove on 1 November 1894; and Stretton and Clay Mills on 1 August 1901.

Politics

Given its early interface with the GNR it is difficult to comprehend why the NSR was so against the S&UR Bill of 1878-1879 which was designed to give the S&UR running powers beyond Uttoxeter and permission for the GNR to enter Stafford. Perhaps it was because the NSR came under such severe criticism for delaying S&UR trains at Bromshall Junction and providing poor facilities at Uttoxeter Bridge Street station for the interchange of passengers and the onward transit of goods or was it perhaps, more realistically, because at this stage the NSR was enjoying such a good relationship with the L&NWR that it did not want this rapport upset by aligning itself with the GNR.

GNR Agent in the Potteries

The GNR established an agent to look after its affairs in the Potteries. This was Thomas W. Dawson who had been born in Upper Tean, Staffordshire in 1844. In 1862 he married Hannah Holdcroft from Burslem at Wolstanton and they had seven children. He was initially employed by the NSR as a goods clerk and was still employed by the NSR in a clerical capacity in 1871, but by 1881 was employed by the GNR and his family was living at 77 Hall Street, Burslem. He then moved to 210 Waterloo Road, Cobridge and operated from there until his death in 1910. His eldest son, Thomas W.J. Dawson, succeeded him as GNR

agent working from 24 Glebe Street, Stoke-on-Trent.

On 22 April 1895, Dawson senior was interviewed by Sir Henry Oakley (Oakley was knighted in 1891) in connection with North Staffordshire traffic. It is not clear whether this was to justify his position or as a result of a request for additional help but Dawson's response in the form of a report dated 29 April 1895, gives us a wonderful insight into the duties of a railway agent. He commenced his report by describing the pottery towns and the surrounding district emphasising coal production, the manufacture of earthenware (fine and course), iron, bricks and tiles. He estimated that there were up to 400 organisations to be canvassed including pottery, brick and tile manufacturers, merchants, builders, colliery proprietors, iron masters, corn merchants, millers and grocers. Some canvassing involved going outside the district and could involve long journeys on foot, presumably from the nearest railway station. He said he received from 16 to 18 letters per day which in themselves created ten to 12 calls per day in addition to his routine canvassing. Claims were fairly numerous and took up a good deal of his time. Emphasising that he also canvassed for passenger traffic, he said he supplied 194 GNR timetables throughout the district, the greater proportion of which were delivered by hand.

He went on to say that in order to cope with all this work he enlisted the help of his sons. He then compared his lot with that of L&NWR and Midland agents and other staff employed at the NSR goods depots at Longton, Stoke, Hanley, Longport and Tunstall, going into great detail to describe the staff and the costs involved. For example, at Hanley the L&NWR employed one agent, five clerks and a foreman at a cost of £426 per annum. There were also ten draymen who were each paid £1 3s 0d (£1.15) per week and carted 25 tons per man per week. The Midland Railway also employed an agent, five clerks and a foreman at this location at a cost of £426 per annum. The Midland had 13 draymen who were also paid £1 3s 0d (£1.15) per week and they

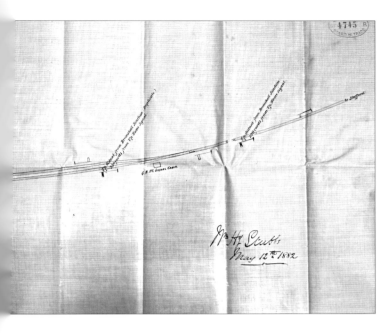

NSR signalling arrangements at Bromshall Junction 1882, as part of GNR instigated improvements to the S&UR after it acquired the railway. NA MT6 307/15

also carted 25 tons per man per week. In contrast the NSR had 27 draymen who each carted 29 tons. We cannot say whether Dawson was granted any assistance but he certainly survived his interview with the general manager which must have been a daunting experience.

Passenger Traffic

In Chapter Seven we described the GNR's passenger service to and from Stafford which at its height amounted to six trains each way on weekdays. All these trains travelled over the NSR between Egginton and Bromshall Junctions and many of them called at the NSR's intermediate stations at Tutbury, Sudbury and Marchington. The GNR's occupancy of the NSR Burton branch between Dove Junction and North Stafford Junction on the Midland main line was so intense that it warranted a separate section in the NSR working time tables. For example, in 1913 on weekdays, there were nine passenger trains in the up direction and ten in the down. These trains were in addition to the NSR's own trains between Tutbury and Burton and, of course, goods trains operated by both companies.

In contrast the NSR never took full advantage of its rights to operate passenger trains over the GNR but, as from 1 May 1878, it did agree to discontinue a passenger service commenced in 1874 to the Midland Railway station at Nottingham which avoided Derby by running via Stenson Junction, Castle Donington and Trent. It was by this route that *The Locomotive* for 14 March 1908 recorded that the NSR once ran a service to Nottingham from Stafford via the S&UR using *outside cylinder tender engines, and outside cylinder tank engines, and also by an old tender engine with a 'Gothic' firebox* (see Chapter Six). Amazingly, when the NSR withdrew its service to Nottingham in 1878, it did not substitute a service via the GNR's new line through Derby, remaining content to run into the Midland Railway station at Derby and terminate there. However, for many years it did operate excursion

trains to Nottingham via the GNR route.

On 26 March 1895 the NSR General Manager, William Douglas Phillipps (1839-1932), wrote to his GNR counterpart saying that it had been drawn to his attention that both the NSR and GNR trains between Uttoxeter and Egginton Junction had been very lightly loaded during the past winter. He suggested that a single service of trains between the two points might suffice during the winter months and that the matter should be referred for discussion between Thomas Trim (1854-1914), NSR Outdoor Assistant and J. Rayner of the GNR District Superintendent's Office, Nottingham. Needless to say Phillipps' proposal was such that the NSR should operate the service so reverting to the practice which prevailed prior to the GNR takeover of the S&UR with passengers to and from Stafford changing at Uttoxeter and Egginton Junction. The NSR proposal was complicated by a suggestion that certain NSR trains from Ashbourne should continue to Stafford and that certain GNR trains in the opposite direction should run through to Ashbourne. Rayner recalled that this Ashbourne initiative had been proposed some seven years earlier but was abandoned owing to the bridges on the Ashbourne branch not being strong enough for GNR locomotives. The dialogue rumbled on for some months but on 24 September 1895 Rayner wrote to Oakley recommending that the existing method of working should not be disturbed as it would greatly inconvenience GNR passengers having to change and waste time at Uttoxeter and Egginton. Moreover, there were some concerns about disruption to milk traffic and the GNR Locomotive Department had calculated that the NSR's proposed method of working would be more expensive.

In the summer of 1902 the NSR commenced running through trains from Derby Midland to Llandudno serving the developing holiday resorts along the North Wales coast. These trains became extremely popular such that the NSR Locomotive Carriage and Wagon Superintendent, John Henry Adams (1860-1915),

CONTINUED ON PAGE 156

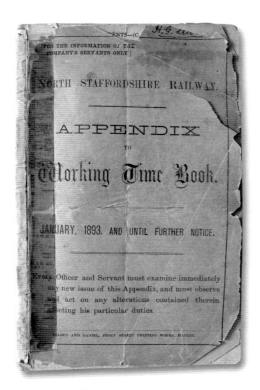

G. N. Passenger Trains.

When the Line between Bromshall Junction and Egginton is obstructed, and there is a probability of Up G. N. Passenger Trains being seriously delayed, the Station Master in whose district the block has occurred must immediately advise by wire the Egginton and Derby G.N. Station Masters, and also telegraph the G.N. District Superintendent, Nottingham, so that any special arrangements necessary may be made.

North Staffordshire Railway working time book January 1893.

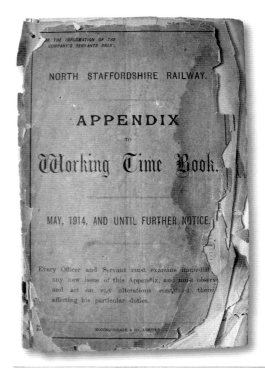

G. N. Passenger Engines.

G.N. Passenger Engines are now being fitted with a connection at the back of the Tender, which prevents the Engine from starting with a Train unless the Vacuum Pipes are coupled between the Engine and Train. When the shackle is lifted (as in coupling) air is admitted through the plug on which the tender pipe rests, and the brake is applied on Engine and Tender.

When necessary to couple these Engines to Wagons not fitted with Vacuum Pipes, or to other Vehicles when it is required to leave the Vacuum Pipes uncoupled, the Wagon or other coupling must be used instead of the Engine shackle.

North Staffordshire Railway working time book May 1914.

North Staffordshire Railway timetables, July, August, September 1889 relating to Great Northern trains.

North Staffordshire Railway timetables, October 1910 relating to Great Northern trains.

North Staffordshire Railway timetables, October 1922 relating to Great Northern trains.

This is the NSR station at Weston and Ingestre on its line from Stone to Colwich which passed under the S&UR just to the south of here. The S&UR gave its station the name Ingestre and Weston to avoid confusion. The NSR station opened at the same time as the line itself on 1 May 1849 and closed to passenger traffic on 6 January 1947, along with the other intermediate stations when the local passenger service was withdrawn. Having said that, it never boasted more than three or four passenger trains per day in each direction. For example the summer 1896 timetable shows four trains in each direction on weekdays and one on Sundays. By the summer of 1921, the service was down to three trains each way and none on Sundays. It never got any better. This view looks north towards Stone and Stoke and dates from the mid 1890s.

A much later view of the former NSR station at Weston and Ingestre, taken in 1951 after it had lost its passenger service, although it remained open for goods traffic until 2 September 1963. The view looks south from the road overbridge which replaced the level crossing over the present A51, Newcastle-under-Lyme to Lichfield road in 1937. The top of the original McKenzie & Holland NSR signal box can be seen to the bottom left. In the far distance the bridge taking the S&UR over the NSR can just about be discerned.

L&GRP NO. 25300

Sandon NSR station in 1957. This was located some two miles or so north of Weston and Ingestre and had the same train service. The far more ornate station building on the right hand, up-side, with the porte-cochère that can just be seen to the extreme right, was a requirement of the Earl of Harrowby, Viscount Sandon. Nearby Sandon Hall was his family seat and the NSR agreed to this rather grand building, with a separate waiting room for the Earl, his family and friends, as the price for him not opposing the line passing through his estate. The Jacobean style red brick building with blue brick diapering was granted Listed Grade II status on 25 April 1980. There was an arrangement for the London trains to be stopped specially for the Earl's purposes, should he so wish. The view looks north.

Sandon again, this time on 20 April 1957 with the 1.16pm ex Stoke, 12.5 pm ex Manchester London Road to Euston train passing. The engine is ex LM&SR Jubilee class 4-6-0 number 45644 Howe, *a Manchester Longsight based engine at the time. Most of the Manchester to London trains that were routed via the North Stafford line used the Stone to Colwich section so as to avoid Stafford. It provided the shortest route between the two cities.*

L&NER Stafford bound train standing at the joint LM&SR-L&NER station, Egginton Junction, sometime in the early-to mid-1930s. This was where the former GNR route from Derby Friargate to Burton-on-Trent joined the NSR for the short section of but a few yards, before curving away on its own formation, to join the NSR again, on its line to Burton-on-Trent at Dove Junction. This was just to the north of Rolleston. The engine is one of the Ivatt 4-4-0 passenger engines number 4079, originally GNR number 1079, built at Doncaster in 1897 and later L&NER class D2, rebuilt to D3 with a larger boiler in 1926. Nevertheless, it was withdrawn in October 1937 so the photograph pre-dates this. In 1922 it was allocated to Grantham but by the time this photograph was taken, the engine had presumably, been transferred to Colwick.

Egginton Junction looking north on 2 June 1957. The lines in the foreground comprise the former NSR route from Willington Junction, where it joined the Midland Railway line from Derby to Burton-on-Trent and on the right, the former GNR line from Derby Friargate. Looking north, the NSR route to Uttoxeter is on the right and the GNR curve, which rejoined the NSR at Dove Junction, thus giving GNR access to Burton-on-Trent, curves away to the immediate left of the signalbox. The former GNR line closed to passenger trains on 9 September 1961 and the former NSR station lost its passenger service on 5 March 1962, although other stations on the line retained a service. The GNR curve closed on 6 May 1968. The former GNR line between Egginton and Derby remained in use for the BR Research Department until 9 July 1990.

Another view of Egginton Junction, looking north again from the former NSR platforms. That is the former GNR station building to the extreme right and the date is 28 May 1957.

Taken on the same day as the previous view, here we have the former GNR platforms at Egginton Junction, a view looking towards Derby. The dairy in the background had a rail connection and a covered van can just be discerned in the siding through the centre bridge arch.

GNR train from Stafford leaving the NSR Tutbury Station in 1911. There is a headboard on the smokebox of the engine displaying the destination DERBY. The locomotive is one of the Stirling 2-4-0 passenger engines, number 818, built at Doncaster in 1889, rebuilt with a larger boiler in July 1909 and withdrawn in January 1924. It was a long time resident of Colwick shed. The train, rather a long one, consists of eight six wheel coaches with a van of some sort at the rear – a horse box perhaps. With two vehicles having brake compartments in the train, presumably it consisted of two otherwise separate rakes. We wonder if this particular train was augmented on this occasion for some special reason? L&GRP 16493

Taken in about the same place as the previous photograph, this is a down GNR train arriving at Tutbury, also in 1911 and it is suggested, on the same day. In this case the train is a shorter one of five coaches, the first of which is a bogie vehicle while those behind appear to be six-wheelers. The engine is one of the Stirling six-coupled goods engines, number 1095, which often seem to have found their way, at least in later years, on relatively short distance passenger trains. This one was contractor built by Dübs & Company of Glasgow in 1897 and was later rebuilt with a larger boiler as L&NER class J5, in 1924. It was withdrawn in April 1934 and was yet another long term resident of Colwick shed. The factory behind the train is a creamery, in later years belonging to the Swiss firm of Nestlé, hence the stack of coal behind the engine in the previous view and wagon in the private siding alongside this one. L&GRP 16492

L&NER up train complete with a milk tank arriving at Tutbury on 27 June 1933 - a Tuesday. The engine is another of the Stirling six-coupled tender engines, in this case number 4094. Dating from 1897 this was another one built by Dübs & Company of Glasgow. It was rebuilt with a larger boiler in December 1917 and not withdrawn until April 1951. Like many of its brethren, for many years a Colwick based engine. Incidentally, the GNR, L&NER and later BR, had a small shed at Derby Friargate; while always a sub-shed of Colwick, it must on occasions have paid host to engines working over the line to Uttoxeter and Stafford. It opened in 1876 and closed in 1955.
H.C. CASSERLEY COURTESY R.M. CASSERLEY

Unfortunately we do not have the number of the locomotive in this case, but it is one of the Ivatt 4-4-0 passenger tender engines. It is an up train at Tutbury, the engine running tender first with the headcode for a class three train, so it could well be a Sunday milk working from Grindley some time after the last war when this would be the only traffic on the former S&UR on a Sunday. As these trains did not go all the way to Stafford, it was not possible to turn the engine round for the return journey.

designed locomotives and carriages especially for use on this service. The passenger stock included three lavatory brakes built in 1907 for through carriage working to Burton, Derby Friargate, Nottingham Victoria and Grantham. They had three third class compartments with side corridor and lavatory, a first class compartment and two first class lavatories arranged transversely, another first class compartment and a small compartment for the guard, making them each self-contained units. In 1910 and 1911, the train did not call at Egginton Junction which meant that the through carriage from the GNR had to be conveyed by the GNR's Stafford service and attached to the Llandudno train at Uttoxeter. Moreover, the NSR's through carriage from Burton had earlier been attached to the GNR's Stafford train at Tutbury and so both these carriages were shunted at Uttoxeter – what ingenuity! The operation was reversed for the return journey. These trains were discontinued during the First World War but were resumed afterwards.

A summary of all NSR stations used by GNR passenger trains is given in Appendix Three together with dates of opening and closing.

Through goods traffic

On 11 April 1895, just over two weeks after Phillipps had proposed the rationalisation of passenger trains between Uttoxeter and Egginton Junction, he again wrote to Oakley saying that when their respective representatives had met, through working of goods trains had also been discussed. Reading over the ensuing correspondence we cannot help but feel that querying the passenger workings was but a smokescreen obscuring the real objective of securing a through working for goods trains. Indeed, in his letter Phillipps stated that a proposal, no doubt previously implanted in the mind of Thomas Trim, had already been discussed whereby GNR engines would work to Stoke and NSR engines to Peterborough on weekdays in accordance with the following schedule:

NSR engine and men with NSR through train

Stoke-on-Trent dep.	8.50pm	Peterborough arr.	5.0am
Peterborough dep.	11.0pm	Stoke-on-Trent arr.	7.15am

GNR engine and men with GNR through train

Peterborough dep.	11.0pm	Stoke-on-Trent arr.	7.15am
Stoke-on-Trent dep.	8.50pm	Peterborough arr.	5.0am

Two sets of engines and men would operate on alternate weekdays with the engines being stabled at Peterborough and Stoke in between turns of duty. Phillipps told Oakley that the NSR had similar arrangements with the L&NWR and the Midland. This approach eventually manifested itself in an arrangement whereby from 6 January 1896 the GNR ran a fast goods train from King's Cross Goods Yard to Stoke and back and, in return, the NSR ran a coal train from Alsager to Colwick returning with empty wagons. The GNR train was timed to leave King's Cross at 9.45pm arriving at Stoke at 8.20am the following morning. En route the train called at the GNR's Clarence Goods Yard at Finsbury Park, Hitchin (for locomotive purposes), Peterborough, Grantham, Colwick, Derby, Egginton, Uttoxeter and Longton.

The train returned from Stoke (Newcastle Junction) at 8.35pm making similar stops to those on the outward trip but with the addition of Tutbury. The train arrived at King's Cross at 7.0am the following morning having left the GNR's East Goods Yard ten minutes earlier. The NSR coal train was scheduled to leave Alsager Junction at 9.10pm arriving at Colwick at 3.15am the following morning having called at Harecastle, Chatterley, Longport, Cliff Vale (if required), Tutbury, Egginton, and Derby. The return empty wagon train left at 5.55pm arriving at Alsager Junction at 12.55am the following morning with stops at Ilkeston, Derby, Egginton, Tutbury, Uttoxeter, Stoke, Grange Junction, Longport, Bradwell Siding and Chatterley. The distance from Egginton to Colwick was 28 miles 63 chains and the distance from Egginton to Stoke was 27 miles 27 chains which represented only a slight difference in mileage worked over each company's system with the small balance in favour of the NSR.

GNR local agent Dawson was closely monitoring the situation at Stoke and for the first five nights he was there to watch the GNR train depart. He then made day by day enquiries through his local contacts in order to produce a report on the performance of the new service for the first four weeks of its operation. This is a summary of what he found:

DATE	SCHEDULED DEPARTURE	ACTUAL DEPARTURE	WAGONS
6 January	8.35pm	9.15pm	26
7 January	8.35pm	9.20pm	39
8 January	8.35pm	9.20pm	35
9 January	8.35pm	9.10pm	41
10 January	8.35pm	9.15pm	40+
11 January	8.35pm	8.55pm	41
13 January	8.35pm	9.45pm	43
14 January	8.35pm	8.50pm	40
15 January	8.35pm	9.00pm	46
16 January	8.35pm	9.15pm	34
17 January	8.35pm	9.00pm	34
18 January	8.35pm	9.05pm	44
20 January	8.50pm	9.05pm	44
21 January	8.50pm	9.00pm	30
22 January	8.50pm	8.50pm	34
23 January	8.50pm	9.05pm	25
24 January	8.50pm	9.25pm	28
25 January	8.50pm	9.00pm	38
27 January	8.50pm	9.10pm	22
28 January	8.50pm	9.10pm	38
29 January	8.50pm	8.55pm	37
30 January	8.50pm	8.50pm	40
31 January	8.50pm	9.15pm	41
1 February	8.50pm	9.00pm	36

The departure time was changed to 8.50pm after two weeks because of the late arrival of trains with wagons for the GNR and busy line occupancy on the NSR up line as no less than seven passenger trains were scheduled at about this time in quick succession. Even so the revised departure time only produced three on time departures during the next two weeks. Scheduled arrival time at Egginton remained unchanged. Dawson was definitely of the opinion that the running of through trains was resulting in

This L&NER train, photographed on 14 February 1941, is the down milk empties just south of Uttoxeter, approaching the East Junction. The engine is one of the Ivatt D2 class 4-4-0 tender engines, L&NER number 4318, rebuilt in 1920 to class D3 when a shorter boiler was fitted. This engine was a long term resident of Colwick shed and would have made frequent appearances on the S&UR.
It was withdrawn in August 1949. The engine is running tender first as the train terminated at Chartley.

Uttoxeter Station about 1908 with the main line to Derby and Burton to the right and the Churnet Valley line platforms to the left. The splendidly attired Station Master, Thomas Mellor (1842-1921) rightly proud of his domain, dominates the scene with a member of his staff, quite properly, standing a few steps behind. The lady to the left is Mellor's wife Emma (née Mottershead).

extra business for the GNR and reported that the down train was also gaining traffic formerly carried by competitors, for example, tea from London, starch from Newark, drugs from Nottingham and ale from Derby. However, the average loading of the down train during January was only 19 wagons, including empties.

Behind the scenes there was a great kerfuffle with regard to the attachment of brake vans. The GNR regulations stipulated that all goods and coal trains running west of Colwick must have two brake vans with a guard in each (one at the front of the train and one at the rear) or a brake van with a guard in the rear and a fully fitted automatic brake van next to the engine whereas the NSR regulations required only one brake van and guard. The GNR was prepared to provide an automatic fitted brake for the trains worked by the NSR from Egginton to Colwick and two brake vans for their trains between Egginton and Stoke to ensure safety on the heavy gradients but the NSR was detaching the front brake at Egginton. Obviously the NSR was doing the shunting!

Very soon after the new arrangement was put in place, Phillipps complained to Oakley that it was not cost-effective for the NSR and again pressed for the NSR to work through to Peterborough or Grantham. He expounded on this in a letter dated 14 January 1896 - just one week after the first through trains had commenced running. During the first two weeks of operation and despite being classified by the GNR as a *Coal Train*, the NSR through train to Colwick conveyed an average of seven goods wagons and 15 coal trucks. The goods wagons were those which missed the GNR through train and so were attached to the NSR train from Alsager at Cliff Vale. The coal was destined to an amazing variety of destinations including Lowestoft, London and Eastbourne, thus exemplifying wagon load traffic at its height of popularity! The suggestion of the NSR running through to Grantham or Peterborough again fell on stony ground until Thomas Trim suggested that a GNR train might run to and from Market Drayton where the NSR made connection with the GWR's line to Wellington in Shropshire. This suggestion immediately aroused the interest of the GNR who foresaw that its earlier aspirations to penetrate further west might at long last be achieved with the help of the GWR. The distance from Market Drayton to Egginton was 43 miles 73 chains, that from Egginton to Grantham being 48 miles 66¼ chains. This proposal had the makings of a breakthrough but very shortly after Trim made the proposal, Phillipps withdrew it! Obviously Trim had made the suggestion on his own initiative without consulting his boss who clearly did not want to risk upsetting the L&NWR by diverting traffic away from the Shrewsbury to Stafford route. We suspect that poor Trim had a rap on the knuckles.

Phillipps and Oakley signed an agreement dated 21 August 1896 setting out the arrangements for through working between the two companies. In view of its great interest the full wording of this agreement is shown below.

AN AGREEMENT made the 21st day of August 1896 BETWEEN the Great Northern Railway Company (hereinafter called "the Great Northern Company") of the one part and The North Staffordshire Railway Company (hereinafter called "the North Staffordshire Company") of the other part.

With a view to the most convenient and economical working and development of through traffic passing between the Systems of the Companies parties hereto it is hereby agreed as follows:

1. *The Great Northern Company shall work certain Goods and Coal trains between Egginton and Stoke or elsewhere over the Railway of the North Staffordshire Company. AND the North Staffordshire Company shall work certain Goods and Coal trains between Egginton and Peterborough or elsewhere over the Railway of the Great Northern Company as shall be arranged from time to time between the General Managers of the respective Companies, (the basis of such arrangements being the equalization of the mileage run by each Company over the Line of the other).*

2. *Each Company shall receive in settlement in respect of the through traffic worked by one Company over the Line of the other under this Agreement the proportion of receipts due to its own Line of Railway subject to no deduction therefrom for working expenses and the Company owning the Line shall be held liable for payment of mileage on rolling stock and sheets used in such working in accordance with the Clearing House Regulations for the time being subject to the proviso in Clause 6 with regard to brakes. The present arrangements and mode of settlement of the receipts of any traffic carried in the trains of one Company over the Line of the other between Bromshall Junction and Egginton and Dove Junction and Burton or elsewhere outside the terms of this Agreement not to be disturbed.*

3. *The train mileage worked by each Company over the Railway of the other under this Agreement shall be recorded and the excess mileage worked by either Company at the rate of 1/1 [5p] per train mile calculated upon the excess.*

4. *The accounts under the last article shall be settled half-yearly to the 30th June and the 31st December in each year.*

5. *Engine stabling provided by either Company for the engines of the other at Stoke and Alsager and Peterborough and Colwick or elsewhere, respectively, shall be paid for at the rate of 10/- [50p] per engine per week inclusive of all charges. Water taken by the engines of either Company on the journey to be paid for at the rate of 1/- [5p] per tank. Coal and other stores to be paid for at fair prices.*

6. *The brake vans of either Company attached to the trains the subject of this Agreement shall be exempt from the mileage charge payable under Clearing House Regulations. Having regard to the requirements of the two Companies in the working of trains over their respective undertakings, and with the view to equalize the cost, the North Staffordshire Company will provide one brake and guard for their trains running on the Great Northern Railway, and the Great Northern Company will provide a second brake and guard when required at their own expense as between Egginton and Colwick or elsewhere for the North Staffordshire Company's coal trains and as between Egginton and Peterborough for the North Staffordshire Company's goods trains and the Great Northern Company will provide one brake and guard for their trains worked over the North Stafford Line and are to be at liberty*

if they elect to do so to send a second guard's brake attached to their own trains when running over the North Staffordshire Railway.

7. *Each Company shall afford to the trains of the other without charge all usual facilities and services such as marshalling and bank engine assistance.*

8. *Each Company shall supply to the other from time to time any instructions for the guidance of servants relating to the lines run over by the other Company under this Agreement and also if required copies of guard's journals relating to the lines worked over.*

9. *In the event of any accident or casualty occurring to the train of one Company upon the Railway of the other the liability to all claims arising directly therefrom shall as between the Companies parties hereto rest with the Company responsible for the occurrence.*

10. *This Agreement may be terminated by one month's notice which may be given by either Company to the other at any time hereafter.*

11. *Any difference between the Companies arising out of or incidental to the subject matter of this Agreement shall be determined by Arbitration under the Arbitration Act 1889.*

For the North Staffordshire   *W.D. Phillipps*
Railway Company

For the Great Northern   *Henry Oakley*
Railway Company   *per W.J. Grinling*

While the Agreement referred to Peterborough, in practice the NSR through train never ran beyond Colwick in spite of further pressure exerted by the NSR. For example, in April 1898, Phillipps wrote to Oakley's successor, Charles Steel (1847-1925), suggesting that the NSR through working might be extended to Newark to pick up malt traffic destined for Warrington, Manchester and Liverpool but the proposal was not entertained. The NSR through train was suspended from 1 September 1901 until 12 January 1902. The GNR train was supplemented from July 1901 by an additional through working from Boston but all through working for both companies ceased with effect from 30 April 1907. From April 1911 until April 1913, the NSR re-instated a through goods train between Stoke (Newcastle Junction) and Colwick but there was no reciprocal GNR working.

Summary

In terms of train movements, we have to conclude that the GNR obtained far more out of the NSR than did the latter over the former. Indeed the GNR could not have reached Burton and Stafford without its statutory rights to run over the NSR. The GNR actually included appropriate extracts from official NSR operating notices in the Appendix to its working timetables. However, it must be remembered that for every mile the GNR ran over the NSR, the NSR collected a fee. We are amazed at the amount of senior management time that was devoted to the question of through trains and the amount of detail entered into in order that the respective general managers could reach an informed decision. This chapter illustrates how two neighbouring pre-grouping railway companies co-existed and interacted to obtain additional traffic from their competitors whilst zealously protecting their own interests. It is a microcosm of railway operating practice in the Victorian and Edwardian eras.

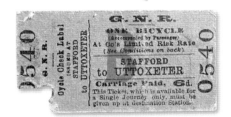
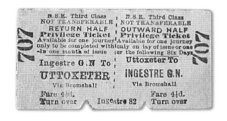

COLLECTIONS ARMAND CHATFIELD & RICHARD DEMPSTER

A busy scene in the NSR Uttoxeter goods yard which was situated just north-west of the station and between Uttoxeter West and Pinfold Crossing signal boxes. There are wagons from several of the pre-grouping companies in the yard including the GNR, along with coal wagons from the Ruabon Coal & Coke Company Ltd, the owners of Hafod Colliery at Johnstown, near Ruabon. The workshops behind are those of Bamfords Limited, agricultural machinery manufacturers and that is St Mary's Church on the skyline. The photograph is undated but probably taken in the period 1900-1913.

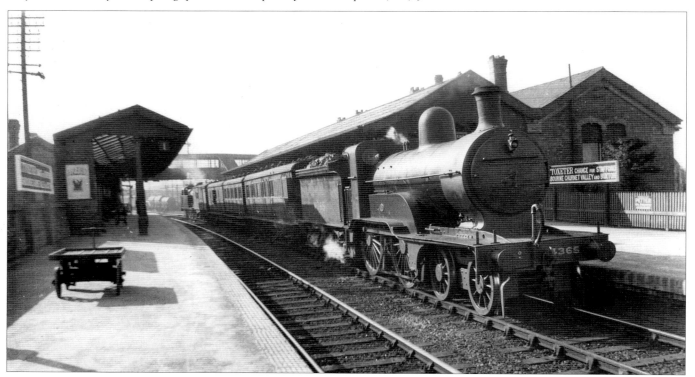

This 1931 photograph shows an up L&NER train at Uttoxeter with one of the, by this date, standard three coach formations used on the Stafford train. However, notice an NSR New L class 0-6-2 tank engine either attaching or detaching vans at the rear, at least one of which appears to be a horse box. The engine is one of the Ivatt 4-4-0 passenger engines once again, number 4365, built at Doncaster in 1899, L&NER class D1. This locomotive, not withdrawn until July 1948, had been allocated to Leicester shed in 1922 but must have migrated to Colwick sometime after that.

L&GRP 1354

A rather nice photograph of Uttoxeter Station taken in 1951, illustrating clearly the Churnet Valley platforms to the left and the main line ones to the right, along with that large and distinctive footbridge and the repeating signal arms to improve visibility. L&GRP 25297

The Crewe to Derby passenger services were the first in North Staffordshire to be turned over to diesel multiple units – although we called them railcars in those days! Here we have the 6.20 pm from Crewe to Derby arriving at Uttoxeter on 19 August 1961, consisting of two three-car BRCW units, later class 104, although these trains usually consisted of only one three car unit. The second one may have been attached to balance an otherwise unbalanced special working although as this was a Saturday, there may have been a football match involved. There is a six-wheel milk tank in the siding to the right and they are the Churnet Valley lines curving away in the foreground.
MICHAEL MENSING

ABOVE: *Pinfold Crossing was the signalbox immediately to the north of Uttoxeter and the site of the original NSR locomotive shed. The train here is the 5.21pm Lincoln to Crewe departing Uttoxeter, consisting of one the three-car Cross-Country diesel multiple units built at Swindon and later class 120, on 12 August 1978. The siding on the left had served a goods yard along with Bamford's agricultural machinery works and in the right distance, is the remains of the other, down side, goods yard.*

MICHAEL MENSING

Bromshall Junction signal box was distinctive in view of its height. This gave the signalman a clear view of traffic on the line to Stafford as well as road traffic, the box also controlling the level crossing.

This and the next two photographs at Bromshall Junction, were all taken on Saturday 19 August 1961 by the intrepid Michael Mensing, who so often seems to have got to places where others did not! In this first view we see a down train of six-wheel milk tanks indicating that milk traffic was still an issue with BR at the time. The train carries express freight headlamps indicating a fitted head, while in fact, tanks of this design were all vacuum fitted. This train is the 4.50pm, Saturdays only, Tutbury to Stoke Yard milk. The engine is one of the former LM&SR Standard Freight engines of class 4F, number 44354 of Uttoxeter shed. The former junction is obscured by the engine's smoke. The signal is the junction up home.   MICHAEL MENSING

The train here is the 12.55pm Saturdays only Llandudno to Derby, where it was due at 4.53pm, reporting number 1T81, drifting down the bank towards Bromshall Junction with a wisp from the safety valves, hauled by Class 5 number 45434. This was a Workington allocated engine at the time and must have been purloined by Llandudno Junction shed to cover this job doubtless due to a problem with the diagrammed engine. The former LM&SR design Class 5 mixed-traffic engines were renowned for getting themselves all over the system irrespective of their home sheds! The signals are the Junction down starter with the Bromshall down distant below.   MICHAEL MENSING

During the electrification works on the west coast main line northwards from Euston, a number of the London to Manchester trains that were routed via Stoke, were diverted to run on the Midland main line from St. Pancras to Derby and then by way of Uttoxeter, to gain their normal route at Stoke-on-Trent. This is such a train, the 1.55pm from St. Pancras hauled on this occasion, by English Electric Type 4 diesel locomotive, later class 40, number D218 Carmania of Longsight shed. This train was due at Stoke at 5.17pm. Notice that at this time, BR was no more capable of keeping its new traction clean any more than the steam locomotives being replaced! The signal on the left with its co-acting twin arms, is the Bromshall Junction up home again.
MICHAEL MENSING

Notes

170 NA RAIL 783/238.
171 35-36 Vic ch cxxxix.
172 NA RAIL 236/552 and MT6 203/11.
173 37-38 Vic ch clviii - Royal Assent 29 June 1874.
174 NA RAIL 236/1099.

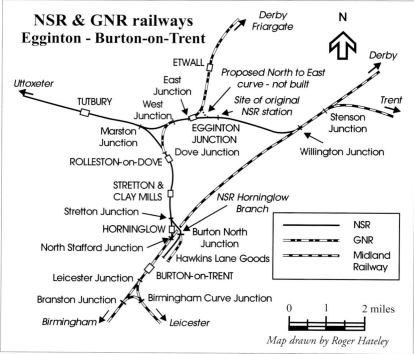

NSR & GNR railways
Egginton - Burton-on-Trent

Map drawn by Roger Hateley

CHAPTER NINE
The L&NER Period 1923-1947

Grouping

On 1 January 1923, by virtue of the Railways Act 1921,[175] the Great Northern Railway became a constituent company of the newly formed London and North Eastern Railway Company – one of the *Big Four*. The others were the London Midland and Scottish Railway, the Great Western Railway and the Southern Railway. The L&NER had 6,590 route miles of railway stretching from London to Scotland and so the newly acquired largely single line from Bromshall Junction to Stafford would, in comparison to the rest of the system, pale into insignificance, especially when to access it running powers were required over the LM&SR of which the former L&NWR and NSR had become constituent parts. One almost immediate difference was a change in livery for the locomotives and rolling stock using Stafford and Uttoxeter stations and a gradual repaint for those stations and those in between to comply with the corporate image of the new owners. At Stafford station, the L&NER limited the length of trains in the *Great Northern bay* to six six-wheeled vehicles and permitted trains of coal slack to run from Stafford LM&SR to Venables signal box without a brake van in the rear provided a man rode in the last or next most convenient vehicle. A separate booking office for L&NER trains remained in use at Stafford station until at least 1932.[176] At Doxey Road, a new sign was erected bearing the legend: *LMS & LNE, Doxey Road, Goods and Coal Depot* illustrating a degree of co-operation but the depot continued to display the sign of *W. Hall & Co. Ltd, Coal Factors* which carried on trading under a new private siding agreement. In the case of an accident or mishap on the line, the L&NER made available a breakdown van at Derby Friargate with the Colwick steam crane being available for more serious breakdowns. By 1947 the L&NER had changed this arrangement relying on the LM&SR breakdown van at Stafford and the steam crane based at Crewe. The L&NER quoted the loading gauge for the line as follows: width of load 9ft 0in; height in centre from rail 13ft 6in; height at side from rail 11ft 0in.

Rationalisation at Bromshall

On 3 January 1924 the L&NER Traffic Committee agreed a rationalisation programme for the double line junction at Bromshall[177] in conjunction with the LM&SR. This involved the closure of the L&NER West Junction signal box and the concentration of all workings on the LM&SR Junction box

L&NER passenger train leaving Stafford, a photograph probably dating from the 1920s. The engine, number 3177, is one of the GNR Stirling design six-coupled goods tender engines, although built at Doncaster in 1900 as GNR number 177, during Ivatt's tenure as Locomotive Engineer. As these engines had five foot two inch diameter driving wheels they proved quite suitable for moderately timed relatively short journey passenger trains. They were thus, a popular choice for use on the S&UR. In L&NER days classified as J4, this one was a long time resident of Colwick shed. It was rebuilt with a domed boiler in December 1918 and withdrawn in April 1936. L&GRP 16606

and the installation of electric tablet working in place of the still existing train staff and ticket working throughout the former S&UR.[178] It was estimated that the services of two signalmen could be dispensed with to produce an annual saving of £346. The cost of the works, part of which would be carried out by the LM&SR, was estimated to be £695. Lt. Col. Alan Henry Lawrence Mount (1881-1955), Inspecting Officer for the Ministry of Transport, viewed the new facilities on 12 April 1926. What follows is based on his report. He stated that the west junction single line facing points were situated 560 yards from the LM&SR box and were operated, together with a 40ft 4in locking bar, by a primary battery point machine, the position of the points being indicated in the box. The superfluous distant signals had been removed, the existing west junction up distant being fixed in the warning position and its light repeated in the box. The existing west junction up and down home signals had become, respectively, the up outer home and down starter for the junction box, the latter signal being 480 yards away from the box. Instruments had been installed to enable the section between Bromshall Junction and Grindley to be worked by the key token system. Auxiliary instruments had also been provided in the LM&SR box and at the down starting signal to permit the delivery, if necessary, of tokens to drivers of down trains when standing at this signal, as an alternative to delivery in the usual manner when passing the box. This additional facility was necessary through trains having to draw up to the down starter to clear the main line if the section to Grindley was blocked.

Mount observed that a track circuit had been provided through the single line facing points, extending for 206 yards to the rear of the up outer home signal. This circuit, when occupied, locked the down starter, which was also electrically controlled by the token. He thought it would have been preferable for the occupation of this track circuit to have either back-locked the up outer home signal or locked the points both normal and reverse. In this respect the installation was not in accordance with current operating practice which would have required an additional track circuit for train waiting purposes but as the traffic on the branch only amounted to four or five trains each way daily he did not insist on any alteration.

Mount noted that the junction box now contained 18 working levers and a gate wheel. The additional locking, both mechanical and electric, was tested and found to be correct but it was such that before the home signal could be lowered the single line facing points had to be set. As a result, when a train was approaching from Grindley, a down train would be brought to a stand on the main line. The LM&SR officers expressed the view that this locking arrangement restricted traffic working on the main line and had the disadvantage that in the event of a train from Grindley over-running the up outer home signal with the points set for the reception of a down train onto the branch, there would be the danger of a resulting head-on collision. In view of this danger and bearing in mind the heavy rising gradient of 1 in 70 on the down branch, Mount was prepared to sanction the removal of the lock between the down outer home signal and the loop facing points provided that: (1) if a train was approaching from Grindley, any down train would be brought to a stand at the down home signal

before being permitted to proceed on the branch line towards the down starter; and (2) there was a lock between the down home and up outer home signals. The 1 in 70 gradient at Bromshall was clearly still exercising the minds of operating staff some 65 years after it was first proposed. The new working arrangements were enshrined in the L&NER WTT Appendix which came into operation on 17 October 1927 and are worth quoting in full.

The section between Bromshall Junction (LMS) and Grindley is worked in accordance with the regulations for train signalling on single lines worked on the Electric Train Tablet System, key token instruments being used for this purpose. An auxiliary key token instrument has been fixed in a hut adjacent to Bromshall Junction down starting signal and telephonic communication provided between the hut and Bromshall Junction Box.

In connection with the Key Token Working, drivers in the ordinary way will receive the key token from the signalman at Bromshall Junction and will only be called upon to obtain one from the auxiliary instrument when drawn up to the branch down starting signal clear of the main line. Trains brought to a stand at Bromshall Junction down starter must proceed towards the signal a sufficient distance to actuate the electric depression bar provided in the rear thereof. The driver must proceed to the hut housing the auxiliary key token instrument and obtain admission thereto by pressing the plunger on the door, and unless the indicator on the key token instrument shows "Free" communicate with the signalman at Bromshall Junction by means of the telephone and act on the instructions received. When the indicator on the instrument shows "Free" a key token must be extracted therefrom, in accordance with the instructions shown on the label attached to the instrument, which instructions are as follows:

When the indicator shows "Free" raise key with the web downwards to top portion of grooves and push in, then turn key one-half turn as indicated by arrow and pull out. When a key token has been obtained from the instrument and the starter has been lowered the train may proceed towards Grindley.

New siding at Ingestre

On 27 May 1929 the L&NER concluded an agreement to provide a siding connection to the dairy at Ingestre. This was with United Dairies (Wholesale) Ltd and London Wholesale Dairies Ltd, as successors to the previous owners.[179] Another agreement was concluded on 15 February 1930 for an extension of the siding. On 30 October 1930 Lt. Col. Edward Philip Anderson (1883-1934) inspected the new facilities which were provided to accommodate the introduction of glass-lined six-wheeled milk tankers.[180] His initial instructions were given some two years' earlier and so there was obviously a backlog of inspections to be undertaken at this time. He noted that the layout of the siding differed slightly from that shown on an L&NER plan dated 8 October 1928, no doubt because of the later authorised extension. The official agreements were concluded after the work had been undertaken. He reported to the Ministry of Transport that the new siding was 100 yards long and formed a new trailing connection from the up platform line. The connection was made with steel rail weighing 85lb per yard ballasted with slag. It was properly trapped and practically level, the main line rising at 1 in 379 away from the siding. The

Another up L&NER passenger train departing from Stafford although on this occasion, taken from the opposite side. The photograph was taken very early in the L&NER period as while on the original print the letters L&NER can be clearly seen on the tender, the engine still bears its pre-grouping number 1116. This is another of the Stirling six-coupled goods tender engines although in this case contractor built by Dübs & Company of Glasgow in 1899. It was rebuilt with a domed boiler as class J5 in June 1923, when one might have expected it to have also been renumbered. The L&NWR Cauliflower 0-6-0 to the extreme right also appears to bear its pre-grouping cast number plates; but then the former L&NWR management was renowned for taking its time with renumbering. The L&NER engine, renumbered as number 4116, was withdrawn in January 1936 being another of the class that became long term residents of Colwick shed and making regular appearances at Stafford. Three coaches would seem to have been the standard loading for passenger trains in the L&NER period.
L&GRP 16601

siding points were worked from Ingestre signal box which at this time had 20 working levers and five spares. The altered locking arrangement was tested and found to be correct and Anderson noted that the tank wagons were hand shunted beyond the trap points. The milk tanks ran from Ingestre to a siding at East Finchley in London under a tripartite agreement between the L&NER, United Dairies (Wholesale) Ltd and Manor Farm Dairies Ltd until 31 January 1935 when the agreement was terminated.

The special provision for the Sunday down milk train to run into the up platforms at Grindley, Chartley and Ingestre continued to prevail throughout the L&NER regime.

Train services
The L&NER did little to attract additional traffic to its Stafford outpost but insofar as passenger traffic was concerned it did maintain the status quo inherited from the GNR by continuing the four trains each day on weekdays between Stafford LM&SR and Derby Friargate. The L&NER public timetables from 22 September 1924 until further notice show departures from Stafford at 9.2am, 2.3pm, 4.30pm and 7.28pm. These trains called at all intermediate stations between Stafford and Uttoxeter, arrival times at Derby being 10.23am, 3.32pm, 6.3pm and 8.56pm, respectively. On Saturdays the 4.30pm departure from Stafford was

extended to Ilkeston. In the opposite direction trains left Derby Friargate for Stafford at 9.23am, 1.43pm, 4.50pm and 7.25pm calling at all stations; arrival times at Stafford being 10.59am, 3.22pm, 6.26pm and 8.52pm. There were no passenger trains on Sundays. Fifteen years later, the L&NER timetable from 3 July to 24 September 1939, which was the one in operation immediately before the outbreak of the Second World War on 3 September, showed a similar pattern of four trains each way on weekdays with only minor variations in the timings. These trains called at all intermediate stations between Stafford and Derby Friargate. The first afternoon departure from Stafford was permitted to pick up loaded cattle wagons from the S&UR intermediate stations on Wednesdays only.

Two sets of carriages were used to work the passenger trains. One set was stabled overnight at Derby Friargate while the other set was kept overnight at Doxey Road Yard, being taken there from Stafford after the last passenger train of the day had arrived from Derby. The following morning an LM&SR light engine left Stafford at 8.3am to collect the empty stock for the first eastbound train of the day.

However, the L&NER did continue to encourage excursion trains from Stafford to Skegness and other east coast resorts, often in the form of local company outings for employees.

This photograph is said to have been taken in 1925 and as it is part of a set with the previous two, they may all date from that year. This is an unusual working, an L&NER goods train passing through the station at Stafford and destined for the S&UR. Doubtless the two locomotives had been engaged in some shunting at the yards to the south of the station because, as far as is known, L&NER trains never ventured away from the immediate station area. Note that the first two vehicles are those distinctive salt vans with their hip-roofs. The train engine is yet another of the Stirling six-coupled goods tender engines, number 4151, built by Kitson & Company of Leeds in 1900 and rebuilt with a domed boiler in January 1916, becoming L&NER class J4. It was another long term Colwick resident. The pilot is one of the Stirling 2-4-0 passenger tender engines with six foot six inch diameter driving wheels that were popular on the line in pre-grouping days. Number 868, still with its GNR number, was built in 1892 and rebuilt with a larger domed boiler in July 1902. As one of the last survivors of the class it was withdrawn in June 1925 so, if the 1925 date for this photograph is correct, it was eking out its final months in service and probably has enough coal in its tender, just have a look, to see its days out! Only two members of this once large class survived beyond the end of 1925 to receive their allocated L&NER numbers.

L&GRP 16608

A rather nice view of the north end of Stafford Station with an L&NER passenger train leaving from the S&UR bay platform. Presumably the goods train in the centre was stopped at signals, albeit the clearing point looks quite short. The engine is one of the later Ivatt design of six-coupled goods tender engines fitted with piston valves, in this case number 3623 of 1901 - later L&NER class J22 - which was allocated to Colwick from when it was built. However, by the time this photograph was taken around 1930, it was at Retford. Note the former Midland Railway Standard Freight 0-6-0 to the right and beyond it, the rear end of a former NSR tank engine.

Henry Venables timber yard with the rails from the S&UR in the foreground. The photograph dates from the 1930s and looks due west. The tall bracket signals visible to the left are on the former L&NWR main line and beyond them is part of the works of W.G. Bagnall Ltd, locomotive builders and railway engineers. The line going off to the left served W. Hall & Company's coal yard.

VENABLES BROTHERS LTD

Although this photograph is taken with the former L&NWR main line in the foreground, it is nonetheless interesting and worthy of reproduction here. It shows the other side of Henry Venables timber yard, looking due east with LM&SR wagons being unloaded in the siding off the LM&SR line. VENABLES BROTHERS LTD

Uttoxeter races remained popular with special trains on race days. For example, on 12 and 13 October 1936 a special train for Uttoxeter left Stafford Town at 12.10pm, Stafford Common at 12.15pm, Ingestre at 12.25pm and Grindley at 12.35pm. First class return fares were 2s 6d (12.5p) from either of the Stafford stations, 2s 1d (10p) from Ingestre and 1s 1d (5p) from Grindley. The corresponding third class fares were 1s 6d (7.5p), 1s 3d (6p) and 8d (3p). Race meetings at Doncaster also attracted special trains as evidenced by an excursion which ran from Stafford to Doncaster on 13 September 1933 in connection with the St. Leger meeting, the journey time being just over four hours. During the summer months, local excursions operated to Alton Towers and to Tissington on the former L&NWR line from Ashbourne to Buxton. Of course this traffic ceased during wartime but the line did witness the occasional troop train and trains carrying children evacuees.

Insofar as freight workings were concerned we have taken a typical weekday during the summer of 1939 in order to describe what went on, assuming, of course, that everything ran in accordance with the timetable. The first movement for the branch would be triggered by the LM&SR signalman at Bromshall Junction accepting the 2.52am from Colwick to Stafford LM&SR goods. This train was due to arrive at Bromshall at 6.38am and depart one minute later. It had started from Colwick Down Goods Yard and had stopped to shunt at Derby, Egginton Junction and Uttoxeter. On the branch it was scheduled to stop at Grindley (3 minutes), Ingestre (13 minutes) and Stafford Common (22 minutes) before arriving at Stafford LM&SR at 7.57am. There was one other down goods and empty wagon train which ran during the afternoon leaving Derby at 12.30pm and terminating at Stafford Common at 4.10pm. This train called at all stations on the branch except Salt. These two trains were the only through workings of the day but there were several local movements between Stafford Common, Doxey Road Yard, Gas Works Siding, Venables Siding and Stafford LM&SR.

In the opposite direction there were two corresponding through freight trains both of which started from Stafford Common during the afternoon. The first was the 4.57pm goods and empty wagon train bound for Derby where it was due to arrive at 8.30pm. Stops were made at all the branch stations, except Salt, with further stops at Uttoxeter, Egginton Junction, Etwall and Mickleover. The second train left Stafford Common at 9.40pm being due to terminate at Derby at 12.56am. On the branch, this train was scheduled to stop at Ingestre and Grindley but could also call at Chartley, if required, to attach or detach cattle vans. Similar activity was also provided for at Ingestre and Chartley. The train went on to call at Uttoxeter, Egginton Junction, Etwall (to attach only) and Derby. During the day, there were again local movements between Stafford LM&SR and Stafford Common which included an LM&SR coal train for the Gas Works Siding. This train left Stafford at 11.20am returning with empty wagons at 1.5pm.

Only one through freight train ran in each direction on Saturdays – the 2.52am departure from Colwick and the 9.40pm departure from Stafford Common. On Sundays the only movement on the entire branch was the milk train which

ran in each direction. The incoming train with vans and empty churns from King's Cross and Finsbury Park left Derby at 1.2pm and called at Etwall, Egginton Junction, Tutbury, Sudbury and Uttoxeter passing Bromshall Junction at 2.44pm. It then called at all the branch stations, except Chartley, arriving at Stafford LM&SR at 4.5pm. Provision was made to attach milk tank wagons at Ingestre for Stafford, if required. The return train left Stafford LM&SR at 4.52pm and called at Stafford Common, Salt, Ingestre, Chartley, Grindley and Tutbury, terminating at Egginton Junction at 7.57pm. The vans were then attached to an express milk train which left Egginton at 9.35pm, arriving at Finsbury Park at 1.55am and King's Cross at 2.40am. The Sunday scene at the branch stations continued to be very animated as the empty and laden churns were man handled from and to the vans.

On Mondays to Fridays three pilot engines were used at Stafford Common as follows:

No.1 - From 7.45am to 4.55pm, using the engine off the local goods train to Stafford Common which left Stafford LM&SR at 6.45am, shunted Venables Siding, and arrived at Stafford Common at 7.45am.

No.2 - From 4.0pm to 9.40pm, using the engine which arrived at 4.10pm on the down goods train from Derby.

No.3 - From 9.20pm to 10.25pm, using the engine which returned the empty coaching stock to Doxey Road Yard following the arrival of the last train of the day from Derby.

On Saturdays just one engine was involved, this being the engine off the 6.45am local goods from Stafford. The pilot engines shunted wagons from the three salt works, Stafford Common Goods Yard, Doxey Road Yard, the Gas Works Siding and Venables Siding, tripping between these locations as required.

As previously mentioned, the single line was worked by electric key token between Bromshall Junction and Grindley. Train staff and metal ticket operation applied between Grindley and Stafford Common. The intermediate branch line signal boxes were closed when trains were not running. For example, on weekdays Grindley box was closed from 10.35am to 1.30pm, from 8.40pm to 9.40pm and from the clearance of the last train from the branch (which left Grindley at 10.12pm) until 6.30am the following morning. The box closure times on Saturdays and Sundays obviously covered longer periods. It is amazing that the line opened on Sundays for that one milk train running in both directions. On weekdays, the milk continued to be conveyed by the passenger trains. By May 1945 the Sunday milk train only ran to and from Grindley where the engine ran round its train for the return journey.

L&NER Motive Power

Following grouping, the older GNR types previously seen on the S&UR were phased out and 4-4-0 tender engines of Classes D1, D2 and D3 became the normal motive power on the passenger trains while goods trains were in the hands of 0-6-0s from Classes J3, J5 and J6. Class K2 2-6-0s were also used on passenger and freight trains and no doubt other types visited the line from time to time especially during the holiday season and race meetings at Uttoxeter. LM&SR motive power was often used on these excursion trains bringing race goers from the West Midlands.

Changes at Stafford Common

In 1926, Chance & Hunt Ltd, owners of the Tillington Salt Works at Stafford Common, became part of the General Chemicals Division of Imperial Chemical Industries Ltd, thereafter becoming part of ICI's Salt Division in 1937. An agreement made with the L&NER on 28 June 1940 transferred the original Chance & Hunt siding agreement to ICI (Salt) Ltd. On 2 September 1929, the L&NER granted an easement to Stafford Corporation to widen the bridge over the railway at Doxey Road and obligated the Corporation to maintain the widened roadway.

On 1 July 1930 Stubbs and Company Ltd, owners of the Crown Salt Works became Manger's Salt Works Limited and the change of name was duly noted by the L&NER with an amendment to the siding agreement. On 1 July 1932 a new agreement was entered into with Manger's for the construction and use of a new siding which we believe to be the sharply curved siding immediately to the west of Stafford Common signal box. This necessitated taking a slice away from the east end of the up platform at the station to accommodate access from a trailing connection from the down line. An additional charge of £5 per annum was made for this new facility. With effect from 12 November 1935, Manger's shunting charges were amended to a fixed payment of 10s 6d (52.5p) per month, plus a penalty of 16s 6d (82.5p) per hour beyond a period of 30 minutes per day. This seems to indicate that the shunting requirement had become excessive and was tying up locomotives and manpower beyond what the L&NER considered reasonable. The matter was dealt with in correspondence.

The L&NER Works Committee at its meeting on 30 October 1947 agreed that the crane stage in the goods yard could be renewed, the contract being awarded to F. Espley and Sons for £310 2s 0d (£310.10p). This was probably the last significant action to be taken by the L&NER insofar as the former S&UR was concerned before nationalisation.

CONTINUED ON PAGE 175

Stafford Common Station with an up passenger train waiting to depart consisting of the usual three coach formation. The engine is one of the Ivatt 4-4-0 passenger tender engines with six foot eight inch diameter driving wheels, later L&NER class D1. This one, number 2399, was built at Doncaster in 1907, the penultimate member of the class and yet another long term resident of Colwick shed. It was withdrawn in May 1946. Notice the fellow standing in the six-foot chatting to somebody on the train — no yellow vests in those days!

Stafford Common signal box in L&NER days with the signalman standing outside and could that be his young son, visiting dad, at the foot of the steps? Manger's Salt Works behind. COLLECTION PHIL JONES

Not a very good photograph but nonetheless an interesting one of Salt station. The train is a down one, for Stafford and consists of four rather than the more usual three passenger coaches, followed by what looks like an L&NWR six-wheel van and a horsebox. The engine is one of the former GNR Ivatt 4-4-0 passenger tender engines and alongside its tender can be seen the timber milk churn loading dock constructed when the passing loop was removed. The fellow surveying the scene is Lewis Foster, son of the Salt station master.

COLLECTION PHIL JONES

Horace Roome relaxing at Salt Station just after the transition from the GNR to the L&NER, circa 1924. He was a footman at nearby Shugborough Hall, family seat of the Earl of Lichfield. It is interesting to see the L&NER 'Skegness is so Bracing' poster. This slogan, which became extremely popular and is still used today, originally appeared on a poster commissioned by the GNR in 1908 along with 'The Jolly Fisherman' whose characterisation can just be seen at the bottom right of this poster. The GNR used the fisherman image and the slogan to encourage excursionists to the resort from stations throughout its system, including those on the Stafford to Uttoxeter line. The pioneer poster was designed by illustrator John Hassall (1868-1948) and is regarded as one of the most famous holiday posters of all time.

STAFFORDSHIRE ARTS & MUSEUM SERVICE

Unfortunately we don't know exactly where this photograph was taken but we do know it's somewhere on the S&UR and reputed to be a down train somewhere between Salt and Stafford Common. The train in L&NER days, consists of the usual three coach formation and the engine is one of the Ivatt 4-4-0 passenger tender engines, in this case number 4363 of class D1 which was allocated to Colwick during this period. It was built in 1899 and withdrawn in June 1939.

A Stafford bound L&NER passenger train on the approach to Weston and Ingestre station at some time in the 1930s. The dead end siding to the left, is the back-shunt to access the goods dock, an arrangement designed to avoid a set of facing points off the main line. The engine is another of the Ivatt 4-4-0 tender engines, L&NER number 4317, of 1898, a class D2 rebuilt to D3 with a shorter boiler in 1913 and withdrawn in 1950. Yet another one of the class that was a long term resident of Colwick shed. COLLECTION MICHAEL A. VANNS

Bursting out of the western, Stafford end, portal of the 321 yard long Bromshall tunnel, is L&NER class D1 number 4353, built in 1899. It was withdrawn in April 1936 so the photograph was taken at an earlier date. It would appear to have been a Colwick engine for all its existence and would, therefore, have travelled this route on numerous occasions.

Stafford bound L&NER train about to join the S&UR at Bromshall Junction in 1934. This was after the former GNR West Junction signal box had closed, hence the fireman is going to the former NSR junction box to collect the single line electric token for the section to Grindley. Strange that the signalman has not brought the token down to save any unnecessary delay - perhaps being an LM&SR man, he felt this was beneath him! Once again the train consists of the usual three coaches with an Ivatt class 4-4-0 from Colwick shed, number 4329 of class D1. This engine was built at Doncaster in 1898 and withdrawn in April 1948; one of the last members of the class to survive.

LM&SR up, Uttoxeter bound, passenger train passing Bromshall Junction around 1930. The engine is one of the former NSR class F, large superheated 0-6-4 tank engines, number 2051, former NSR number 117 of 1916; it was withdrawn in 1935. The bridge in the background was a footbridge for a public footpath from Bromshall to a small wood known as the Wellbank Plantation and the Picknal Brook, a tributary of the River Dove, both on the south side of the S&UR. There was an occupation crossing over the less busy S&UR. It would seem that this public right of way was abolished under war time regulations when the ROF at Bramshall was established, the bridge subsequently being dismantled.

W.A. CAMWELL - SLS COLLECTION

Although some way off the S&UR, this is a Stafford bound train at Derby Friargate in June 1933. The engine is taking water for which the driver assumes control, while the fireman trims the coal. Yet another of the Colwick based Ivatt 4-4-0 tender engines, in this case number 4302, one of the earliest members of the class built at Doncaster in 1897 and later L&NER class D3. In 1922 it was allocated to Ardesley shed in Leeds but must have migrated to Colwick sometime after that. It had been rebuilt to what became L&NER class D3, by Gresley in March 1916, with a larger boiler, hence the slightly shorter chimney than on the others of the type illustrated in this chapter. It was withdrawn in February 1948.

H.C. CASSERLEY COURTESY R.M.CASSERLEY

Closure to Passenger Traffic

On 3 November 1938, the Green Bus Co. Ltd of Rugeley applied to the West Midlands Traffic Licensing Commissioners at Birmingham for powers to operate a bus service from Stafford to Uttoxeter. This was successful and the bus service commenced early in 1939. This move unfortunately and perhaps all too conveniently for the L&NER, heralded the demise of railway passenger services. On 2 October 1939, the L&NER introduced its emergency timetable which provided for only one passenger train each way between Stafford and Derby. There was a morning departure from Stafford at 9.3am arriving at Derby at 10.24am; the return working left Derby at 7.25pm due into Stafford at 8.44pm. Neither of these trains called at Chartley and Stowe station which was effectively closed to passenger traffic from that date. The solitary weekday service continued to operate for another two months before finally being withdrawn with effect from 4 December 1939, bringing to an end 72 years of scheduled passenger trains on the S&UR. Salt station closed completely but the other intermediate stations at Stafford Common, Ingestre and Weston, Chartley and Stowe and Grindley remained open for goods traffic.

While the success of the Green Bus Company's new local service and the onset of war brought about the demise of regular passenger services, the line accommodated trains of child evacuees during the war (see Chapter Twelve) and excursion trains after the war while the line remained operational to Bromshall Junction. It also benefitted from wartime freight traffic.

RAF 16 Maintenance Unit, Stafford

In September 1939 the Treasury authorised the purchase of 362 acres of land to the south east of the former S&UR just beyond Stafford Common station for use by the Royal Air Force (RAF). On 1 December 1939, No.16 Maintenance Unit (16MU) was formed under strong pressure to bring RAF Stafford to operational status as quickly as possible. The main function of the unit was to serve as a maintenance and supply depot for RAF planes and equipment. The first storage sheds became available in March 1940 and additional sheds and engineering facilities were provided throughout the war years. The principal contractor was Sir Alfred McAlpine (Northern) Limited at a contract price of £1.51m. This company may have used locomotives to assist in the construction works but, if so, details are lacking. This construction work, completed by 1943, had top priority such that domestic accommodation for RAF officers, airmen and civilian staff was provided in tents and huts for the duration of the war.

16 MU comprised several sites and four of these, No. 1, No. 5, No. 7 and the HQ sites, were rail connected. Connection with the main line was in place by June 1940 from a spur controlled by a ground frame just to the east of the Sandon Road overbridge. The cost of the connection was £826 borne by the Ministry of Transport.[181] Once inside Air Ministry property, the line split into three reception sidings running parallel to the main line but at a lower level before converging into a headshunt at the far end. Near this location a line curved south east into No. 7 site, there splitting into two dead-end sidings between five large sheds.

Another line curved back south into the HQ site, with a run-round loop from which three sidings trailed back into the coal store. The line then continued through the HQ site, serving two large sheds with run-round loops and a substantial brick built two-road locomotive shed, until at the far end it split to form a triangular junction. From the eastern apex of this junction a line ran into No. 5 site, splitting into two sidings, each with several run-round loops, serving five storage sheds. From the western apex a line ran under the A513 main road to No. 1 site. Once clear of the overbridge a siding trailed back parallel to the road to form a headshunt for two sidings which ran southwards with run-round loops to serve two storage sheds. The main siding also continued south with run-round loops to serve a further two sheds. At its peak, the extent of the rail network within 16MU amounted to about five miles.

A fleet of diesel locomotives was acquired by the Air Ministry to shunt the works area as well as the incoming and outgoing trains. The system commenced operations with two diesel mechanical 0-4-0 locomotives built by Robert Stephenson & Hawthorns Ltd of Newcastle-upon-Tyne in 1940. These were joined in 1941 by two diesel mechanical 0-4-0s built by John Fowler & Co. Ltd of Leeds with another two locomotives from Fowler being delivered in 1943 and 1944 as the unit continued to expand. Details of these and all other locomotives used to service 16MU can be found in Appendix Eight. In addition to components for repair and spares there was a significant traffic in coal which was used for heating. The presence of 16MU gave a great boost to traffic

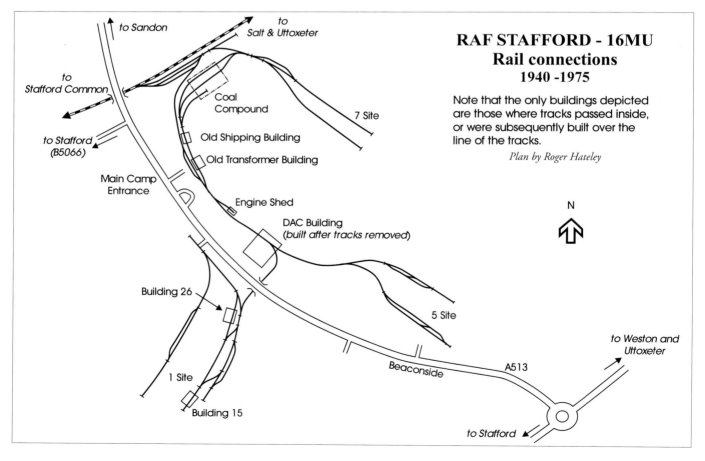

RAF STAFFORD - 16MU
Rail connections
1940 -1975

Note that the only buildings depicted are those where tracks passed inside, or were subsequently built over the line of the tracks.

Plan by Roger Hateley

The Air Ministry No. 16 Maintenance Unit at Stafford was established in the early part of the last war and colloquially known to the locals, as 16MU. Motive power on the internal railway system was always with diesels and here is one of them, AMW (Air Ministry Works) number 218, an 0-4-0 with mechanical transmission built by John Fowler of Leeds in 1941. This and the next four photographs were all taken on 28 August 1975.
S.A. LELEUX

Another locomotive of the same design was AMW number 212, also built by John Fowler in 1941. This was a standard design of the builder at that time and the Air Ministry had a number of them at various establishments round the country. S.A. LELEUX

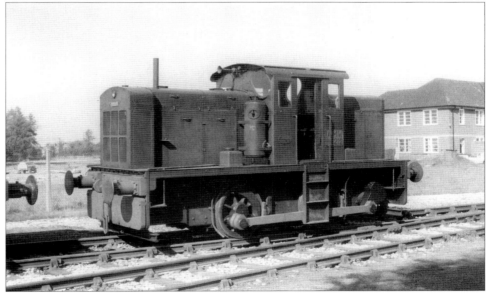

These two views show AMW number 212 shunting in the exchange sidings with BR just beyond Stafford Common. Notice the wide range of freight vehicles illustrating the variety of rail traffic being handled at the time. In the second view, the former S&UR is behind the fence on a gently raising embankment as it climbed Hopton bank towards Salt.
S.A. LELEUX

AMW number 212 busy shunting a covered van inside the Air Ministry complex. S.A. LELEUX

This is a typical example of the many large storage buildings within the 16MU site. They were all equipped to be serviced by both rail and road transport.

S.A. LELEUX

RIGHT: *In this undated view, looking east from Stafford Common, the former S&UR line is on the left, climbing towards Salt, with the connection into 16MU on the right. Notice the gate and the trap-points protecting the connection.*

handled over the former S&UR and substantially increased the strategic importance of the railway. We are aware that previous authors have mentioned the operation of special passenger trains conveying RAF personnel to 16MU but, in spite of an extensive search, we can find no evidence to support this. Moreover, the barracks for the unit were on the opposite side of the line to the reception sidings making access extremely difficult for any potential passengers.

The L&NER General Appendix to the WTT effective from 1 November 1947 permitted a maximum of 40 wagons to be propelled from Stafford Common to the Air Ministry sidings with a propelling limit of 12 wagons in the reverse direction. Other propelling movements permitted on the line at this time were from Venables to Stafford (LM&SR) for freight trains without a brake van and from Bromshall Junction to Grindley subject to a limit of two vans and in clear weather only. The mind boggles as to the reason for the latter.

Royal Ordnance Factory, Bramshall

This was one of numerous such factories constructed for the Ministry of Supply during the Second World War. It was situated in the fork formed between the former S&UR and NSR lines at Bromshall Junction (note the difference in spelling) and was completed by September 1942. The factory's basic function was to store and service ammunition for which there were a number of underground bunkers. There were two rail connections, one to the former NSR line and the other to the former S&UR. Ammunition filled at the Royal Filling Factory at Swynnerton came to ROF Bramshall for storage, some of which was routed via Badnell Wharf on the LM&SR west coast main line and Stafford Common. The new connections at Bromshall were completed by September 1942 but were not inspected until 17 October 1945 when Major George Robert Stewart Wilson (1896-1958) carried out that task and reported his findings to the Director General, Ministry of War Transport.[182] He said the factory sidings were served at the western end by facing and trailing connections in the up and down LM&SR lines respectively at Bromshall Crossing and at the eastern end by a trailing connection in the up L&NER line where it became double at the approach to Bromshall Junction. He recorded that the new connections were made with steel rails weighing 95lb per yard in stone ballast and that the running lines were adequately protected by trap points. He went on to say that that a new signal box had been constructed at Bromshall Crossing containing a frame of 17 working levers, including two detonator placers, with three spares. At the Bromshall Junction end of the new arrangement, the connection was worked by a two-lever ground frame electrically released from the existing LM&SR box at Bromshall Junction. This box had a frame of 18 working levers plus a gate wheel. The road over the crossing had been widened in 1942 to improve access to the new depot.[183] Wilson reported that the locking in both boxes was correct and that neither of the signalmen had any complaints. He also observed that the factory was being used by that time for the disposal of equipment and was only served by one up and down freight trains daily. He said the traffic remained at about wartime levels with daily movements of about 15-20 wagons inwards and about the same number outwards. The connection to the S&UR passed out of use in the 1950s but the site, latterly a Ministry of Works Storage Depot, survived until December 1968. Details of the locomotives used on the site can be found in Appendix Eight, including those that were introduced after the war.

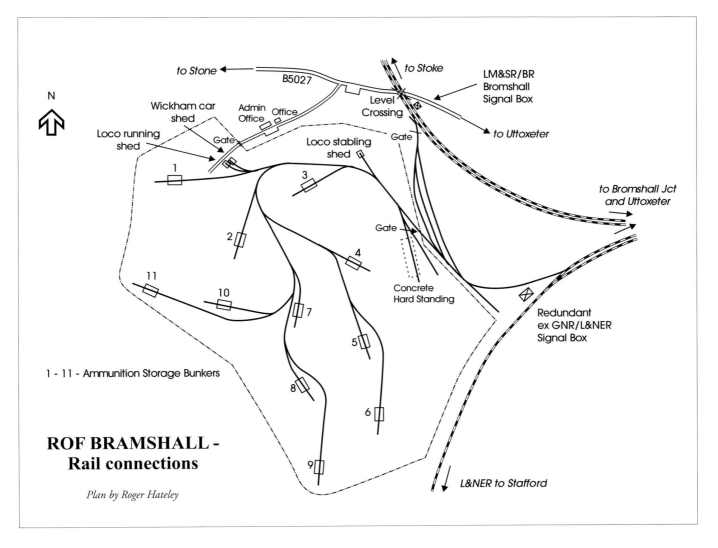

ROF BRAMSHALL -
Rail connections

Plan by Roger Hateley

1 - 11 - Ammunition Storage Bunkers

Accidents

Unfortunately two fatalities occurred in the mid-1930s, the first took place on 25 April 1934 involving the 9.40pm Stafford Common to Derby goods train which stopped at Chartley and Stowe to shunt livestock which involved attaching and detaching cattle trucks. The guard was Walter Edward Cross of Derby who slipped and fell in front of the engine, receiving multiple injuries. His mutilated body was transferred by ambulance to the Staffordshire General Infirmary, Stafford but he died shortly after admission.

On 14 August 1937, George Wignal, the fireman of the 9.20am Derby to Stafford passenger train on approaching the foot of Hopton bank in heavy rain caught the glimpse of what appeared to be a bundle of clothing near the line. On arrival at Stafford Common, Wignal and his driver examined the engine but found nothing untoward. However, they reported their concern to the station master who immediately sent the senior porter, William Dix, to investigate. As he walked the line towards Uttoxeter he eventually came across the body of Samuel Preston, aged 65, a farm labourer from Bridge Farm, Hopton. At an inquest, held at Stafford two days later, a jury returned a verdict of suicide whilst temporarily of unbalanced mind.

On the night of 15 December 1939 the 9.40pm Stafford Common to Derby goods train booked to arrive at Bromshall Junction at 10.10pm was long overdue. The train comprised 26 loaded wagons and was hauled by an L&NER Class J1 0-6-0 tender engine. It was not until 12.57am that the LM&SR signalman at Bromshall Junction received train on line from the Grindley L&NER signalman. An LM&SR train was due to pass Bromshall Junction at 1.05am. This was the 12.58am Pinfold Sidings to Longton goods train and on this occasion comprised 37 wagons hauled by an LM&SR 2-6-4 tank engine. Signalman Allen at Bromshall Junction, keeping his L&NER up home and distant signals at danger, cleared the line for the Longton goods train. Knowing that the signals were safely set against the late running 9.40pm goods train from Stafford to Derby, signalman Allen watched the LM&SR

Longton bound train pass his box on time when suddenly there was a dreadful noise as the locomotive of the L&NER train hit the 22nd wagon of the LM&SR train. The J1 0-6-0 turned at 90° to the track on the level crossing and overturned onto its offside, its chimney leading up the lane to Bramshall village. The tender reared up simultaneously throwing all the coal forward and trapping Driver Robert Godfrey of Gelding in his cab, while the surge of the water in the tender tank lifted the filler cap and literally washed the fireman off the footplate. There was a huge pile of wreckage from the two goods trains and as the first two wagons of the L&NER train contained potatoes, Bramshall crossing was knee deep in spuds!

Signalman Allen belled obstruction danger to Hockley Crossing, Leigh and Grindley signal boxes and advised Stoke Control. The Leigh signalman received the message just in time to stop the 6.3pm Ellesmere to Beeston freight train which was running late with loaded petrol tanks! An inevitable conflagration of potential enormous proportions was thus averted. By 5.30am two breakdown cranes were at the scene but it was not until about 2.0am the following morning that normal working was resumed. Because of wartime restrictions an official report on this accident was never published. However, the responsibility for it must have fallen on the driver of the L&NER train for running through signals set at danger on that falling gradient of 1 in 70 towards Bromshall Junction. The much feared gradient had at last claimed a victim.

Adverse weather conditions disrupted the Stafford to Derby freight service during February 1946. Torrential rain caused flooding such that the supports of a bridge carrying the former NSR line over the Hilton Brook between Marston Junction and Egginton Junction were swept away on the night of 8 February, consequently all traffic had to reverse at Dove Junction. The following day severe flooding affected Uttoxeter and Stafford where the lines through the main station were swamped with three feet of water halting all LM&SR and L&NER traffic for 36 hours. Doxey Road goods yard was flooded and L&NER trains bound for Derby continued to reverse at Dove Junction for several days.

Extract from Wood, Mitchell's Railway, Bus & Tram Time Table - June 1927.

Notes

175 11-12 Geo V ch lv. Royal Assent 19 August 1921.
176 Letter in *The Railway Magazine*, Vol. 100, April 1954, from Dr. James Bernard Woolley (1915-1965) who travelled from Stafford to Oakamoor at the beginning of school terms at Cotton College between 1926 and 1932.
177 NA RAIL MT29/84.
178 NA RAIL 390/58.
179 During 1920-1921 several companies, including Metropolitan and Great Western Dairies Ltd, consolidated their London wholesale milk business under the name London Wholesale Dairies Ltd and that of the provincial creameries under the name United Dairies (Wholesale) Ltd.
180 NA MT 29/85.
181 NA RAIL 390/74 L&NER Traffic Committee minute 4333, 27 June 1940.
182 NA MT 29/94.
183 NA RAIL 418/42 LM&SR Land & Works Committee minute 1070, 24 September 1942.

CHAPTER TEN

The Station Masters

Personnel

Throughout this book we have been at pains to highlight those who were involved with the S&UR and its successors. We have already devoted separate chapters to the directors and principal officers of the original railway company and wherever possible we have mentioned employees in relevant parts of the text and in the captions to photographs where they feature and their details are known. In this chapter we have singled out the station masters who also acted as goods agents at Stafford Common and the other intermediate stations on the branch. We have done this because they were important figures within the community served by the stations and were the prime interface between the railway and its customers. The list is not exhaustive but it is based on all information known to us.

The stations recalled

Before dealing with the individual station masters, it is appropriate to summarise the history of the stations on the line and their various renamings which can sometimes cause confusion. We start at Stafford Common and work eastwards towards Bromshall Junction. Stafford Common station was first known simply as Common. It was not one of the original stations being opened later than the rest on 1 July 1874. It was renamed Stafford Common on 1 November 1881 after the GNR takeover and replaced by a new station east of Marston Road in 1882.

Salt and Sandon station, originally named Salt, was opened along with all the other intermediate stations on 23 December 1867; it was renamed in 1904 following the station's rebuilding the previous year. Ingestre and Weston, originally Weston, was renamed Ingestre for Weston in December 1869 and is shown as such on many Railway Clearing House maps. However, the final name board used at the station, which survived until 1957, clearly shows the station as Ingestre and Weston, as did the GNR 1903 book of plans. Grindley was the only station to retain its original name throughout its entire existence. Chartley and Stowe station, originally Stowe, was renamed on 3 October 1874 and was the first to lose its passenger service on 2 October 1939. The passenger service from the remaining stations was withdrawn on 4 December 1939; Salt and Sandon station was also closed to goods traffic on that date. The other stations closed to goods traffic on 5 March 1951. Houses for the station masters and their families were eventually provided at all the intermediate stations except Stafford Common. The station masters are listed under the stations for which they were responsible with the period of their term of office. Some of the names appear more than once as there was some switching between stations. Following the list we have singled out certain individuals where further biographical details are available. These include all the known station masters at Stafford Common, the most important station on the line, and others with particularly long service and interesting careers.

Stafford Common

Charles Roden	1880
Charles Jervis	1884-1908
John Milburn Foster	1908-1933

Salt and Sandon

Charles Roden	1872-1880
John Colin Osborne	1884-1900
John Boul	1904-1916
Frank Rackham	1924

Ingestre and Weston

George Kendrick	1876
John Harris	1880-1884
Richard Maddison	1888
William Epton	1892-1904
George Harvey Valance Wyman	1908
Frederick Tebb	1912
Thomas Edwards	1916
Percival Edwards	1924
Thomas William Smithson	1929-1951

Chartley and Stowe

Henry Warner	1884
William Warner	1888
Alfred Byrd	1892
William Musson	1896
John Boul	1900
George Harvey Valance Wyman	1904
William Walker	1908
Albert Ernest Short	1912
Thomas William Smithson	1915-1929

Grindley

William Warner	1884-1888
William Hodson	1892
John Crockford	1896-1900
William Berry	1904-1908
William H. Littledyke	1912-1916
William Barratt	1924

John Boul

John Boul was born in Quadring, Lincolnshire on 2 February 1852. He was the son of Isaac and Elizabeth (née Wyles) Boul. In 1871 he was lodging at Barkston, Lincolnshire and working as a journeyman blacksmith following the profession of his father. On 5 March 1872 he married Rebecca Lowis after which he decided to change his profession and become a railway signalman with the GNR. The birth places of his five children reflect his moves around the system: Emma at Retford in 1873, Edward and Nellie at Tuxford in 1874 and 1877, Ethel at Claypole in 1883 and Elizabeth at Burton-on-Trent in 1886. In 1891 the family was living in March Road, Belgrave, Leicestershire where John was still employed as a signalman. By 1900 he had become the station master at Chartley and Stowe transferring to the rebuilt station at Salt and Sandon in 1904 where he remained until 1916. He died in Skegness on 31 January 1943.

John Milburn Foster

John Milburn Foster was born at Lincoln in 1871 being the son of William and Mary Foster. By 1891 he was a booking clerk at Derby Friargate station taking lodgings nearby at 9 Campion Street. In 1897 he married Julia Chaplin at Ashby de la Zouch and by 1901 he was a railway clerk living at Belgrave, Leicester, perhaps working at Leicester Belgrave Road station. He became station master at Stafford Common in 1908 and remained there for some 25 years until he retired in 1933, being employed for the last ten years by the L&NER. The 1911 census records John and Julia living at 11 Common Road, Stafford together with their two sons and two daughters: Mary and William born at Belgrave in 1899 and 1902; Edward born at Humberstone, Leicestershire in 1905; and Marjorie at Stafford in 1910. John Milburn Foster died in Stafford in 1954 aged 82 years.

Charles Jervis

Charles Jervis was born at Acton Hill in Staffordshire in 1846 being the eldest child of Joseph and Mary Jervis. The 1851 census describes his father as an agricultural labourer. Ten years later Charles was a lodger in Stafford in Peel Street at the home of Charles Rhodes who was the night foreman at Stafford engine shed. Charles Jervis, aged 15, was described as Clerk at Railway and since 1 April 1860 had been employed by the L&NWR as a delivery clerk at a salary of £19 10s (£19.50) per annum rising to £26pa with effect from 1 January 1862. At Stafford in 1866 he married Elizabeth Weeks who hailed from Lockerley in Hampshire. On 1 April 1869 he was transferred from Stafford Goods Department to become Station Master at Handforth in Cheshire at a salary of £60pa. He became Station Master at Wilmslow on 1 September 1871 and Station Master at Chelford on 1 October 1872 by which time his salary had increased to £80pa, increasing further to £90pa by 1 July 1874. However, by 1881 the family was again living in Stafford at 22 Bellasis Street where Charles was described as Railway Station Agent. This was at the time when the GNR was in the midst of the S&UR acquisition proposals and we suspect that he was attracted by the new opportunities about to be offered and became GNR Agent at Stafford canvassing for new business. He soon became Station Master and Goods Agent at the rebuilt station at Stafford Common and in 1891 was recorded as such living with his family at Field Place, Tillington. He was still there in 1901 when his residence was described as Station Villas, Field Place and he remained as Station Master, Stafford Common until succeeded by John Milburn Foster.

LEFT: *John Milburn Foster (1871-1954) became Station Master at Stafford Common in 1908 and remained there until he retired in 1933. The 1911 census return records him living at 11 Common Road, Stafford and this view shows him at that address in his back garden complete with top hat.*

ABOVE: *Another view of Station Master Foster at exactly the same location but in uniform.*

ABOVE RIGHT: *A third view of Station Master Foster but this time on duty on the down platform of Stafford Common Station circa 1920. The Crown Salt Works of Stubbs & Co. can be seen in the background.*

Charles Roden

Charles Roden was baptised at Market Drayton, Salop on 9 June 1833. He was the son of Adam and Sarah (née Holmes) Roden. His father was a farmer but was listed in Kelly's Directory for 1870 as an Agent to the Great Western Railway. Charles entered the service of the L&NWR as a parcel porter at Whitmore station on 21 February 1854 being paid 17s 6d (87.5p) per week for the privilege; prior to that he had been a carter. On 13 July 1855 he was transferred to Rugeley (Trent Valley) station as a porter on the same rate of pay. On 8 October 1855 he returned to Whitmore to marry Elizabeth Langwell Woodgate from Sidmouth, Devon at Whitmore Parish Church. The 1861 census describes Charles (29) as a L&NWR porter resident with his wife (34) and son, Henry Langwell Roden (4) at Rugeley railway station. Charles must have been among the first employees to join the S&UR as by 1871 he had become the station master at Salt and was living at Station House with his wife and son. He gave evidence to Captain Tyler during his investigation of the fatal accident which occurred at Hopton on 1 February 1873 (see Chapter Six). On that occasion he was described as Inspector of the Line which indicates that he had a dual role. Sadly his wife died on 10 April 1880 by which time he had become station master at Stafford Common. On 8 March 1881 he married his second wife Mary Lowndes at Little Drayton parish church in Shropshire by which time he had retired from the S&UR. The 1881 census describes him as Retired Railway Officer. Perhaps his new marriage and the impending takeover by the GNR prompted him to seek a new life. Unfortunately, he did not live long to enjoy his new circumstances as he died at Providence House, Little Drayton on 13 December 1890 aged 57 and was buried in Stafford Cemetery alongside his first wife. His personal estate amounted to £76 13s 6d (£76.67½p) and his will was proved at Shrewsbury on 17 March 1891 by his son, Henry, who at that time had become the station master at Douglas on the Isle of Man Railway.

A relic from Charles' employment with the S&UR has survived in the form of a whistle and disc attached to a chain. The disc is inscribed on one side:

CHARLES RODEN

S. & U. RY. CO. SALT,

STAFFORDSHIRE

and on the other:

ANY PERSON RETURNING

THESE KEYS WILL BE

SUITABLY REWARDED.

Presumably Charles handed back the keys but held on to the whistle!

Charles Roden (1833-1890) commenced his railway career on the L&NWR but by 1871 he had become the Station Master at Salt. As such he must have been among the first employees to join the S&UR. He also had the role of Inspector of the Line and by 1880 was the Station Master at Stafford Common. However, the 1881 census, completed just before the GNR takeover, suggests that by then he had retired. JOHN NEWCOMBE

Charles Roden's whistle linked to a single Albert chain. TIMOTHY NEWCOMBE

The wording on the whistle fob. TIMOTHY NEWCOMBE

Thomas William Smithson

Thomas William Smithson spent over 40 years of his working life on the S&UR being employed by the GNR, L&NER and British Railways. He was born at Bottesford in Leicestershire in 1888 being the first child of Robert Smithson, a GNR porter, and his wife, Elizabeth. In 1901 the family was living at Harby in Leicestershire and his father had been promoted to the position of signalman. Thomas followed in his father's footsteps and pursued a career on the railway, initially at Melton Mowbray but in 1909 he was appointed as a signalman with the GNR at Ingestre and Weston. During the following year he married Fanny Dix at Stafford and the 1911 census duly records the couple living at Weston. In 1913 he took up a position in Lincolnshire but returned in 1915 to become the station master at Chartley and Stowe Station remaining there until 1929 when he took the same position at Ingestre and Weston Station. He remained in this post until the line closed to freight traffic on 5 March 1951 after which he retired. However, very appropriately, he was once again present on the platform at Ingestre and Weston station on 23 March 1957 to witness the arrival of the very last train after a gap of over six years when no trains had run and the line remained undisturbed – see Chapter Eleven. Thomas William Smithson died at Stafford in 1966 aged 77.

George Harvey Valence Wyman

George Harvey Valence Wyman was born at Finsbury Park, London about 1872 and baptised at St. Barnabas, Hornsey Road, Islington on 27 July 1873, being the son of William and Sarah Wyman. He married Jenny Franklin at Biggleswade in 1895 and their first child was born in Dewsbury, Yorkshire in 1897. By 1901 he and his wife were living with their three children at Wood Walton, Huntingdonshire where he was employed as a GNR signalman. He then had his flirtation with the former S&UR as he was the Station Master at Chartley and Stowe in 1904 and the Station Master at Ingestre and Weston in 1908. By 1911 he had moved away and was the Station Master at Old Leake Station in Lincolnshire and in 1928 he was the Station Master at Humberstone in Leicestershire working for the L&NER. He died at Market Harborough in Leicestershire in 1947 aged 74.

One wonders if this young fellow, standing in the four-foot, might have been the son of Stafford Common Station Master Foster, or some other member of the staff - a platelayer perhaps? Notice milepost 10 to the right which identifies the location as towards the top of Hopton bank. The view looks towards Uttoxeter and the bridge in the distance is No. 34 at nine miles and 70 chains, known as Kent's, an occupation bridge of brick construction with an elliptical arch of 28 ft span.

These three images are of a GNR station lamp from the collection of Richard Dempster. The lamp bears the legend INGESTRE on a brass plate and presumably, came from that station. It may be the lamp held by the former Station Master in the photograph on page 197.

CHAPTER ELEVEN

Nationalisation and Closure 1948-1975

British Railways

On 1 January 1948, along with all other main line railways in Great Britain, the former S&UR was nationalised, all the assets being vested in the British Transport Commission (BTC). The railways were controlled by a Railway Executive (RE) under the guise British Railways (BR) and the line from Stafford to Uttoxeter came within BR's Eastern Region. This meant that for a while former L&NER locomotives could still be seen at Stafford. These were normally 0-6-0 tender engines shedded at Colwick (code 38A) or its sub-shed at Derby Friargate but there was an unusual appearance of a tank engine in the form of Class N2 0-6-2T No. 69552 when the turntable at Stafford locomotive shed was under repair. However, with effect from 2 April 1950 control passed to BR's London Midland Region (LMR) which introduced an immediate change in operating practice. Trains travelling from Stafford to Uttoxeter were now described as travelling in the down direction with trains from Uttoxeter to Stafford becoming up trains. This was a reversal of the former L&NER and GNR practice and a return to the original S&UR arrangement.

In 1948, following its reconstruction, responsibility for the Stone Road Bridge (No.42) together with its approaches was transferred to the Ministry of Transport under the Trunk Roads Act 1946. The reconstruction had originally been approved by the L&NER at a total cost of £5,614 11s 5d (£5,614.57p) to be charged to the Ministry of War Transport. The successful contractors were Fletcher & Co. (Contractors) Ltd. Also in 1948 there were changes in the ownership of two of the salt works at Stafford Common. In that year, Manger's Salt Works Ltd joined forces with the Stafford Salt & Alkali Company Ltd and Geo. Hamlett & Sons of Cheshire to form Vacuum Salt Ltd. The new company was merged into Amasal Ltd in 1950 which was then taken over by the Staveley Coal & Iron Group in 1959 to form part of their subsidiary company, British Soda.

Submission for partial closure

On 15 December 1950 a submission was sent to the Chief Secretary of the BTC proposing closure of the line from the Air Ministry sidings of 16 Maintenance Unit (16MU) at Stafford to Bromshall Junction, a distance of 10 miles 72 chains.[184] The goods depots at Doxey Road and Stafford Common and six private sidings at the Stafford end of the branch were to be retained *in view of the heavy traffic involved*, receipts from this traffic amounting to £64,098 in 1948. The submission pointed out that the area served by the line was a sparsely populated agricultural district. There was a private siding at Ingestre provided and maintained at railway cost for the use of United Dairies (Wholesale) Ltd. The agreement for that siding was terminable on either party giving twelve months' notice. At Bromshall Junction the branch siding belonging to the Ministry of Supply, although disused and not subject to a written agreement, could not be removed without the Ministry's approval.

The train service in 1950 comprised of two through freight trains on weekdays and Saturdays and one milk train from Grindley to Derby which ran every day, including Sundays. The ultimate destinations for the milk were Winchmore Hill and Finsbury Park in London. The freight trains called at Grindley, Chartley and Stowe and Ingestre and Weston stations as required. Revenue from this traffic in 1949 totalled £4,264 broken down as follows:

			£ Receipts
By passenger train:			
124,000 gallons of milk forwarded in churns			1,320
By freight train:	Tons forwarded	Tons received	
Merchandise	44	173	452
Minerals	444	3,016	2,420
Coal		96	29
Livestock	Head	Head	
	12	41	43
Total receipts			4,264

The freight traffic forwarded was described as mainly sugar beet while the freight received was chiefly wet beet fertilisers, feeding stuffs and coal. For some reason the sugar beet traffic must have been classified as 'mineral'. An average of eight tons of butter per week was despatched by rail from Ingestre and there was also some traffic in *smalls* and parcels. Having analysed the traffic and receipts in the way shown above, the submission, without a proper explanation, quotes the estimated annual loss of receipts as £7,109 made up as follows: milk - £3,000; butter - £3,000; other traffic - £1,109.

It was explained that the £3,000 for loss of milk traffic also included the potential loss of traffic in churns from Sudbury and Tutbury following the cancellation of the milk train. Clearly it was anticipated that some of the freight traffic would be retained, possibly by diverting it to the nearby former NSR station of Weston & Ingestre but this was not clarified. It was accepted that the small amount of coal delivered to the Ingestre dairy would be lost. The estimated annual reduction of expenditure resulting from the closure was estimated at £24,607 as follows:

	£
Repair and renewal of way and works and estate property	4,531 (minimum)
Repair and renewal of locomotives	5,500
Repair and renewal of coaching stock	2,400
Train working expenses, including staff	9,693
Station expenses – staff (saving of 14 posts)	2,444
Station expenses – stores	39
Estimated annual reduction in expenditure	24,607

This interesting photograph was taken in the summer of 1961. At that time civil engineering works were under way on the west coast main line in preparation for the electrification - notice the newly erected stanchion for the overhead line equipment to the extreme right. The work required, among a whole range of issues, a number of overbridges being rebuilt to increase the clearance so that the existing loading gauge could be maintained despite the erection of the overhead power lines. One such bridge was this one at Stafford known as Bagnall's Bridge, which takes Castle Street over the railway and gave access to the W.G. Bagnall Ltd locomotive works. For bridge reconstruction works railway breakdown cranes had since time immemorial, been borrowed by the civil engineers to assist in the works and this was one such occasion. The Crewe North 50 ton Cowans Sheldon steam crane, number 1005/50, is being shunted into position for a lift which required the use of the S&UR as a head-shunt. At that time the late Geoff Sands was the Shedmaster at Crewe North and a keen enthusiast – he was in fact, responsible for one of the authors starting his railway career at Crewe North. It was Geoff's practice to use what might otherwise be considered unusual engines for such work on these jobs and as they were usually on Sundays; at a shed like Crewe North, he would have plenty to choose from! Here then we have Princess Royal pacific number 46209 Princess Beatrice, *which was a Crewe North engine at the time. As the turntable at Stafford was not long enough to turn a pacific, the breakdown train would have had to return to Crewe with the engine running tender first. We wager the crew were not impressed! By this date the former W. Hall & Co. coal yard to the right, had lost its rail connection.*

JOHN BUCKNALL

The annual saving was thus quantified as £17,498 (£24,607 minus £7,109) It was explained that if closure did not take place, approximately £61,000 would shortly need to be incurred on track renewals and that essential repairs to bridges during the next two years would amount to £5,070. There was also a suggestion that the proposal might enable Derby Friargate (ex L&NER) motive power depot to be closed saving expenditure of £9,500 on its reconstruction which had been approved previously. As events turned out, the shed actually remained in use until 1955.

On a positive note the submission highlighted a deposit of gypsum which was being developed at Stowe, half a mile distant from Chartley and Stowe station and two miles from Ingestre and Weston. The submission concluded with a recommendation in support of the closure and the recovery of the redundant assets subject to the temporary retention of a small section of line at

Bromshall Junction to give access to the Ministry of Supply sidings and to the section from Stafford Common to Ingestre pending the possible development of the potential gypsum traffic at Stowe. It was made clear that there would be a continuing liability for the maintenance of slopes, fences, culverts, bridges, level crossings, easements and protection against infestation until the land occupied by the railway had been sold.

Consultation and closure decision

The farmers and sugar beet growers had been consulted and were not in favour of the closure proposals neither were the owners of the dairy at Ingestre even though a combined road-rail service had been offered at no extra cost. It should be borne in mind that at this date the BTC was also responsible for the nationalised British Road Services. On 1 January 1951 the Chief Secretary of

At one point during the bridge reconstruction operation described in the previous caption, the whole breakdown train and crane had to be moved to allow trains to pass. Here then is the pacific number 46209 Princess Beatrice, *nicely framed by trees, just beyond Venables signal box waiting the re-call. That is one of the relieving bogies of the crane to the extreme right. These were used to reduce the axle loading of the crane by spreading its weight over additional axles, when in train formation as opposed to when it was being used in lifting operations.*

JOHN BUCKNALL

the BTC advised the Chairman of the RE that the Commission concurred with the closure proposal and had advised the Ministry of Transport accordingly. The BTC minute recording formal approval of the closure is dated 30 January 1951.[185] The actual closure and the consequential cessation of through working on the former S&UR took place with effect from 5 March 1951.

Left to slumber

Demolition proved to be a very protracted affair. Because the original cost of the assets exceeded £25,000, a bureaucratic direction to the RE required the organisation to seek the prior approval of the BTC before any dismantling could take place and so the same members who agreed to the closure had to agree to the demolition. A second submission to the BTC received on 14 September 1952 made it clear that the works to be removed, rather obviously, included the permanent way, the station buildings at Grindley, Chartley and Stowe stations and the iron girder superstructure of bridge No. 20. It was intended to infill bridges Nos. 3, 11 and 12. The quantity of the materials to be recovered was estimated as follows:

	Usable Tons	Scrap Tons	Total Tons
Steel in rails	95	640	735
Cast iron in chairs	76	430	506
Fittings	8	50	58
Wrought iron from bridge No. 20	24		24
TOTAL tonnage	203	1,120	1,323
	Number	Number	Number
Sleepers	2,220	11,500	13,720

The estimated value of the recoverable material was £23,479 against which it was estimated that there would be recovery costs amounting to £12,381, leaving a net credit of £11,098. The

estimated original cost of the assets to be displaced was £44,532. In a letter dated 23 September 1952, Michael Robert Bonavia, Principal Works and Development Officer for the BTC, informed the RE that the demolition process could proceed between Bromshall Junction and Ingestre, further dismantling to be subject to the possibility of developing the gypsum traffic at Stowe. On 20 October 1952 the RE informed the BTC that the gypsum proposal had been dropped and that a scheme for the recovery of assets for the whole of the closed line was being prepared. From 1953 all the former GNR signals were removed, except for the fixed distant near Eccleshall Road and after 1954 the signal boxes at Grindley and Ingestre were demolished but, for some reason, nothing else happened. The track on the closed section remained and the line slumbered.

The 'SLS Special'

The Stephenson Locomotive Society (SLS) was founded on 11 December 1909. It has stood the test of time and is now the oldest railway society in the world. During the 1950s one of its members, William Arthur Camwell (1906-1995), always known as 'Cam', organised a great many rail tours with unusual locomotive power often over lines closed to passenger traffic. As the Society's Midlands Area Secretary, he became very adept at persuading BR to agree to his requests. The *SLS Journal* for February 1957 reported that the former S&UR branch was scheduled for dismantling between Bromshall Junction and RAF 16MU sidings, near Stafford Common, with effect from 1 April 1957. It went on to say: *Accordingly negotiations were completed on 7th February for a special LAST TRAIN (a push/pull set) to run on Saturday afternoon, 23rd March next, leaving Stafford about 3-15 p.m. and arriving back about 7 p.m. The special will run to a point just short of Bromshall Junction, as the actual junction has been removed; and will halt en route wherever possible. The fare is 8/6d (42.5p).* How 'Cam', a bank manager, developed enough clout to

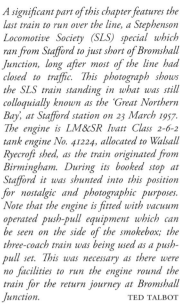

A significant part of this chapter features the last train to run over the line, a Stephenson Locomotive Society (SLS) special which ran from Stafford to just short of Bromshall Junction, long after most of the line had closed to traffic. This photograph shows the SLS train standing in what was still colloquially known as the 'Great Northern Bay', at Stafford station on 23 March 1957. The engine is LM&SR Ivatt Class 2-6-2 tank engine No. 41224, allocated to Walsall Ryecroft shed, as the train originated from Birmingham. During its booked stop at Stafford it was shunted into this position for nostalgic and photographic purposes. Note that the engine is fitted with vacuum operated push-pull equipment which can be seen on the side of the smokebox; the three-coach train was being used as a push-pull set. This was necessary as there were no facilities to run the engine round the train for the return journey at Bromshall Junction.

TED TALBOT

Here is the crew involved with that last train, photographed at Stafford alongside the engine before the start of the trip. From left to right they are:

Les Davis – known to his colleagues as 'Big Les', as he was well over six feet tall. Les was a Stafford based goods guard. He was however, a former L&NER man based at Stafford who therefore, had knowledge of the route to Bromshall. Les acted as the conductor guard, necessary because the train guard, a Walsall based man, did not know the road. **Les Gun** –This Les was a Stafford based operating inspector who accompanied the train. **Jimmy Tidesley** – Jimmy was a Stafford driver who acted as the conductor as the Walsall, Ryecroft crew were, of course, not familiar with the road. Jimmy had been over the line several times during the previous week or so, to familiarise himself with the route and to work a train recovering some materials. **Sid Cooper** – Sid was the Ryecroft driver. **Bill Mason** – Bill was the Ryecroft fireman. **Ken Holmes** – Ken was the Walsall-based guard.

The authors had the great pleasure of a long interview with Les Davis, living in retirement at Hopton, when he was able to relate his experiences as an L&NER shunter at Stafford Common and his memories of this last trip over the line.

COLLECTION RICHARD DEMPSTER

Photograph taken from the special train at the start of the journey having just left the main line. The W. Hall & Co. coal yard is to the right with its rail connection. Ahead of the train is Venables timber yard. Compare with the photograph on page 45.

COLLECTION PHIL JONES

persuade BR to run a special passenger train over a former goods only branch which had closed some six years earlier beggars belief but that was just what he did and he did it with panache! Prior to the running of the special, much cutting of hedges and the removal of saplings in and around the permanent way had to take place in order to clear a path for the train. No doubt many keys also had to be hammered home or replaced in the chairs. Those undertaking this work included Head Ganger Jack Williams and Reg Durose who drove the petrol-engined permanent way trolley that was based at Chartley and bore the number TP15P. This was manufactured by D. Wickham & Co. Ltd of Ware, Hertfordshire and delivered to the L&NER at Chartley on 12 October 1933 (maker's number 1283). It was designated a Wickham Type 17 and was powered by a JAP 1100cc air cooled engine. A Type 17T trailer was delivered the following day (maker's number 1322) and both vehicles were kept at Chartley, the motorised trolley being kept in a locked shed. Following the clearance work, the Permanent Way Inspector at Stafford, H.L.C. Reynolds, said that the metals and sleepers were found to be in extraordinary good condition and were fit for any type of train. The sidings were still intact and the condition of the points and crossings was excellent. On the three consecutive Sundays prior to the running of the SLS train, an ex LM&SR Class 4F Fowler 0-6-0 hauled four wagons with a brake van at either end over the S&UR to collect large platform paving slabs from Ingestre and Weston, Chartley and Stowe and Grindley Stations. The slabs were re-used on the West Coast main line at Baswich to assist in containing the ballast for the super-elevation of the curved tracks through the Trent Valley.

The fully booked special train, a three-coach non-corridor push/pull set headed by 2-6-2T No. 41224 built at Crewe in October 1948, started from Birmingham New Street at 1.45pm and was scheduled to arrive at Stafford at 2.31pm. It bore the famous SLS SPECIAL headboard, carried reporting number W711 and was due to leave Stafford at 2.51pm. Passengers travelling from Birmingham had to book their own day return tickets to Stafford at a cost of 5s 10d (29p). The driver from Birmingham was Sid Cooper of Walsall (3C) locomotive shed, always known as Ryecroft, where the engine was based but from Stafford he was accompanied by Jimmy Tidesley from Stafford shed (code 5C) acting as conductor. The fireman was Bill Mason from Walsall and other members of the train crew were guard Ken Holmes from Walsall, guard Les Davis from Stafford and Les Gun, Inspector from Stafford. The SLS warned its members against looking out of the windows in parts of the line where hedges had not been cut and during the passage of Bromshall tunnel. The train left Stafford a few minutes late because 'Cam' had successfully insisted on the train starting from the 'Great Northern Bay' at the north end of the station into which the train was duly propelled. As the train passed Stafford shed there was an exchange of whistles with 2P 4-4-0s Nos. 40443 and 40461, Jinty No. 47665 and a Super D 0-8-0. Moreover, there was a further exchange with Britannia Pacific No. 70033 *Charles Dickens* which roared by with a Euston to Manchester express. A Traffic Inspector (from Crewe) took charge of the train staff from Venables ground frame to 16MU sidings frame and, at the far end of the line, a signalman had to display a red hand signal at a point

a quarter of a mile from the end of the line at Bromshall.

The event was widely reported in the local media as evidenced by the following description based on a report in the *Staffordshire Evening Sentinel* with some choice quotations. *Locomotive 41224 started on a well-kept length of track but as it joined the old Uttoxeter line the track became rusty, and bushes and grass growing in between the lines became increasingly abundant. Branches of trees growing on the bank poked their way nearly into the carriage windows.* Harold D. Bowtell, a distinguished SLS member, was on board and as the train sped through the former station at Salt he noted that the local parson and his flock were there to wave the train on its way. As the train pulled into Ingestre and Weston station, where it was scheduled to call at 3.30pm, Thomas William Smithson, a former station master there in L&NER days, held high *a battered old railwayman's lamp* and was joined by his brother-in-law and former platelayer, William John Dix, *a sprightly 72-year old* who prior to his enlistment in the army in 1916 had been a railway porter. After a brief stop, *out of the carriages swarmed more than 200 railway enthusiasts.* The train then called at Chartley and Stowe station (scheduled arrival 3.45pm) which was *once a railhead for pottery going to the Continent by train ferry wagons* and then passed through Grindley station with its staggered platforms similar to those at Ingestre. *Both Chartley and Ingestre had immense milk traffic at one time. Then the train went through the 300-yard* [sic] *Bromshall Tunnel to Bromshall Junction. There, with a great amount of whistling, was journey's end.* As there were no turning facilities at Bromshall the train was propelled back to Stafford with push-pull coach No. M24417M leading. It called only at Grindley as the train did not stop there on the outward journey and, unlike at Salt, it was deemed safe to do so. Its return through Stafford Common and arrival at Stafford's *Great Northern Bay* was accompanied by the explosion of detonators strategically placed on the track and by long blasts on the whistle, including one to comply with the instruction to *WHISTLE FOR CEMETERY CROSSING* which was obeyed for the very last time by the driver of a passenger train – a fitting death knell. At Stafford the train was shunted for the return to Birmingham New Street. Departure time was scheduled for 7.16pm with arrival in Birmingham at 8.05pm after a call at Wolverhampton High Level. It had been a poignant journey.

Another little known 'Special'

Demolition did not commence immediately probably because an expression of interest in preserving the line was mooted by the Railway Preservation Society (RPS). In 1959 the Railway Society from Queen Mary's Grammar School, Walsall managed to persuade BR to organise another outing over the line using the Wickham trolley and trailer. On the appointed day some 20 or so boys and a teacher duly assembled at Stafford Common station for the trip to Bromshall and back. Reg Durose drove the trolley accompanied by Jack Williams and a BR Inspector. Brian Holmes (see Chapter Twelve) was also present together with Bill Ives from the RPS. The trolley plunged into the broom and sycamore bushes which were once more encroaching on the track; a stop being made at Weston and Ingestre for the engine to cool down. At Bromshall, Reg and Jack transferred the trailer to the rear of the trolley for the return journey to Stafford Common where the S&UR's final passengers alighted. They watched in silence as the trolley left to return to its shed at Chartley for the very last time.

Demolition

The *Stafford Newsletter* for 10 October 1959 reported that a contract for removal of the rails and sleepers between Grindley and Bromshall Junction had been obtained by Cox and Danks Ltd of Oldbury, Birmingham and that work had already commenced. It was estimated that about 650 tons of metal, including the rails, chairs (some dating back to 1923) and fishplates, together with some 7,000 sleepers, would be removed by road to the firm's depot at Langley Green. The firm was responsible for demolishing the station building, an old cottage and all the platelayers' huts. It was also responsible for the demolition of Grindley station road bridge and infilling the cutting to take a new road but no authority had been given to seal or fill Bromshall tunnel. The newspaper went on to say that BR had invited tenders for the demolition of the section from Grindley to the RAF 16MU sidings near Stafford Common. However, this line still did not want to die as, shortly after work had commenced, Cox and Danks Ltd went into voluntary liquidation and work was stopped. It took until the early 1960s for all derelict track to be removed. Hopton cutting was filled using Stafford Corporation refuse and the spoil from the embankment at Salt was used in A51 trunk road improvements at Sandon.

Economies at Stafford

While the majority of the line slumbered, economies were also slowly taking place on the remaining operational section at the Stafford end on the branch. From 22 May 1955, the Stafford Common branch, as the remaining operational part of the S&UR had become known, was singled by the removal of the former up line from 110 yards west of bridge No. 44, which was the one crossing the River Sow, to a point 440 yards east of that bridge. This required the installation of two new upper quadrant signals and the installation of ground frames at Venables and Stafford Common, thus making the two signal boxes at those locations redundant. They quickly became derelict and vandalised. Ex LM&SR Class 3F 'Jinty' 0-6-0 tank engines from Stafford shed (code 5C) became the usual motive power until the end of steam traction. However, it is known that ex LM&SR Stanier Class 8F 2-8-0s and Class 5 4-6-0s very occasionally ventured onto the branch.

Royal Occasions

We have two noteworthy occasions to record which occurred late in the life of the remaining active part of the branch to Stafford Common. The first arose during the visit of Queen Elizabeth II and the Duke of Edinburgh to Cheshire and Staffordshire in 1955. Following a visit to Johnson's Pottery at Hanley and the Wedgwood factory at Barlaston on 2 November, the Royal train arrived at Stafford. After the Royal party alighted from the train for an official reception, the stock was hauled back onto the S&UR by Stafford's ex L&NWR Super D 0-8-0 No. 49410. The empty stock was later propelled back into the station for the royal party to re-embark and then once again hauled the train back onto the S&UR where it remained overnight complete with the Queen and Duke and the Super D which provided the steam for the carriage heating. In the meantime, the train engine went light engine to and from Crewe for attention in readiness to take the train on to London the following morning.

The second occasion was altogether different and involved the visit of ex LM&SR Princess Royal Class 8P Pacific No. 46209 *Princess Beatrice*. Geoff Sands, the shedmaster at Crewe North, was a keen enthusiast and it was his practice to allocate unusual engines to jobs involving the shed's 50 ton Cowans Sheldon steam crane. In the late summer of 1961 No. 46209 headed south to Stafford with the crane to assist in the reconstruction of Bagnall's Bridge as part of the electrification scheme. The bridge took Castle Street across the railway and once provided access to the Castle Engine Works of locomotive builder, W.G. Bagnall Ltd – hence its name. The work involved the locomotive using the remains of the S&UR as a head shunt and at one stage the whole breakdown train and crane ventured on to the branch. *Princess Beatrice* must have been the largest ever locomotive to do so.

Final closure

In the early 1950s, the goods stations at Doxey Road and Stafford Common were still in use with full facilities, including parcels traffic, being offered at the latter where the five ton capacity hand operated crane was still used when required. The Railway Clearing House Hand-Book of Railway Stations for 1956 listed the following private sidings as still extant going eastwards from Stafford: Lilleshall Company Ltd, Venables, Central Electricity Authority, West Midlands Gas Board, Manger's Salt Works Ltd, ICI Tillington Salt Works, Stafford Salt & Alkali Company Ltd and Air Ministry 16MU. The Lilleshall siding had not been used for landsale coal since that company was vested in the National Coal Board on 1 January 1947. Later events saw the ICI Salt Works closing in 1958, the Stafford electricity generating station closing in 1959, Stafford gas works ceasing production in 1964 and the Crown Salt Works siding agreement being terminated on 20 November 1965. Stafford Common goods yard closed in August 1968 and in that same month the remains of Stafford Common Station were demolished. In August 1970 the vehicular gates at the notorious Blackford Lane level crossing were removed and replaced by fencing and wicket gates provided for use by local workpeople. Later that year salt production in Stafford was banned as a result of serious subsidence occurring to the north of the town. This heralded the closure of the former Stafford Salt & Alkali Works at Stafford Common which, ironically, was the first to exploit the salt beds; it had the honour of being the last open-pan salt producing plant in the UK. On 15 August 1972, a Weekly Traffic Notice issued by the Chief Operating Manager at Crewe[186] reported that until further notice redundant track was being removed from the down and up sidings between 12¾ and 12¼ mile posts, including Stafford Doxey Road. This action probably heralded the removal of all the redundant sidings between Stafford and 16MU to avoid the maintenance of the point frogs as traffic to and from that location was by then the only movement over the truncated Stafford Common branch. The same weekly notice reported that under the control of Stafford No. 5 signal box, the shunting signal at the points in the up fast line of the trailing connection to the 16MU sidings had been repositioned on the cess side of the line. Formal closure of the line from the junction at Stafford to milepost 10¾ took effect from 19 November 1973 but the line remained operational for the occasional movement to and from 16MU.

The finale came on 28 November 1975 when the last train within the 16MU site was flagged off by Group Captain Alan Francis Britton. Eric Bruce with 30 years' service was the driver and his brother, Terry, with 13½ years' service was the shunter. The train continued its journey from the exchange sidings behind a BR Class 08 0-6-0 diesel electric shunter. Rail services were

officially withdrawn from 16MU with effect from 1 December 1975 but on 4 April 1976, Fowler diesel locomotives AMW Nos. 212, 218 and 241 were noted at Stafford Salop Sidings which means they must have travelled over the line after the official closure date. The 08 diesel electric shunters had replaced 204hp Drewry 0-6-0 diesel mechanicals (Nos. D2221, D2236 and D2385) which had, in turn, replaced the 'Jintys' when Stafford shed closed on 19 July 1965. The junction with the main line was severed in 1981 and the remaining track was subsequently lifted in 1982. In the meantime 16MU had been transformed by the RAF into a Density Activity Complex which, when opened in 1977, was widely publicised as the largest warehouse in North West Europe. Alas, it was no longer served by rail.

A view taken in 1967 looking west with the footbridge situated just east of the River Sow crossing in the distance. The footbridge took a path leading from the Stafford to Eccleshall road to serve a cemetery which was situated on both sides of the line. The bridge is No. 43B at 12 miles and eight chains.

Train of empty coal wagons crossing the bridge over the River Sow en-route from the gas and electricity works siding to Stafford station on 26 February 1963. The engine is former LM&SR class 3F shunting tank, No. 47354. TED TALBOT

Two views of Stafford Common taken on 18 March 1962 looking towards Stafford. Notice the recovery of coping stones from the platforms and the disused connection into the Crown Salt Works.

F.W. SHUTTLEWORTH

On 26 February 1963, former LM&SR 3F shunting tank engine No. 47354 pauses during shunting operations at Stafford Common with the signal box to the left and part of the ICI Salt Works to the right.

TED TALBOT

Photograph taken in early BR days and before through services from the Eastern Region ceased. The engine standing outside Stafford Common signal box is former L&NER Gresley designed N2 0-6-2 tank engine number 69552, former L&NER number 9552 and before that number 2585, built by Beyer Peacock of Gorton, Manchester in 1925. It was allocated to Colwick (38A) and lasted until withdrawn in May 1960. As it was not renumbered into the BR list until May 1949 and as control passed to the LMR with effect from 2 April 1950, this photograph was presumably taken between those dates. The tank engine was used because the turntable at Stafford Shed (5C) was out of commission at the time.

Stafford Common on 23 March 1957. The siding to the left served Manger's Crown Salt Works while the works on the right is the Common Works of the former Stafford Salt and Alkali Company, by this time part of Amasal Ltd. There was an occupation level crossing over Blakeford Lane just behind the photographer, not one of the original crossings as the lane post-dated the railway, or at least the extension of it over the line did.

Stafford Common signal box on 18 March 1962. This was one of the boxes built by the GNR after it took over the S&UR and part of its major re-signalling and general refurbishing of the route. Notice that by this date, the connection into Manger's Salt Works to the left of the box has been disconnected. F.W. SHUTTLEWORTH

Two photographs taken on the morning of Saturday 23 March 1957, the day of the SLS special last train over the line. Two platelayers, Reg Durose and Jack Williams, both former L&NER men who had been involved with the line, are engaged in some final tightening of the rail keys before the train arrived. The first view looks west in Hopton cutting ...

... and the second, where they are accompanied by their Wickham motorised trolley number TP15P, is at the same location but looking in the opposite - east - direction. The bridge in the distance is No. 33 at nine miles 55 chains taking a road to serve Hopton Heath over the railway.

Ingestre and Weston Station during the long period of dereliction on Boxing Day 1954. The view looks west towards Stafford illustrating the wooden platform on the down line and the fact that the platforms here were staggered. The platform on the other, up side, is of later concrete construction and was built to serve the milk traffic from the dairy. The Trent & Mersey Canal can just be discerned passing under the railway in the dip in the ground beyond the station. F.W. SHUTTLEWORTH

The derelict signal box at Ingestre and Weston taken at the same time as the previous view. As can be seen, the box was just designated as Ingestre. It appears that the frame has been removed from the box and of course, all the signals have been taken away. When the last train ran, the SLS special, all the points were clipped and locked for through line running, which in the case of Ingestre, was on the up line. F.W. SHUTTLEWORTH

This is the up side platform and buildings at Ingestre and Weston, also seen on Boxing Day 1954. The platform here was of more substantial construction and would have been the original one when the line was first built. F.W. SHUTTLEWORTH

Three views of the SLS special last train on the line while it called at Ingestre and Weston on 23 March 1957. The train stopped here on its outward journey when passengers were allowed to disembark, have a look around and take photographs if they so wished. Note that the train carried express train headlamps, one over each buffer, and that a small boy is managing to have a look in the cab of the engine.
TED TALBOT

This is a very happy view of part of the welcoming party for the SLS special train at Ingestre and Weston station. It is particularly interesting as two former L&NER employees are part of the group. On the extreme right holding one of the original station lamps is former station master Thomas William Smithson, still resident in the village. He had charge of the station from 1929 until the last goods train ran in March 1951. To his immediate right is his brother-in-law, William John Dix, 72 years old at that time and a former platelayer on the line.

Three views of the SLS special train while it stopped at Chartley and Stowe on its outward journey. Here again passengers were able to leave the train and have a look around. TED TALBOT

We have included this photograph as it shows the late and legendry William Arthur Camwell (1906-1995) for so long such a staunch supporter of the Stephenson Locomotive Society and for many years editor of its Journal. He was largely responsible for organising numerous special trains on behalf of Society members, very often over lines shortly to be closed or perhaps, devoid of any normal passenger service. However, in the case of the special that ran over the S&UR long after it had closed to all traffic, he excelled himself, as described at length in the text. The person to the right of 'Cam' with the cameras is Doctor Arthur Lionel Barnett (1908-2007) at that time a long serving member of the Railway Correspondence & Travel Society and later to become the President of the Railway & Canal Historical Society.
ROBERT B. PARR COURTESY JAN AND FONS DE JONG

Platelayers Durose and Williams were kept very busy on the morning of the SLS special train attending to the track to ensure safe passage of the train. They had of course, been giving the line attention for some time previously, while this was a final run over it before the special train ran. Here they are at Parkhill, between Chartley and Stowe and Grindley.

Parkhill on the morning of 12 March 1957, prior to the running of the SLS Special train. The bridge is No 12, just on the Uttoxeter side of Grindley station at three miles and 29 chains, this is the east face looking towards Stafford. Compare with an earlier photograph of the same bridge in Chapter Three (page 62).

Grindley Station with its staggered platforms on Boxing Day 1954, a view looking towards Uttoxeter.   F.W. SHUTTLEWORTH

Taken at the same time as the previous view, the signal box at Grindley which, like the others on the disused part of the line, appears to have had its lever frame recovered along with all the associated signals.

On its outward journey the SLS last day special did not call at Grindley, but it did on the way back to Stafford, where once again the passengers were allowed to alight and have a look around. Note that the driving coach of the push-pull set now carries a black headlamp rather than the white tail lamp in the earlier views.

These two views at Grindley were taken on 27 July 1981 and show the former Station Master's house and the hand pump used for raising water from the station itself, to a tank in the house. The pump was located in that small hut to the bottom right, which was located on the down side platform. A. HENSHAW

A view from the SLS special train as it is about to enter Bromshall tunnel on its outward journey. Notice Durose and Williams with their Wickham inspection trolley at the trackside on the right having lifted it off the track while the train passed. TED TALBOT

The SLS special train at the end of its outward journey standing alongside the former GNR Bromshall West Junction signal box. This box had been taken out of use in 1926 with all the signalling operations transferred to the former NSR Bromshall Junction box. When this photograph was taken, most of the passengers had walked along the short section of track to the junction as the train only went to this point which as can be seen, was then the commencement of the single line.

Here they are! This view looks down from the signal box, which stood at quite a height to give the signalman good visibility. The former NSR main line curves away to the right with the S&UR to the left. The special train is out of sight in this view. The main line connections were still in place, but clipped out of use.

This is a much later view of Bromshall Junction, or the site of it, on 19 August 1961. The train is the 4.15 pm Derby to Crewe consisting of two three car BRCW (later class 104) diesel multiple units. The signal box remained in use as a block post as it controlled a road level crossing. The site of the junction can just be seen to the right of the train at the side of the box.   MICHAEL MENSING

This is Bromshall signalbox on the former NSR main line, a photograph taken on 28 March 1965. The box and crossing were situated just to the west of Bromshall Junction – this view looks south. As can be seen the box also controlled a road level crossing; the two crossings, Bromshall and Bromshall Junction, were only about half a mile apart. This is a replacement of the original NSR box, required in connection with the construction of a Royal Ordnance Factory, actually a storage and ammunition servicing depot, known as ROF Bromshall, in the apex between the NSR and S&UR lines, during the last war. Siding connection was provided from both lines – NSR and S&UR – and in the case of the former, the additional signalling and track work arrangements necessitated a larger lever frame and therefore, a bigger signal box. Hence this LM&SR standard design box. The new arrangements came into operation in September 1942. In the early 1960s the ROF storage facility fell out of use but in February 1967, it was re-commissioned as WD Bromshall, as a temporary facility for the United States Air Force after General DeGaulle un-ceremoniously booted it out of France. Shortly after this, in late May and early June the same year, the box and associated signals were abolished and replaced by automatic half lifting barriers to control the level crossing. The siding connection and crossover road were then operated by a new ground frame which was unlocked by Hockley Crossing signal box, as by this date Bromshall Junction box had also been abolished and the crossing controlled by automatic half barriers (known as Loxley Lane). Hockley Crossing was the next block post towards Uttoxeter. Telephone communication was provided between the frame and the signal box. The US Air Force moved out in December 1968 and shortly after this, the connection was removed. F.W. SHUTTLEWORTH

LEFT: This is a somewhat earlier view of Bromshall looking north west. The crossover road and connection to the ROF sidings can be seen, out of use at this time and before the US Air Force arrived on site. The NSR house on the left is much larger than normally provided for crossing keepers, as there had been a station at this point and this was originally the station house. The station was one of the original ones when the line opened but it closed due to lack of patronage, on 1 January 1866. Despite several attempts by the locals and over several years, to have it reopened, it never was.

THE LATE DR. J.R. HOLLICK

This is the replacement ground frame to control movements in and out of the former ROF Bramshall. The view looks towards Uttoxeter and notice that the ground frame is designated as Bramshall, while the signal box was Bromshall. There are some covered vans in the siding just discernible in the centre.

RIGHT: *Stafford Common Station on 23 March 1957 looking towards Stafford. The connection with the Crown Salt Works can be seen in the right foreground; the siding agreement for this connection was terminated on 20 November 1965. The railwayman is Mr. Hall, the Foreman in charge.*

The joint LM&SR L&NER Goods Depot at Stafford Common.

COURTESY JAN AND FONS DE JONG

Although just off the route itself, a photograph of the former NSR Uttoxeter shed will not go amiss. Dating from 1901, it replaced an earlier establishment at Pinfold and doubtless on occasion, the GNR and L&NER engines would have sought refuge here! Always a sub-shed of Stoke, although in later LM&SR and BR days it had its own shed-code of 5F and its own allocation of engines, they were regularly supplemented by others from the parent shed. This was to cover maintenance requirements, along with additional diagrams at holiday times, the local races and the like. In fact the two engines here that we can identify, the class 4 tank No. 42454 and the Hughes/ Fowler Crab on the right, No. 42926, were both Stoke allocated engines and they almost certainly allow us to date this photograph as between June 1962 when the tank engine was transferred from Bletchley and August the same year when the Crab went to Buxton. There is the possibility the Crab had already moved to Buxton, having worked through on the line via Ashbourne, but it still dates the photograph as the summer of 1962, as the tank engine was withdrawn while still allocated to Stoke in December that year. The shed closed in December 1964.

An ex LM&SR Jinty shunts at Stafford Common in the mid-1950s. Note the logo Amasal on the lorry between the signal box and the bunker of the Jinty. Amasal Ltd took over the salt works formerly operated by Manger's and the Stafford Salt & Alkali Company in 1950.

JIM FOLEY COLLECTION

Notes

184 NA AN13/1727.
185 Minute No. 4/91.
186 BR 31012, WE1-No. 34.

CHAPTER TWELVE
Reflections and Remains

Clog and Knocker

Nowadays the S&UR is often referred to as the Clog and Knocker Line but we suspect this is a comparatively new pseudonym as there is no mention of the term in contemporary reports of journeys over the line or in the considerable publicity that announced and reported on the 1957 SLS Special. Other railways were similarly termed. Phil Jones in the introduction to his book on the line published by the Oakwood Press in 1981 thought the term was adopted due to the *enthusiastic engine driving on the gradients at both ends of the line.* There are other explanations but this is the one we like best, imagine the sound of a loose coupled goods train pounding up the 1 in 70 grade to Hopton with the locomotive's exhaust echoing off the cutting sides and then clanking down the 1 in 75 to Salt.

Authors' Lament

Neither of the authors was able to sample the delights of travel over the S&UR as passenger services had ceased long before we were born and we both missed out on the significance of travelling on the 1957 SLS Special. At that time we were more interested in copping *namers* on the West Coast Main Line! However, one of the authors did on more than one occasion journey from Stoke to former GNR territory at Grantham. This was accomplished by travelling over the former NSR main line through Uttoxeter to Derby Midland and then walking through the town to Derby Friargate for the onward journey to Grantham via Nottingham Victoria. This at least replicated what it must have been like to travel over part of the route followed by former GNR/L&NER through services from Stafford to Nottingham. We both recall photographing the derelict structures on the remains of the branch between Stafford and Stafford Common while the track was still in use and reflecting on how remarkable it was that the GNR managed to penetrate so far west. Compared to similar local structures, the different architectural styles of the surviving signal boxes at Venables and Stafford Common and Stafford Common station itself certainly bore witness to a more enterprising past and aroused our interest which is now manifested in this book.

There now follows a few descriptions of the line in past times and reminiscences from those who knew it well.

Thomas Richard Perkins (1872-1952)

This gentleman, a pharmacist, was once described by Cuthbert Hamilton Ellis as the doyen of all interested in the travel and history of branch lines. Perkins was born in Wolverley, Worcestershire in 1872 and often was wont to tell of his experiences of travelling from Stafford to London, not via the L&NWR but via the GNR to Derby and Grantham and thence to King's Cross[187]. The distance from Stafford to Euston is 133½ miles whereas the distance from Stafford to King's Cross via the S&UR was 179½ miles. He was a budding railway enthusiast

and had experienced a casual sighting of NSR and GNR trains when passing through Stafford station which had clearly aroused his interest. Moreover, just prior to his trip in May 1893 he had spent an evening at Stafford and noticed that the fare from there to King's Cross was the same as that to Euston. His journey was planned to commence with the 6.25am departure from Stafford where he had arrived in the early hours from Wolverhampton. He was pleased to watch the GNR locomotive back onto the train and noted that it was a 2-4-0 but of very different appearance from those of the L&NWR looking curious with its domeless boiler, rounded cab and leading wheels set well forward under the centre of the smokebox. He noted the grass-green livery with the GNR initials on the tender, the number painted on the cab sides, the polished brass safety-valve cover and the chocolate coloured frames. The varnished teak carriages were of the old flat-roofed type, rather narrow, but well upholstered with four or six wheels. One point that appeared strange to him was that most of the third class compartments shared an oil-lamp with their neighbours, the lamp cavities being immediately above the partitions. We will now let Perkins tell the tale in his own words.

The time for departure had nearly arrived before the booking clerk appeared; evidently passengers by that train were not usually many. My request for a ticket to King's Cross occasioned surprise and a little delay, but eventually I obtained it, and was hurried into the now overdue train, which started almost before I had taken my seat. I had brought with me Cassell's guide to the GNR and so was able to follow my journey intelligently; the excellent panoramic maps assisted very much in this. In fact, having studied my route pretty thoroughly during the previous week, I knew what to look for as we proceeded, and didn't miss much of interest.

We diverged almost at once from the LNWR main line, and entered upon the GNR branch to Uttoxeter, a single line – but double as far as Common station – some 13 miles in length, soon to draw up at Stafford Common, the first station. Here all was strange and unfamiliar – the somersault signals, the yellow gravel ballasted track, and many other minor details, all emphasising the fact that I was on a 'foreign' system. At most of the succeeding stations, churns of milk were taken on board; quite a quantity of Staffordshire milk still finds its way to King's Cross I believe. The country passed through was undulating and decidedly picturesque, becoming more level as we approached the valley of the Dove at Uttoxeter. At Bromshall Junction we ran on to the main line of the North Staffordshire Railway, over which we continued – by virtue of running powers – for some 11 miles to Egginton Junction.

Perkins eventually arrived at King's Cross behind a Stirling 2-2-2 having changed at Netherfield and Colwick into a through coach on a train from Nottingham. The through coach was shunted into a siding at Grantham and then attached to the rear

For this Chapter we have again decided to take a trip along the line from the Stafford end. This is the junction of the S&UR at Stafford on 17 August 1971, looking south with the station, and Stafford No. 5 signal box just visible through the arch of Bagnall's Bridge. Towering above is the coaling tower of the by then closed Stafford shed. The former W.G. Bagnall Ltd locomotive works is to the right, then part of the GEC Group. On the left is the site of the siding into the former W. Hall & Co. coal yard. This was still in use as a coal yard, albeit without rail traffic.

The two junctions at the north end of Stafford Station are seen here. On the left is the former Shropshire Union line to Wellington and on the right the S&UR, with the west coast main line striking away in the centre. The line from Stafford to Crewe had originally been double track; it was quadrupled in the period 1875-1876. The pick-up goods train (judging by its head lamp code) coming off the Wellington line on 4 March 1961, is hauled by ex LM&SR class 4F No. 44434 of Burton-on-Trent shed. The photograph is taken from Bagnall's bridge with the W.G. Bagnall locomotive works prominent. Beyond is the works of the Universal Grinding Wheel Company.   MICHAEL MENSING

of the express to London. It should be borne in mind that at the time of Perkins' journey, Nottingham Victoria station did not exist.

The Locomotive

This magazine, which was founded as *Moore's Monthly Magazine* in 1896, contains an article on the S&UR in its issue for 14 March 1908. Most descriptions of the line, like our own, commence from Stafford but this feature is unusual in that it describes the line westwards from Uttoxeter.

Running out of Uttoxeter the line passes into hilly country through the only tunnel on the line at Loxley, about 300 yards in length, and crosses the Blythe river to Grindley (five miles from Uttoxeter), then passing near the ivy-covered towers of Chartley Castle, reaches Chartley and Stowe (7½ miles). About two miles further on, the NSR line is crossed between Colwich and Stone, just before arriving at Ingestre and Weston (9¼ miles), near Ingestre Hall, the seat of the Earl of Shrewsbury and Talbot. There were extensive salt works adjoining Weston station, the buildings of which still remain, although the works are now out of use. Considerable quantities of salt were turned out here up to about 20 years ago. After successfully crossing the Trent and Mersey Canal and the River Trent, the line passes near Sandon Hall, the Earl of Harrowby's seat. A lofty column, seen over the trees was erected in 1806 to the memory of the Right Hon. William Pitt. It is of grey local stone and is 75ft high. The next halt is at Salt and Sandon station (10¾ miles), and leaving here the line passes through a short cutting, and a little further on through what may perhaps be considered the heaviest bit of engineering work on the line, viz., the Hopton cutting, nearly half a mile in length, and in places nearly 60 feet in depth; in fact, it is so extensive that the question naturally arises whether it would not have been cheaper to tunnel this piece of work instead of blasting away the many thousands of tons which had to be removed. It is, perhaps, the prettiest feature of the whole line, and in the summer time is particularly beautiful, foliage, yellow broom and ferns abounding in rich profusion. The summit of this portion of the line occurs in the middle of the cutting, and when viewed from the cab of the engine, the line seems to climb to this point (just under the bridge) and then to disappear altogether.

The next station is at Stafford Common, and here is the chief depot and goods station of the line, and also the extensive salt works of the Stafford Salt & Alkali Co. and Messrs Stubbs, with siding accommodation from the railway. Some very large chemical works are to be established here by Messrs Chance & Hunt Ltd, which the line will serve. Stafford Common is 13¾ miles from Uttoxeter. The line soon after crosses the river Sow and terminates at Stafford LNWR station.

Hugh Bryan Oliver (1901-1980)

Hugh Bryan Oliver vividly recalled the line between the years 1910-1914 as a small boy enjoying his annual four-week family summer holiday in a cottage on Sandon Bank[188]. His father, the Rector of St. John's Church at Longton, was keen on railways and instilled his enthusiasm into his son. Hugh recalls watching distant railway activity from the cottage bedroom window. Each weekday morning he waited for the GNR train to Stafford which left Uttoxeter at 7.15am to pass over the NSR main line exactly as the 7.0am train from Stoke to Colwich passed underneath. In his words: *I used to strain my eyes looking from this bedroom window, high up on Sandon Bank, to see the puffs of smoke as these two trains passed each other. Soon after, at about 7.45am, one could hear the GNR 2-4-0 or 0-6-0 tender engines tackling the adverse gradient of the Hopton Cutting and the noise made was memorable.* Hugh also recalled that he often went with his father to Ingestre station to see the passing of the only two trains of the day which actually crossed at that point. These trains were due at Ingestre at 2.33pm and 2.34pm and were, respectively, the 11.30am ex Grantham to Stafford and the 2.15pm ex Stafford to Derby. Alas such animated scenes today can only be recreated by rummaging through Bradshaw. We have checked Hugh's timings against a 1912 edition and they marry perfectly.

L&NER and BR Reminiscences

The following reminiscences have been collected by Jim Foley of Stafford and kindly made available for our use.

Roy Yates began employment with the L&NER at Stafford Common in 1934. *We had quite a large booking office with a staff consisting of a Station Master (Mr. Simons) three clerks and myself. The office was positioned on top of the Common Road Bridge jutting out over the platforms and spanning the railway line. From the booking hall there was a wooden stairway about six feet wide which led down to each of the two platforms. There was a toilet under the stairway on each platform. On the platform for the trains from Stafford to Derby there was a parcels office, ladies and gents waiting rooms and a porters' room. At the end of that platform was the signal box operated by my uncle, Fred Saunders.*

Mrs. A. Brain of Station House, Salt, prompted by the running of the SLS 'Special', wrote to the *Stafford Newsletter* on 19 April 1957. She recalled the late Lord Harrowby's car arriving to meet the first train to Salt from Stafford at 8.40am. This train brought his lordship's daily papers and sometimes fresh fish which the chauffeur would collect. Lord Harrowby would also meet any new maids for the hall at the station. She commented that parcels and passenger traffic was always light and recalled one week *when the whole weekly takings at Salt amounted to seven pence – a ticket from Salt to Stafford and just a parcel or two.* Her observation is certainly borne out by the L&NER Summary of Monthly Totals of Passenger Train Traffic for 1938. The entry for Salt shows a total of 576 third class tickets issued producing total receipts of only £17 5s 11½d (£17.30p) for the entire year. During November only 19 tickets were sold. After the outbreak of the war in 1939, Mrs. Brain recalled being told that a trainload of Ramsgate children evacuees was coming down the line. *We took stools and chairs on to the station platform and gave them a real good welcome. The train was full of excited children brought to safer homes out of the bombing area.* She added that many of those children still visited the people they stayed with at Salt.

Lillian Peake went to work for the L&NER as a signalwoman at Ingestre and Weston station during the Second World War when she was 18. *The Station Master was Mr. Smithson who lived nearby in the Station Master's house. We had to put up shutters in the signal box during 'blackout'. Soldiers from an army unit based* at Ingestre Hall used to come to unload explosives from goods trucks at Weston Goods Yard. It was mostly ammunition for the RAF. There was a team of four platelayers who travelled up and down the railway line on a trolley. Percy Preston, who lived at Chartley, was the driver in charge. The trolley was kept at Chartley and two or three times a week the team used to travel from Chartley to Stafford Common and back. There was an RAF Air Ammunition Park at nearby Bagot's Wood and no doubt the ammunition to which Lillian referred was destined for this location.

Lawrence Dowd was a goods guard who worked for the L&NER and BR at Stafford Common. He recalls that the freight staff consisted of two sets of enginemen one of the drivers of whom was Ernie Copper. There were two guards, including himself, a shunter and two foremen: Ted Thompson and Bill Nix. Two brothers comprised the permanent way staff - Alf Middleton, the ganger and Tom Middleton, the platelayer. There was a carriage and wagon examiner, a goods clerk, a goods porter and, of course, the signalmen. Lawrence recalls the race specials to Uttoxeter, the animals and equipment from Bertram Mills Circus being unloaded in Stafford Common goods yard, fly shunting into ICI's Salt Works and the fact that engines were never allowed over the bridge which crossed the River Sow on the gas works branch. Sufficient wagons were attached to the front of the engine to ensure that the wagons destined for the gas works reached their required position without the engine having to cross the bridge. This was not always the practice as goods guard Les Davis who came to Stafford on 17 June 1944 clearly remembers the locomotives crossing the bridge in readiness to fly shunt the wagons for the gas and electricity works sidings. A capstan was used to position the wagons once they were off railway property. The bridge over the river probably weakened in later years so prohibiting the engines from crossing. Both Lawrence and Les recalled that the ICI salt wagons were always kept in good condition whereas those belonging to Manger's and the Stafford Salt and Alkali Company were often stopped for repairs because of overheated axle boxes.

The Brian Holmes Story

Brian Holmes lives at Drointon and well recalls the closed portion of the S&UR during its long slumber in the 1950s. This is his story which he has kindly made available to us.

Back in 1954, I was trainspotting at Penkridge station with a pupil of Stafford Grammar School. 'There's an old branch line near Stafford - grass is growing in the tracks and all the stations are full of tickets and posters - you can pick them up off the floor!' Thus began my early memories of the derelict Stafford and Uttoxeter Railway. Between 1954 and 1957 I made several visits walking the track from the main line junction at Stafford right through to Bromshall crossing. Stafford Common station signal box was still in use as was the section of line to the RAF sidings.

On the first visit, I remember a small BR tank engine shunting trucks. A steam crane worked sluggishly in Venables timber yard and the dismal interior of the salt works was visible from the railway. Leaving the outskirts of the town, the branch line ran through a deep cutting at Hopton where saplings of some size were already taking root in the permanent way. Using the sleepers to pace the walk,

sometimes balancing on the rusty rail, the journey began in earnest. The cast iron chairs on which the rails rested bore the initials GNR. The goal was to reach the end of the line wherever that was and to achieve this before dark. We had done no research beforehand and had only Bartholomew's half inch to the mile map of the Vale of the Trent as a guide. Fortunately all the stations were shown so we were expecting the approach of Salt. There was evidence of a stand for milk churns and possibly a cattle loading ramp. Broken windows, smashed doors, dereliction and abandonment - even the former station master's house, although I think still occupied, seemed to want to hide in shame. The platform once swept and colourful with seaside posters and summer flowers was now overgrown and strewn with slate debris from the roof and broken glass from the booking hall. Nothing seemed to have escaped the reckless vandalism of those who seemed to want to obliterate the place. It was almost verging on a feeling of hatred, as though here were memories so bitter that only extreme destruction would satisfy some hidden desire. A place well ordered, a neat and predictable world of luggage, parcels and pigeon baskets, had been violated.

Walking an old railway is certainly nostalgic. You are constantly aware of the men and machines who had built it with much pride and care, only to have their efforts discarded. Like so many canals before them which outlived their original use, branch lines which had become an economic liability were ruthlessly cut off and the rural communities they once served were isolated. Dr. Richard Beeching had still to make his infamous purge and many an unsuspecting byway basked in the false hope of survival at the dawn of the age of the family car. With mixed feelings we left this sad scene behind and passed under an old bridge emerging between thickly wooded banks alive with scurrying creatures and cuckoos. Out into open countryside, green meadows watered by a glistening river seemed to raise our spirits - over the valley, a fine view of the Pitt memorial in Sandon Park.

As we slowly made our way towards the next station - Ingestre and Weston, the tracks beneath our feet were colonized by wild flowers and small silver birch bushes - here and there a rabbit dived off the line into the encroaching briar. Litter from the main road above us casually dumped in heaps of human detritus - an old gas cooker, bricks from a wall, filthy clothes and a broken pram - straddled the rusty rails. On the lea of Weston Bank, the outline of the stone hall its windows gaping to the sky added to the general feeling of waste and destruction.

Crossing the canal on a painted metal bridge, we entered Ingestre and Weston station on the edge of the village green. Once in the early years, villagers had the choice of two railway stations. Now only one remained, where trains no longer came. [The former NSR station had been demolished shortly after closure on 6 January 1947]. However, the dairy was still in full swing and white steam hung in the air around the clattering lorries discharging the milk from a hundred farms. Others reversed noisily over cobbles in the yard ready to begin the daily delivery round. The station name board was still intact - its large wooden letters proclaiming its identity to the unseeing passenger on a non-existent train. As landowner, the Earl of Shrewsbury's former home at Ingestre was given first place on the name board even though the station was situated in the middle of the village of Weston. The same thing happened at Stowe - the

Two views taken on 17 August 1968, of a very derelict Venables signalbox.

Venables ground frame on 17 August 1968. This had controlled the Gas Works Siding and was unlocked from the signal box.

LEFT: *Bridge No. 44 at 12 miles and 23 chains taking the railway over the River Sow, a view looking towards Stafford on 17 August 1968. This bridge was originally constructed to suit a single line of rails laid on the section to the right over the span with cast iron girders where the track has been removed. The newer span, on the left, has wrought iron girders.*

RIGHT: *Bridge No. 44 on the same occasion as the previous photograph, this time looking in the opposite direction towards Stafford Common. The footbridge in the distance, No. 43B at 12 miles and eight chains is not one of the original bridges; it connected the two parts of the council cemetery divided by the railway. Built at the cost of and maintained by, Stafford Corporation, the three spans were 31ft 2ins, 29ft 9ins and 31ft 2ins, with steel girders and a concrete floor.*

View looking east on 17 August 1968 towards Stafford Common Station with the derelict former goods yard on the right.

This is yet another August 1968 view, looking east with the remains of the closed Stafford Salt & Alkali Company works on the right. The sidings going off to the left had served the Chance & Hunt, later ICI, Salt Works.

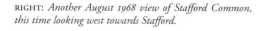

RIGHT: Another August 1968 view of Stafford Common, this time looking west towards Stafford.

The remains of Stafford Common Station looking towards Stafford on 17 August 1968. Notice the clock, stopped at 6 o'clock on the former booking office.

The platforms of Stafford Common Station with the derelict signal box in the left distance on 17 August 1968. Notice the brazier on the right hand platform formerly used to prevent the locomotive water supply column from freezing in inclement weather.

station was called Chartley and Stowe, the Chartley estate and its ancient castle, owned by Earl Ferrers, being some distance away from the village of Stowe. The station buildings at Ingestre and Weston had somehow survived the vandals' eager eyes. Secure and impenetrable, the sanctum of the inner rooms had yet to be defiled. A caring hand had boarded the windows - perhaps the last act of a former employee, a railwayman who still had pride in what had been his charge? We wondered how long it would be before the same fate that had despoiled the station at Salt would overtake this place too.

It was nearly midday and miles of rusty track snaking off into distant fields beckoned us. We crossed the main road on a substantial brick built bridge its pediments ivy covered and graffiti daubed. On an upward gradient we found ourselves above a well used double track railway. An express approached heading towards Colwich. For a blissful moment, we allowed ourselves to be enveloped in its smoke and steam as it thundered past under our trembling bridge. As the air cleared around us the reality of the faded branch line contrasted with the pure silver seams below. The main line was like an artery, active, a vital link in a national network serving the country, connecting people. The single track seemed like a withered arm, almost a joke, so pointless now, so helpless.

The gradient increased beneath our feet and soon we were amidst swaying corn and barley fields either side of the track. Over to the south and slightly behind us was Hixon airfield the wind sock showing a gentle breeze. A wayside shed came into view. Here at least was evidence of active conservation in the form of oiled locks and the smell of fuel, tools and waterproof clothing hanging neatly in an inner workshop visible through a crack in the wooden door. Oh joy! An ancient motorised trolley sat quietly in this untroubled spot, its canopy painted white with the wheels and decking displaying an old burnt orange. There was also another treasure - on a section of track by the side of the shed stood a four-wheeled vehicle complete with a brake formerly used by the platelayers. It would not take much to lift it onto the line but our enthusiasm was dampened when we discovered it was chained!

It was not on this visit - but later that we realised this dream. For now the shed was left undisturbed as we made for the over-bridge in Chartley by Stowe. On gaining view of the neat little station, we were again impressed with the name board - blue and white, the colours of the Eastern Region of British Railways. The station master's house was intact and occupied - the Victorian cast iron gentleman's lavatory was still in situ on the platform - in fact we used the facilities offered! An empty signal box and evidence once again of mindless vandalism - smashed windows, broken doors and frames. Here we collected the old ledgers and publicity sheets for bygone trains. Some were scattered in abandoned rooms, others on the platform. We stood behind the ticket window and pretended to serve tickets to passengers in the booking hall.

Leaving Chartley by Stowe, we climbed the bank towards Grindley, across the fields to the north stood the Crusaders' castle. From the railway, the main road is hidden and the castle's curtain wall and keep seemed isolated on a green bank in the middle of nowhere. At the top of the incline we came across a lonely gatekeeper's cottage. A simple four roomed house with a slate roof and small windows. The building could easily have been renovated and although damp and smelly was structurally sound. What a forlorn place for a crossing. Life

for the keeper and his family must have dragged - not even a farm in the near vicinity or anyone to talk to. We thought that the cottage had not been occupied for many years. It was outside that I found a GNR cast iron notice warning of the consequences of trespass on the company's railway - I still have it today!

The track plunged into woodland moist and lush on the edge of Chartley Moss. In many places mud had consumed the permanent way and rusty rails had been almost swallowed by the earth itself. There was now no one to tend the ditches, dredge the culverts and discourage the coppice. Soon there would be no visible sections of track to show that there ever had been a branch line at this location. We turned the curve and were confronted with a high road bridge immediately before the forgotten station at Grindley. Lupins festooned the cutting like silent watchers. Once part of the station garden, they had seeded themselves everywhere in defiance of the closure of the line. The banks either side were ablaze with colour. Hidden almost in the depth of broom and coppice, a smiling faced vicar suddenly emerged from the carcass of the old Grindley signal box carrying some wooden planks from the fabric of the building. What use he had in mind for these appendages, I do not know, but clearly the word had got around that materials from the old railway could be plundered at will.

Moving further down the track on a left curving bend in the line were the main station buildings - the Stafford platform, as at Ingestre and Weston, being staggered on the curve. It was inside this place that we found wonderful ledgers detailing all the movement of munitions during the Second World War, for storage in Bagots Wood. Once again the vandals had been active leaving a trail of debris and destruction. Eventually, the mouth of the Loxley Tunnel - known for some strange reason as the Bromshall Tunnel - loomed out of the damp cutting in front of us. An old notice proclaimed its length as 321 yards. You could see right through to the other end and so, fearlessly, we began to trudge through thinking it would not take too long. It was dark, cool and not unpleasant - till we noticed the large cracks in the lining of the roof. Probably they were settlement defects, but it suddenly came home to us that we were after all trespassing! Half way through and the other end seemed just as far away as it had at the beginning. Our eyes were now accustomed to the gloom and we became aware of the old refuges either side of the single line, encrusted with a hundred years of soot and grime from the passing trains. We began to imagine ghosts of the old platelayers who had maintained this passage under the hill, only to witness the revenge of Mother Nature on their work as stalactites dripped endlessly. Our feet were suddenly in water either side of the track as drains were blocked and water flowed freely out of the other end. As we emerged into bright sunlight bats from the tunnel roof fluttered out then circled and returned to their cave. The opening looking back seemed smaller and darker than we expected. Above us, set deep in the brick fascia of the tunnel entrance were two huge cast iron plates supporting the wall against movement. Rusty and redundant now they were lost in undergrowth which hung down over the entrance threatening to hide it like a lost city. We had reached our goal.

Some months later the old railway beckoned once again. Tales of the abandoned stations and tunnel had been exchanged amongst school friends and several lads were eager to explore the track and walk the tunnel. A junior hacksaw was purchased and in the school holidays following the Christmas of 1957, a small group stood huddled over the

The last of the August 1968 views illustrates the connection with the Air Ministry 16MU sidings which left the main line of the S&UR to the right. Notice the ground frame controlling the connection, the gate guarding the site and the loading gauge for outgoing vehicles. The ground frame was released by the single-line token.

A very derelict Salt Station looking east towards Uttoxeter.

ABOVE: *Another slightly earlier view of the derelict Salt Station and before so much foliage had grown. Notice the distinctive bay window in the station building. This had housed a ground frame to control the remaining signals after the signal box ceased to be used as such.*

LEFT: *This is the former station master's house at Salt on 27 July 1981. It abutted the station buildings which were single storey, while the house, due to a fall in the ground, had two storeys. The approach road served both the house and the station.* A. HENSHAW

rusty chain holding the four wheeled truck to a section of track beside the shed at Chartley - the home of the motorised inspection trolley. It took several minutes before the link could be prized open enough to free the chain around the wheel and with a swift jerk the truck was liberated. Five eager pairs of hands lifted the vehicle bodily onto the track. The next hour or so was sheer delight. Five trespassers on an old truck hurtled at some speed over rusting tracks on a downhill gradient of 1 in 100 sufficient to carry us to Ingestre and Weston non stop! We felt that we had breathed new life into the line; thoughts of preservation and reopening were in our minds. Although rules had been broken somehow our 'vandalism' seemed pale and insignificant beside the wanton damage in evidence all around. We 'cared' about the railway and by using the wheels on the permanent way it felt that for a short time the Stafford and Uttoxeter lived again. Several trips were undertaken in the succeeding months, each time the truck was carefully returned to its base and the chain re-threaded on the wheels. One of the most exciting sections was the bank down from the old crossing into Chartley and Stowe station - the thrill of clattering over the points and on down the hill was like something the 'Famous Five' in an Enid Blyton adventure story. No damage (except to the chain) was ever done and we had no accidents. For several wonderful months we were Railway Kings playing trains on a branch line that nobody wanted.

Remaining infrastructure and surviving relics

Following the removal of the track, the deep cutting at Hopton was filled in with refuse and the spoil from the embankment at Salt was used in connection with road improvements to the A51 at Sandon. Elsewhere the line fell into a more gradual decay. The brick lined tunnel at Bromshall remains intact although it is in-filled at its eastern end. The western stone faced portal is accessible, although the tunnel itself can be flooded with up to three feet of water. The bridge over the former NSR main line at Weston has been demolished as have the bridges over the River Trent and the Trent & Mersey Canal although the latter survived until 1996. Happily the main line bridge over the River Sow at Stafford has survived and now supports a footpath and cycleway. Other bridges survive and can be viewed on Jim Foley's excellent Picasa website mentioned in the acknowledgements. A coloured photograph of bridge No. 2 taken at Loxley in 1996 is particularly grand as the sunlight superbly contrasts the red brickwork of the arch and parapet with the Staffordshire blue bricks of the remaining structure. At Stafford Common an unusual signal used to warn pedestrians of impending movements over Blackford

Lane level crossing still survives in the undergrowth. At Salt the much renovated Station House has recently been advertised for sale by a local estate agent for £499,950.

The happiest survivor of all must be the slate-roofed wooden waiting room from Chartley and Stowe station. This has been beautifully restored and repainted by members of the Staffordshire Industrial Archaeology Society and now resides on the 2ft 6in gauge Amerton Railway at Stowe-by-Chartley, very close to the former route of the S&UR. This pleasure line on Amerton Working Farm was created in order to find a permanent home for ISABEL[189], a 0-4-0 saddle tank locomotive built by W.G. Bagnall Ltd of Stafford for the Cliff Hill Granite Co., Markfield, Leicestershire in 1897 (maker's number 1491). Since its withdrawal in 1946 the locomotive has led a charmed life having been cosmetically restored at least twice before being restored to working order by the Stafford Narrow Gauge Railway Society in time to haul the first revenue earning service on the Amerton Railway on 19 July 1992. The railway has since been extended and is a great success. Less successful was an attempt by the Railway Preservation Society to purchase a cast iron urinal also from Chartley station back in 1962. It was painted grey and embedded in concrete when BR agreed a selling price of £6. Unfortunately it was stolen along with lengths of rail by three men before it could be retrieved. The men concerned were convicted at Stafford Magistrates Court on 11 December 1962, each being fined £10 and ordered to share payment of a total of £92 13s 6d (£92.67½p) costs and restitution. A lady member of the bench asked whether the *thing* had been recovered. She was told it had not and so an ornate piece of cast iron much appreciated by gentlemen over the years receded into history.

Smaller relics remain in private collections including paperwork, tickets and timetables. Relics from Salt include a whistle, inkpots, keys and the station seal; a signal lamp has survived from Ingestre; a station lamp from Chartley and a cast iron seat plate from Grindley. Bridge plates Nos. 2, 6 and 9 have survived, as has a block instrument from Venables signal box. An Annett's key for Ingestre ground frame has also survived, together with a leather pouch and a tablet for the section between Ingestre and Stafford Common. Perhaps more importantly, the line is still remembered with affection by those who knew it well and we hope that our efforts will help keep those memories alive for many years to come. We also hope that those who enquire about the Stafford and Uttoxeter Railway in future years will appreciate and benefit from our research.

Surviving relics from Grindley station; lamp glass and cast iron seat plate. COLLECTION ARMAND CHATFIELD

Ingestre and Weston Station on 17 March 1957 after the down side platform and signal box had been demolished. The view looks west towards Stafford and as can be seen, the dairy is still functioning with its smoking chimney.

The last and little-known trip over the line by members of the Queen Mary's Grammar School at Walsall in July 1959. Here is the group at Ingestre and Weston with platelayers Reg Durose and Jack Williams involved; they can be seen on the left. The Wickham trolley and on this occasion its un-powered trailer were involved, the stop at Ingestre was to allow the engine to cool down.

BRIAN HOLMES

A rather nice photograph of Chartley and Stowe station again looking towards Uttoxeter showing the crossover road to give access from the loop to the milk dock. By this date, probably just after the last war, the loop has been secured out of use with the right hand road used for running in both directions. Notice the polished railhead.

One of the Chartley station lamps of GNR design.

PHIL JONES

Chartley and Stowe Station on 17 March 1957 looking east towards Uttoxeter.

This is a much later photograph of the cutting and site of Grindley and Stowe Station taken on 29 September 1962, after the track had been removed. The small hut to the left, housed the hand pump used for pumping water up to the Station Master's house which is off the picture to the left. Notice to the right, the remains of the down side platform.

Bridge No. 17 at five miles and 45 chains on 27 July 1981. This bridge carries the Amerton to Stowe road near Chartley, over the former railway and as can be seen in this view, it has been supported by brick pillars and a steel raft. The original girders are cast iron. This would have been less costly than removal of the bridge and filling in the gap, or realigning the road. It would also have caused less disruption to road traffic.

West portal of Bromshall tunnel on 17 March 1957.

Bridge No. 3 after track lifting. Compare with the earlier view of this bridge in Chapter 3 (page 66). It is situated at 47 chains from Bromshall Junction and adjacent to Loxley Park. This is the opposite east face looking towards Stafford.
JIM FOLEY

View looking towards Stafford at Bromshall with the derelict former GNR West Junction signal box. Just to the right of the box is the site of the former connection, through the gate, into the ROF. By this time, 23 August 1957, while there was still activity at the former ROF, the only rail connection was the one from the NSR line.

The site of the S&UR connection to the NSR line at Bromshall Junction on 30 March 1968. The sign, the rear of which can be seen under the central arch of the footbridge, is a whistle sign for the level crossing situated behind the photographer.

The train here, consisting of a three-car Birmingham Railway Carriage & Wagon Company (BRCW), later class 104, diesel multiple unit, is the 5.15pm Uttoxeter to Crewe where it was due at 6.22pm, on 19 August 1961. Bromshall Junction signal box can be seen to the right background along with the formation of the former junction of the S&UR.

MICHAEL MENSING

A very much reduced Uttoxeter Station on 21 April 1979. By this time the complete Churnet Valley side had disappeared along with the footbridge and West Junction signal box. The train departing is the 1.35pm Lincoln to Crewe consisting of a BR Swindon built Cross-Country diesel multiple unit, later class 120. The signal is the Pinfold Crossing down home with the Hockley Crossing down distant mounted below it.

MICHAEL MENSING

One item that has survived, is the former station building from the Uttoxeter side platform at Chartley, splendidly restored on the Amerton Railway. This is a two-foot gauge enthusiast run system located within the Amerton Working Farm at Stowe-by-Chartley.

ANNE & JIM ANDREWS

Notes

187 *The Railway Magazine* Vol. 84, February 1939.
188 NRM H.B. Oliver Collection, Volume 9.
189 ISABEL is named after Isabel Fitzmaurice, née Bennion (1871-1905) wife of John Rupert Fitzmaurice, founder of the quarry company.

Acknowledgements

In compiling this book the authors have tried hard to spread their net far and wide in their endeavour to tell as complete a story as possible. In doing so they have had help and assistance from numerous individuals and organisations. Wherever possible primary source documents and records have been consulted in an attempt to ensure the story is an accurate account of the railway's history. Bearing in mind that the Stafford & Uttoxeter Railway ceased to be an independent undertaking over 130 years ago, it is perhaps not surprising that we have had some difficulty in this respect. We have for example, been unable to locate the railway's minute books despite the fact that the Act of Parliament authorising the acquisition of the railway by the Great Northern, stipulated that the books should be handed over to the new owners. Had this been done, it seems inconceivable that they have not survived to form part of the British Transport Historical Records (BTHR) now held within the National Archives at Kew, along with all the other records of the Great Northern Railway. We can only assume that they were in fact, not passed over. We have however, been able to consult the records of the NSR, L&NWR and GNR, which form part of the BTHR at Kew. The records of the Board of Trade and Ministry of Transport, in regard to the statutory inspections of railway works are also held at Kew.

Within the Staffordshire & Stoke-on-Trent Archives in the Country Record Office at Stafford, there is much material relating to the railway. This encompasses both official documents, for example the Parliamentary deposits, including the plans and sections of railways, both those actually built and others that did not advance beyond the planning stage, along with bequests made by individuals. The Parliamentary Archives held at the House of Lords Record Office contain duplicate copies of the deposits made by potential railway companies as well as the actual transcriptions of the various Select Committee debates and of course, the actual Acts of Parliament. Russell Wear was instrumental in letting us know that the Ferrers family archive was located at the Record Office for Leicestershire, Leicester & Rutland. We have also consulted papers and documents in the custody of the British Newspaper Library at Colindale, the Imperial War Museum, the Museum of Science & Industry in Manchester and the National Railway Museum. The staff at all these locations have been extremely considerate and helpful. We have also had help and assistance from the Great Northern Railway Society, Stephenson Locomotive Society, Staffordshire Industrial Archaeology Society and the Wellington History Group.

Several individuals are deserved of special mention. Phil Jones was the first author to research and write a detailed history of the railway, published by the Oakwood Press back in 1981. He has unreservedly placed his entire collection at our disposal for which we are extremely grateful. Armand Chatfield has amassed a significant number of documents and artefacts relating to the railway which have been made available to us. Richard Dempster likewise, has a collection and these too have been placed at our disposal. Richard introduced us to his father-in-law, Les Davis – Big Les – who was the guard on the last train to traverse the line, the SLS special in March 1957. The authors spent an interesting few hours with Richard and Les when we were able to learn a lot about the later days of the line. Les started his railway career with the L&NER at Colwick, transferring to Stafford in June 1944 where he eventually became a goods guard, his work occasionally encompassing trains over the line.

Ken Plant has made an extensive study of surviving records inherited by Network Rail from BR and these have been made available to us. Peter Trewin, the former secretary of BRB (Residuary) Limited, kindly allowed copies to be made of the plans in its custody that did not pass to Railtrack and later NetworkRail when BR was privatised. Included in this archive are the complete plans of the S&UR, a selection of which are included in these pages.

In addition to the above many individuals have freely shared with us their knowledge of the S&UR, allowed us to inspect surviving relics and memorabilia in their collections, provided photographs which they have allowed us to use and disclosed information about their ancestors who were connected with the railway. We list them in alphabetical order: John Alsop, Anne and Jim Andrews, David Bathurst, Paul Blurton, Robert Brown, John Bucknall, Richard Casserley, Allen Civil, John Clarke, Neil Clarke, Lawrence Dowd, Jim Foley (and his Picasa Web Album), Alan Fozard, Allan John Frost, Martin Fuller, Terry Godridge, Geoff Harrison, Brian Holmes, J.R. Hollick, George Howe, Basil Jeuda, Frank Jux, Sydney Leleux, Phil Jones, Jan and Fons de Jong, Trevor Lodge, Michael Mensing, John Newcombe, Timothy Newcombe, Col. William A. Oakeley (ret) US Army, H.B. Oliver, Jo Probert, F.W. (Tim) Shuttleworth, Hillary Snape, Peter Smith, Ted Talbot, Allan Turner, Keith Turton, Michael A. Vanns and Ken Wood.

If perchance, we have missed any individual or organisation, this has certainly not been our intention and we offer our most sincere apologies.

We have also made good use of the internet and have found the following websites (accessed 30 May 2014) particularly helpful:

www.amertonrailway.co.uk   www.lancashire.gov.uk
www.ancestry.co.uk   picasaweb.google.com/clogandknocker
www.forgottenrelics.co.uk   www.search.staffspasttrack.org.uk

Except where otherwise acknowledged, the photographs and other illustrations are from our own collections. Several of the maps and diagrams have been specially drawn for us by Roger Hateley whose cartographic skills are greatly appreciated. The computer skills of David Rodgers in assisting the processing of the draft and some of the illustrations is also very much appreciated.

We cannot close these remarks without expressing thanks to our publisher Neil Parkhouse, for taking on this work, along with Stephen Phillips who has been responsible for the origination. Sorting out the manuscript and the multifarious documents and photographs has been Stephen's lot and we hope readers will agree that he has made a splendid job of it. Last but by no means least, Angela and Darral our wonderful wives, who constantly put up with our strange ways, not least locked away in studies for hours on end, record offices and other dark and dismal depositories here and there. As a sort of midway point between High Halden and Brough, a certain public house in Grantham has, it has to be added, on occasion considerably increased its takings when the authors have met there to debate and discuss how this work should be progressed!

It goes without saying that any errors of fact or how we have interpreted the information at our disposal, omissions and anything else a diligent reader might detect, is our responsibility and ours alone. The authors would however, be more than happy to hear from any reader, via the publisher, who can add to or amend our story. One never knows, a second edition might one day be considered appropriate.

Appendix One

STAFFORD AND UTTOXETER RAILWAY
LOCOMOTIVE DIMENSIONS AND IDENTITY OF NLR LOCOMOTIVE

	Shrewsbury and Talbot	*Ingestre* (as rebuilt)
Wheel arrangement/type	2-4-0 side tank	0-4-4 saddle tank
Inside cylinders: diameter × stroke	14in × 20in	16in × 24in
Leading wheel diameter	3ft 3½in	not applicable
Coupled wheel diameter	5ft 0½in	5ft 0in
Trailing wheel diameter	not applicable	2ft 8in
Total wheelbase	13ft 4in	20ft 10in
Heating surface: tubes	552 sq ft	858 sq ft
Heating surface: firebox	54 sq ft	68 sq ft
Heating surface: total	606 sq ft	926 sq ft
Grate area	10.5 sq ft	13 sq ft
Coal capacity	13 cwt	1 ton 5 cwt
Water capacity	420 gals	800 gals
Weight in working order	25 tons 5 cwt	40 tons 19 cwt 2 qtr

In Chapter Six mention is made of a conundrum regarding the possible identity of the former North London Railway locomotive *Ingestre* that came to the S&UR in 1873. It has been generally accepted by various authors, that the engine was the former NLR No. 41, one of the two out of the five in the class (the other one was said to have been No. 38), that had been rebuilt in 1868 at the Bow Works. This would have been under the direction of William Adams the Locomotive Engineer, with one of his patent four-wheel bogies in replacement for the original single trailing radial axle. The NLR Locomotive, Stores & Traffic Committee minutes however, are silent on the issue.[190] The earliest published reference to the locomotives insofar as the S&UR is concerned, is a 1908 article on the railway in *The Locomotive Magazine*,[191] where the outline drawing of the engine in Chapter Six came from. It is identified in the article as former NLR No. 41. We have seen in Chapter Six that the S&UR Receiver & Manager purchased a locomotive from Hendry & Co. in May 1873 and that NLR No. 41 had been sold to J.H. Johnson of Wigan; the sale date recorded in the NLR minutes for No. 41 is 27 September 1872. However, despite the minutes on 4 June 1872 recording the offer of Messrs Hendry & Co. to buy all five of the NLR engines (following a decision of the members of the committee to advertise their availability[192]), the minutes later record that only No. 40 was sold to Messrs Hendry & Company, in this case on 4 June 1873. All five incidentally, were sold via an un-named broker on a commission basis.

A series of anonymous articles in *The Locomotive Railway Carriage & Wagon Review* in 1942-1943, attribute former NLR No. 40 as sold in 1873 to Aberdare Rhondda Company.[193] However, the Industrial Railway Society (IRS) in *Industrial Locomotives of Mid & South Glamorgan*,[194] have former NLR No. 39 as going in October 1872, directly from the NLR to Aberdare Rhondda Steam Coal Company, while the minutes have it as

sold on 25 October 1872, to W.H. Williams of Redlands, Bristol. In *The Industrial Locomotive*,[195] the late John Bates attempts to unravel the later history of all five of these locomotives having, like the present authors, consulted the NLR minute books. He discusses two adverts placed in *The Engineer* by T.E. Minshall, a dealer of Queen Street in Wrexham, which on the face of it, would appear to refer to some of these NLR locomotives. On 14 February 1873 he was advertising three tank locomotives by Beyer Peacock, *second-hand, 16 inch cylinders, six-wheel, four-coupled, two fitted with patent bogie*. Later, on 30 May the same year, *tank locomotives, two by Beyer Peacock, four-wheel coupled 5ft diameter driving wheels, one with patent bogie, the other with trailing wheels 3ft 6inch diameter*. It should be mentioned at this juncture that it was by no means unusual for dealers to advertise locomotives they did not own, on behalf of others in the hope of getting a commission on any sales they might facilitate. On the face of it, it is difficult to discount these adverts as not referring to some of the NLR locomotives. There is a discrepancy in the first advert as *six-wheel, four-coupled*, cannot refer to an engine with a four-wheel bogie. However, bearing in mind Minshall would have been attempting to sell the engines on behalf of a broker, perhaps not too much importance should be attached to this. As the second advert would appear to be correct, the discrepancy may be no more significant than the way the wording of the first advert was compiled.

John, in accepting these adverts to be correct and there is no evidence to suggest they were not, comments that the only locomotives remaining unsold by the NLR in February 1873, were Nos. 38, 40 and 42. Of these No. 40 was sold on 4 June 1873 - only five days after the advert appeared - leading him by process of deduction, to conclude that the two engines rebuilt with the trailing bogie were in fact, Nos. 38 and 40; not 41 as previously assumed.

The above deduction is supported by the order book of Fletcher Jennings & Company of Whitehaven. The locomotive that went to J.H. Johnson of Wigan is recorded as having worked for the Strangeways Hall Coal Company, of which he was manager, the company owning pits at Bickershaw and Stangeways Hall. C.H.A. Townley, F.D. Smith and J.A. Peden, in their *Industrial Railways of the Wigan Coalfield, Part One - West and South of Wigan*,[196] tell us that the locomotive was found to be too heavy for the track at the collieries and in 1877, was sold to Fletcher Jennings, a firm the company had been buying new locomotives from. The locomotive appears in the Whitehaven firm's order book,[197] as its order No. 154. The book tells us that an engine was purchased from Messrs Crompton & Shawcross of Wigan in part payment for a new 12 inch cylinder engine, *it being too heavy for the track, inside cylinders, 16×24 inch, six wheels, leading four-coupled, put in a new steel firebox and new iron tubes and repainted. It was originally on the North London Railway.* Fletcher Jennings advertised the locomotive for sale in August 1876,[198] subsequently hiring it to Whitehaven Collieries before being sold in 1884, to the Colne Valley & Halstead Railway in Essex. Of particular significance is an outline sketch of this locomotive in the surviving Fletcher Jennings order book, clearly illustrating it as an 0-4-2 saddle tank and not an 0-4-4. The foregoing led John Bates to conclude that the locomotive that went to the S&UR was former NLR No. 40 and as mentioned above, this was the one rebuilt at Bow with a trailing bogie and not No. 41. The present authors continue to have an open mind on the actual identity of the locomotive the S&UR acquired, being conscious that other authors, albeit unidentified, writing over 100 years ago, had concluded it to have been former NLR No. 41. It is a pity that the NLR surviving records do not tell us which of the locomotives were converted with a trailing bogie – the previously accepted version identifying numbers 38 and 41, coming from secondary sources. Similarly the GNR Locomotive Committee minute books don't help as while they record when the S&UR locomotives were acquired, no details of their type or manufacture are given.[199]

Notes

190 NA RAIL 529/45-46.
191 Vol. XIV, 1908 - March issue.
192 *The Engineer*, 21 June 1872.
193 Vol. XLIX 1943 - May issue.
194 Author Geoffrey Hill, 2007, ISBN 978-1-90-901556-34-6.
195 Journal of the Industrial Locomotive Society. Vol. 8 1996-1998, No. 87 and subsequent correspondence Vol. 9 1998-2001, No. 93. In a letter from Geoffrey Hill the author of the IRS book, he tells us that a Mr William Hole Williams, an accountant of Bristol, was one of the original subscribers of the Aberdare Rhondda Steam Coal Company Ltd when it was registered in May 1871. This would seem to confirm that former NLR No. 39 was the engine that went to Aberdare & Rhondda having been purchased by Williams on behalf of the colliery company.
196 Runpast Publishing, 1991 ISBN 1-870754-18-2.
197 Original held at the National Railway Museum.
198 *The Engineer*, 25 August 1876. This would suggest the 1877 sale date quoted by Townley, Smith & Peden in their book is incorrect. In fact, the last new Fletcher Jennings locomotive the firm had was supplied in 1874, which would imply that the former NLR locomotive had a very short sojourn at the collieries.
199 NA RAIL 236/197 GNR Locomotive Committee Minute Book No. 4, Minute 282 5 October 1882.

Given the more recent research as summarised above, in particular the primary source material, the balance of evidence does seem to suggest that the S&UR engine was former NLR No. 40 and not No. 41 as previously accepted.

To conclude this dissertation, it is opportune to mention briefly the fate of the two locomotives of the five, not already mentioned. No. 38 was sold on 2 October 1873 to a Mr Grice of the Cwmbran Works at Newport, later the Patent Nut & Bolt Company Ltd. No. 42 was sold on 2 October 1873 to a Mr McConnochie. A John McConnochie was the Engineer of the Bute Trustees, of the Bute Docks in Cardiff and it seems likely that Mr Connochie, as recorded in the NLR minutes and John McConnochie, are one and the same individual.

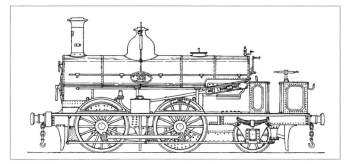

NLR No. 38.

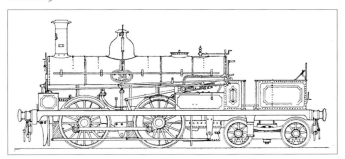

NLR No. 38 as rebuilt.

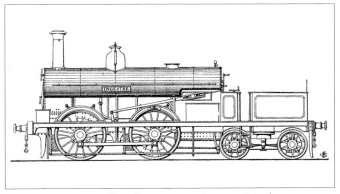

INGESTRE *as portrayed in The Locomotive Magazine - March 1908.*

The above images can also be found in Chapter Six but are repeated here for ease of reference.

Appendix Two

STAFFORD AND UTTOXETER RAILWAY - HIRE OF LOCOMOTIVES 1870-1881

DATE		HIRED FROM/BY	£ COST	(DECIMAL)
June	1870	L&NWR	£10 10s 0d	(£10.50)
1 November	1871	Isaac Watt Boulton	£50 0s 0d	
4 December	1871	Isaac Watt Boulton	£50 0s 0d	
30 January	1872	L&NWR	£7 10s 0d	(£7.50)
31 January	1872	L&NWR	£4 6s 0d	(£4.30)
2 February	1872	L&NWR	£8 1s 0d	(£8.05)
8 February	1872	L&NWR	£20 2s 6d	(£20.13)
26 February	1872	L&NWR	£12 1s 6d	(£12.08)
1 March	1872	L&NWR	£16 2s 0d	(£16.10)
7 March	1872	Isaac Watt Boulton	£16 1s 5d	(£16.07)
7 March	1872	L&NWR	£20 2s 6d	(£20.13)
11 March	1872	L&NWR	£12 1s 6d	(£12.08)
16 March	1872	L&NWR	£20 2s 6d	(£20.13)
23 March	1872	Roden, Inspector of the Line	£24 3s 0d	(£24.15)
1 April	1872	Roden, Inspector of the Line	£20 2s 0d	(£20.10)
6 April	1872	Roden, Inspector of the Line	£32 4s 0d	(£32.20)
12 April	1872	Roden, Inspector of the Line	£26 3s 3d	(£26.16)
19 April	1872	Roden, Inspector of the Line	£32 4s 0d	(£32.20)
26 April	1872	Roden, Inspector of the Line	£32 4s 0d	(£32.20)
4 May	1872	L&NWR	£32 4s 0d	(£32.20)
9 May	1872	Roden, Inspector of the Line	£32 4s 0d	(£32.20)
16 May	1872	Roden, Inspector of the Line	£32 4s 0d	(£32.20)
27 May	1872	Roden, Inspector of the Line	£32 4s 0d	(£32.20)
1 June	1872	Roden, Inspector of the Line	£32 4s 0d	(£32.20)
7 June	1872	Roden, Inspector of the Line	£32 4s 0d	(£32.20)
17 June	1872	Roden, Inspector of the Line	£32 4s 0d	(£32.20)
29 June	1872	Roden, Inspector of the Line	£34 4s 3d	(£34.21)
8 July	1872	Roden, Inspector of the Line	£32 4s 0d	(£32.20)
15 July	1872	Roden, Inspector of the Line	£32 4s 0d	(£32.20)
19 July	1872	Roden, Inspector of the Line	£32 4s 0d	(£32.20)
29 July	1872	Roden, Inspector of the Line	£33 4s 2d	(£33.21)
3 August	1872	Roden, Inspector of the Line	£32 4s 0d	(£32.20)
16 August	1872	Roden, Inspector of the Line	£30 3s 9d	(£30.19)
16 October	1872	Isaac Watt Boulton (Balance of engine hire)	£16 10s 0d	(£16.50)
6 February	1873	L&NWR	£15 2s 0d	(£15.10)
6 February	1873	L&NWR	£50 0s 0d	
24 February	1873	L&NWR (Including removal of broken carriages and engine)	£46 1s 6d	(£46.08)
27 March	1873	East & West Junction Railway	£35 0s 0d	
29 April	1873	East & West Junction railway	£35 0s 0d	
17 December	1873	East & West Junction Railway (Hire of rolling Stock – may or may not include locomotives)	£188 9s 6d	(£188.48)
7 September	1875	Roden, Inspector of the Line	£28 7s 0d	(£28.35)
3 December	1875	Burton, General Manager	£1 17s 9½d	(£1.89)
3 December	1875	Burton, General Manager	£9 19s 6d	(£9.98)
7 December	1875	Burton, General Manager	£12 18s 3d	(£12.91)

DATE		HIRED FROM/BY	£ COST	(DECIMAL)
25 February	1876	Duffill, General Manager	£4 4s 0d	(£4.20)
21 April	1876	Duffill, General Manager	£4 4s 0d	(£4.20)
25 April	1876	Duffill, General Manager	£12 0s 0d	
1 July	1876	NSR	£8 11s 2d	(£8.56)
3 August	1876	Duffill, General Manager	£37 1s 3d	(£37.06)
10 August	1876	Duffill, General Manager	£36 4s 6d	(£36.23)
17 August	1876	Duffill, General Manager	£25 14s 6d	(£24.73)
23 August	1876	Duffill, General Manager	£41 13s 9d	(£41.69)
4 September	1876	Duffill, General Manager	£59 10s 11d	(£59.55)
10 December	1877	William Moss, contractor	£6 0s 0d	
6 February	1879	L&NWR	£54 11s 9d	(£54.59)
2 April	1879	L&NWR	£10 10s 0d	(£10.50)
2 April	1879	L&NWR	£9 4s 10d	(£9.24)
5 September	1879	L&NWR	£26 7s 1d	(£26.35)
25 October	1879	Firmin Hill & Co.	£7 0s 0d	
1 November	1879	Firmin Hill & Co.	£7 0s 0d	
8 November	1879	Firmin Hill & Co.	£7 0s 0d	
14 November	1879	Firmin Hill & Co.	£7 0s 0d	
24 November	1879	Firmin Hill & Co.	£7 0s 0d	
1 December	1879	Firmin Hill & Co.	£7 0s 0d	
9 December	1879	Firmin Hill & Co.	£7 0s 0d	
22 December	1879	Firmin Hill & Co.	£14 0s 0d	
8 January	1880	Firmin Hill & Co.	£14 0s 0d	
19 January	1880	Firmin Hill & Co.	£14 0s 0d	
27 January	1880	Firmin Hill & Co.	£14 0s 0d	
4 February	1880	Firmin Hill & Co.	£14 0s 0d	
10 February	1880	Firmin Hill & Co.	£14 0s 0d	
19 February	1880	Firmin Hill & Co.	£50 0s 0d	
3 April	1880	Firmin Hill & Co.	£50 0s 0d	
12 May	1880	Firmin Hill & Co.	£50 0s 0d	
25 October	1880	L&NWR	£91 0s 7d	(£91.03)
24 December	1880	L&NWR	£223 8s 8d	(£223.43)
4 February	1881	L&NWR	£76 6s 8d	(£76.33)
3 March	1881	L&NWR	£78 4s 6d	(£78.23)
19 April	1881	L&NWR	£220 11s 8d	(£220.58)
27 April	1881	L&NWR	£25 4s 0d	(£25.20)
2 May	1881	L&NWR	£75 12s 0d	(£75.60)
7 May	1881	L&NWR	£25 4s 0d	(£25.20)
16 May	1881	L&NWR	£25 4s 0d	(£25.20)
23 May	1881	L&NWR	£25 4s 0d	(£25.20)
28 May	1881	L&NWR	£25 4s 0d	(£25.20)
13 June	1881	L&NWR	£25 4s 0d	(£25.20)
20 June	1881	L&NWR	£25 4s 0d	(£25.20)
27 June	1881	L&NWR	£25 4s 0d	(£25.20)
6 July	1881	L&NWR	£25 4s 0d	(£25.20)
13 July	1881	L&NWR	£25 4s 0d	(£25.20)
16 July	1881	L&NWR	£25 4s 0d	(£25.20)
26 July	1881	L&NWR	£25 4s 0d	(£25.20)
6 August	1881	L&NWR	£40 1s 2d	(£40.06)

Appendix Three

NSR STATIONS USED BY GNR PASSENGER TRAINS

STATION NAME	OPENING DATE		CLOSING DATE	
Egginton Junction	1 July	1878	5 March	1962
Horninglow	1 August	1883	1 January	1949
Marchington	February	1854	15 September	1958
Rolleston-on-Dove	1 November	1894	1 January	1949
Stretton and Clay Mills	1 August	1901	1 January	1949
Sudbury	11 September	1848	7 November	1966
Tutbury	11 September	1848	7 November	1966
Uttoxeter Bridge Street	7 August	1848	1 October	1881
Uttoxeter	1 October	1881	Still open	

GNR trains only used Uttoxeter Bridge Street station from 1 to 30 September 1881.

Egginton Junction station was jointly owned by the NSR and GNR. L&NER passenger trains from Stafford and Burton-on-Trent ceased to use the station from the date of their withdrawal on 4 December 1939.

Tutbury station was reopened on a slightly different site on 3 April 1989 and renamed Tutbury and Hatton. It remains open.

Appendix Four

STAFFORD AND UTTOXETER RAILWAY
RECEIVER AND MANAGERS' ACCOUNTS 1868-1881

The following sets of accounts were prepared by Robert Daniel Newill who was appointed Receiver and Manager pursuant to an order made in the Court of Chancery on 2 May 1868.

	£ RECEIPTS	£ PAYMENTS	£ BALANCE DUE TO RECEIVER
1st Account 2 May 1868 to 2 May 1869	1,578	2,346	768
2nd Account 2 May 1869 to 2 May 1870	2,523	3,330	807
3rd Account 2 May 1870 to 2 May 1871	2,090	2,760	670
4th Account 2 May 1871 to 2 May 1872	2,784	3,378	594
5th Account 2 May 1872 to 2 May 1873	7,059	7,803	744
6th Account 2 May 1873 to 2 May 1874	8,788	9,869	1,081
7th Account 2 May 1874 to 2 May 1875	5,787	6,112	325
8th Account 2 May 1875 to 2 May 1876	4,646	4,857	211
9th Account 2 May 1876 to 2 May 1877	5,705	6,137	432
10th Account 2 May 1877 to 2 May 1878	5,196	5,815	619
11th Account 2 May 1878 to 13 July 1878	752	1,278	526

The following sets of accounts were prepared by Henry Cecil Newton who was appointed Receiver and Manager pursuant to an order made in the High Court of Justice, Chancery Division, on 4 February 1879. The 1st Account shows a large drop in receipts and payments which is odd but may be partially explained by the Company being in disputes as noted by the Board of Trade in respect of the year 1878 - see Appendix Six.

1st Account 13 July 1878 to 13 July 1879	1,944	1,926	18 (Credit)
2nd Account 14 July 1879 to 13 July 1880	5,764	5,753	11 (Credit)
Final Account 14 July 1880 to 15 November 1881	5,509	5,561	52

Appendix Five

STAFFORD AND UTTOXETER RAILWAY – CAPITAL 1872-1880

	1872 £	1873 £	1874 £	1875 £	1876 £	1877 £	1878 £	1879 £	1880 £
AUTHORISED CAPITAL									
By shares and stock	180,000	180,000	180,000	180,000	180,000	180,000	180,000	193,731	196,460
By loans and debenture stock	59,900	59,900	59,900	59,900	59,900	59,900	59,900	150,000	150,000
Total	**239,900**	**239,900**	**239,900**	**239,900**	**239,900**	**239,900**	**239,900**	**343,731**	**346,460**
PAID UP STOCK & SHARE CAPITAL									
Ordinary stock	134,260	134,260	113,903	113,903	113,903	113,903	113,893	113,893	113,893
Rate of dividend paid	nil	nil	nil	nil	nil	nil	nil	nil	nil
Preferential stock		79,838	79,838	79,838	79,838	79,838	79,838	79,838	81,418
Preferential rate of dividend	5%	5%	5%	5%	5%	5%	5%	5%	5%
Rate of dividend paid	nil	nil	nil	nil	nil	nil	nil	nil	nil
Total	**134,260**	**214,098**	**193,741**	**193,741**	**193,741**	**193,741**	**193,731**	**193,731**	**195,311**
CAPITAL RAISED BY LOANS & DEBENTURE STOCK									
Loans	59,900	18,600	10,600	10,600	500	500	500	nil	nil
Rate of interest	5%	5%	5%	5%	5%	5%	5%	nil	nil
Debenture stock		72,015	86,440	86,440	98,754	98,754	99,154	115,119	115,446
Rate of interest		5%	5%	5%	5%	5%	5%	5%	5%
Total	**59,900**	**90,615**	**97,040**	**97,040**	**99,254**	**99,254**	**99,654**	**115,119**	**115,446**
TOTAL CAPITAL PAID UP & RAISED BY LOANS & DEBENTURE STOCK									
	194,160	**304,713**	**290,781**	**290,781**	**292,995**	**292,995**	**293,385**	**308,850**	**310,757**

Appendix Six

STAFFORD AND UTTOXETER RAILWAY – REVENUE & EXPENDITURE 1872-1880

	1872 £	1873 £	1874 £	1875 £	1876 £	1877 £	1878 £	1879 £	1880 £
RECEIPTS FROM PASSENGERS									
1st Class	540	437	551	319	313	351	N/A	306	225
2nd Class	780	526	394	373	303	357	N/A	248	213
3rd Class (inc. Parliamentary)	1,672	1,776	2,101	2,067	1,929	2,082	N/A	1,738	1,746
Season tickets	8	6	nil	10	nil	nil	N/A	22	25
Excess luggage, parcels, carriages, horses, dogs, etc.	48	42	91	138	165	67	N/A	100	164
Total	**3,048**	**2,787**	**3,137**	**2,907**	**2,710**	**2,857**	**N/A**	**2,414**	**2,373**
RECEIPTS FROM GOODS TRAFFIC									
Merchandise	109	279	646	627	848	1,076	N/A	879	868
Live stock	82	94	133	317	132	131	N/A	76	108
Minerals	19	nil	254	138	324	351	N/A	135	246
Total	**210**	**373**	**1,033**	**1,082**	**1,304**	**1,558**	**N/A**	**1,090**	**1,222**
MISCELLANEOUS									
Rents, tolls, etc.	**nil**	**nil**	**nil**	**44**	**nil**	**28**	**N/A**	**9**	**21**
TOTAL RECEIPTS FROM ALL SOURCES	**3,258**	**3,160**	**4,170**	**4,033**	**4,014**	**4,443**	**N/A**	**3,513**	**3,616**
WORKING EXPENDITURE									
Maintenance of way, works, etc.	1,280	1,285	1,118	908	1,236	1,330	N/A	881	764
Locomotive power	811	1,207	1,454	1,277	2,041	1,115	N/A	1,343	1,743
Carriage and wagon repairs and renewals	53	152	349	208	104	164	N/A	141	132
Traffic expenses (coaching and merchandise)	390	376	1,027	1,351	1,537	1,440	N/A	1,487	1,445
General charges	436	459	470	688	608	685	N/A	680	909
Rates and taxes	34	40	40	36	39	83	N/A	47	42
Government duty	21	8	8	108	113	106	N/A	80	63
Compensation for personal injury	nil	nil	230	nil	nil	nil	N/A	nil	nil
Compensation for damage and loss of goods	nil	nil	15	4	15	17	N/A	8	nil
Legal and Parliamentary expenses	nil	nil	nil	7	nil	82	N/A	19	nil
Miscellaneous	100	1,100	126	nil	87	98	N/A	36	45
Total	**3,125**	**4,627**	**4,837**	**4,587**	**5,780**	**5,120**	**N/A**	**4,722**	**5,143**
TOTAL REVENUE	**3,258**	**3,160**	**4,170**	**4,033**	**4,014**	**4,443**	**N/A**	**3,513**	**3,616**
PROFIT OR (LOSS)	**133**	**(1,467)**	**(667)**	**(554)**	**(1,766)**	**(677)**	**N/A**	**(1,209)**	**(1,527)**

NB - No returns were submitted for 1878 'owing to the Company being engaged in disputes.'

Appendix Seven

GNR ESTIMATES FOR IMPROVEMENTS TO S&UR STATIONS WHEN THE LINE WAS TAKEN OVER

STAFFORD COMMON STATION (Goods and Passengers)

Goods Shed (100ft × 40ft × 23ft deep)	£1,533 0s 0d	
Office	100 0s 0d	
Rail Weighbridge	180 0s 0d	
Engine Shed for 4 engines, £400 per engine including Tank House and Shops	1,640 0s 0d	
Fencing to platforms - 200 yards	60 0s 0d	
Platform - 600ft long	690 0s 0d	
Timbered Crossing	15 0s 0d	
Waiting Sheds	250 0s 0d	
Coke Stage	120 0s 0d	
Wharf Wall - 84 yards	168 0s 0d	
10 ton Crane and Foundations	750 0s 0d	
40ft Turntable	850 0s 0d	
Road Weighbridge	120 0s 0d	
Weight Office and Foundations for Weighbridge	150 0s 0d	
Permanent Way - 1,590 yards	1,590 0s 0d	
P/Way - 19 Switches	304 0s 0d	
P/Way - 17 Acute Crossings	272 0s 0d	
P/Way - 4 sets Obtuse Crossings	128 0s 0d	
Metalling 12in thick - 4,420 yards	331 10s 0d	(£331.50)
Entrance Gates	50 0s 0d	
Pulling out old road, clearing away old Platform, Goods Shed, Engine Shed and Wharf	200 0s 0d	
Contingencies 10%	950 10s 0d	(£950.50)
Total	**£10,452 0s 0d**	

SALT STATION

Platform - 108 yards	372 12s 0d	(£372.60)
Platform - 92 yards	184 0s 0d	
Timbered Crossing	15 0s 0d	
Fencing behind platforms - 200 yards	60 0s 0d	
Waiting Shed	100 0s 0d	
Contingencies 10%	73 8s 0d	(£73.40)
Total	**£805 0s 0d**	

INGESTRE STATION

Platform - 137 yards	472 9s 0d	(£472.45)
Platform - 64 yards	128 0s 0d	
Timbered Crossing	15 0s 0d	
Waiting Shed	100 0s 0d	
Permanent Way - 158 yards	158 0s 0d	
P/Way - 3 sets of Switches	48 0s 0d	
P/Way - 3 Acute Crossings	48 0s 0d	
Pulling out old road including excavation for new	10 0s 0d	
Fencing behind platforms - 137 yards	41 2s 0d	(£41.10)
Fencing taken down and refixed - 63 yards	4 14s 6d	(£4.73)
Contingencies 10%	102 14s 6d	(£102.73)
Total	**£1,128 0s 0d**	

CHARTLEY STATION

Platform - 140 yards	483 0s 0d	
Platform - 60 yards	120 0s 0d	
Waiting Sheds	100 0s 0d	
Fencing - 200 yards	60 0s 0d	
Timbered Crossing	15 0s 0d	
Permanent Way - 330 yards	330 0s 0d	
P/Way - 4 Switches	64 0s 0d	
P/Way - 8 Acute Crossings	128 0s 0d	
P/Way - 2 sets of Acute Crossings	64 0s 0d	
Loading Wharf - 27 yards	54 0s 0d	
Removing and rebuilding Plaster Shed	25 0s 0d	
Pulling up old road	5 0s 0d	
Contingencies 10%	144 0s 0d	
Total	**£1,592 0s 0d**	

GRINDLEY STATION

Platform – 200 yards	690 0s 0d	
Fencing behind platform - 200 yards	60 0s 0d	
Timbered Crossing	15 0s 0d	
Waiting Shed	100 0s 0d	
Pulling out old siding	3 0s 0d	
Contingencies 10%	86 0s 0d	
Total	**£954 0s 0d**	

Appendix Eight

INDUSTRIAL LOCOMOTIVES (from *Industrial Locomotives of North Staffordshire*, Allan C. Baker, Industrial Railway Society).

AIR MINISTRY (RAF) 16 MAINTENANCE UNIT, STAFFORD					
No. 172	0-4-0DM	RSHN	6989/1940	Delivered new	(1)
No. 173	0-4-0DM	RSHN	6990/1940	Delivered new	(2)
AMW No. 212	0-4-0DM	JF	22959/1941	Delivered new	(3)
AMW No. 214	0-4-0DM	JF	22961/1941	Delivered new	(4)
AMW No. 218	0-4-0DM	JF	22965/1941	(a)	(5)
AMW No. 241	0-4-0DM	JF	22995/1943	(b)	(6)
AMW No. 244	0-4-0DM	JF	23001/1943	Delivered new	(7)
AMW No. 268	0-4-0DM	JF	23009/1944	Delivered new	(8)
24	0-6-0DM	HE	1721/1933	(c)	(9)
25	0-4-0DM	DC	2047/1934	(d)	(10)

ROYAL ORDNANCE FACTORY, BRAMSHALL					
BRAMSHALL No. 1	0-4-0DMF	JF	22982/1942	Delivered new	(11)
BRAMSHALL No. 2	0-4-0DMF	JF	22289/1942	Delivered new	(11)
BRAMSHALL No. 3 (Later ROF 15 No. 2)	0-4-0DMF	JF	22975/1942	(e)	(12)
BRAMSHALL No. 4 (Later ROF 14 No. 4)	0-4-0DMF	JF	22979/1942	(f)	(13)
	2w-2PMR	W	7438/1956	Delivered new	(14)
813	4wDM	RH	411319/1957	(g)	(15)
867	0-4-0DM	AB	342/1940	(h)	(16)
842	0-4-0DM	AB	368/1945	(i)	(17)
9020	2w-2PMR	W	8084/1958	(j)	(18)

ABBREVIATIONS

DM	Diesel Mechanical Locomotive
DMF	Diesel Mechanical Flameproof Locomotive
LM&SR	London Midland and Scottish Railway
MOD	Ministry of Defence
PMR	Petrol Mechanical Railcar
RAF	Royal Air Force
ROF	Royal Ordnance Factory
WD	War Department

LOCOMOTIVE MANUFACTURERS

AB	Andrew Barclay, Sons & Co. Ltd, Caledonia Works, Kilmarnock
DC	Drewry Car Co. Ltd, London
HE	Hunslet Engine Co. Ltd, Hunslet, Leeds
JF	John Fowler & Co. (Leeds) Ltd, Hunslet, Leeds
RH	Ruston & Hornsby Ltd, Lincoln
RHSN	Robert Stephenson & Hawthorns Ltd, Newcastle-upon-Tyne
W	D. Wickham & Co. Ltd, Ware, Hertfordshire

NOTES

(a) Ex Air Ministry, Heywood, Lancashire, via JF, 6/3/1956
(b) Ex Air Ministry, Ruislip, Middlesex, via JF, 30/7/1954
(c) Ex LM&SR 7052 on loan 8/1940
(d) Ex LM&SR 7050 on loan 8/1940
(e) Ex ROF Bescot, Staffordshire by 8/1948
(f) Ex ROF, King's Newton, Derbyshire by 4/1960
(g) Ex WD, Weedon, Northamptonshire 2/6/1961
(h) Ex Army Department, Sudbury, Derbyshire 18/1/1967
(i) Ex Ruddington Depot, Nottinghamshire 20/11/1967
(j) Ex Bicester Depot, Oxfordshire 27/6/1967

(1) To Air Ministry, Cardington, Bedfordshire
(2) To Air Ministry, Henlow, Bedfordshire by 3/1950
(3) Repaired by JF 9/1954; to Air Ministry, Leuchars, Fifeshire 1/1951, returned ex Hartlebury Depot, Worcestershire 27/3/1974. To Hughes Bolckow Ltd, Northumberland circa 8/1976
(4) Repaired by JF 2/1956; to Air Ministry, Cardington, Bedfordshire 6/2/1956
(5) Repaired by JF 3/1956; to Ministry of Defence, RAF Leuchars, Fifeshire circa 5/1976
(6) Repaired by JF 7/1954; to George Cohen, Sons & Co. Ltd, Kingsbury, Warwickshire by 8/1976
(7) Repaired by JF 4/1954; to Air Ministry, Pembroke Dock, Cardiganshire 12/4/1954
(8) Repaired by JF 1/1957; to Ministry of Defence, Air Force Department, Hartlebury, Worcestershire 12/10/1970
(9) Returned to LM&SR 2/1942
(10) This locomotive was also allocated English Electric/Dick Kerr maker's number 874/1934; to Air Ministry, Leuchars, Fifeshire 10/1940; later became WD 224
(11) To ROF Paradise, Coven, Staffordshire 8/1948
(12) To WD, Bicester 8/1961; became WD 8310
(13) To WD, Bicester 3/1962; became WD 8302
(14) To MOD, Yardley Chase Depot, Northamptonshire by 11/1964; became WD 9044
(15) To WD, Asfordby, Leicestershire 19/3/1964
(16) To Army Department, Sudbury, Derbyshire 15/8/1968
(17) To Bicester Depot, Oxfordshire 31/7/1968
(18) To Bicester Depot, Oxfordshire 15/8/1968

Appendix Nine

GREAT NORTHERN RAILWAY – REPORT ON BRIDGES, VIADUCTS, TUNNELS & CULVERTS

References to bridge numbers and distances used in this book are taken from an official list prepared by the Great Northern Railway. The pages presented here are from a ledger entitled:

GREAT NORTHERN RAILWAY
ENGINEER'S DEPARTMENT
DERBYSHIRE DISTRICT
REPORT ON BRIDGES, VIADUCTS, TUNNELS & C.
ENGINEER'S OFFICE No. 131

[Revised and reprinted April, 1921]

The ledger is leather bound and measures 16¾" × 13½".

Bridge numbers and distances commence at the eastern (Uttoxeter) end of the line, from a zero datum at Bromshall Junction.

Bridge numbers run from 1 to 48. Curiously there is no Bridge No. 15 listed, although there is a Bridge No. 43A, so the total of numbered bridges is 48.

Bromshall Tunnel is not numbered, being one of 30 other bridges listed without numbers, including 27 culverts, one pipe and one footbridge (maintained by Stafford Corporation).

Bridge No. 31, Bodkin's cattle creep at 9m 15ch, located between Salt and Stafford Common. Brick built with a 9ft span, typical of many cattle creeps along the line. Note the bridge number post top left.

No.	Between what Stations	Mileage. M.	Mileage. Ch.	Local Name.	Under or Over	Public or Occupation.	Date of Reconstruction.	Span in feet. Square.	Span in feet. Skew.	DESCRIPTION.	Maintenance of Roads and Approaches.	Last Examined.	Last Painted.	Remarks as to Condition.
										REPORT ON BRIDGES.		STAFFORD AND UTTOXETER RLY. 119		
										Single Line.				
										Unless otherwise shown, bridges constructed in 1867.				
	STAFFORD AND UTTOXETER RAILWAY. OPENED SINGLE LINE, ——?									Incorporated with G.N.R. Co., 1881.				
	Widened to Double Line from Stafford Common to Stafford, 1882.													
1	Uttoxeter and Grindley	0	16	Statham's Cattle Creep	Under	Occupation		11′ 10″		Brick abutments and segmental arch. **L.R.**				
2	Do.	0	19	Bromshall Brook	Under	Stream		2 spans each 4′ 0″		Brick abutments, pier and semi-circular arches, 2 spans. **L.R.**				
	Do.	0	36	Culvert	Under			3′ 0″ dia.		Brick barrel.				
3	Do.	0	47	Milnes'	Over	Occupation		28′ 0″		Brick abutment and elliptical arch. Width between parapets 12′ 4″.				
4	Do.	0	68	Phillips	Over	Occupation		27′ 10″		Brick abutment and elliptical arch. Width between parapets 12′ 1″.				
	Do.	1 to 1	7 21	**Bromshall Tunnel** Length, 321 yards				14′ 9½″		Brick egg-shaped arch, 5 refuges on Down side, 4 on Up side. Headway at centre, 15′ 3½″ above rails.				
5	Do.	1	47	Durose's	Under	Occupation		9′ 1″		Brick abutments and segmental arch. **L.R.**				
6	Do.	1	58	Upton's	Under	Occupation		9′ 1″		Brick abutments and semi-circular arch. **L.R.**				
	Do.	1	60	Culvert	Under			2′ 0″ dia.		Brick barrel.				
	Do.	1	60	Culvert	Under			0′ 9″ dia.		G. E. pipe.				
7	Do.	1	70	Lee's Mill	Under	Cattle Creep		2 spans each 8′ 11″		Brick abutments, pier and segmental arches, 2 spans. **L.R.**				

No.	Section			Name	Over/Under	Carries	Span	Arch	Description
	Uttoxeter and Grindley	2	2	Culvert	Under		2' 0" dia.		Brick barrel.
8	Do.	2	12	River Blyth	Under	River	20' 3" (2 spans)	23' 4" (arch)	Brick abutments, pier and segmental arches, 2 spans. **L.R.**
9	Do.	2	12		Up side of line		14' 11"		Brick abutments. Timber face and centre longitudinals and flooring. Width between parapets 9' 8½"
	Do.	2	24	Culvert	Under		2' 0" dia.		Brick barrel.
10	Do.	2	30	Farnsworth's Cattle Arch	Under	Occupation	11' 11"		Brick abutments and segmental arch. **L.R.**
11	Grindley and Chartley	2	68	Grindley Road	Over	Public	24' 0" / 28' 0" / 24' 0"		Brick abutments, piers and segmental arches. 3 spans, viz.:— Over Down side cutting. „ Main Line. „ Up side cutting. Width between parapets 25' 2".
	Do.	2	78	Culvert	Under		2' 0" dia.		Brick barrel.
12	Do.	3	29	Deville's	Over	Occupation Road	23' 11" / 28' 0" / 24' 1"		Brick abutments, piers and segmental arches. 3 spans, viz.:— Over Down side cutting. „ Main line. „ Up side cutting. Width between parapets 12' 1".
	Do.	3	49	Culvert	Under		2' 0" dia.		Brick barrel.
	Do.	3	53	Culvert	Under		3' 1" dia.		Brick barrel.
13	Do.	3	70	Park Hill	Under	Occupation	9' 0"		Brick abutments and segmental arch. **L.R.**
14	Grindley and Chartley	4	61	Cage Hill	Under	Occupation	11' 10"		Brick abutments and segmental arch. (Filled in.) **L.R.**
	Do.	4	61	Culvert	Under		3' 0" dia.		Brick barrel (Disused).
16	Chartley and Ingestre	5	20	Uttoxeter and Stowe	Over	Public	27' 2"	30' 4½"	Brick abutments. C.I. face and longitudinal girders. Brick jack arches. Width between parapets 20' 9". **L.N. & M.N.**
17	Do.	5	45	Hamilton Road	Over	Public	27' 11"	28' 10"	Brick abutments. C.I. face and longitudinal girders. Brick jack arches. Width between parapets 21' 9". **L.N. & M.N.**
18	Do.	5	73	Shirley Wick	Over	Public	28' 1"	32' 5"	Brick abutments and elliptical arch.
	Do.	6	7	Culvert	Under		2' 0" dia.		Brick barrel.
19	Do.	6	22	Deakins	Under	Cattle Creep	9' 0"		Brick abutments and segmental arch. **L.R.**
	Do.	6	39	Culvert	Under		4' 0" dia.		Brick barrel.
	Do.	6	40	Culvert	Down side of line		4' 0" dia.		Brick barrel.
20	Do.	6	49	North Staffordshire Railway	Under		29' 9"	34' 4"	Brick abutments. W.I. main and cross girders. Timber longitudinals and flooring. Main girders strengthened 1907. **T.R.**
21	Do.	6	70	The Old Turnpike	Under	Public	34' 7"		Stone abutments. W.I. main and cross girders. Timber longitudinals and flooring. Main girders strengthened 1907. **T.R.**

No.	Section	M.	C.	Name	Over/Under	Carries	Date	Dim. 1	Dim. 2	Description	Authority
22	Ingestre Station	7	4	Salt Works Lane	Under	Public	1913	12' 0"		Stone abutments. W.I. parapet girders. Steel trough flooring. **T.R.**	
	Ingestre and Salt	7	14	Culvert	Under			3' 0" dia.		Brick barrel.	
23	Do.	7	15	Grand Junction Canal	Under	Canal		31' 0"	50' 5"	Stone abutments, W.I. main and cross girders. Timber longitudinals and flooring. **T.R.**	
24	Do.	7	17	Shaw's	Under	Occupation		12' 0"		Brick abutments and segmental arch. **L.R.**	
	Do.	7	29	Culvert	Under			4' 0" dia.		Brick barrel.	
25	Do.	7	42	Stafford to Uttoxeter Road	Over	Public		27' 10"	32' 7"	Stone abutments and elliptical arch. Width between parapets 30' 10".	Stafford County Council, 10/2/94.
26	Do.	7	48	River Trent	Under	River		30' 0" / 30' 0" / 30' 0"		Stone abutments and piers. C.I. parapet and main girders. Timber cross-bearers, longitudinals and flooring. 3 spans, viz.:— Over East cess and River. ,, River and cess. ,, West cess. **T.R.**	
	Do.	7	57	Culvert	Under			2' 0"		Brick semi-circular arch.	
	Do.	7	66	Culvert	Under			2' 0" dia.		Brick barrel.	
27	Do.	7	69		Under	Cattle Creep		6' 0"		Stone abutments. Brick segmental arch. **L.R.**	
28	Do.	8	16	Sandon Road	Over	Public		28' 0"	36' 6"	Stone abutments. Brick segmental arch. Width between parapets 25' 10"	
	Do.	8	23	Culvert	Under			2' 2"		Brick segmental arch.	
29	Salt and Stafford Common	8	41	Brook Lane	Under	Public		11' 11"		Brick abutments and segmental arch. **L.R.**	
30	Do.	8	59	Old Lane	Under	Public		9' 0"		Brick abutments and segmental arch. **L.R.**	
		9	8	Culvert	Under			2' 0" dia.		Brick barrel.	
31	Do.	9	15	Bodkin's	Under	Cattle Creep		9' 0"		Brick abutments and segmental arch. **L.R.**	
32	Do.	9	19	Fenton's	Under	Cattle Creep		9' 0"		Brick abutments and segmental arch. **L.R.**	
	Do.	9	21	Culvert	Under			2' 0" dia.		Brick barrel.	
33	Do.	9	48	Highbridge (Main road)	Over	Public		28' 0"		Brick abutments and semi-circular arch. Width between parapets 20' 1".	
34	Do.	9	70	Kent's	Over	Occupation		28' 0"		Brick abutments and elliptical arch. Width between parapets 11' 11".	
35	Do.	10	15	Stafford to Hopton	Under	Public		25' 0"		Brick abutments and segmental arch. **L.R.**	
	Do.	10	16	Culvert	Under			3' 0" dia.		Brick barrel.	
36	Do.	10	38	Bird's	Under	Cattle Creep		9' 0"		Brick abutments and segmental arch. **L.R.**	
	Do.	10	51	Culvert	Under			2' 0" dia.		Brick barrel.	
37	Do.	10	52	Bird's	Under	Occupation		12' 0"		Brick abutments and segmental arch. **L.R.**	
	Do.	10	68	Culvert	Under			2' 0" dia.		Brick barrel.	

No.	Line	M.	C.	Road	Over/Under	Type	Span	Skew	Description	Authority	Notes
38	Salt and Stafford Common	10	74	Stafford to Sandon	Over	Public	28' 0"	31' 3"	Brick abutments and elliptical arch. Width between parapets 35' 2".	Stafford County Council, 10/2/94.	
	Do.	10	78	Culvert	Under		1' 6" dia.		Brick barrel.		
39	Do.	11	8	Chance and Hunt's	Under	Cattle Creep	9' 0"		Brick abutments and segmental arch. L.R.		
	Do.	11	12	Culvert	Under		2' 0" dia.		Brick barrel.		
40	Do.	11	17	Chance and Hunt's	Under	Cattle Creep	12' 1"		Brick abutments and segmental arch. L.R.		
	Do.	11	18	Culvert	Under		4' 0" dia.		Brick barrel.		
DOUBLE LINE.											
41	Stafford Common	11	42	Stafford to Marston Road	Over	Public	31' 2" / 25' 0"	28' 6"	Brick abutments. C.I. face and longitudinal girders. Brick jack arches and staircases. Smoke boards over Down and Up Main. 2 spans, viz.:— Under Booking Office. „ Road. 6" gas main over bridge. Width between parapets 29' 11". L.N. & M.N.		
42	Stafford Common and Stafford (L. & N. W. Rly.)	11	68	Stafford to Stone Road (North Street)	Over	Public	26' 10"	28' 7"	Brick abutments. C.I. face and longitudinal girders. Brick jack arches. 6" gas main 7" from W. parapet. 4" water main 5' 6" from E. parapet. Width between parapets 30' 2". L.N. & M.N.	Stafford Borough Council, 22/11/10.	*This bridge & approaches was transferred to the Minister of Transport under Trunk Roads Act 1946.*
	Do.	11	74	Pipe	Under		2' 0" dia.		G. E. pipe.		
43	Stafford Common and Stafford (L. & N. W. Rly.)	12	1	Stafford to Eccleshall Road	Over	Public	26' 10"	28' 7"	Brick abutments. C.I. face and longitudinal girders. Brick jack arches. Gas main on E. side. Water main on W. side. Width between parapets 30' 1". L.N. & M.N.	Stafford County Council, 10/2/94.	
	Do.	12	8	Footbridge	Over	Public	31' 2" / 29' 9" / 31' 2"		Brick abutments and piers. Steel girders and concrete flooring. Built and maintained by the Stafford Corporation. *3 spans, viz.:— Over Down side cutting. „ Down and Up Main. „ Up side cutting. Width between parapets 8' 8½".		
43A	Do.	12	18	Flood opening	Under		9' 1½"		Timber face and centre longitudinals and flooring. Built on piles. L.R.		
44	Do.	12	23	River Sow	Under	Stream	30' 0" (2 spans each)		Brick abutments and trussed timber piers, 2 spans. Under Down side footway. C.I. parapet girder. Timber bearers and flooring. Under Down Main. W.I. main, cross and longitudinal girders and flat plate flooring. Under Up Main. Brick abutments and pier, 2 spans. C.I. parapet and main girders. Timber cross bearers and flooring. L.R.		
	Do.	12	29	Culvert	Under		3' 0" dia.		Brick barrel.		
45	Do.	12	37	Flood opening	Under		10' 0" / 9' 3"		Timber trestles, trussed longitudinal girders and flooring, 2 spans. L.R.		

No.	Between what Stations	Mileage M.	Mileage Ch.	Local Name.	Under or Over.	Public or Occupation.	Date of Recon-struction.	Span in feet. Square	Span in feet. Skew	DESCRIPTION.	Maintenance of Roads and Approaches.	Last Examined.	Last Painted.	Remarks as to Condition.
										REPORT ON BRIDGES.	**STAFFORD AND UTTOXETER RLY. DOUBLE LINE.** **STAFFORD GAS WORKS BRANCH. SINGLE LINE.** 126			
										Unless otherwise shown, bridges constructed in 1867.				
46	Stafford Common and Stafford (L. & N. W. Rly.)	12	43	Flood opening	Under			4′ 1″		Timber face and centre longitudinals and flooring. L.R.				
	Do.	12	47	Culvert under approach road Doxey Road	Down side of line			3′ 0″ dia.		Brick barrel.				
47	Do.	12	48	Doxey Road	Over	Public		28′ 0″		Brick abutments and elliptical arch. Gas main (Stafford Corporation) on E. side. Width between parapets, 15′ 5″.	Stafford Borough Council, 22/4/10.			
			STAFFORD GAS WORKS BRANCH, SINGLE LINE. OPENED, 1891.											
48	Stafford Common and Gas Works	12	50	Flood opening	Under			2 spans each 16′ 0″		Timber face and centre longitudinals and flooring. Built on piles, 2 spans. L.R.				

NETWORK RAIL ARCHIVE

Park Hill occupation bridge No. 13 at three miles 70 chains, located between Grindley and Chartley. Brick built with a nine foot span.

Bridge No. 27, an unusual stone-built cattle creep with a six foot span between Ingestre and Salt at seven miles 69 chains.

Bridge No. 43A, a flood opening at twelve miles 18 chains near Stafford.

Bridge No. 45, a timber trestle flood opening at twelve miles 37 chains.

Appendix Ten

STAFFORD COMMON SIGNALLING DIAGRAM

This diagram of the signalling at Stafford Common accompanied a submission to the Board of Trade regarding new and revised connections. The Inspecting Officer was Colonel Edward Druitt and his report was dated 14 April 1910. He mentions a new facing connection laid in the up line leading to some new sidings, a new frame having been provided in the box with 24 working levers and four spares. This was part of the connections to both Chance & Hunt's and Stubbs & Companies' Salt Works. He also mentions an old trailing connection to the down line that was formerly worked from Stafford Common Yard Box. This box had been closed and replaced by a two lever ground frame bolt locked from the Common Box. This was the Uttoxeter end connection into the goods yard. The new arrangements and interlocking being correct, he recommended that the Board of Trade sanction the works. All these arrangements can be readily seen on the diagram.

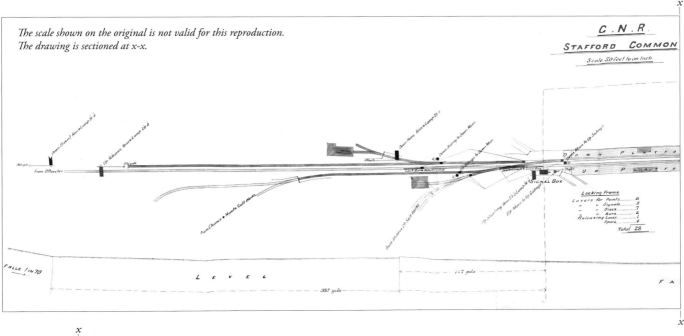

The scale shown on the original is not valid for this reproduction. The drawing is sectioned at x-x.

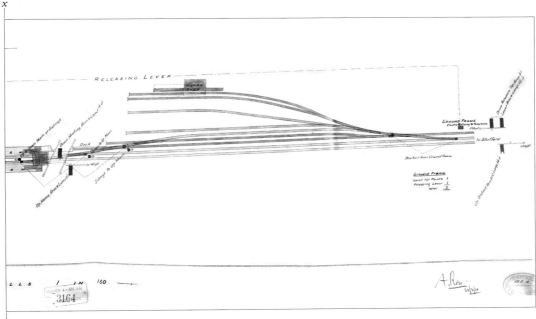

Appendix Eleven

BRB (RESIDUARY) LIMITED – PLANS OF THE LINE

When Britain's railways were privatised in the early 1990s, no provision was made in the relevant Act of Parliament, to disband the British Railways Board (BRB). This followed a decision that Railtrack, the new company formed to own the infrastructure of the railways, would not acquire ownership of any land etc., formerly owned by the BRB, that was not required for operational purposes. At this point it is worth mentioning that the BRB had a very large portfolio of non-operational land. This included many miles of track beds of closed lines involving in some cases, bridges, tunnels and other engineering works, a good number of which were listed structures. Some years later a new company was formed, BR (Residuary) Limited, to manage this portfolio

and to continue a process that had been underway for many years, in gradually disposing of this otherwise surplus property. To this end a number of plans were retained by the BRB and in this Appendix are a few relevant examples regarding the S&UR. The plans in question are those of the former L&NER Surveyors Department that had been located at London's Liverpool Street Station. They are particularly interesting in that they often show when and to whom, parcels of land were disposed of after the track had been removed. We are particularly grateful to Peter Trewin, one time Secretary of BR (Residuary) Limited and a former colleague of one of us, for allowing access to these plans

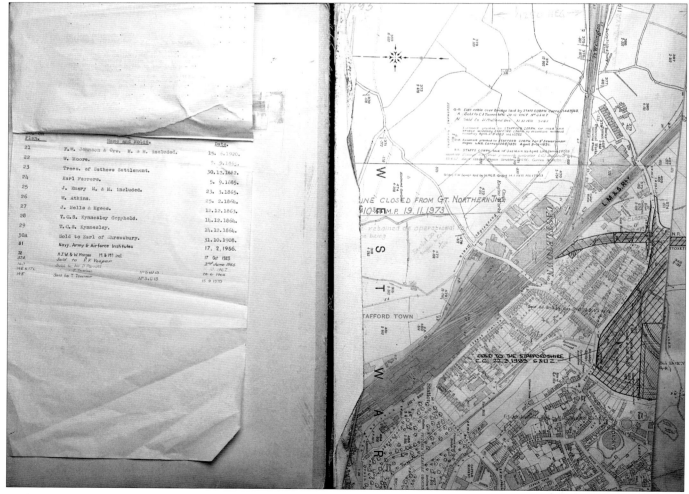

Stafford Junction.

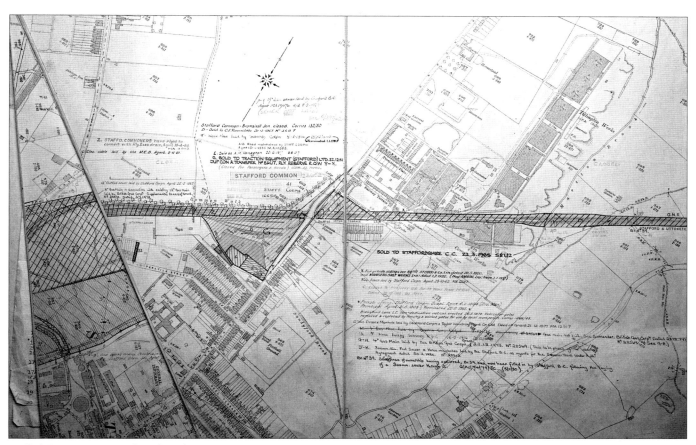

Stafford Common Station and Goods Yard.

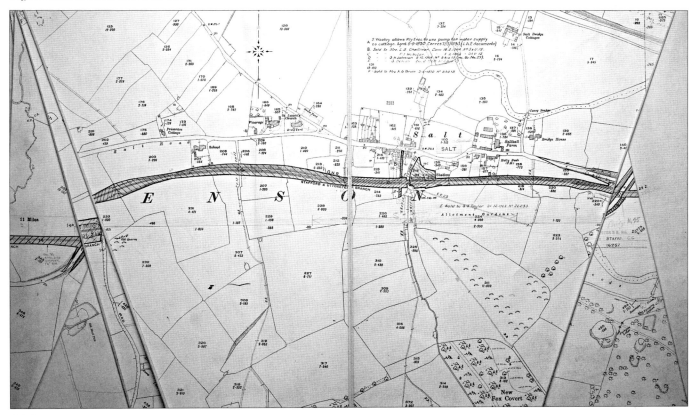

Salt Station.

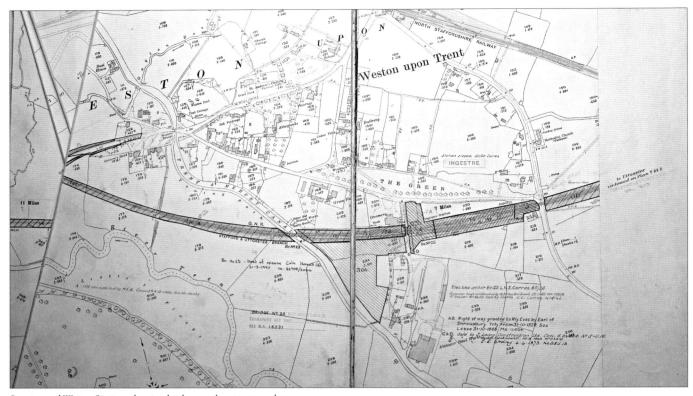

Ingestre and Weston Station, showing bridge numbers 21, 22 and 23.

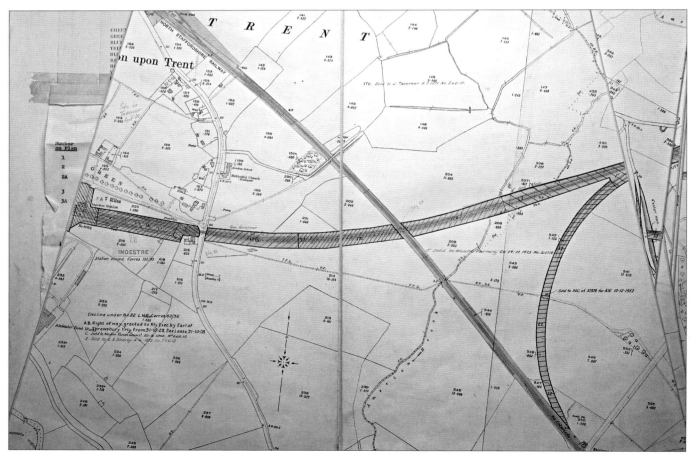

Ingestre and Weston showing bridge number 20 crossing the NSR main line.

Chartley & Stowe Station.

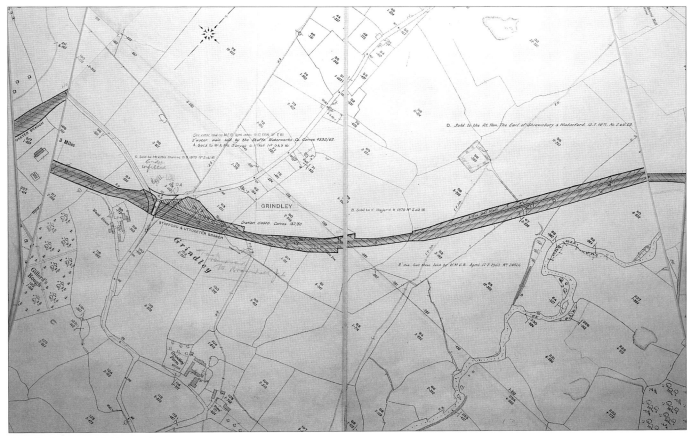

Grindley Station and bridge number 11.

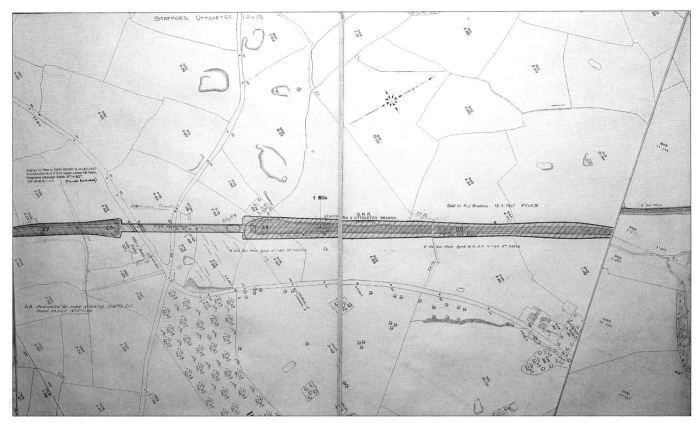

Bromshall Tunnel.

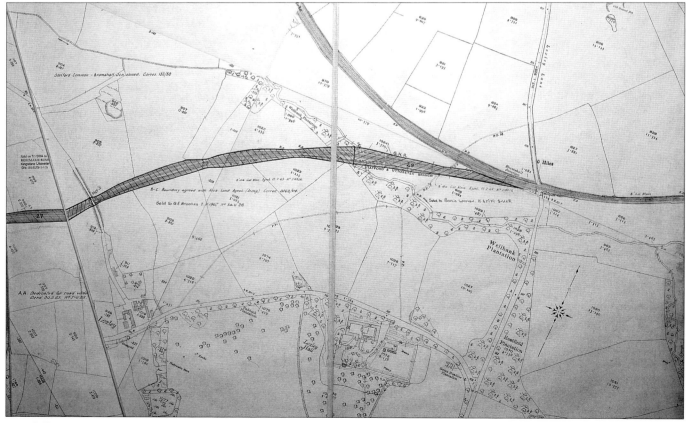

Bromshall Junction.

Bibliography

ANONYMOUS
The Stafford & Uttoxeter Railway, The Locomotive, Volume 14, 14 March 1908.
The North London Railway, The Locomotive, Volume 69, 15 May 1943.
Our Heading, SLS Journal, Volume 28, July 1952.

BAKER, Allan C.
Industrial Locomotives of North Staffordshire, Industrial Railway Society 1997. ISBN 0 901096 97 0.

BAKER, Allan, C. and FELL, Mike G.
The Railway through Uttoxeter, Railway Archive No. 37, Lightmoor Press 2012. ISSN 1477-5336.

BAXTER, Bertram
British Locomotive Catalogue 1825-1923, Great Northern Railway, Volume 5B, Moorland Publishing Company, 1988. ISBN 0 903485 86 9.

BENNETT, A.R. *The Chronicles of Boulton's Siding*, The Locomotive Publishing Company 1927.

BIGG, James
Bigg's General Railway Acts: A Collection of Public General Acts for the Regulation of Railways 1830-1838, Waterloo & Sons 1898.

BIRD, George Frederick
The Locomotives of the Great Northern Railway, The Locomotive Publishing Company, 1903.

BRADSHAW'S *Railway Manual, Shareholders' Guide and Directory* - various issues.

BURKE, Ashworth Peter
Burke's Peerage, Baronetage and Knightage, 1914 Edition.

CAMWELL, William Arthur
The Stafford and Uttoxeter Railway, Railway World, Volume 18, May 1957.
Some Railway Schemes in Mid-Staffordshire, Railway World, Volume 18, June 1957.

CHRISTIANSEN, Rex
A Regional History of the Railways of Great Britain, Volume 7 The West Midlands, David & Charles 1973.

CHRISTIANSEN, Rex and MILLER, R.W. *The North Staffordshire Railway*, David & Charles 1971. ISBN 0 7153 5121 4.

CLINKER, C.R.
Railways of the West Midlands – A Chronology 1808-1954, Stephenson Locomotive Society 1954.

CORSER, W.J.L.
Wings on Rails: Industrial Railways in the Logistic Support of Britain's Air Defence Forces 1914-1994. Arcturus Press 2003, ISBN 0 907322 85 9.

De SALIS, Henry Rodolph
Bradshaw's Canals and Navigable Rivers of England and Wales, Henry Blacklock & Co. Ltd., 1904; new edition, David & Charles (Publishers) Limited, 1969, ISBN 7153 4689 X.

DIX, Charles
Running Powers and Working Arrangements (1) Great Northern Railway and (5) North Staffordshire Railway, The Railway Magazine, Volume 22, April 1908 and Volume 24, April 1909.

FROST, Allan John
Wellington's Past: The Story of Barbers established 1848
AJF Paperback Originals, 2004, ISBN 0 9538085 3 X.

GRINLING, Charles H.
The History of the Great Northern Railway, George Allen & Unwin, new edition 1966.

GROVES, Norman
Great Northern Locomotive History, Volume 2 (second revised edition) and Volume 3a, Railway Correspondence and Travel Society, 1991 and 1990. ISBN 0 901115 76 6 and 0 90115 69 X.

HIGGINSON, Mark
The Friargate Line, Golden Pringle Publishing, 1989, ISBN 0 9513834 0 X.

JONES, Phil
The Stafford & Uttoxeter Railway, Oakwood Press, 1981, ISBN 0 85361 277 3.

KEYS, Robert
North Staffordshire Railway: 'Foreign Relations' with the Great Northern Railway, private paper.

LEAD, Peter
The Caldon Canal and Tramroads, Oakwood Press, second edition, 1990, ISBN 0 85361 404 0.

LEWIN, Henry Grote
The Railway Mania and its Aftermath 1845-1852, The Railway Gazette, 1936.

'MANIFOLD'
The North Staffordshire Railway, J.H. Henstock Ltd., Ashbourne 1952

MacDERMOT, E.T.
History of the Great Western Railway Vol. 1, Part 1 1833-1863, Great Western Railway Company, 1927.

MILLAR, John
William Heap and his Company, Published privately, 1976.

NEELE, George Potter
Railway Reminiscences, McCorquodale & Co., London 1904, reprinted EP Publishing Limited, 1974, ISBN 0 85409 950 6.

PERKINS, Thomas Richard
My Red-Letter Day, The Railway Magazine, Volume 84, February 1939.

POPPLEWELL, Lawrence
A Gazetteer of the Railway Contractors and Engineers of Central England 1830-1914, Melledgen Press, 1986, ISBN-0-906637-09-0.

READ, R.E.G.
The NSR and its Neighbours, Parts I and II, The Railway World, Volume 15, March and April, 1954.

REED, M.C. *The London & North Western Railway*, Atlantic Transport Publishers 1996. ISBN 0 906899 66 4.

STAFFORDSHIRE INDUSTRIAL ARCHAEOLOGY SOCIETY
100 Years of Business in Stafford 1900-2000, private publication, 2000.

VANNS, Michael A.
An Illustrated History of Great Northern Railway Signalling, OPC, 2000.

WROTTESLEY, John. *The Great Northern Railway, Volume I, Origins & Development*, Batsford 1979. ISBN 0 7134 1590 8.

WROTTESLEY, John. *The Great Northern Railway, Volume II, Expansion & Competition*, Batsford 1979. ISBN 0 7134 1592 4.

WROTTESLEY, John. *The Great Northern Railway, Volume III, Twentieth Century to Grouping*, Batsford 1981. ISBN 0 7134 2183 5.

YATE, Bob
The South Staffordshire Railway, Volumes One and Two, Oakwood Press, 2010 & 2011, ISBN 978-0-85361-700-6 & 978-0-85361-717-4.

YEOMANS, G.A.
Great Northern to Burton and Stafford, private publication, 1977.
Centenary of the Derbyshire Extension of the GNR, SLS Journal, Volume 54, April 1978.
Egginton Junction, SLS Journal, Volume 54, July 1978.

Index

While this Index is by no means comprehensive, it should prove useful in conjunction with the detailed breakdown of the individual sections of the Chapters as listed on the Contents pages. In view of this, with the occasional exception, the S&UR itself is not indexed. There is a small amount of cross referencing. Page numbers in bold type refer to illustrations, but not necessarily photographs and in many cases, there are also references in the main text on the same page.